Course   Taking Sides: Clashing Views
in Family and Personal
Relationships, 10/e

Course Number   **by David M. Hall**

http://create.mcgraw-hill.com

ISBN-10: 1308098197   ISBN-13: 9781308098197

Contents

Credits

Preface

Human beings naturally seek out relationships. While these relationships vary depending on whether they are among family, coworkers, friends, acquaintances, or significant others, relationships with intimate others can be the most rewarding and challenging. From a public policy and social interaction perspective, they can also be the most controversial. The ways in which our personal and family relationships are understood and respected can influence not just our intimate relationships but also our social relationships and livelihood. Too often in the national media our family and relationship diversity is approached from a controversial perspective that can foster division and animosity. *Taking Sides: Family and Personal Relationships* is intended to provide thoughtful discourse, standing in sharp contrast with the divisive portrayals and rhetoric too often found in the national media.

The tenth edition of *Taking Sides: Family and Personal Relationships* provides thoughtful discourse from diverse perspectives on some of the most controversial issues in American society today. This volume contains provocative questions with thoughtful and engaging viewpoints that are designed for readers not just to reinforce but also to challenge their existing perspectives and values. Each chapter includes an *introduction* from the editor, which provides a context for this debate. The *introduction* may cite important statistics, pertinent history, and an overview of the debate. The *introduction* is followed by two competing views on the controversial question. Following the competing viewpoints are *critical questions* and *common ground* from the editor, which will examine suggestions for further thought, research, or action to the topic posed in the issue. The section *Additional Resources* provides a list of sources that will help further the reader's understanding about the topics in this volume.

Taking Sides: Family and Personal Relationships, 10/e will challenge readers to examine divergent viewpoints on some of the most contentious issues in American society today. Topics relate to parenting, cyberspace, infidelity, sexual orientation, sexual decision–making and many other issues that are sensitive and often difficult to discuss openly. Each issue will provide the reader with an opportunity to reinforce what they already believe while also challenging some of their already held beliefs and convictions.

A word to the instructor An *Instructor's Resource Guide with Test Questions* provides multiple-choice and essay questions related to this text for help with assessment of student reading. While the *Instructor's Resource Guide with Test Questions* is tailor-made for this specific volume, educators can also reference *Using Taking Sides in the Classroom*, which provides an overview of ways in which instructors can manage discussions about divergent viewpoints within their classroom. For an online version of *Using Taking Sides in the Classroom* and a correspondence service for *Taking Sides* adopters, please visit www.mhhe.com/createcentral.

McGraw-Hill provides a dynamic list of titles in this series in addition to *Taking Sides: Family and Personal Relationships* that can be used in a wide variety of courses, ranging from titles that relate to specific course content to utilizing any of the volumes in teaching students how to write and debate persuasively. If interested in reviewing other thought-provoking editions, please visit the Taking Sides Collection on McGraw-Hill Create™ at www.mcgrawhillcreate.com/takingsides.

Acknowledgments

First and foremost, let me thank McGraw-Hill's Jill Meloy. Writing and editing can be so very personal and therefore challenging. However, Jill could not have been more thoughtful and collaborative throughout this process. Her feedback and support would almost instantaneously follow my emails and phone calls. She has been an invaluable resource in creating this edition. Jill's timely, thoughtful feedback combined with their support for my goals in creating the best edition possible have been critical to the creation of this volume. Had it not been for Jill, this edition would never have reached publication with this level of quality.

I would also like to thank:

- William J. Taverner, Editor-in-Chief of the *American Journal for Sexuality Education* and editor of *Taking Sides: Human Sexuality*, for his generous spirit of collaboration and mentorship. I have learned so very much from Bill's intellect and creativity. It is unlikely that I would be editor of this volume had it not been for Bill.

- Lauren Ewaniuk, a gifted educator and curriculum author, for serving as Contributing Editor to the Instructor's Manual that accompanies this book. Lauren has put extensive work into significantly expanding the book's Advisory Board to help ensure that the issues meet the needs and objectives of those who are assigning it. Lauren has been an invaluable partner in this edition. Her work on expanding the Advisory Board will have a lasting impact not just on this edition but also on future editions to this text.

- My dear spouse, Annie Hall. With three young children, there were days when much more was asked of her as a mother so that this book could be completed with the necessary quality. She never complained and always provided our kids with exciting enrichment each and every time.

- The authors featured in this edition. I am fortunate to have had the opportunity to collaborate with bright and talented scholars who have framed a powerful debate that will enhance not only learning but also public discourse.

Remember that when reading this volume you may very well find viewpoints that you find challenging and even offensive. This is why I want to end by acknowledging you, the reader, for the courage to challenge your deeply held convictions in reading these chapters. It is difficult to entertain positions that one finds morally wrong, but doing so leads to stronger moral and intellectual growth. Thank you for taking the time to read and interact with this book.

This book is dedicated to my three children, who inspire me to be a better person. Despite their youth, they never hesitate at taking sides.

David M. Hall, PhD
Delaware Valley College

Editor of This Volume

DR. DAVID M. HALL, a distinguished corporate diversity trainer and educator, is the author of *Allies at Work: Creating a Lesbian, Gay, Bisexual, and Transgender Inclusive Work Environment* and the editor of *Taking Sides: Family and Personal Relationships*, a college text. He is the creator of *BullyShield*, a bullying prevention mobile application for the iPhone and Droid. Dr. Hall is the recipient of teaching and humanitarian awards at the national, state, and local level. Those awards include the Gay, Lesbian, and Straight Education Network Educator of the Year Runner-Up Award, Teacher as Hero Award from the National Liberty Museum, Outstanding Alumnus from Widener University, and Outstanding Pennsylvanian from the Pennsylvania Jaycees. Dr. Hall's long list of clients includes JP Morgan Chase, Merck, the U.S. Department of Energy, PSE&G, The Hershey Company, Blue Cross Blue Shield of Florida, Safeway, The University of Pennsylvania, and many others.

Academic Advisory Board Members

Members of the Academic Advisory Board are instrumental in the final selection of articles for Takings Sides books and ExpressBooks. Their review of the articles for content, level, and appropriateness provides critical direction to the editor(s) and staff. We think that you will find their careful consideration reflected in this book.

Bill Anderson
Illinois State University

David Ayers
Grove City College

Yvonne Barry
John Tyler Community College

Laurence Basirico
Elon University

Timothy Baylor
Lock Haven University of Pennsylvania

Zsuzsa Berend
University of California–Los Angeles

Amy Blackstone
University of Maine

John Bodinger de Uriarte
Susquehanna University

Kathryn Bonach
Indiana University of Pennsylvania

Carolyn Bradley
Monmouth University

Corby Caffrey-Dobosh
Waynesburg University

Stanley Clawar
Rosemont College

Theodore Cohen
Ohio Wesleyan University

John Conahan
Kutztown University of Pennsylvania

Jason Lee Crockett
Kutztown University of Pennsylvania

Regina Davis-Sowers
Santa Clara University

Nancy DeCesare
Chestnut Hill College

Eli DeHope
West Chester University of Pennsylvania

Evelyn Doody
College of Southern Nevada

Cynthia Drenovsky
Shippensburg University

John Durst
Ohio Wesleyan University

Monica Faulkner
University of Texas–Austin

Julie Fennell
Gallaudet University

Diane FerreroPaluzzi
Iona College

Laci Fiala
Walsh University

Bernard Fitzpatrick
Naugatuck Valley Community College

Sheila Fox
Immaculata University

Cynthia Franklin
University of Texas–Austin

Anita Garey
University of Connecticut

Sara Garner
Southeast Missouri State University

Craig Goforth
Mars Hill College

Melissa Gosdin
Ohio University

Ruby Gourdine
Howard University

Laura Groves
Cabrini College

C. Margaret Hall
Georgetown University

Brent Harger
Albright College

Joann Haws
DeSales University

Terrell Hayes
High Point University

Susan Herrick
West Liberty University

Gary Jones
Cabrini College

Eric Jorrey
Ohio University–Athens

Kara Joyner
Bowling Green State University

Antonia Keane
Loyola University

Rina Keller
Rosemont College

Jo Anna Kelly
Walsh University

Caitlin Killian
Drew University

John Kovach
Chestnut Hill College

Michelle Kozimor-King
Elizabethtown College

Jackie Krasas
Lehigh University

Werner Lange
Edinboro University of Pennsylvania

Monica Longmore
Bowling Green State University

Wade Luquet
Gwynedd Mercy College

Mark Lynch
Saint Francis University

Heidi Lyons
Oakland University

J. Beth Mabry
Indiana University of Pennsylvania

Cameron Macdonald
University of Wisconsin–Madison

Andrew Marks
Texas State University–San Marcos

Christine McCormick
Rosemont College

Katrina McDonald
Johns Hopkins University

Susan Milstein
Montgomery College

David Miyahara
Azusa-Pacific University

Maya Nadkarni
Swarthmore College

Patricia E. Neff Claster
Edinboro University of Pennsylvania

Kei Nomaguchi
Bowling Green State University

Catherine O'Conor
Bucks County Community College

Elizabeth Osborn
St. Mary's College of Maryland

Aurea Osgood
Winona State University

Caree Oslislo-Wizenberg
Anne Arundle Community College

Naoko Oyabu-Mathis
University of Mount Union

Manacy Pai
Kent State University

Varsha Pandya
Kutztown University of Pennsylvania

Michael Patte
Bloomsburg University

Vania Penha-Lopes
Bloomfield College

Catherine Petrissans
Clarion University of Pennsylvania

Liz Piatt
Hiram College

Erica Polakoff
Bloomfield College

Beth Pomeroy
University of Texas–Austin

Doug Rice
California State University–Sacramento

Karen Rice
Millersville University of Pennsylvania

Karen Rich
Marywood University

Lauren Rinelli McClain
Savannah State University

Susan Roxburgh
Kent State University

Cynthia Schellenbach
Oakland University

Prakash Sharma
Rider University

Jonathan Singer
Temple University

Carrie Lee Smith
Millersville University

Nora Smith
Monmouth University

Karrie Ann Snyder
Northwestern University

Catherine Solomon
Quinnipiac University

Cynthia L. Sutton
Thiel College

Dianne Sykes
Gardner-Webb University

Kathryn Tillman
Florida State University

Deanna Trella
North Michigan University

Kielty Turner
Marywood University

Kourtney Vaillancourt
New Mexico State University

Joseph Ventimiglia
University of Memphis

Glenda Warren
University of the Cumberlands

Suzanne Weaver
Cedar Crest College

Casey Welch
Flagler College

Anita Woolery
Ocean County College

Michelle Young
McDaniel College

Elizabeth Ziff
Rutgers University

Jane Zupancic
California University of Pennsylvania

Correlation Guide

The Taking Sides series presents current issues in a debate-style format designed to stimulate student interest and develop critical-thinking skills. Each issue is thoughtfully framed with an issue summary, an issue introduction, learning outcomes, and key end-of-issue instructional and discussion tools. The pro and con essays—selected for their liveliness and substance—represent the arguments of leading scholars and commentators in their fields.

Taking Sides: Clashing Views in Family and Personal Relationships, 10/e is an easy-to-use reader that presents issues on important topics such as *parental decision-making, divorce, children's rights, nontraditional families,* and *relationship issues.* For more information on Taking Sides and other *McGraw-Hill Create™ Contemporary Learning Series* titles, visit www.mcgrawhillcreate.com.

This convenient guide matches the issues in **Taking Sides: Family and Personal Relationships**, 10/e with the corresponding chapters in two of our best-selling McGraw-Hill Sociology textbooks by DeGenova et al. and Lauer/Lauer.

TAKING SIDES: Family and Personal Relationships, 10/e	Intimate Relationships, Marriages, and Families, 8/e by DeGenova et al.	Marriage and Family: The Quest for Intimacy, 8/e by Lauer/Lauer
Is It Beneficial If Adoptive Parents Adopt Only Within Their Own Racial/Ethnic Group?	**Chapter 11:** Family Planning and Parenting **Chapter 13:** Parent-Child Relationships	**Chapter 2:** Diversity in Families **Chapter 12:** Becoming a Parent
Does Divorce Have a Negative Impact on Children?	**Chapter 16:** The Family and Divorce	**Chapter 14:** Separation and Divorce
Is Homeschooling Kids in Their Best Interest and Ours?	**Chapter 9:** Power, Decision Making, and Communication	**Chapter 11:** Work and Home
Should Pharmacists Be Able to Deny Emergency Contraception to Potentially Pregnant Women?	**Chapter 11:** Family Planning and Parenting	**Chapter 12:** Becoming a Parent
Should Illegal Immigrant Families Be Able to Send Their Children to Public Schools?	**Chapter 1:** Intimate Relationships, Marriages, and Families in the Twenty-First Century **Chapter 8:** Work, Family Roles, and Material Resources	**Chapter 1:** Marriage and Family in America: Needs, Myths, and Dreams **Chapter 2:** Diversity in Families
Should Parents Be Able to Choose Their Baby's Sex?	**Chapter 11:** Family Planning and Parenting **Chapter 12:** Pregnancy and Childbirth	**Chapter 12:** Becoming a Parent
Should Grandparents Have Visitation Rights for Their Grandchildren?	**Chapter 14:** Parents and Extended Family Relationships **Chapter 15:** Conflict, Family Crises, and Crisis Management	**Chapter 1:** Marriage and Family in America: Needs, Myths, and Dreams **Chapter 2:** Diversity in Families **Chapter 13:** Family Crises
Should Courts Be Able to Discriminate Against Immigrant Fathers?	**Chapter 1:** Intimate Relationships, Marriages, and Families in the Twenty-First Century **Chapter 9:** Power, Decision Making, and Communication **Chapter 13:** Parent-Child Relationships	**Chapter 2:** Diversity in Families
Do Parents Have the Right to Deny Their Children Lifesaving Medical Care Due to Their Religious Convictions?	**Chapter 9:** Power, Decision Making, and Communication **Chapter 13:** Parent-Child Relationships	**Chapter 10:** Power and Conflict in Marriage **Chapter 12:** Becoming a Parent
Does the Federal Government Discriminate Against Same-Sex Couples If It Refuses to Recognize Their Marriage?	**Chapter 1:** Intimate Relationships, Marriages, and Families in the Twenty-First Century **Chapter 2:** Gender: Identity and Roles **Chapter 10:** Sexual Relationships	**Chapter 4:** Sexuality **Chapter 8:** Getting Married
Should Private Sexual Acts Between Gay Couples Be Illegal?	**Chapter 10:** Sexual Relationships	**Chapter 4:** Sexuality
Are Traditional Families Better Than Nontraditional Families?	**Chapter 1:** Intimate Relationships, Marriages, and Families in the Twenty-First Century **Chapter 11:** Family Planning and Parenting **Chapter 13:** Parent-Child Relationships	**Chapter 1:** Marriage and Family in America: Needs, Myths, and Dreams **Chapter 2:** Diversity in Families

(Continued)

TAKING SIDES: Family and Personal Relationships, 10/e	Intimate Relationships, Marriages, and Families, 8/e by DeGenova et al.	Marriage and Family: The Quest for Intimacy, 8/e by Lauer/Lauer
Is Hookup Culture on College Campuses Bad for Heterosexual Girls?	**Chapter 1:** Intimate Relationships, Marriages, and Families in the Twenty-First Century **Chapter 2:** Gender: Identity and Roles **Chapter 3:** Being Single **Chapter 4:** Attraction and Dating **Chapter 10:** Sexual Relationships	**Chapter 3:** Gender Roles: Foundation for Intimacy **Chapter 4:** Sexuality
Are Teenagers Too Young to Become Parents?	**Chapter 11:** Family Planning and Parenting **Chapter 13:** Parent-Child Relationships	**Chapter 12:** Becoming a Parent
Is Cybersex "Cheating"?	**Chapter 15:** Conflict, Family Crises, and Crisis Management **Chapter 10:** Sexual Relationships	**Chapter 1:** Marriage and Family in America: Needs, Myths, and Dreams **Chapter 10:** Power and Conflict in Marriage **Chapter 13:** Family Crises
Is Internet Pornography Harmful to Teenagers?	**Chapter 9:** Power, Decision Making, and Communication **Chapter 15:** Conflict, Family Crises, and Crisis Management	**Chapter 4:** Sexuality **Chapter 13:** Family Crises
Are Statutory Rape Laws Effective at Protecting Minors?		
Do Reality Television Shows Have a Negative Influence on Teenage Pregnancy and Parenting?	**Chapter 11:** Family Planning and Parenting **Chapter 13:** Parent-Child Relationships	**Chapter 9:** The Challenge of Communication
Should There Be Harsh Penalties for Teens Sexting?	**Chapter 10:** Sexual Relationships	**Chapter 4:** Sexuality
Are Open Relationships Healthy?	**Chapter 1:** Intimate Relationships, Marriages, and Families in the Twenty-First Century **Chapter 9:** Power, Decision Making, and Communication **Chapter 10:** Sexual Relationships	**Chapter 1:** Marriage and Family in America: Needs, Myths, and Dreams **Chapter 9:** The Challenge of Communication

Topic Guide

This topic guide suggests how the selections in this book relate to the subjects covered in your course.

All the issues that relate to each topic are listed below the bold-faced term.

Adolescence

Are Teenagers Too Young to Become Parents?
Do Reality Television Shows Have a Negative Influence on Teenage Pregnancy and Parenting?
Does Divorce Have a Negative Impact on Children?
Is Internet Pornography Harmful to Teenagers?
Should There Be Harsh Penalties for Teens Sexting?

Adoption

Are Traditional Families Better Than Nontraditional Families?
Is It Beneficial If Adoptive Parents Adopt Only Within Their Own Racial/Ethnic Group?

Biotechnology

Should Parents Be Able to Choose Their Baby's Sex?

Child Development

Does Divorce Have a Negative Impact on Children?
Is Homeschooling Kids in Their Best Interest and Ours?

Children

Are Teenagers Too Young to Become Parents?
Are Traditional Families Better Than Nontraditional Families?
Does Divorce Have a Negative Impact on Children?
Is It Beneficial If Adoptive Parents Adopt Only Within Their Own Racial/Ethnic Group?
Should Courts Be Able to Discriminate Against Immigrant Fathers?
Should Parents Be Able to Choose Their Baby's Sex?

Civil Rights

Do Parents Have the Right to Deny Their Children Lifesaving Medical Care Due to Their Religious Convictions?
Should Courts Be Able to Discriminate Against Immigrant Fathers?
Should Illegal Immigrant Families Be Able to Send Their Children to Public Schools?
Should There Be Harsh Penalties for Teens Sexting?

Constitutional Law

Are Statutory Rape Laws Effective at Protecting Minors?
Should Private Sexual Acts Between Gay Couples Be Illegal?
Should There Be Harsh Penalties for Teens Sexting?

Criminal Behavior

Should There Be Harsh Penalties for Teens Sexting?

Cultural Anthropology

Is Hookup Culture on College Campuses Bad for Heterosexual Girls?

Discrimination

Are Traditional Families Better Than Nontraditional Families?
Is It Beneficial If Adoptive Parents Adopt Only Within Their Own Racial/Ethnic Group?
Should Courts Be Able to Discriminate Against Immigrant Fathers?
Should Illegal Immigrant Families Be Able to Send Their Children to Public Schools?
Should Private Sexual Acts Between Gay Couples Be Illegal?

Disease

Should Parents Be Able to Choose Their Baby's Sex?

Divorce

Does Divorce Have a Negative Impact on Children?

Ethics

Should Parents Be Able to Choose Their Baby's Sex?
Should Pharmacists Be Able to Deny Emergency Contraception to Potentially Pregnant Women?

First Amendment

Should There Be Harsh Penalties for Teens Sexting?

Gender

Is Hookup Culture on College Campuses Bad for Heterosexual Girls?

Government Regulation

Should Illegal Immigrant Families Be Able to Send Their Children to Public Schools?

Health Care

Do Parents Have the Right to Deny Their Children Lifesaving Medical Care Due to Their Religious Convictions?
Should Pharmacists Be Able to Deny Emergency Contraception to Potentially Pregnant Women?

Homosexuality

Does the Federal Government Discriminate Against Same-Sex Couples If It Refuses to Recognize Their Marriage?
Should Private Sexual Acts Between Gay Couples Be Illegal?

Human Development

Should Parents Be Able to Choose Their Baby's Sex?

(Continued)

Human Rights

Does the Federal Government Discriminate Against Same-Sex Couples If It Refuses to Recognize Their Marriage?
Should Private Sexual Acts Between Gay Couples Be Illegal?

Immigration

Should Courts Be Able to Discriminate Against Immigrant Fathers?
Should Illegal Immigrant Families Be Able to Send Their Children to Public Schools?

Inequality

Are Traditional Families Better Than Nontraditional Families?
Does the Federal Government Discriminate Against Same-Sex Couples If It Refuses to Recognize Their Marriage?
Is Hookup Culture on College Campuses Bad for Heterosexual Girls?
Should Courts Be Able to Discriminate Against Immigrant Fathers?
Should Illegal Immigrant Families Be Able to Send Their Children to Public Schools?
Should Private Sexual Acts Between Gay Couples Be Illegal?

Internet

Is Cybersex "Cheating"?
Is Internet Pornography Harmful to Teenagers?

Law Enforcement

Are Statutory Rape Laws Effective at Protecting Minors?
Should Private Sexual Acts Between Gay Couples Be Illegal?
Should There Be Harsh Penalties for Teens Sexting?

School Reform

Is Homeschooling Kids in Their Best Interest and Ours?
Should Illegal Immigrant Families Be Able to Send Their Children to Public Schools?

Marriage

Are Traditional Families Better Than Nontraditional Families?
Does the Federal Government Discriminate Against Same-Sex Couples If It Refuses to Recognize Their Marriage?

Medicine

Do Parents Have the Right to Deny Their Children Lifesaving Medical Care Due to Their Religious Convictions?
Should Pharmacists Be Able to Deny Emergency Contraception to Potentially Pregnant Women?

Parenting

Are Teenagers Too Young to Become Parents?
Are Traditional Families Better Than Nontraditional Families?
Do Parents Have the Right to Deny Their Children Lifesaving Medical Care Due to Their Religious Convictions?
Do Reality Television Shows Have a Negative Influence on Teenage Pregnancy and Parenting?
Does Divorce Have a Negative Impact on Children?
Is Homeschooling Kids in Their Best Interest and Ours?
Is It Beneficial If Adoptive Parents Adopt Only Within Their Own Racial/Ethnic Group?
Should Courts Be Able to Discriminate Against Immigrant Fathers?

Pornography

Is Internet Pornography Harmful to Teenagers?

Pregnancy

Are Teenagers Too Young to Become Parents?
Do Reality Television Shows Have a Negative Influence on Teenage Pregnancy and Parenting?
Should Pharmacists Be Able to Deny Emergency Contraception to Potentially Pregnant Women?

Public Health

Do Parents Have the Right to Deny Their Children Lifesaving Medical Care Due to Their Religious Convictions?
Should Pharmacists Be Able to Deny Emergency Contraception to Potentially Pregnant Women?

Relationships

Are Open Relationships Healthy?
Is Cybersex "Cheating"?
Should Grandparents Have Visitation Rights for Their Grandchildren?

Sex Crimes

Are Statutory Rape Laws Effective at Protecting Minors?
Should There Be Harsh Penalties for Teens Sexting?

Sex Discrimination

Is Hookup Culture on College Campuses Bad for Heterosexual Girls?

Social Change

Does the Federal Government Discriminate Against Same-Sex Couples If It Refuses to Recognize Their Marriage?
Is Cybersex "Cheating"?
Is Hookup Culture on College Campuses Bad for Heterosexual Girls?
Is Internet Pornography Harmful to Teenagers?

Social Values

Are Traditional Families Better Than Nontraditional Families?
Should Grandparents Have Visitation Rights for Their Grandchildren?

State and Local Government

Does the Federal Government Discriminate Against Same-Sex Couples If It Refuses to Recognize Their Marriage?
Should Illegal Immigrant Families Be Able to Send Their Children to Public Schools?
Should There Be Harsh Penalties for Teens Sexting?

Taxes

Should Illegal Immigrant Families Be Able to Send Their Children to Public Schools?

Television

Are Teenagers Too Young to Become Parents?
Do Reality Television Shows Have a Negative Influence on Teenage Pregnancy and Parenting?

Introduction

*T*aking Sides: Family and Personal Relationships is released at a time when American society is reconstructing its concept of families and relationships. More children are growing up in nontraditional homes than ever before. In fact, concepts of the traditional family that were once considered a universal norm are not reflective of the diverse families that exist. These changes can be a source of societal conflict. Conversely, these changes can also be a source of societal strength and growth.

Pluralistic nations thrive by demonstrating a willingness to cooperate despite existing differences. In order for this to occur, the citizenry must engage in thoughtful and respectful discourse. In that spirit, this volume examines the diversity of views in American society as they relate to family and personal relationships to provide a context for weighing more carefully not just one's own values but also opposing values. Most readers will find that their responses to issues raised in this volume are anchored in a moral or intellectual foundation. Four such frameworks are identified in this introduction to assist the reader in providing a larger context for the issues debated in this volume.

Many readers will find themselves conducting further research on the topics raised in each chapter. Today, issues in this volume often permeate discourse in society, families, the law and education. *Taking Sides: Family and Personal Relationships* is designed to provide an intellectual foundation for much of this discourse.

Carefully evaluate the arguments made throughout this book. Readers should be able to identify statements of fact, statements of value and the credibility of research used to support the author's thesis. While such evaluation is important when reading persuasive essays, higher-level thinking skills can be used to examine each issue through a variety of frameworks.

This introduction outlines four potential frameworks: political ideology, religion, linguistics and legal theory. Try applying one or more frameworks to the issues addressed in this book. How would you compare and contrast your conclusions for each issue in this book? Are there areas in which competing frameworks create a conflict for you? If so, how would you reconcile these differences?

Let us now examine the four frameworks that can be used for analysis throughout this volume.

Political Ideology Framework

Many of the topics raised in this book are political and can sometimes be significant issues in campaigns and elections. The political ideology continuum contains the following stages: reactionary, conservative, liberal and radical (see Table 1). Reactionary ideology supports going back to a previous way of doing things. Reactionaries believe that most social problems are the result of democratic excesses that favor the masses at the expense of proven tradition. Conservative ideology believes in defending the status quo and making only small changes. Liberal ideology believes in change that guarantees greater individual rights. Radical ideology, typically the antithesis of reactionary, favors fundamental restructuring of society to ensure equality.

If the reader chooses, for example, to examine the issue of whether or not open relationships are healthy, a reactionary view would oppose open relationships as well as support changing marriage laws to make divorce more difficult. In fact, they would probably argue that cultural acceptance of divorce will ultimately lead to polygamy. A conservative perspective would likely oppose open relationships and same-sex marriage but support leaving divorce laws as they stand. A liberal view would likely support allowing same-sex marriage but voice opposition for polyamory. A radical perspective would favor fundamentally reconstructing the culture of marriage so that polyamory is as much the expected norm as monogamy.

The political ideology framework can be used for any topic within this book. Is your political ideology the same for adoption as it is for marriage? How about with other topics in this book? What does this comparison and contrast reveal about your overall political ideology?

Religious Framework

Many people have views about sexual orientation and gender identity that are the result of their religious upbringing. However, religious views vary not just from one religion to the next but also within certain faiths themselves. Debate over acceptance, tolerance and rejection based on sexual orientation is dividing many places of worship. Dr. James Nelson, a Christian minister, created a continuum for religious responses to lesbian, gay and bisexual individuals, which consists of Rejecting Punitive, Rejecting Non-Punitive, Qualified Acceptance and Full Acceptance (see Table 2). Readers who come from a strong religious background may want to consider where their faith falls along this continuum and whether their personal views correspond with their faith. When reading

Table 1

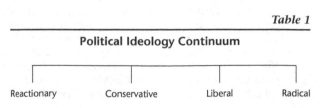

Political Ideology Continuum

| Reactionary | Conservative | Liberal | Radical |

Table 2

Nelson Continuum

| Rejecting Punitive | Rejecting Non-Punitive | Qualified Acceptance | Full Acceptance |

each issue, consider how religious values may impact your views on particular issues.

A Rejecting Punitive place of worship would expel anyone who identifies as lesbian, gay, bisexual or transgender. Rejecting Non-Punitive values are found in places of worship where lesbian, gay, bisexual and transgender individuals are welcome to attend but will regularly hear sermons about the immorality of their identity. Qualified Acceptance is found in a place of worship in which one will never hear hatred from the pulpit and generally feel accepted. However, if one day a gay attendee offers to teach his child's Bible study group, a committee at the church might meet and decide that gay members of the church may not teach children. Full Acceptance is featured in a place of worship that holds same-sex weddings and allows for the full inclusion of all lesbian, gay, bisexual and transgender members, including serving as clergy.

When reading the sections involving LGBT issues and definitions of family, try and identify if your response has a religious foundation. Where does your school community fall on this continuum? Where does your home community fall on this continuum? What do you believe is the most ethical response on this continuum and why?

While Nelson uses this framework in the context of religious faith and sexual orientation, it can be applied to any of the topics found in this book.

Linguistics Framework

Professor of Linguistics George Lakoff utilizes a Nation as Family framework for examining political rhetoric. Lakoff argues that Americans view the nation as a family, which is evidenced by metaphors such as "founding fathers," "daughters of the American revolution," and "sending our sons off to war." Using the Nation as Family model, Lakoff contends that Republicans tend to support what he calls Strict Father Morality and that Democrats tend to support what he calls Nurturant Parent Morality. A Lakoffian framework is pertinent to this particular volume in the *Taking Sides* series as it demonstrates that our concept of family applies not just to our personal lives but also to our sense of patriotism and national psyche.

Strict Father Morality rests upon a patriarchal system that values adherence to past moral standards to ensure future success. Strict Father Morality would not only support defining marriage as between a man and a woman but also argue that a nation's success comes from such a traditional family structure. Conversely, Nurturant Parent Morality values independent thinking that will strengthen the family. Nurturant Parent Morality would support marriage being reconstructed to include same-sex couples as an issue of fairness and equality for all members of the familial society. Nurturant Parent Morality argues that such change will strengthen American society.

Few people fit entirely into either Strict Father or Nurturant Parent Morality. For example, a person can adhere to Strict Father Morality about social welfare programs but Nurturant Parent Morality about funding for education. Are your Nation as Family views regarding family and personal relationship issues consistent across issues in this volume? How do your Nation as Family views on topics raised within this volume compare and contrast with your views on other issues within American society?

Legal Framework

The two primary competing legal philosophies are Originalism and Living Constitution. This framework can be applied to any article involving law and policy. Originalism is the belief that judges should base their decisions on the original meaning of the text of the Constitution. Their understanding of the intent is based on the writings of the framers and the debates at the Constitutional Convention. In the case of constitutional amendments, advocates of Originalism would consider the writings and discussions at the time of the amendment's adoption. In contrast, Living Constitution is the belief that the Constitution was written with the intent that its interpretation would evolve in response to an ever-changing society. Those who believe in Living Constitution believe it is against the spirit and intent of the Constitution to interpret contemporary legal issues with a nineteenth-century mindset.

The Fourteenth Amendment guarantees equal protection under the law. Sexual orientation was not debated during passage of this amendment. As a result, an Originalist would argue that such protection refers only to race since the intent was to protect newly freed slaves and that it therefore categorically denies protection based on sexual orientation. However, adherents of a Living Constitution perspective argue that the equal protection guarantee was written without mention of any identity, including race, so applications of this right could be applied differently for successive generations. Supporters of the Living Constitution perspective would support extending equal protection rights based on biological sex as well as sexual orientation. How would Originalism and a Living Constitution apply to issues related to immigration, parental rights and medical treatment, grandparents' visitation rights and other related topics?

Conclusion

During early American history, someone caught having sex outside of marriage was likely to be severely punished. Within marriage, sex for procreation was typically the expected norm. In fact, married couples lacked a defined, constitutional right to contraception until the 1960s. Over the past 50 years, accepted norms of family and personal relationships have been fundamentally reconstructed. Today Americans are living in an era in which society is openly grappling with a wide variety of changes related to family and personal relationships.

The debate over rights for nontraditional families is sometimes referred to as part of a culture war. While there is no protracted physical battle, the passion associated with many people's deeply held beliefs is at stake in the issues addressed in this volume. In some cases, individual livelihoods and even lives are threatened. The use of such a violent metaphor as *culture war* reflects the strong feelings and deep divisions that exist within American society when people discuss many of the issues addressed in this volume.

Each essay provides an engaging examination of both sides of each issue. Readers may find that they will be challenged in some of their beliefs and that they need to conduct further research. It is important not only to read about these issues but also to work for better understanding of the diversity of views that are expressed in this volume. A willingness to consider diverse views will allow for growth and mutual collaboration, thereby strengthening America's pluralistic society.

David M. Hall
Delaware Valley College

Unit 1

Parental Decision Making: What's Best for Children . . . Or What's Best for Parents?

*U*se of the oft-quoted "it takes a village to raise a child" is still met with understanding, thoughtful nods as we appreciate the concept that many people beyond the family structure play key roles in raising children. There are, however, numerous factors that contribute to, interfere with, detract from, and otherwise affect how parents raise their children. Parenting styles vary. The so-called village includes the government, which is met with open arms by some and skepticism and mistrust by others. This section examines questions that society often asks relating to parenting issues.

Selected, Edited, and with Issue Framing Material by:
David M. Hall, Ph.D., *Delaware Valley College*

ISSUE

Is It Beneficial if Adoptive Parents Adopt Only Within Their Own Racial/Ethnic Group?

YES: **Tony Dokoupil**, from "Raising Katie: What Adopting a White Girl Taught a Black Family About Race in the Obama Era," *The Daily Beast* (April 22, 2009)

NO: **Ezra E. H. Griffith and Rachel L. Bergeron**, from "Cultural Stereotypes Die Hard: The Case of Transracial Adoption," *Journal of the American Academy of Psychiatry Law* (vol. 34, pp. 303–14, 2006)

Learning Outcomes
After reading this issue, you will be able to:
• Identify the major arguments made for and against transracial adoption.
• Compare and contrast the competing challenges caused by transracial adoption depending on the race of the parents and children.
• Evaluate the implications of contemporary views about race in the United States and how that informs the controversy related to transracial adoption.

ISSUE SUMMARY

YES: Tony Dokoupil is a staff writer at *Newsweek* and *The Daily Beast*. Dokoupil writes about different issues affecting national life, often related to diversity. In this chapter, he writes about the increasing number of transracial adoptions in the United States in recent years but notes that we are seeing limited examples of African American families adopting white babies. When an African American family adopts a white baby, a unique set of challenges is created, he argues, due to deep-seated views about race in American society today. Dokoupil explores questions related to what this reveals about contemporary views on race in American society.

NO: Ezra Griffith and Rachel Bergeron, both faculty members of the Yale University School of Medicine's psychiatry department, argue that requiring racial and ethnic matching, although an appropriate effort, would leave too many children of color languishing in the foster and adoption systems. By maintaining that only in-race adoption is the best and ideal situation, they ask rhetorically, does our society actually do more to reinforce cultural stereotypes or to truly serve children needing homes?

The practice of adopting children is nothing new; adoptions have been documented in the United States going back to the late nineteenth century. In the twentieth century, international adoptions in the United States increased at the end of World War II, a logical response to the number of children orphaned when families were uprooted or eradicated by the war's violence. This increase was also documented after the Korean and Vietnam wars, and more recently as violence continues to mar various countries worldwide and the number of children needing homes grows.

This means that many of the adults who have adopted and are currently adopting children are from a different racial or ethnic group than their adoptive chil-

dren. In the most recent U.S. census, just over 17 percent of adopted children under age 18 had adoptive parents of a different racial background than theirs. One thing that we are learning is that the public has different views depending on which race(s) are involved in transracial adoption.

Although adoption as a practice is much less stigmatized today, adopting children outside one's own racial or ethnic group remains controversial in some circles. Some believe that raising a child in a family outside the child's racial group impedes the child from forming a healthy identity and from coping effectively in the world. In 1972, in response to the increase in transracial adoptions, the National Association of Black Social Workers (NABSW) produced a resolution stating, in part, that "black children belong physically and psychologically and culturally in black families where they can receive the total sense of themselves and develop a sound projection of their future. Only a black family can transmit the emotional and sensitive subtleties of perceptions and reactions essential for a black child's survival in a racist society." Although this statement is specifically about black and African American children, the 2003 position statement of the National Association of Social Workers (NASW) about foster care and adoption includes all racial and ethnic backgrounds.

Others argue that love is the most important component of any family, that parents of any racial or ethnic background can invest time and resources to teach their children about their racial or ethnic heritage and history and connect them with social supports to ensure that their children integrate whatever identity best fits them. It is better, these individuals argue, to give a child a home, regardless of the different racial or ethnic backgrounds of the family members, than to let a child languish in foster care. Another controversial aspect of this debate is that these same individuals argue that there is an implicit bias in the NABSW and NASW guidelines, that they assume an adoptive family that is white; there are no guidelines or discussions around placing white children with families of color.

Indeed, the controversy over transracial adoption has typically focused on Caucasian families adopting children of color. These positions have been made in the larger context of a growing number of transracial adoptions. However, transracial adoptions have historically been discussed involving white couples adopting children of color. What role does race play in public perception when the adoptive parents are African American? What about when the African American couple is adopting a white child?

In the following selections, one side reflects on African American parents raising an adopted white child. How does race and power interject in public views and interactions regarding such families? The opposing side cites research demonstrating, they assert, that children of transracial adoptions can develop strong identities and high self-esteem, the difference between their and their family's backgrounds notwithstanding.

As with any discussion of race, culture, or ethnicity, presumptions, perceptions, and biases can all affect how a person forms her or his opinion about this sensitive topic.

Consider your reactions to the readings—would your views change at all if the discussion were not about two parents of the same racial or ethnic background adopting a child from a different background, but rather about a man and a woman of two different racial or ethnic background choosing to procreate together? Why or why not? In doing so, the couple is intentionally creating a child who will have a race or ethnicity that is different from—albeit a combination of—their own. If adopting outside one's own group is okay—or not okay—with you, what about planned procreation, done within the context of a long-term, committed relationship?

What makes good parents? Think about this for a moment, then make a list. Many people will begin their list with characteristics (e.g., patience) that are not related to race, religion, ethnicity, or other forms of identity. If you were in charge of an adoption agency, what criteria would you look for in finding suitable parents for adoption? Does race play a role? Is income important? What about religion? Would you apply the same criteria to Christians, Muslims, Scientologists, and atheists? What role does marital status play? What about sexual orientation or gender identity or expression? If these identities are on your list, how important are they? Are they a primary or a secondary concern?

The compelling question in this case, for most people, is: What is in the best interest of the child? What role does racism play in American society that affects the ways in which people see this topic? How does it change a child's sense of self-involving their own race?

Also, consider your own racial or ethnic makeup—how, do you think, does this come into play as you think about your position for or against transracial adoption? What role does our own identity play in how we might view issues such as this?

Later in this edition, we will discuss adoption by same-sex parents. Keep the thoughts you had in response to this topic in mind as you read the later issue, and see whether your arguments can be applied to a same-sex couple adopting a child who may be heterosexual.

YES ↵

Tony Dokoupil

Raising Katie: What Adopting a White Girl Taught a Black Family About Race in the Obama Era

Several pairs of eyes follow the girl as she pedals around the playground in an affluent suburb of Baltimore. But it isn't the redheaded fourth grader who seems to have moms and dads of the jungle gym nervous on this recent Saturday morning. It's the African-American man—six feet tall, bearded and wearing a gray hooded sweatshirt—watching the girl's every move. Approaching from behind, he grabs the back of her bicycle seat as she wobbles to a stop. "Nice riding," he says, as the fair-skinned girl turns to him, beaming. "Thanks, Daddy," she replies. The onlookers are clearly flummoxed.

As a black father and adopted white daughter, Mark Riding and Katie O'Dea-Smith are a sight at best surprising, and at worst so perplexing that people feel compelled to respond. Like the time at a Pocono Mountains flea market when Riding scolded Katie, attracting so many sharp glares that he and his wife, Terri, 37, and also African-American, thought "we might be lynched." And the time when well-intentioned shoppers followed Mark and Katie out of the mall to make sure she wasn't being kidnapped. Or when would-be heroes come up to Katie in the cereal aisle and ask, "Are you OK?"—even though Terri is standing right there.

Is it racism? The Ridings tend to think so, and it's hard to blame them. To shadow them for a day, as I recently did, is to feel the unease, notice the negative attention, and realize that the same note of fear isn't in the air when they attend to their two biological children, who are 2 and 5 years old. It's fashionable to say that the election of Barack Obama has brought the dawn of a post-racial America. In the past few months alone, *The Atlantic Monthly* has declared "the end of white America," *The Washington Post* has profiled the National Association for the Advancement of Colored People's struggle for relevance in a changing world, and National Public Radio has led discussions questioning the necessity of the annual Black History Month. Perhaps not surprising, most white and black Americans no longer cite racism as a major social problem, according to recent polls.

But the Ridings' experience runs counter to these popular notions of harmony. And adoption between races is particularly fraught. So-called transracial adoptions have surged since 1994, when the Multiethnic Placement Act reversed decades of outright racial matching by banning discrimination against adoptive families on the basis of race. But the growth has been all one-sided. The number of white families adopting outside their race is growing and is now in the thousands, while cases like Katie's—of a black family adopting a nonblack child—remain frozen at near zero.

Decades after the racial integration of offices, buses, and water fountains, persistent double standards mean that African-American parents are still largely viewed with unease as caretakers of any children other than their own—or those they are paid to look after. As Yale historian Matthew Frye Jacobson has asked: "Why is it that in the United States, a white woman can have black children but a black woman cannot have white children?"

That question hit home for the Ridings in 2003, when Terri's mother, Phyllis Smith, agreed to take in Katie, then 3, on a temporary basis. A retired social worker, Phyllis had long been giving needy children a home—and Katie was one of the hardest cases. The child of a local prostitute, her toddler tantrums were so disturbing that foster families simply refused to keep her. Twelve homes later, Katie was still being passed around. Phyllis was in many ways an unlikely savior. The former president of the Baltimore chapter of the National Association of Black Social Workers, she joined her colleagues in condemning the adoption of black children by white families as "cultural genocide"—a position she still holds in theory, if not in practice. She couldn't say no to the "charming, energetic" girl who ended up on her front doorstep.

Last November, after a grueling adoption process—"[adoption officials] pushed the envelope on every issue," says Mark—little Irish-Catholic Katie O'Dea, as pale as a communion wafer, became Katie O'Dea-Smith: a formally adopted member of the African-American Riding-Smith family. (Phyllis is her legal guardian, but Mark and Terri were also vetted as legal surrogates for Phyllis.)

To be sure, it's an unconventional arrangement. Katie spends weekdays with Phyllis, her legal guardian. But Mark and Terri, who live around the corner, are her de facto parents, too. They help out during the week, and welcome Katie over on weekends and holidays. As for titles: Katie calls Phyllis "Mommy" and Terri "Sister," since technically it's true. Mark has always been "Daddy" or "Mark."

"Let me just put it out there," says Mark, a 38-year-old private-school admissions director with an appealing blend of megaphone voice and fearless opinion, especially when it comes to his family. "I've never felt more self-consciously black than while holding our little white girl's hand in public." He used to write off the negative attention as innocent curiosity. But after a half-decade of rude comments and revealing faux pas—like the time his school's guidance counselor called Katie a "foster child" in her presence—he now fights the ignorance with a question of his own: why didn't a white family step up to take Katie?

Riding's challenge hints at a persistent social problem. "No country in the world has made more progress toward combating overt racism than [the United States]," says David Schneider, a Rice University psychologist and the author of "The Psychology of Stereotyping." "But the most popular stereotype of black people is still that they're violent. And for a lot of people, not even racist people, the sight of a white child with a black parent just sets off alarm signals."

Part of the reason for the adoptive imbalance comes down to numbers, and the fact that people tend to want children of their own race. African-Americans represent almost one third of the 510,000 children in foster care, so black parents have a relatively high chance of ending up with a same-race child. (Not so for would-be adoptive white parents who prefer the rarest thing of all in the foster-care system: a healthy white baby.) But the dearth of black families with nonblack children also has painful historical roots. Economic hardship and centuries of poisonous belief in the so-called civilizing effects of white culture upon other races have familiarized Americans with the concept of white stewardship of other ethnicities, rather than the reverse.

The result is not only discomfort among whites at the thought of nonwhites raising their offspring; African-Americans can also be wary when one of their own is a parent to a child outside their race. Just ask Dallas Cowboys All-Pro linebacker DeMarcus Ware and his wife, Taniqua, who faced a barrage of criticism after adopting a nonblack baby last February. When *The New York Times* sports page ran a photo of the shirtless new father with what appeared to be a white baby in his arms (and didn't mention race in the accompanying story), it sent a slow shock wave through the African-American community, pitting supporters who celebrated the couple's joy after three painful miscarriages against critics who branded the Wares "self-race-hating individuals" for ignoring the disproportionate number of blacks in foster care. The baby, now their daughter, Marley, is in fact Hispanic. "Do you mean to tell me that the Wares couldn't have found a little black baby to adopt?" snarled one blogger on the *Daily Voice,* an online African-American newspaper.

For the relatively few black families that do adopt non-African-American children, and the adoptive children themselves, the experience can be confusing. "I hadn't realized how often we talked about white people at home," says Mark. "I hadn't realized that dinnertime stories were often told with reference to the race of the players, or that I often used racial stereotypes, as in the news only cares about some missing spring-break girl because she is blonde."

Katie, too, has sometimes struggled with her unusual situation, and how outsiders perceive it. When she's not drawing, swimming, or pining after teen heartthrob Zac Efron, she's often dealing with normal kid teasing with a nasty edge. "They'll ignore me or yell at me because I have a black family," she says. Most of her friends are black, although her school is primarily white. And Terri has noticed something else: Katie is uncomfortable identifying people by their race.

Is she racially confused? Should her parents be worried? Opinions vary in the larger debate about whether race is a legitimate consideration in adoption. At present, agencies that receive public funding are forbidden from taking race into account when screening potential parents. They are also banned from asking parents to reflect on their readiness to deal with race-related issues, or from requiring them to undergo sensitivity training. But a well-meaning policy intended to ensure colorblindness appears to be backfiring. According to a study published last year by the Evan B. Donaldson Adoption Institute, transracial parents are often ill equipped to raise children who are themselves unprepared for the world's racial realities.

Now lawmakers may rejoin the charged race-adoption debate. Later this year the U.S. Commission on Civil Rights, an independent federal think tank, is expected to publish a summary of expert testimony on adoption law—much of which will ask Congress to reinstate race as a salient consideration in all cases. The testimony, from the Evan B. Donaldson Institute and others, will also suggest initiatives currently banned or poorly executed under existing policies, including racial training for parents and intensifying efforts to recruit more black adoptive families.

Would such measures be a step back for Obama's post-racial America? It's hard to tell. The Ridings, for their part, are taking Katie's racial training into their own hands. They send her to a mixed-race school and mixed-race summer camps, celebrate St. Patrick's Day with gusto and buy Irish knickknacks, like a "Kiss Me I'm Irish" T shirt and a mug with Katie's O'Dea family crest emblazoned on it. But they worry it won't be enough. "All else being equal, I think she should be with people who look like her," says Mark. "It's not fair that she's got to grow up feeling different when she's going to feel different anyway. She wears glasses, her voice is a bit squeaky, and on top of that she has to deal with the fact that her mother is 70 and black."

But even if Katie feels different now, the Riding-Smiths have given her both a stable home and a familiarity with two ethnic worlds that will surely serve her well as she grows up in a country that is increasingly blended. And it may be that hers will be the first truly post-racial generation.

TONY DOKOUPIL is a staff writer at *Newsweek* and *The Daily Beast*. Dokoupil writes about different issues impacting national life, often related to diversity. In this article, he writes about the increasing number of transracial adoptions in the United States in recent years but notes that we are seeing limited examples of African American families adopting white babies. When an African American family adopts a white baby, a unique set of challenges are created, he argues, due to deep-seated views about race in American society today. Dokoupil explores questions related to what this reveals about contemporary views about race in American society.

**Ezra E. H. Griffith
and Rachel L. Bergeron**

Cultural Stereotypes Die Hard:
The Case of Transracial Adoption

The adoption of black children by white families, commonly referred to as transracial adoption in the lay and professional literature, is the subject of a debate that has persisted in American society for a long time.[1] On one side of the divide are those who believe that black children are best raised by black families. On the other are the supporters of the idea that race-matching in adoption does not necessarily serve the best interests of the child and that it promotes racial discrimination.[2]

Coming as it does in the midst of myriad other discussions in this country about black-white interactions, transracial adoption has occupied an important place in any debate about adoption policy. But in addition, as can be seen in language utilized by the Fifth Circuit Court in a 1977 case,[3] there is a long-held belief that since family members resemble one another, it follows that members of constructed families should also look like each other so as to facilitate successful adoption outcomes.

> [A]doption agencies quite frequently try to place a child where he can most easily become a normal family member. The duplication of his natural biological environment is part of that program. Such factors as age, hair color, eye color, and facial features of parents and child are considered in reaching a decision. This flows from the belief that a child and adoptive parents can best adjust to a normal family relationship if the child is placed with adoptive parents who could have actually parented him. To permit consideration of physical characteristics necessarily carries with it permission to consider racial characteristics [Ref. 3, pp 1205–6].

In utilizing this language, the court acknowledged that transracial adoption ran counter to the cultural beliefs that many people held about the construction of families. Still, the court concluded that while the difficulties attending transracial adoption justified the consideration of race as a relevant factor in adoption proceedings, race could not be the sole factor considered. With a bow to both sides in the transracial adoption debate, the argument could only continue.

As the debate marches on, mental health professionals are being asked to provide expert opinions about whether it would be preferable for a particular black child to be raised by a black family or by a family or adult of a different ethnic or racial group. There are, of course, different scenarios that may lead to the unfolding of these adoption disputes. For example, the question may arise when a black child is put up for adoption after having spent a number of months or years in an out-of-home placement. The lengthy wait of black children for an adoptive black family may understandably increase the likelihood of a transracial adoption. In another situation, the death of a biracial child's parents, one of whom was white and the other black, may lead to competition between the white and black grandparents for the right to raise the child. In a third possible context, the divorce of an interracial couple may result in a legal struggle for custody of the biracial child, with race trumpeted at least as an important factor if not the crucial factor to be considered in the decision about who should raise the child. Mental health professionals should therefore make an effort to stay abreast of the latest developments around this national debate if they intend to provide an informed opinion about the merits or problems of a potential transracial adoption.

We have already alluded to two significant factors that have played a role in the evolution of adoption policy concerning black children, particularly with respect to the question of whether race-neutral approaches make sense and whether transracial adoption is good practice. One factor has been judicial decision-making. In a relatively recent review, Hollinger[4] reminded us that, in general, racial classifications are invalidated unless they can survive the "strict scrutiny" test, which requires meeting a compelling governmental interest. Hollinger suggested that the "best-interest-of-the-child" standard commonly used in adoption practice would serve a substantial governmental interest. Such argumentation would allow the consideration of race as one element in an adoption evaluation. Following this reasoning, while race-neutral adoption may be a lofty objective, the specific needs of a particular child could legally allow the consideration of race.

The second factor to influence the evolution of adoption policy in this arena has been the academic research on transracial adoption.[5–9] This work has cumulatively demonstrated that black children can thrive and develop strong racial identities when nurtured in families with white parents. Transracially adopted children also do well on standard measures of self-esteem, cognitive development, and educational achievement. However, neither judicial decision-making nor scholarly research has settled the debate on transracial adoption policy.

In this article, we focus on a third factor that emerged as another mechanism meant to deal with transracial adoptions and the influential race-matching principle. These statutory efforts started with the Multiethnic Placement Act, which Hollinger stated "was enacted in 1994 amid spirited and sometimes contentious debate about transracial adoption and same-race placement policies."[4] We will point out that even though the statutory attempts were meant to eliminate race as a controlling factor in the adoption process, their implementation has left room for ambiguity regarding the role that race should play in adoption proceedings. Consequently, even though the statutes were intended to eliminate adoption delays and denials because of race-matching, they may have allowed the continued existence of a cultural stereotype—that black children belong with black families—and may have facilitated its continued existence. This article is therefore principally about statutory attempts in the past decade to influence public policy concerning transracial adoption. Secondarily, we shall comment on potential implications of these developments for the practice of adoption evaluations.

We emphasize once again that in referring to transracial adoption, we mean the adoption of black children by white parents. This is the focus of the statutes we consider. The adoption by Americans of children from other countries (international adoptions) and other transcultural adoptions (such as the adoption of Native American children by Anglos) are explicitly outside the parameters of this article. We also do not wish to suggest that although transracial adoption has been the subject of a significant national debate, it is a numerically common phenomenon. Later in this article, we review the available data on transracial adoption.

Brief Review of Race-Matching in Adoption

Feelings about who should raise a black child have run high in the United States for a long time. These feelings come from different groups for different reasons. Kennedy[1] presented a number of historical cases to illustrate this. Among the cases he described, Kennedy told the early 1900s story of a white girl who was found residing with a black family (Ref. 1, p 368). The authorities concluded that the child had been kidnapped and rescued her. They then placed her with a white family. When it was learned later that the child was black, she was returned to the black family because it was not proper for the black child to be living with a white family. This case, along with others described by Kennedy, is part of the fabric of American racism and racial separatist practices. Kennedy also pointed to the practice during slavery of considering "the human products of interracial sexual unions"

as unambiguously black and the mandate that they be reared within the black slave community as an attempt to undermine any possibility of interracial parenting (Ref. 1, pp 367–8).

Whites have not been the only ones to support the stance of race-matching—the belief that black or white children belong with their own group. In 1972, the National Association of Black Social Workers (NABSW) stated unambiguously that white families should never be allowed to adopt black children.[10] The NABSW opposed transracial adoption for two main reasons: the Association claimed that transracial adoption prevents black children from forming a strong racial identity, and it prevents them from developing survival skills necessary to deal with a racist society.

Since its 1972 statement, the NABSW has remained steadfast in its opposition to transracial adoption. In testimony before the Senate Committee on Labor and Human Resources in 1985, the President of the NABSW reiterated the Association's position and stated that the NABSW viewed the placement of black children in white homes as a hostile act against the black community, considering it a blatant form of race and cultural genocide.[11]

In 1991, the NABSW reaffirmed its position that black children should not be placed with white parents under any circumstances, stating that even the most loving and skilled white parent could not avoid doing irreparable harm to an African-American child.[12] In its 1994 position paper on the preservation of African-American families, the NABSW indicated that, in placement decisions regarding a black child, priority should be given to adoption by biological relatives and then to black families.[13] Transracial adoption "should only be considered after documented evidence of unsuccessful same race placements has been reviewed and supported by appropriate representatives of the African American community" (Ref. 13, p 1).

The NABSW's position was reflected in the 1981 New York case of *Farmer v. Farmer*.[14] Mr. Farmer, a black man, sought custody of his six-year-old daughter after he and his white wife divorced. He argued that his daughter, who looked black, would do better being raised by him than by her white mother and that her best interests could be achieved only by awarding custody to him, the parent with whom she would be racially identified by a racially conscious society. Three experts testified on his behalf. Each addressed the importance of racial identity problems that the child would face and the importance of her identification with her black heritage, but none would state categorically that custody of the child should be determined by her dominant racial characteristic. The judge rejected Mr. Farmer's race-based argument, finding that "between two natural parents of different races who have opted to have a child, neither gains priority for custody by reason of race alone. Nor can race disqualify a natural parent for custody" (Ref. 14, pp 589–90). He awarded custody to the mother based on the determination of the best interests of the child. In this determination race was not a dominant, controlling, or crucial factor, but was weighed along with all other material elements of the lives of the family.

Race-matching has been and remains an influential and controversial concept regarding how best to construct adoptive families. Matching, in general, has been a classic principle of adoption practice, governing non-relative adoptions for much of the 20th century. Its goal was to create families in which the adoptive parents looked as though they could be the adopted child's biological parents. Matching potential adoptive parents and children on as many physical, emotional, and cultural characteristics as possible was seen as a way of insuring against adoptive failure.[5] It was not uncommon for potential adoptive parents to be denied the possibility of adoption if their hair and eye color did not match those of a child in need of adoption.[5] Differences among family members in constructed families were seen as threats to the integration of an adopted child and the child's identification with the adoptive parents. Race, along with religion, was considered the most important characteristic to be matched, and it continued to be important even as the matching concept regarding other characteristics began to shift.[5] For example, in 1959, in its *Standards for Adoption Service* (SAS), the Child Welfare League of America (CWLA) recommended that

> . . . similarities of background or characteristics should not be a major consideration in the selection of a family, except where integration of the child into the family and his identification with them may be facilitated by likeness, as in the case of some older children or some children with distinctive physical traits, such as race [Ref. 5, pp 3–4].

The CWLA reiterated its view in its discussion of the role of physical characteristics: "Physical resemblances should not be a determining factor in the selection of a home, with the possible exception of such racial characteristics as color" (Ref. 5, p 4). It was not until 1968 that the CWLA omitted any reference to color as a criterion for adoption: "Physical resemblances of the adoptive parents, the child or his natural parents should not be a determining factor in the selection of a home" (Ref. 5, p 6). By 1971, the CWLA considered characteristics that had been encompassed in the matching concept to be broad guidelines rather than specific criteria and the weight afforded them depended on the potential adoptive parents (i.e., their desire for a child similar to them in particular ways should be taken into consideration).[5] While not identified as a strict criterion of adoption, matching continued to be a broad principle in adoption practices. For example, the CWLA's 1988 *Standards for Adoption Service* and its 1993 statement of its children's legislative agenda reflected its belief that the developmental needs of black adopted children could best be met by black adoptive parents.[5,6]

> Children in need of adoption have a right to be placed into a family that reflects their ethnicity or race. Children should not have their adoption

denied or significantly delayed, however, when adoptive parents of other ethnic or racial groups are available. . . . In any adoption plan, however, the best interests of the child should be paramount. If aggressive, ongoing recruitment efforts are unsuccessful in finding families of the same ethnicity or culture, other families should be considered [Ref. 5, p 32].

Matching, of course, continued to influence child placement decisions outside of adoption agencies, as evidenced by the comments of the Drummond court. Following that court's decision, the general rule has been that trial courts may consider race as a factor in adoption proceedings as long as race is not the sole determinant.[15,16]

Statutory Attempts at Remedies

As we previously noted, in 1972 the National Association of Black Social Workers (NABSW) issued a position paper in which the Association vehemently opposed the adoption of black children by white families.[10] The Black Social Workers had a quick and striking effect on transracial adoption policy. Following the appearance of the paper, adoption agencies, both public and private, either implemented race-matching approaches or used the NABSW position to justify already existing race-matching policies. As a result, the number of transracial adoptions were estimated to drop significantly—39 percent within one year of the publication of the NABSW statement.[17] Although robust data were lacking, it was thought that the number and length of stay of black children in out-of-home placements increased as social workers and other foster care and adoption professionals, believing that same-race placements were in the best interest of the child, searched for same-race foster and adoptive parents. Agencies and their workers had considerable discretion in deciding the role race played in placement decisions. States, while generally requiring that foster care and adoption decisions be made in the best interest of the child, varied in their directions regarding the extent to which race, culture, and ethnicity should be taken into account in making the best-interest determination.[18]

While race-matching policies were not the sole determinant of increasing numbers of black children in institutions and out-of-home placements, there was growing concern that such policies, with their focus on same-race placement and their exclusion of consideration of loving, permanent interracial homes, kept black children from being adopted.[19] Because he was concerned that race had become the determining factor in adoption placements and that children were languishing in foster care homes and institutions, Senator Howard Metzenbaum introduced legislation to prohibit the use of race as the sole determinant of placement.[19] Senator Metzenbaum believed that same-race adoption was the preferable option for a child, but he also believed that transracial placement was far preferable to a child's remaining in foster care when an appropriate same-race placement was not available.[19]

Multiethnic Placement Act

Congress passed the Howard Metzenbaum Multiethnic Placement Act (MEPA) and President Clinton signed it into law on October 20, 1994.[20] MEPA's main goals were to decrease the length of time children had to wait to be adopted; to prevent discrimination based on race in the placement of children into adoptive or foster homes; and to recruit culturally diverse and minority adoptive and foster families who could meet the needs of children needing placement.[18] In passing MEPA, Congress was concerned that many children, especially those from minority groups, were spending lengthy periods in foster care awaiting adoption placements.[19] Congress found, within the parameters of available data, that nearly 500,000 children were in foster care in the United States; tens of thousands of these children were waiting for adoption; two years and eight months was the median length of time children waited to be adopted; and minority children often waited twice as long as other children to be adopted.[21]

Under MEPA, an agency or entity receiving federal funds could not use race as the sole factor in denying any person the opportunity to become an adoptive or foster parent. Furthermore, an agency could not use race as a single factor to delay or deny the placement of a child in an adoptive or foster care family or to otherwise discriminate in making a placement decision. However, an agency could consider a child's racial, cultural, and ethnic background as one of several factors—not the sole factor—used to determine the best interests of the child.[22] MEPA stated:

> An agency, or entity, that receives Federal assistance and is involved in adoption or foster care placements may not—(A) categorically deny to any person the opportunity to become an adoptive or a foster parent, solely on the basis of the race, color or national origin of the adoptive or foster parent, or the child involved; or (B) delay or deny the placement of a child for adoption or into foster care, or otherwise discriminate in making a placement decision, solely on the basis of the race, color, or national origin of the adoptive or foster parent, or the child involved.[23]

However, MEPA also contained the following permissible consideration:

> An agency or entity . . . may consider the cultural, ethnic, or racial background of the child and the capacity of the prospective foster or adoptive parents to meet the needs of a child of this background as one of a number of factors used to determine the best interests of a child.[24]

So, under MEPA, agencies could consider a child's race, ethnicity, or culture as one of a number of factors used to determine the best interests of the child, as long as it was not the sole factor considered, and they could consider the ability of prospective parents to meet the needs of a child of a given race, ethnicity, or culture.[22]

Following the passage of MEPA, the Department of Health and Human Services (DHHS), Office of Civil Rights, provided policy guidance to assist agencies receiving federal financial assistance in complying with MEPA.[25] The guidance permitted agencies receiving federal assistance to consider race, culture, or ethnicity as factors in making placement decisions to the extent allowed by MEPA, the U.S. Constitution and Title VI of the Civil Rights Act of 1964.[25]

Under the Equal Protection Clause of the Fourteenth Amendment, laws or practices drawing distinctions on the basis of race are inherently suspect and subject to strict scrutiny analysis.[26] To pass such analysis, classifications or practices based on race have to be narrowly tailored to meet a compelling state interest.[26] The Supreme Court has not specifically addressed the question of transracial adoption. It has considered race as a factor in a child placement decision in the context of a custody dispute between two white biological parents when the mother, who had custody of the child, began living with a black man, whom she later married. The Court found the goal of granting custody on the basis of the best interests of the child to be "indisputably a substantial government interest for purposes of the Equal Protection Clause" (Ref. 27, p 433). The DHHS guidance on the use of race, color, or national origin as factors in adoption and foster care placements addressed the relevant constitutional issues and indicated that the only compelling state interest in the context of child placement decisions is protecting the best interests of the child who is to be placed.[25] So, under MEPA, consideration of race or ethnicity was permitted as long as it was narrowly tailored to advance a specific child's best interests.[25] Agencies receiving federal funds could consider race and ethnicity when making placement decisions only if the agency made a narrowly tailored, individualized determination that the facts and circumstances of a particular case required the contemplation of race or ethnicity to advance the best interests of the child in need of placement.[18,25] Agencies could not assume that race, ethnicity, or culture was at issue in every case and make general policies that applied to all children.[18] The guidance also specifically prohibited policies that established periods during which same-race searches were conducted, created placement preference hierarchies based on race, ethnicity, or culture, required social workers to justify transracial placement decisions or resulted in delayed placements to find a family of a particular race, ethnicity, or culture.[18]

The DHHS policy guidance did address MEPA's permissible consideration of the racial, cultural, or ethnic background of a child and the capacity of the prospective foster or adoptive parents to meet the needs of a child of this background as one of a number of factors in the best-interest-of-the-child determination. The guidance allowed agencies to assess the ability of a specific potential adoptive family to meet a specific child's needs related to his or her racial, ethnic, or cultural background, as long as the assessment was done in the context of an individualized assessment[18,25]:

> As part of this assessment, the agency may examine the attitudes of the prospective family that affect their ability to nurture a child of a particular background and consider the family's ability to promote development of the child's positive sense of self. The agency may assess the family's ability to nurture, support, and reinforce the racial, ethnic, or cultural identity of the child, the family's capacity to cope with the particular consequences of the child's developmental history, and the family's ability to help the child deal with any forms of discrimination the child may encounter [Ref. 18, pp 9–10].

However, agencies were not allowed to make decisions based on general assumptions regarding the needs of children of a specific race, ethnicity, or culture or about the ability of prospective parents of a specific race, ethnicity, or culture to care or nurture the identity of a child of a different race, ethnicity, or culture.[18]

To increase the pool of potential foster or adoptive parents, MEPA also required states to develop plans for the recruitment of potential foster and adoptive families that reflected the ethnic and racial diversity of the children needing placement.[28] The recruitment efforts had to be focused on providing all eligible children with the opportunity for placement and on providing all qualified members of the community with an opportunity to become an adoptive or foster parent.[18] As a result, while MEPA sought in a reasonable way to recruit a broad racial and cultural spectrum of adoptive families, the law was at the same time underlining the idea that there was something special about a black child's being raised by a black family.

Those who objected to the permissive consideration of race in MEPA asserted that it allowed agencies to continue to delay adoptions of minority children based on race concerns.[21] They also argued that race-matching policies could and did continue under MEPA. Social workers could, for example, use race as a factor to support a finding that a transracial adoption was not in a given child's best interest. Supporters of MEPA reached their own conclusion that it did not accomplish its goal of speeding up the adoption process and moving greater numbers of minority children into foster care or adoption placements and that the permissive consideration of race allowed agencies legitimately to continue race-matching to deny or delay the placement of minority children with white adoptive parents.[22] Senator Metzenbaum himself agreed with this conclusion about MEPA and worked for its repeal.[29] As we shall see later, the arguments and counterarguments about the effectiveness of MEPA were being made in the absence of robust data.

The Interethnic Adoption Provisions

MEPA was repealed when on August 20, 1996, President Clinton signed the Small Business Job Protection Act of 1996. Section 1808 of the Act was entitled "Removal of Barriers to Interethnic Adoption" (The Interethnic Adoption Provisions; IEP).[30] MEPA's permissible consideration provision was removed and its language changed. (The words in brackets were part of MEPA and do not appear in the IEP.)

> A person or government that is involved in adoption or foster care placements may not—(a) [categorically] deny to any individual the opportunity to become an adoptive or a foster parent, [solely] on the basis of race, color, or national origin of the individual, or the child involved; or (b) delay or deny the placement of a child for adoption or into foster care [or otherwise discriminate in making a placement decision, solely] on the basis of race, color, or national origin of the adoptive or foster parent, or the child, involved [Ref. 22, pp 1616–17].

Under the IEP, states were still required to "provide for the diligent recruitment of potential foster and adoptive families that reflect the ethnic and racial diversity of children in the State for whom foster and adoptive homes are needed."[28]

Failure to comply with MEPA was a violation of Title VI of the Civil Rights Act of 1964[17]; failure to comply with the IEP is also a violation of Title VI.[31] Under MEPA, an agency receiving federal assistance that discriminated in its child placement decisions on the basis of race and failed to comply with the Act could forfeit its federal assistance[17] and an aggrieved individual had the right to bring an action seeking equitable relief in federal court[32] or could file a complaint with the Office of Civil Rights. The IEP added enforcement provisions that specified graduated fiscal sanctions to be imposed by DHHS against states found to be in violation of the law and gave any individual aggrieved by a violation the right to bring an action against the state or other entity in federal court.[33]

The Department of Health and Human Services issued two documents to provide practical guidance for complying with the IEP: a memorandum[34] and a document in question-and-answer format.[35] According to the guidance, Congress, in passing the IEP, clarified its intent to eliminate delays in adoption or foster care placements when they were in any way avoidable. Race and ethnicity could not be used as the basis for any denial of placement nor used as a reason to delay a foster care or adoptive placement.[34] The repeal of MEPA's "permissible consideration" provision was seen as confirming that strict scrutiny was the appropriate standard for consideration of race or ethnicity in adoption and foster care placements.[34] DHHS argued that it had never taken the position that MEPA's permissible consideration language allowed agencies to take race into account routinely in making placement decisions because such a view would be inconsistent with a strict scrutiny standard.[34] It reaffirmed that any decision to consider race as a necessary element in a placement decision has to be based on concerns arising out of the circumstances of the particular situation:

> The primary message of the strict scrutiny standard in this context is that only the most compelling reasons may serve to justify consideration of race and ethnicity as part of a placement decision. Such reasons are likely to emerge only in unique and individual circumstances. Accordingly, occasions where race or ethnicity lawfully may be considered in a placement decision will be correspondingly rare [Ref. 34, p 4].

The guidance again made clear that the best interest of the child is the standard to be used in making placement decisions. So, according to the guidance, the IEP prohibits the routine practice of taking race and ethnicity into consideration ("Public agencies may not routinely consider race, national origin, and ethnicity in making placement decisions" (Ref. 35, p 2)), but it allows for the consideration of race, national origin, and ethnicity in certain specific situations ("Any consideration of these factors must be done on an individualized basis where special circumstances indicate that their consideration is warranted" (Ref. 35, p 2)). Once again, such language seems to suggest that, in certain contexts, the adoptive child may well benefit from placement in a same-race family.

The DHHS guidance seemed to frame the possibility for adoption agencies to continue the practice of race-matching.[22] For example, while warning that assessment of a prospective parent's ability to serve as a foster or adoptive parent must not act as a racial or ethnic screen and indicating that considerations of race must not be routine in the assessment function, the guidance conceded that an important aspect of good social work is an individualized assessment of a prospective parent's ability to be an adoptive or foster parent.

Thus, it allows for discussions with prospective adoptive or foster care parents about their feelings, preferences, and capacities regarding caring for a child of a particular race or ethnicity.[22,35]

Data Collection

Hansen and Simon[36] have pointed out that the Adoption and Safe Families Act (ASFA) of 1995 created an adoption incentive program that paid bonuses to states that increased the number of adoptions of children from foster care. The incentive program also provided an incentive for data collection, using a system known as the Adoption and Foster Care Analysis and Reporting System (AFCARS). States must submit data to AFCARS on each adoption in which a public child welfare agency was involved in any fashion. AFCARS issues periodic reports, and others (such as the Child Welfare League of America) use the AFCARS data to publish analytic reports from time to time. AFCARS

Table 1

Children Waiting to Be Adopted from the Public Foster Care System, by Race, by Fiscal Year

	On Sept. 30, 2002*		On Sept. 30, 2003[†]	
	Number	%	Number	%
Black/non-Hispanic	54,832	43	47,630	40
White/non-Hispanic	58,975	46	43,820	37
Total	127,942	100	119,000	100

*Reference 37.
[†]Reference 38.

Table 2

Children Adopted from the Public Foster Care System, by Race, by Fiscal Year

	Fiscal Year 2002*		Fiscal Year 2003[†]	
	Number	%	Number	%
Black/non-Hispanic	18,957	36	16,570	33
White/non-Hispanic	27,272	52	20,940	42
Total	52,138	100	50,000	100

*Reference 37.
[†]Reference 38.

reports may be preliminary, interim, or final as data continue to be submitted by states over many months.

Tables 1 and 2 show that in fiscal year (FY) 2002 and in FY 2003, more whites were adopted than blacks in the public foster care system. The two fiscal years show some difference between whites and blacks in terms of the comparative number of whites and blacks waiting for adoption. The data for FY 2003 show that more whites than blacks were in the foster care system. Of course, these numbers of children in the foster care system must be viewed in light of their representation in the general population. Data from the 2000 U.S. Census . . . show that of the total population under age 18 years, 68.6 percent (49,598,289) are white and 15.1 percent (10,885,696) are black. Consequently, a substantially greater proportion of blacks (.4%), in comparison to whites (.09%), were awaiting adoption in September 2003. Still, of the children awaiting adoption in September 2002, 30 percent of black children were adopted in FY 2003 in comparison to 36 percent of white children.

The AFCARS data from FY 2001 have been the subject of greater analysis, which has led to the following conclusions.[36,39] In FY 2001, mean time for adoption of black children was 18 months compared with 15 months for white children. It was also estimated that about 17 percent of black children adopted in FY 2001 were adopted transracially by white, non-Hispanic parents. This figure of transracial adoptions (about 2,500) provided for the public foster care system is not significantly above estimates given for earlier years—about 2,574 in 1971. However, the FY 2001 data do not include private sector adoptions. This has led Hansen and Simon[36] to conclude that there has been no clear increase in transracial adoptions, at least in the arena of public child welfare agency adoptions. In 2003, McFarland[40] published a report pointing out that while AFCARS is now producing robust data about public sector adoptions, information about private sector adoptions is scant.

Nevertheless, it has been estimated that in 2001, about 127,000 children were adopted in the United States,[41] including public, private, and intercountry adoptions. These adoptions arise out of the estimated 500,000 children in out-of-home placements in the United States.

Discussion

The IEP addresses individual cultural elements such as race, color, or national origin and does not address the broad role of culture in placement decisions. The DHHS guidance notes:

> There are situations where cultural needs may be important in placement decisions, such as where a child has specific language needs. However, a public agency's consideration of culture would raise Section 1808 [IEP] issues if the agency used culture as a proxy for race, color, or national origin. Thus, while nothing in Section 1808 directly prohibits a public agency from assessing the cultural needs of all children in foster care, Section 1808 would prohibit an agency from using routine cultural assessments in a manner that would circumvent the law's prohibition against the routine consideration of race, color, or national origin [Ref. 35, p 2].

This raises questions about the role of cultural capacity or cultural competence of parents in adoption and foster care decisions. In response to a question regarding whether public agencies may assess the cultural capacity of all foster parents, the DHHS responded in the negative, but seemed to open the door to such assessment, at least of particular parents:

> Race, color, and national origin may not routinely be considered in assessing the capacity of particular prospective foster parents to care for specific children. However, assessment by an agency of the capacity of particular adults to serve as foster parents for specific children is the heart of the placement process, and essential to determining what would be in the best interests of a particular child [Ref. 35, p 2].

The DHHS guidance makes a similar statement regarding cultural competency:

> The term "cultural competency," as we understand it, is not one that would fit in a discussion of adoption and foster placement. However, agencies should, as

a matter of good social work practice, examine all the factors that may bear on determining whether a particular placement is in the best interest of a particular child. That may in rare instances involve the consideration of the abilities of prospective parents of one race or ethnicity to care for a child of another race or ethnicity [Ref. 35, p 5].

Such language is obviously far from being lucid and specific. It grants the potential importance of considering race and cultural competence, but cautions against general and routine use of these factors, while contemplating their utility in particular situations.

In considering the best interests of a child who is being placed for adoption, DHHS is suggesting that there could be special circumstances uniquely individualized to the child that require consideration of ethnicity and race of the potential adoptive parents. Presumably this should not be done routinely and should not be seen as serving as a proxy for a consistent and mundane contemplation of ethnicity or race in the adoption context. Undoubtedly, what constitutes special circumstances in the practices of any given adoption agency is likely to be a matter of interpretation. While agencies can readily assert what their routine practices are, much may turn on how vigorously supervised are the claims that special circumstances exist with respect to a particular black child that dictate consideration of ethnicity and race in that child's case. As a practical result, while it appears no one is now allowed to claim that every black child needs a black family, it may still be reasonable and practicable to claim that a black child requires adoption by a black family, as dictated by consideration of the best interests of that child. For example, Kennedy (Ref. 1, p 416) has raised the possibility that an older child might say he or she wanted to be adopted only by a black family. Such a context could indeed make it difficult for the child's wish to be refused outright, without any consideration whatsoever.

Such reasoning is articulated starting from the point of view of the child. Giving consideration to the interests of the potential adoptive parent is another matter. In other words, what should we consider about the adoptive parent's interest in raising black children and the parent's ability to do so? The opinions about this matter remain divided. Kennedy (Ref. 1, pp 416, 434) and Bartholet[42] have proposed that prospective adoptive parents be allowed to state a preference for adopting a child from a particular ethnic group. This is, in their view, permissible race-matching that ultimately serves the best interests of the child. After all, what would be the use of forcing a family to adopt a child they really did not want? In addition, both authors also have argued that state intervention in such racial selectivity in the formation of families would be akin to imposing race-based rules on the creation of married couples. However, Banks[43] has opposed this accommodationist stance, where in practice adoption agencies would simply show prospective adoptive parents only the class of ethnic children the adoptive parent was interested in adopting. Banks thought this merely perpetuated the status quo, as white adoptive parents had little interest in black children. This would result in black children's continuing to languish in out-of-home placements, and their time spent awaiting adoption would remain prolonged.

Kennedy and Bartholet were permissive in their attitude toward the racial selectivity of prospective adoptive parents, respecting parents' choice to construct families as they wish.

There has been and continues to be strong support for the belief that black children belong with black adoptive parents. It is not only the NABSW, which has called for the repeal of the IEP,[13] that has taken this position. For example, in a 1998 letter to the Secretary of the Department of Health and Human Services, a former executive director of the Child Welfare League of America strongly disagreed with the DHHS's interpretation of MEPA/IEP, stating that prohibiting any consideration of race in adoptive and foster care placement decisions contradicts best-practice standards in child welfare:

> CWLA standards for adoption and foster care services clearly state that the best practice requires consideration of race. . . . Children in need of adoption have a right to be placed into a family that reflects their ethnicity or race. . . . These standards—calling for the explicit consideration of race in adoption and foster care placement decisions—reflect the best thinking of child welfare experts from across the country [Ref. 44, p 2].

The CWLA, in its most recent *Standards of Excellence for Adoption Services* (2000), reiterated its belief that race is to be considered in all adoptions and that placement with parents of the same race is the first choice for any child. Other placements should be considered only after a vigorous search for parents of the same race has failed:

> All children deserve to be raised in a family that respects their cultural heritage. . . . If aggressive, ongoing recruitment efforts are unsuccessful in finding families of the same race or culture as the child, other families should be considered to ensure that the child's adoptive placement is not delayed [Ref. 45, p 68].

In its most recent policy statement on foster care and adoption (2003), the National Association of Social Workers also reiterated its position that consideration of race should play a central role in placement decisions:

> Placement decisions should reflect a child's need for continuity, safeguarding the child's right to consistent care and to service arrangements. Agencies must recognize each child's need to retain a significant engagement with his or her parents and extended family and respect the integrity of each child's ethnicity and cultural heritage [Ref. 46, p 147].

The social work profession stresses the importance of ethnic and cultural sensitivity. An effort to maintain a child's identity and his or her ethnic heritage should prevail in all services and placement actions that involve children in foster care and adoption programs [Ref. 46, p 148].

The placement of choice should be within the child's family of origin, among relatives (kinship placement) who can provide a more stable environment for the child during the period of family crisis. If no such relatives are available, every effort should be made to place a child in the home of foster parents who are similar in racial and ethnic background to the child's own family. The recruitment of foster parents from each relevant racial and ethnic group should be pursued vigorously to meet the needs of children who require placement [Ref. 46, p 150].

Others[47–49] have espoused the view that inracial adoption is the preferred option for a black child because black families inherently possess the competence to raise children with strong black identities and the ability to cope with racism. While questions of cultural competence to raise a black child often arise about prospective white adoptive parents, no such questions are posed about prospective black adoptive parents.[1] The competence of black families to raise black children is regularly referred to as though black families are culturally identical or homogeneous and all are equally competent to raise black children and equip them to live in our society.[1,50] We may all think about black cultural competence as though it is a one-dimensional concept. Indeed, we may all be referring simply to stereotypical indicators of what we think it means to be black. We may be referring to our own personal preferences for the stereotypic activities of black people: involvement in a black church; participation in a community center where black-focused programs are operating; viewing movies with a clearly black theme; reading literature authored by blacks. What is rarely considered is that some black families are drawn to rap music, others to jazz greats, and still others to traditional classical music. Indeed, some families obviously manage to exhibit an interest in all these genres of music. With respect, therefore, to even these stereotyped indicators of what it means to be black, black families vary in the degree of their attachment to the indicators. This is to say that blacks differ in their level of commitment to the salience of black-oriented culture in their individual and family lives. As a result, there is considerable cultural heterogeneity among black families. Such variability may well lead to differences in black families' ways of coping with racism.[50]

To date, the statutory attempts to deal with transracial adoptions have not been considered as spectacularly successful, especially in the case of MEPA. Nevertheless, efforts have been made to limit the routine consideration of race and ethnicity in adoption, with the result that black children may be remaining for shorter periods in undesirable out-of-home placements. (National data are not yet able to demonstrate clear trends.[36,40]) However,

DHHS guidance still permits consideration of race and ethnicity in specific cases, with the apparent concession that some black children may need a black family for the realization of the child's best interests.

The burden is on forensic psychiatrists and other mental health professionals who perform adoption evaluations to point out cogently and logically two points: first, whether race is a factor that is relevant in the adoption evaluation; and second, whether there is something unique or particular about that adoption context that requires race to be considered. It will require special argumentation for the evaluator to claim that a particular black child could benefit more from placement with a black family than with a non-black family. As stated earlier, the evidence is clear that black children can do well in transracial placements. The pointed objective, therefore, in future evaluations will be to show that a particular black child has such unique and special needs that he or she deserves particular consideration for placement in a black family. It will be interesting to see whether our forensic colleagues, in striving for objectivity, will consider the factor of race in their evaluations only when something unique about that particular adoption context cries out for race to be considered so that the best-interest-of-the-child standard can be met. It seems clear that forensic professionals must be careful not to state that they routinely consider race in their adoption evaluations unless they intend to argue clinically that race is always relevant. And even then, they should be cautious about not articulating a general preference for inracial over transracial adoptions.

Despite federal statutory attempts to remove race as a controlling factor in adoption and foster care placement decisions, the debate over transracial adoption is not over. Indeed, strains of the debate are evidenced in the statutes and their implementation guidelines and the argument continues among our mental health colleagues. For example, following passage of MEPA and the IEP, a group of adoption experts from different disciplines was assembled by the Stuart Foundation to reconsider the controversies surrounding racial matching and transracial adoption. The Adoption and Race Work Group concluded that "race should not be ignored when making placement decisions and that children's best interests are served—all else being equal—when they are placed with families of the same racial, ethnic, and cultural background as their own" (Ref. 51, p 169). The Work Group decided that the research to date was insufficient, even though research has supported transracial adoption.

The ultimate outcome of the group's deliberations is perhaps the clearest indication of how difficult it is in this debate to meld passion and scholarship. The ongoing debate exemplifies Courtney's conclusion that "those with strongly held views are likely to maintain their convictions: advocates of TRA will continue to believe that the research supports their beliefs, while opponents will contend that TRA is harmful, or that the jury is still out" (Ref. 52, p 753). After two years of work analyzing racial matching and transracial adoption, the Stuart work group acknowledged that thinking about the debate in terms of those who oppose or support transracial or inracial adoptions may get us nowhere. "It may be more productive to regard the issue in terms of assessing, deciding, and documenting when the law allows us to place more or less emphasis on race and racial matching and when good social work practice calls for it" (Ref. 52, p 177). This may be a concession to the notion that, with respect to transracial adoption, cultural stereotypes die hard.

References

1. Kennedy R: Interracial Intimacies: Sex, Marriage, Identity and Adoption. New York: Pantheon Books, 2003
2. For further commentary on the debate, see: Griffith EEH, Duby JL: Recent developments in the transracial adoption debate. Bull Am Acad Psychiatry Law 19:339–50, 1991. Griffith EEH: Forensic and policy implications of the transracial adoption debate. Bull Am Acad Psychiatry Law 23:501–12, 1995
3. Drummond v. Fulton County Department of Family and Children's Services, 563 F.2d 1200 (5th Cir. 1977)
4. Hollinger JH: A Guide to the Multiethnic Placement Act of 1994 as Amended by the Interethnic Adoption Provisions of 1996. National Resource Center on Children and the Law. . . .
5. Simon RJ, Alstein H: Adoption, Race and Identity: From Infancy to Young Adulthood. New Brunswick, NJ: Transaction Publishers, 2002
6. Vroegh KS: Transracial adoptees: developmental status after 17 years. Am J Orthopsychiatry 67:568–75, 1997
7. Griffith EEH, Adams AK: Public policy and transracial adoptions of black children, in Family, Culture and Psychobiology Edited by Sorel E. Ottawa, ON, Canada: Legas Press, 1990, pp 211–33
8. Griffith EEH, Silverman IL: Transracial adoptions and the continuing debate on the racial identity of families, in Racial and Ethnic Identity: Psychological Development and Creative Expression. Edited by Harris HW, Blue HC, Griffith EEH. New York: Routledge, 1995, pp 95–114
9. Burrow AL, Finley GE: Transracial, same-race adoptions, and the need for multiple measures of adolescent adjustment. Am J Orthopsychiatry 74:577–83, 2004
10. National Association of Black Social Workers: Position Statement on Transracial Adoptions. September 1972. . . .
11. Testimony of William T Merritt, President of the National Association of Black Social Workers, Hearings Before the Committee on Labor and Human Resources, United States Senate, 99th Congress, June 25, 1985
12. Institute for Justice: Separate is not equal: striking down state-sanctioned barriers to interracial adoption. . . .

13. National Association of Black Social Workers: Preserving Families of African Ancestry. Washington, DC: NABSW, 2003
14. Farmer v. Farmer, 439 N.YS.2d 584 (N.Y Sup. Ct. 1981)
15. Farrell T, Gregor R, Payne A, *et al:* Adoption § 138 Interethnic Adoption. Am Jur 2d: 138, 2004
16. Zitter JM: Race as a factor in adoption proceedings. ALR 4th 34:167, 2004
17. Marby CR: "Love alone is not enough!" in transracial adoptions: scrutinizing recent statutes, agency policies, and prospective adoptive parents. Wayne Law Rev 42:1347–23, 1996
18. Bussiere A: A Guide to the Multiethnic Placement Act of 1994. ABA Center on Children and the Law. . . .
19. Metzenbaum HM: S. 1224—In Support of the Multiethnic Placement Act of 1993. Duke J Gender Law Policy 2:165–71, 1995
20. 42 U.S.C. § 5115a (1994)
21. Varan R: Desegregating the adoptive family: in support of the Adoption Antidiscrimination Act of 1995. J Marshall Law Rev 30:593–625, 1997
22. Campbell SB: Taking race out of the equation: transracial adoption in 2000. SMU Law Rev 53:1599–626, 2000
23. 42 U.S.C. § 5115a (a) (1)(A)-(B) (1994)
24. 42 U.S.C. § 5115a(a) (2) (1994)
25. Hayashi D: Policy Guidance on the Use of Race, Color or National Origin as Considerations in Adoption and Foster Care Placements. Washington, DC: Office of Civil Rights, Department of Health and Human Services. . . .
26. Adarand Constructors, Inc. v. Pena, 515 U.S. 200 (1995)
27. Palmore v. Sidoti, 466 U.S. 429 (1984)
28. 42 U.S.C. § 622(b)(9)
29. Statement of the Honorable Howard Metzenbaum: Testimony Before the Subcommittee on Human Resources of the House Committee on Ways and Means. Hearing on Interethnic Adoptions, September 15, 1998. . . .
30. 42 U.S.C.S. § 1996 b(l) (2003)
31. 42 U.S.C.S. § 1996 b(2) (2003)
32. 42 U.S.C.S. § 5115a(b) (1994)
33. 42 U.S.C.S. § 674(d) (2003)
34. Hayashi D: Interethnic Adoption Provisions of the Small Business Job Protection Act of 1996. Memorandum, Office for Civil Rights, Department of Health and Human Services. June 4, 1997. . . .
35. Questions and Answers Regarding the Multiethnic Placement Act of 1994 and Section 1808 of the Small Business and Job Protection Act of 1996. Office for Civil Rights, Department of Health and Human Services. . . .
36. Hansen ME, Simon RJ: Transracial Placement in Adoptions With Public Agency Involvement: What Can We Learn From the AFCARS Data? . . .
37. National Data Analysis System. . . .
38. U.S. Department of Health and Human Services, Administration for Children and Families: The AFCARS Report 10. . . .
39. The Multiethnic Placement Act. National Data Analysis System. . . .
40. McFarland MC: Adoption Trends in 2003: A Deficiency of Information. National Center for State Courts, 2003. . . .
41. National Adoption Information Clearinghouse: How Many Children Were Adopted in 2000 and 2001? . . .
42. Bartholet E: Private race preferences in family formation. Yale Law J 107:2351–6, 1998
43. Banks RR: The color of desire: fulfilling adoptive parents' racial preferences through discriminatory state action. Yale Law J 107: 875–964, 1998
44. Letter from David Liederman, Former CWLA Executive Director to Donna Shalala, HHS Secretary, December 21, 1998. . . .
45. Child Welfare League of America: Standards of Excellence: Standards of Excellence for Adoption Services (revised edition). Washington, DC: Child Welfare League of America, Inc., 2000
46. National Association of Social Workers: Foster care and adoption, in Social Work Speaks: National Association of Social Workers Policy Statements, 2003–2006 (ed 6). Washington, DC: NASW Press, 2003, pp 144–51
47. Chimezie A: Transracial adoption of black children. Social Work 20:296–301, 1975
48. Jones E: On transracial adoption of black children. Child Welfare 51:156–64, 1972
49. Bowen JS: Cultural convergences and divergences: the nexus between putative Afro-American family values and the best interests of the child. J Family Law 26:487–531, 1987–88
50. Griffith EEH: Culture and the debate on adoption of black children by white families, in American Psychiatric Press Review of Psychiatry (vol 14). Edited by Oldham JM, Riba MB. Washington, DC: American Psychiatric Press, 1995, pp 543–64
51. Brooks D, Barth RP, Bussiere A, *et al:* Adoption and race: implementing the Multiethnic Placement Act and the Interethnic Adoption Provisions. Social Work 44:167–78, 1999
52. Courtney ME: The politics and realities of transracial adoption. Child Welfare 76:749–79, 1997

Ezra E. H. Griffith, MD, is a Professor Emeritus of Psychiatry and African American studies at Yale University, as well as Deputy Chair for diversity and organizational ethics and Senior Research Scientist in the Yale Department of Psychiatry.

Rachel L. Bergeron is Assistant Clinical Professor of Psychiatry at the Yale School of Medicine. Griffith and Bergeron argue that requiring racial and ethnic matching, although an appropriate effort, would leave too many children of color languishing in the foster and adoption systems. By maintaining that only in-race adoption is the best and ideal situation, they ask rhetorically, does our society actually do more to reinforce cultural stereotypes or to truly serve children needing homes?

EXPLORING THE ISSUE

Is It Beneficial if Adoptive Parents Adopt Only Within Their Own Racial/Ethnic Group?

Critical Thinking and Reflection

1. What are some of the arguments made by each side with which you agree or disagree?
2. What are the strengths and weaknesses of the two positions argued in this chapter?
3. Pick the side with which you most agree. What are some additional arguments you would make to strengthen the case for or against transracial adoption?
4. Think more broadly of the issue of transracial adoption. What are the benefits of homogeneous family structures and what are the benefits of heterogeneous family structures? What are the weaknesses or limitations?

Is There Common Ground?

Everyone wants children to have the best childhood possible, and everyone knows that parents' loving a child is the most important factor. At the same time, our nation has a long and complicated history related to race, and that history cannot be easily separated or removed from the subject of transracial adoption. Why is transracial adoption more controversial with some races than with others? How does this affect children when they learn about attitudes regarding race and traditional families? Are there certain situations that would be more ideal for transracial adoption than others?

Create Central

www.mhhe.com/createcentral

Additional Resources

H. M. Dalmadge, *Tripping on the Color Line: Black-White Multiracial Families in a Racially Divided World* (Piscataway, NJ: Rutgers University Press, 2000).

H. Fogg-Davis, *Ethics of Transracial Adoption* (Ithaca, NY: Cornell University Press, 2001).

J. Lang, *Transracial Adoptions: An Adoptive Mother's Documentary of Racism, Injustice, & Joy* (Universe, Incorporated, 2002).

S. Patton, *Birthmarks: Transracial Adoption in Contemporary America* (New York: New York University Press, 2000).

R. J. Simon and H. Altstein, *Adoption Across Borders: Serving the Children in Transracial and Intercountry Adoption* (Lanham, MD: Rowman & Littlefield Publishers, Inc., 2000).

R. J. Simon and R. Roorda, In *Their Own Voices: Transracial Adoptees Tell Their Stories* (New York: Columbia University Press, 2000).

G. Steinberg and B. Hall, *Inside Transracial Adoption* (Indianapolis, IN: Perspectives Press, Inc., 2000).

J. J. J. Trenka, S. Y. Shin, J. C. Oparah, and S. Y. Shin, eds., *Outsiders Within: Writing on Transracial Adoption* (Cambridge, MA: South End Press, 2006).

Internet References . . .

American Adoptions: Transracial Adoptions

www.americanadoptions.com/adopt/
transracial_adoption

Child Welfare: Transracial Adoption

www.childwelfare.gov/pubs/f_trans.cfm

Interracial Adoption and Parenting

http://interracial.adoption.com/

Selected, Edited, and with Issue Framing Material by:
David M. Hall, Ph.D., *Delaware Valley College*

ISSUE

Does Divorce Have a Negative Impact on Children?

YES: Sarah Werthan Buttenwieser, from "Does Divorce Have a Negative Impact on Children?," revised from *Taking Sides: Family and Personal Relationships* (2009)

NO: Jane Johnson Struck and Angela Thomas, from "Solo Act: Single Mom Angela Thomas Reflects on Raising Kids Alone," *Today's Christian Woman* (May/June 2008)

Learning Outcomes
After reading this issue, you will be able to:
• Identify the major challenges that divorce causes parents and children.
• Compare and contrast the competing arguments made for and against divorce in this issue.
• Evaluate issues that authors raise about how they will help create a more peaceful divorce (e.g., communication and collaboration, religious faith).

ISSUE SUMMARY

YES: Sarah Werthan Buttenwieser is a writer and lives in Northampton. She earned her BA at Hampshire College and her MFA from Warren Wilson College. Contributor to many magazines, newspapers, and online publications, she has a blog called "Standing in the Shadows," which can be found at www.valleyadvocate.com.

NO: Jane Johnson Struck and Angela Thomas are the authors of *My Single-Mom Life*, published by Thomas Nealson. Thomas, a mother of four, possesses a Masters degree from the Dallas Theological Seminary. Thomas writes that being a single mom was not God's design for parenting. She believes in children being raised by a man and a woman in love. Despite her beliefs and the challenges she has faced through divorce, her belief is that God and Jesus protect her and her children when they are in need. She argues that faith in God is what people need to protect them from the challenges of being a single mother and a child of a divorced family.

In the United States today, 63 percent of children grow up with both biological parents. The highest divorce rates in the United States are found in Nevada and Arkansas, while the lowest divorce rates are found in Washington, DC; Massachusetts; and Pennsylvania. Divorces lead to a division of parenting responsibility as well as finances. Almost 7.8 million Americans pay approximately $40 billion each year in child and spousal support. While there has been a slight decline in divorces over recent years, there has been a corresponding decrease in marriage as well.

Couples today are often focused on the well-being of the children in the family. How, then, do we assess the impact of separation on children? Marriage and cohabitation laws vary across the states. These laws are often based on the belief that marriage will provide greater family and societal stability by keeping couples together. Over the last 50 years, American values related to marriage and cohabi-

tation have changed significantly. It was not until 1967, in the case of *Loving v. Virginia*, that the U.S. Supreme Court ruled to strike down state laws forbidding interracial marriages. During more recent times, some courts have struck down state laws prohibiting cohabitation, policies intended to discourage living together out of wedlock.

The history of marriage is diverse and fluid. It can be a story of extraordinary love and joy. It can also be a story of great pain and even abuse. Across time, the meaning of marriage and love has been reconstructed. What was once often a financial arrangement is today something that is much more likely to have a foundation in love. In the United States today, the economic necessity to remain married, or even to get married in the first place, is less than it ever has been in this nation's history.

Considering the decrease in marriage, the challenges of separation now extend well beyond the martial relationship. Many unmarried couples with children choose to cohabitate. In fact, the frequency of cohabitation with children is four times higher today than it was in 1970. With a sizable number of children born out of wedlock, the concept of parents staying together extends well beyond marriage and divorce.

Clearly, concepts of family and matrimony are being reconstructed in American society. Virtually every reader has experience with these changes. It is difficult to grow up in American society today without having personal experiences or knowing someone well who comes from a divorced family. Additionally, there are many families today where two parents, whether married or not, are raising a child. The same challenges and questions for staying together face them as those challenges that face married couples.

The focus of debate in this chapter is whether or not couples should stay together for the sake of their children. If the reader refers to the Political Ideology Continuum featured in the Introduction to this book, reactionaries or conservatives would be more likely to support staying together for the sake of the children. In contrast, liberals and radicals tend to support ending the relationship if they think that is best. However, those labels tend to stop at the level of political theory and are limited in translating it into affecting personal lives. Indeed, many conservatives have their marriages end in divorce while their children are young. Meanwhile, a significant number of liberals stay in their relationships for the sake of their children. In fact, the writers in this chapter prove that there are limitations when applying the Political Ideology Continuum too rigidly. Specifically, when taking a close look at Buttenwieser's article, readers will notice a sometimes liberal but often nonpolitical framework for a position that is traditionally associated with conservative values. In contrast, the opposing article is written through a traditionally Christian framework.

When reading, give consideration to how these views shared fit into the Political Ideology Continuum. Apply these views to experiences in your own world, either in your own family or the relationships of others you know well.

One of the ways to avoid becoming an unhappy married couple is to work on entering healthy relationships and work on ensuring that a relationship remains healthy. However, this is a challenging goal, and unhealthy relationships, or even relationships that are just not right, are inevitable. Despite this fact, little time is invested in helping teenagers identify the qualities of a healthy relationship and to further develop the skills of making relationships work.

While an equal relationship does not guarantee a happy relationship, it is a critical component. Dating and domestic violence organizations will often cite the following qualities in a healthy relationship: negotiation and fairness, nonthreatening behavior, respect, trust and support, honesty and accountability, responsible parenting, shared responsibility, and economic partnership. In all relationships, including happy ones, it is typically necessary to work on ensuring that both individuals are treated equally and feel valued and respected within their relationship.

If separation is inevitable for a couple, it is critical to examine what can make this experience work as well as possible for the children involved. WebMD lists nine do's and don'ts in helping children with divorce. This advice can also be applied to non-marital cohabitation as well:

Don't confide in your children about adult concerns like your disagreements with your spouse or your money worries. Find a friend or counselor to confide in instead.

Don't criticize your ex. If you have a dispute with your ex-spouse, don't expose your children to your conflicts and frustration.

Don't quiz your child about the other parent or what goes on at the other parent's house. It's fine to ask general questions about your child's time there, but don't snoop.

Don't introduce major changes in your child's life if you can help it. Try to keep to your usual family routines and community ties.

Do continue to parent as you always have. You may feel guilty that your children have to cope with divorce, but it won't help to give them special presents or let them stay up late. They'll feel more secure if you're firm and consistent.

Do encourage children to call the other parent when they have news or just to talk. Keep the other parent informed about school events and other activities.

Do learn more about how to help your child cope with divorce.

Do get help for a child having trouble coping with divorce. A young child may show regressive behavior like excessive clinginess or bedwetting, while an older child may become angry, aggressive, withdrawn, or depressed, or have problems in school. A therapist can provide a safe place for your child to express his or her feelings.

Do seek help if you and your ex can't interact without hostility. A family therapist or professional mediator can help you develop a more friendly communication style—one with fewer negative effects on your children.

How would you assess WebMD's list? What advice is most important to adhere to? What advice is most challenging to adhere to?

Although there are differences regarding whether unhappy couples should separate for the sake of their children, there are good and bad ways to go about separation, not only for the children but also for the former couple. Adhering to these guidelines can help limit the struggles associated with divorce or separation.

YES

Sarah Werthan Buttenwieser

Does Divorce Have a Negative Impact on Children?

We all know that Tolstoy was right: "Happy families are all alike; every unhappy family is unhappy in its own way." And so often, unhappy couples decide that their ticket to happiness, their shot at it, begins with divorce.

From divorce, there is possibility—of freedom and of a love relationship working out the next time around.

What about the couple's children? Does divorce have a negative impact on them?

Yes, divorce probably does have a negative impact on children.

Why? Because divorce creates a fissure in a family's life and for the child or children: divorce assumes a great deal of disruption—two households rather than one. Contact with both parents becomes chopped up or the contact with one parent is lost, simultaneously shifting all responsibility onto one parent's shoulders.

That doesn't mean divorce can't have many positive effects, too. It definitely can—and often does. But a happier outcome doesn't happen magically; it takes work.

Divorce can ultimately turn out well for the children *if* the parents decide that a healthy divorce—one that benefits the children—is worth the hard work that it entails. This so-called ideal divorce could be dubbed a peaceful divorce, a friendly divorce, or even a loving divorce. I'd like to share some ideas about how to make divorce work well for the children.

Before I begin, let me make an exception. This is critical: Safety is the top priority. If anyone in a family—spouse or child—is being abused, physically or emotionally, that person's safety is a stand-alone and nonnegotiable consideration.

The premise of a divorce that has a positive impact upon children begins with a commitment from both parents—and any future partners—to work hard for the sake of a peaceful coexistence, and to forge a family that works for the kids—even if it occurs in two places. Some people use the phrase "a family apart" to ensure the child envisions family as a complete entity, even if divided by geography and other life changes. Whatever it's called, a positive divorce scenario for the kids almost inevitably requires a lot of work on the part of the adults. It's harder to have a positive divorce than a happy, uninterrupted marriage.

While marriage is a contract with a legal route to dissolution in its makeup, children come with no equally simple and clear documentation. That's why children do not resemble finances or even custody; they cannot be divvied up like furniture or real estate and remain emotionally intact. And unlike even marriage, children are *the* lifelong commitment parents make. Far more than roof over head and food in bellies, parents owe children a version of a happy family, even if it's post-divorce and a family-apart model rather than a family-together one.

I believe that any couple contemplating divorce should think long and hard about whether they could really commit to a good divorce. I don't think sticking it out until the kids leave is a great alternative. Whether a couple chooses to stay together or separate, children benefit from their parents honestly and earnestly working through either choice toward what is essentially a happy ending. A marriage that vanishes as soon as the child leaves for college, and any sense of goodwill with it, that's like an illusion: a thing that seemed real crumbling into dust.

Once kids appear, whether in a solid, happy marriage, a primarily disappointing marriage, or a divorce, parents need to remain focused on their children's best interests. In order to do so, they need to remain flexible in thought and in action in order to accommodate their children's needs. That's really the main message here. And it's a different message than neglecting your own needs because you are focused upon your children; it's more of a plea to remember what a huge responsibility you've assumed by becoming a parent.

Ideally, everyone's happiness lines up like stars on a perfect evening, like ducks in a row, like that equation we hope is true, that "happy parent equals happy child." However, by choosing one's own adult happiness, one's child's happiness does not inevitably follow. Parents cannot protect children from all unhappiness (nor should they; learning to deal with disappointment and unhappiness is an essential part of life, indeed of a happy life). But parents should try to protect their children, and in so doing, should—I believe—place their children's happiness, if not on a pedestal, in a safe place.

That's why I'm advocating that if parents are divorcing, they should: (1) remain focused on the child or children, (2) remain flexible, and (3) remain willing to put their child's happiness above their own sometimes.

Full disclosure: I'm a (grown) child of divorce contemplating this issue from within a very happy marriage (with four kids). In the case of my parents' divorce, obviously I had no say in whether it happened. Although I cannot rewrite history, I do think all of our lives were better for their choosing to part ways. My parents' was a protracted and ambivalent and messy split. Once it was finally finished, what came next was an improvement upon the uneasy marriage or the mercurial uncertainty that endured for a few more years.

Even though divorce turned out to be better than my parents' staying married, my experience convinced me that divorce is almost inevitably difficult for the children. Having your daily life split between households is unsettling, even if that's the routine. If I close my eyes, I can still picture the small, rectangular, flowery suitcase that I carried between my mother's house and father's house during many childhood years. The green was a bit olivey; the reds contained a bit of magenta; the flowers were rendered with a seventies aesthetic. The case had a plastic, rectangular handle and a gold-brass clasp—as might be on a journal—that slid into place. I absolutely hated it. Not the suitcase itself; I hated what it represented. We went back and forth at a dizzying rate. The prevailing wisdom of the time was that young children should not be separated from their mothers for very long, so we had a staccato rhythm that had us at our dad's a night, our mom's for two, our dad's again for sometime, our mom's, our dad's . . . working out to five days with our father out of every fourteen. My sister—nearly three years my junior—and I were in constant motion. Divorce required that we keep track of our schedule and our stuff and each other.

More so, divorce—at least the peripatetic version I experienced—made me feel that I lacked something I truly longed for: a home. Read carefully: a home, one home, you know, of the "there's no place like home" variety. Two houses do not equal a home. Two houses are more houses, less home.

I am not arguing stay-in-it-for-the-kids'-sake. I'm noting, though, that it makes sense to try really hard before letting go of a marriage in process. But let's assume that you do decide to divorce and want to figure out how to do right by your kids. Begin by remembering that your kids did not ask you to marry, have them, or divorce. What I'm really trying to say here holds whether parents stay together or live apart: it's that parents can sabotage their children's happiness by pitting kids in the middle of angry impasses, warring tactics, and dysfunctional communication. That is not fair. While it is extremely hard to parent like a good crew team, pulling oars in unison, winning a race isn't the goal. Unison doesn't have to mean complete agreement to ensure good coparenting. Rather than attempting to win a race, try to get the rowboat across the lake in reasonable fashion.

A key reason that divorce has a negative impact on children is that it very well may place them in the middle of a rift. As each adult endeavors to create his or her new, solid life, the kids travel between those lives or at least are aware of the two new worlds their parents occupy

while their "constant" is that chasm, the space between. Even if both parents are thriving, the children are missing pieces of those experiences. They remain in transit. If one or both parents struggle, the children are extremely aware of that, too.

Now that I'm an adult, I have a number of friends with kids who have divorced. It seems so hard for my friends to fathom that for their kids, there's ongoing loss in the form of dislocation. Sometimes, it seems they try not to think too hard about their children's experiences. They think about the children and parent them when they are present, but they minimize how difficult it might be to negotiate two households constantly and to have to miss a parent and to have to reconnect, in a sense, twice as often as either parent does. Trying to imagine what it's like for the child negotiating two households, two spaces, and two sets of expectations seems critical.

What makes a good divorce? Supposing the couple has tried hard to make a marriage work and remain well supported by the couples or family therapist they toiled with, they can continue to garner support from that person through the untangling of their shared lives into two more separate lives with the large overlapping factor of continuing attachment to their child or children.

What I observe: The "best" divorces—for the kids—are the ones in which the parents remain, in some fashion, friends (in the best marriages, couples are friends as well). Really. I have divorced friends who discuss their children and their own dating lives with similar ease, and who continue to share certain chores or time hanging out with their kids. While there are tensions—if the relationship were perfectly easy, they might still be together—they decided to override those tensions for the sake of their children. Some people let the kids stay in one place and they cycle in and out of the family home, for that first year or for a few years, depending on circumstances.

There's no single perfect formula for a positive divorce. The idea, though, is to keep things comfortable enough that decisions aren't battles and that the adults aren't seething. Without gigantic tensions between the parents, they are more easygoing and can present a more unified front about the most important issues and support one another's choices (where they differ) than they could back when less-than-happily-married.

It seems that the best divorces—again, like the best marriages—have room for flexibility. A special out-of-town friend is visiting at the other house? Stay another night. A kid needs something from the other house? We'll get it. If what's needed is the other parent, we'll get the other parent. Flexibility assumes that parents can still talk to one another, and thus that the kids are safe to rely upon their parents as a team when necessary. Flexibility doesn't mean a complete disregard for the comfort—for all involved—of structure. There's a comfortable interplay between the two, ideally.

Fast-forward through holidays and birthday parties, plays, and sports competitions, and you probably reach graduations, weddings, births, and other family milestones. Even if a couple divorces, once they have children, they are either in one another's lives through these events at the very least, or all events—those significant and lesser events—become somewhat more chopped up for the kids (which parent comes to which occasion?).

A divorce that remains open—I think you could call it "warm"—assumes this underlying principle: The adults want the best not only for their children, but for one another. That's the underlying principle for a good marriage, too.

There's a pattern here: So much that is necessary for a good marriage is also essential for a good divorce. This probably means the best divorces do not emerge from the worst marriages.

I'm sure there are physics involved in these things, and that there's a point where the momentum of one's work within a marriage no longer contributes to its forward movement. There must be some place from which a couple can split with enough positive energy left to propel those energies toward a reasonably happy divorce. Long before reaching that point, though, any unhappy couple—or even more specifically, each member of an unhappy couple—should seek support, through friends, through counseling, and through practicing a whole lot of patience.

Parenting is a very stressful undertaking, after all. Work can be stressful.

Growing into adulthood and adult responsibilities is often stressful. With so much to push through in one's life, it's no wonder that two people, each trying to navigate his or her way along, struggle to negotiate these challenges together. In families, there are an awful lot of moving parts.

No doubt time is a factor, too. Now that my husband and I have reached adolescence with one child, we're very clear that the early years of parenthood—sleepless nights, nap strikes, diapers, crumbs, runny noses, minute-to-minute vigilance—are grueling. Those early years are wonderful—they are fun; they are funny—and grueling. For most of us, those years caring for very small children are not the most romantic ones, and they are not the easiest ones on a marriage.

It's hard in a culture that's so oriented to quick fixes and instant gratification to counsel patience. However, it might be worth weathering those periods before calling a marriage quits if for no other reason than starting anew—as in a next phase that includes a blended family, for example—is not so easy a feat, either. While I am in no way suggesting to anyone to throw up arms and forgo having a satisfying relationship, I'm all for realism. Love and family are work. If possible, it makes more sense to work on finding happiness within the marital relationship before seeking the next phase and the next relationship. Put another way: when kids are involved, divorce is a big deal, and the children ensure that even most divorces don't sever two parents' ties to one another. Even divorce, pulled off with compassion, is a substantive emotional commitment.

In all of this, kids are innocent creatures. Parents really do owe their children protection and love and as stable a foundation as possible. The muse I'd listen to in a troubled marriage with kids is not Tolstoy. Nor would I consult a romantic poet extolling the virtues of true love. Instead, I'd cue Mick Jagger: "You can't always get what you want, but if you try sometimes, you just might find, you get what you need." If what you need is a divorce, remember to be sure you include your children's needs in its construction.

Sarah Werthan Buttenwieser is a freelance writer and blogger in Northampton, Massachusetts. She earned her BA degree at Hampshire College and her MFA degree from Warren Wilson College. Her work has appeared in numerous publications, including the *New York Times*, *Brain Child Magazine*, and *USA Today*. She has a blog called "Standing in the Shadows," which can be found at www.valleyadvocate .com.

**Jane Johnson Struck
and Angela Thomas**

Solo Act: Single Mom Angela Thomas
Reflects on Raising Kids Alone

"**I** don't think any woman ever envisions herself a single mom," Angela Thomas, author of *My Single-Mom Life* (Thomas Nelson), candidly admits. Angela, 45, is a well-known speaker and author who holds a master's degree from Dallas Theological Seminary. The mom of four—Taylor, 17, Grayson, 14, William, 12, and AnnaGrace, 10—Angela's been divorced for more than six years. Here, she gives TCW readers a firsthand look at the challenges—and blessings—of being a single mom.

Question: Before your divorce, did you harbor any misperceptions about single moms?

Answer: Divorce carries such judgment in the church. I'm sure years ago I judged others the way I've occasionally been judged as a divorced mom.

I didn't fully understand the lives of so many women around me. And I definitely didn't realize the loneliness of that life, the difficulty of parenting alone, or the lost feeling of not being able to lean on anyone. When you solo-parent, no one's coming home to take over. No one's there to bounce ideas off, cover your back, or reinforce your decisions. There's no one to hold you through a tough choice and whisper, "I know you're worn out; I'll handle this."

I've learned to avoid making decisions—about spending, dating, or relocating—out of loneliness. I've also learned some good news about loneliness: it won't kill me—even though at times I feel it might.

I love to tell other single moms, "Receive the lessons loneliness wants to teach."

Question: Today's culture rarely blinks an eye at women intentionally choosing to raise a child outside marriage.

Answer: True. But I know for sure being a single mom is not God's design for parenting. God meant for children to be raised by a mom and dad who love each other, love their children, and live in the same house.

Several of my never-married girlfriends have adopted orphans from all over the world. I applaud these women's selflessness. But even they will tell you single parenting is hard and a child's ideally supposed to have two parents.

Question: You've written, "'Difficult' doesn't even come close to describing [single parenting]." What's the biggest challenge for you?

Answer: It's being afraid—even though I belong to God, trust him, and pray without ceasing. Sometimes I think, The kids seem to be overcoming the damage inflicted by this divorce. Their hearts are tender. God has us. We're going to be OK. But when one of them comes home from school distant and sulky, fear whispers to me, Your children will drag around these wounds forever. Then I begin the spiritual battle to fight back fear again.

But from the very beginning, I've believed Jesus's blood covers my children. I choose not to believe even one negative statistic about children raised in a single-parent home. I trust that when children grow up in a home where God is, they can become amazing, productive, whole people.

Question: What's your opinion on single-mom dating?

Answer: If you're working toward healing, addressing your loneliness issues, experiencing spiritual renewal, and finally seeing clearly, having a dinner and a great conversation with a fun date is OK. I try not to spend time with someone out of loneliness or desperation just to be with anyone. I find it easier to make wise choices about a relationship when I sit across the table from a respectable person who shares my values and commitments.

But dating should take place apart from your relationship with your children. Go to dinner when the kids are visiting their dad. Have lunch while they're in school. Men shouldn't parade through your home. That just isn't fair to your kids.

Question: Do married women find you threatening?

Answer: My single mom-ness doesn't threaten my married girlfriends at all. In fact, they're absolutely sure their husband's not interested in running off with a woman with four kids!

The married men on my street have been more than wonderful to coach my boys in sports, take them camping, or help out with home-repair emergencies. I'm sure these husbands are glad to leave my crazy house and get back to their quiet home with their wife.

However, for the sake of appearances, I never talk to a married man unless his wife's with us. I'm not interested in private conversations with married men; that safeguard keeps my interactions appropriate.

Question: How do you fit into the couples-culture of the church—and even society?

Answer: While some single moms love belonging to a single-parent class at church or a single-mom support group, I love hanging out with couples and their families. Most of my social gatherings involve my suburban neighborhood; that support system works great for me. But everybody needs community. I tell other single moms to keep looking for the right mix of people with whom to connect.

Most of the time, I forget I'm a single mom. My four kids and I are a family. The only time I remember I'm a solo parent is when I'm introduced from a platform or interviewed. Then I remember, Oh yeah, that label again.

Question: What message about single parenting would you most like to share with married moms?

Answer: Be sensitive to the Holy Spirit. A friend told me yesterday, "Remember all those years ago when I ran into you at a conference? I knew your light was gone, but I had no idea you were going through a divorce." Then she said, "I wish I'd listened to my heart that day and stayed closer to you."

If you sense the light's gone from your friend's face, let God lead you to love your friend with compassion.

And remember, if, somehow, some way, you become a single mom, God will amaze you with his love, protection, and provision.

Ultimately the question for everyone—married and single moms alike—is, "This day, in these circumstances, how will I bring glory to God?"

ANGELA THOMAS is the author of *My Single-Mom Life*, published by Thomas Nealson. Thomas, a mother of four, possesses a Master's degree from the Dallas Theological Seminar. Thomas writes that being a single mom was not God's design for parenting. She believes in children being raised by a man and a woman in love. Despite her beliefs and the challenges she has faced through divorce, her belief is that God and Jesus protect her and her children when they are in need. She argues that faith in God is what people need to protect them from the challenges of being a single mother and a child of a divorced family.

EXPLORING THE ISSUE

Does Divorce Have a Negative Impact on Children?

Critical Thinking and Reflection

1. What are some arguments made by each side with which you agree or disagree?
2. What are the strengths and weaknesses of the two positions argued in this chapter?
3. Pick the side with which you most agree. What are some additional arguments you would make to strengthen the case for or against home divorce?
4. Think more broadly of the issue of divorce. What sort of support network do families need when parents are in conflict, whether they are going through divorce or not?

Is There Common Ground?

Both authors agree that there are challenges with divorce, but that there are circumstances and ways to make divorce work best for children. How is the role of faith an issue that affects people on all sides of this question? What can we learn about communication and the best interests of the child from Buttenwieser's article? In many ways, this is an issue in which there is agreement of the challenges but a disagreement over the best path for the family.

Create Central

www.mhhe.com/createcentral

Additional Resources

Helpguide.org provides advice for helping children through divorce:

www.helpguide.org/mental/children_divorce.htm

Kids Health helps young children understand what divorce is:

http://kidshealth.org/kid/feeling/home_family /divorce.html

Coach Christina McGhee helps parents provide an environment so that their children can thrive after divorce:

www.divorceandchildren.com/

The highly respected Mayo Clinic provides advice for helping children through divorce:

www.mayoclinic.com/health/divorce/HO00055

The Children and Divorce web site provides a wide array of resources for parents, children, and professionals:

www.childrenanddivorce.com/

Internet References . . .

ACAP: Children and Divorce

    www.aacap.org/AACAP/Families_and_Youth
/Facts_for_Families/Facts_for_Families_Pages
/Children_and_Divorce_01.aspx

Help Guide: Children and Divorce

    www.helpguide.org/mental/children_divorce.htm

UCLA: Divorce and Children

    http://smhp.psych.ucla.edu/qf/divorce.htm

Selected, Edited, and with Issue Framing Material by:
David M. Hall, Ph.D., *Delaware Valley College*

ISSUE

Is Homeschooling Kids in Their Best Interest and Ours?

YES: Laura Grace Weldon, from "Erasing My Homeschooling Misconceptions: A Parent Dispels Six Myths about Educating Your Own Children," *LILIPOH* (Spring, 2013)

NO: Dana Goldstein, from "Liberals, Don't Homeschool Your Kids: Why Teaching Children at Home Violates Progressive Values," *Slate.com* (February 16, 2012)

Learning Outcomes
After reading this issue, you will be able to:
• Identify the major arguments made for and against homeschooling.
• Compare and contrast the competing arguments made for and against homeschooling in this chapter.
• Evaluate the implications of homeschooling on the impact this has on the larger American society in preparing children for their future.

ISSUE SUMMARY

YES: Laura Grace Weldon argues that for most of human history, children have been educated by their parents. Homeschooling follows this long and proud tradition in which schools were an unnecessary institution. She contends that with the test-heavy approach of public schooling, homeschooling frees parents to create a hands-on educational system that more fully engages their child.

NO: Dana Goldstein argues that homeschooling is bad for children and for the larger society. The children who are homeschooled suffer from the lack of diversity. Goldstein argues that these children often come from privileged families, at least families privileged enough in which one parent can stay home. She explains that poor children perform better when in class with middle-class students.

Education for children in the United States was not originally required; it was up to parents to decide whether and how to educate their children, including whether to send them to school. In 1850, however, Massachusetts became the first state to pass a law requiring "schooling" for children. Some of this took place in school buildings, and some was done by parents at home—but requiring that children be educated became more and more commonplace as time went on. And as early as the beginning of the twentieth century, there were proponents who believed that school-based education failed children, and that children were better off educated at home. Much changed regarding the views and role of public education over the next 100 years.

President George W. Bush expanded the role of federal education standards by requiring states that wanted federal funds to develop clear standards in reading and mathematics. This legislation, often referred to as No Child Left Behind, fundamentally changed the emphasis on reading and math skills in many schools across America. President Barack Obama championed Race to the Top, building on No Child Left Behind. Race to the Top encouraged states to compete for federal funding by adherence to developing national standards that include but are not limited to reading and mathematics, reforming teacher evaluation systems, expanding charter schools, and plans to reform what are regarded as and classified as failing schools. While these laws do not take away the rights of homeschooled children, these laws create a greater role for the federal government in schools, all based on the rationale that there is a compelling federal interest in more centralized standards and academic development of our nation's students.

According to the Home School Association of California, the homeschooling that took place between then and the 1970s tended to be a bit more clandestine and to be found in rural areas. The early 1980s saw the emergence of homeschooling publications and groups that were associated specifically with conservative and religious (in particular, Christian) ideologies. Fearing the "godlessness" of public school, members of these groups received ongoing support for teaching their children at home. As we moved into the 1990s, homeschooled children in the United States increased, with a federal government survey in 1999 estimating that nearly 900,000 children are being homeschooled in this country, a number that can only have increased over the past years.

In your opinion, what are some of the benefits of children being taught by a certified, professional teacher or teachers? What are some of the benefits of teaching children at home, within the context of one's own family values and without the distractions of other people, noise, and social pressures? There are clear arguments on each side, some of which are expressed in the following selections.

There is limited research available about how effective school-based education is as opposed to homeschooling, much of which cannot control the myriad factors that come into play. For example, most states exempt children who are homeschooled from standardized testing. In schools, factors include teacher experience, school and district leadership, the socioeconomic status of the community in which the school is located, and more. In homeschooling, issues include whether a parent can afford financially to stay home and devote the time and energy necessary to homeschool effectively, whether the parent(s) can facilitate a social life for their child(ren) that is comparable to their school-based peers, and whether the child(ren) can still access nonacademic activities such as organized sports, theater, and student clubs.

Ask young people who have been homeschooled whether they liked it, and you will receive a range of responses. A website, WikiAnswers.com., asked people to comment on what they felt the longer-term effects of homeschooling were; here is what several people had to say:

"I was home-schooled for 1st–9th grade. I attended 10th and part of 11th grade. I took my proficiency test and attended community college on and off for 6 years. My younger brother was home-schooled from 1st–8th grade and attended 9th–12th grade. He did not attend college. Almost all the kids I hung out w/ were homeschooled also. We were both socially impaired by it; our parents made a point to keep us in sports and try to keep us socializing w/other kids. But it wasn't enough. Most of our friends were also home-schooled too. Some of us turned out OK, some didn't."

"I am 30 years old now, and was homeschooled through junior high and high school. . . . Part of the answer to [the] question is this: Socialization with adults is improved, while socialization with peers is hindered. . . . There are so many social do's and don'ts that are very arbitrary and are pounded home by peer pressure, teasing, cliques, etc."

"I home-schooled through junior high and high school. I agree that there are some social disadvantages to home-schooling, but I think that they can be avoided or changed. I realized when I was 15 that I was awkward around most of my peers and so I worked really hard at changing that. If parents are careful to involve their children in social groups, the kids will be able to learn the necessary skills. I was lucky; there is a big homeschooling community where I live, with many children to interact with. . . . I am now in college and I don't have any qualms about participating in social-groups with other students, whether home-schooled or not. If done right don't think home-schooling interferes a whole lot with social skills" (from www.faqfarm.com/Q/What_are_the_long-term_effects_of_home-schooling).

Clearly, those who have gone through homeschooling, like those who have gone through public schooling, do not speak with one voice. How do the views of these homeschooled students change or reinforce your views about homeschooling? Keep these diverse views in mind when reading this issue.

YES

Laura Grace Weldon

Erasing My Homeschooling Misconceptions: A Parent Dispels Six Myths about Educating Your Own Children

I never planned to homeschool. I am the daughter, niece, and granddaughter of excellent public school teachers. I cheerfully volunteered in my children's classrooms and worked on parent committees. **I believed in doing my best to change a flawed system from within.**

Yet I kept seeing school wasn't a good fit for my children. Our four-year-old already knew how to read, but had to practice sight words in preschool anyway. Our sweet but inattentive second-grader was deemed a good candidate for Ritalin by his teacher.

Our fifth-grader could do college level work, but due to cuts in the gifted program had to follow grade-level curriculum along with the rest of her class. Our freshman was an honors student but detested school, not only the hours of homework but the trial of dealing with a few teens who were harassing him.

We became homeschoolers overnight when those teens pulled a gun on my oldest in the school hallway, telling him he wouldn't live to see the end of the day. School officials, who had done nothing to ease the harassment, didn't even call the police.

The next morning every reason I had to avoid homeschooling stared me in the face. So did my kids. They were eager to learn on their own terms.

Here are a few of the misconceptions homeschooling erased for me.

1. Education that counts happens in school.

My kids were growing up in an enriching home. We read aloud every day and enjoyed wide-ranging conversations. We went to parks, museums, and plays. But I was raised to believe that formal education is something separate and measurable.

Still, I saw that my kids learned most eagerly when filled with the aliveness we call curiosity. That's true of all of us: learning sticks when we're interested. When we're not, much of what we learn tends to become inaccessible after the grade is earned.

Hard as it is to believe, **studies show that that shallow thinking is actually related to higher test scores.** *(Maybe we acknowledge this reality when we prepare kids for tests by saying, "Don't overthink it.")*

When we're curious we not only retain what we learn, we're also inspired to pursue the interconnected directions it leads us. I saw this the summer before we began homeschooling.

My eight-year-old, the one who barely paid attention in school, was playing with balsa airplanes brought to a picnic by a family friend who piloted his own plane. Other kids gave up after the planes broke, but my son worked to fashion the pieces into newly workable aircraft. This gentleman showed him a few modifications and the unlikely looking planes flew.

After that my son was on a quest. He loaded up on books at each library visit, telling us about *Bernoulli's principle*, aviation history, and experimental aircraft. He begged for balsa to make models of his own design, which became more sophisticated as he overcame earlier mistakes.

The next time we met up with this friend, my son was offered a ride on his Cessna. That was the highlight of his summer. His interest in planes eventually waned, but not the knowledge he gained. He'd taught himself history, science, math, and more importantly, shown himself just how capable he was.

His pursuit is what researcher Carol Dweck, author of *Mindset: The New Psychology of Success,* **calls a** *growth mindset.* It's the understanding that achievement comes from purposeful engagement, that talent and smarts are not fixed traits but are developed through persistence.

A growth mindset is linked to resilience and accomplishment throughout life. That's education that counts!

2. Kids have to follow grade-level standards.

I once thought homeschoolers had to follow conventional school standards. You know what I mean—if it's second grade it's time to learn about ancient Rome, multiplication, and adverbs. For my family, an overly schoolish approach never made sense. I can give dozens of reasons, but here's one that springs to mind.

Kids develop unevenly. They may be way ahead in reading and struggle in math, able to make up imaginative stories but not coordinated enough to easily to write or type them. If they don't advance evenly in school, quite a bit of attention is focused on where they're lacking (extra help, easier and more repetitive work, labels, poor grades).

Weldon, Laura Grace. From *LILIPOH*, Spring 2013. Copyright © 2013 by Laura Grace Weldon. Used with permission of the author. Laura Grace Weldon is the author of *Free Range Learning: How Homeschooling Changes Everything* (Hohm Press, 2010). www.lauragraceweldon.com

But outside of school it's easy to emphasize their strengths while other areas are mastered gradually without ever being considered "deficiencies." This has a basis in current research which shows that children are remarkably good at self-regulating. They're cued to ignore information that's too simple or too complex, but instead are drawn to learn from situations that offer the right amount of challenge.

For example, it's well known in the homeschooling community that many kids aren't ready to read at five or six. Some aren't ready until they're several years older. In school that's a crisis, because every subject is taught using reading. **The child who can't read not only grows disheartened, he also feels stigmatized.**

But as a homeschooler he remains immersed in a learning-rich lifestyle whether he reads or not because homeschooling is infinitely adaptable. Stories abound of homeschooled children who move quickly move from non-reading to zipping through Harry Potter books once they're ready.

A recent study showed that homeschooled children whose parents don't push them to learn to read, but instead emphasize the joy of reading, **end up with kids who are avid readers no matter if these kids started reading early or late.**

In our family, we found our kids eagerly accomplished far more in a whole range of subjects over time. **"Grade-level" expectations were, to us, limitations.**

3. The parent has to be teacher/coach/principal.

Being a mother to my children has always been richly rewarding *(okay, maybe not in the colicky phase)*. I didn't want to take on other roles. Turns out I didn't have to. We found homeschooling to be an immediate stress reduction. My kids got enough sleep, woke rested, and don't have to rush through the day.

Instead they had ample time for conversation, reading, indulging in art projects and experiments, finding the answers to questions, and going on adventures. **Our lives were guided by fascination, not bells. Much less control on my part was required.**

I find that our cultural emphasis on adult-led activities is somewhat counterproductive. We assume children benefit from the newest educational toys and electronics, coached sports, lots of lessons, and other adult-designed, adult-led endeavors. Well-intentioned parents work hard to provide their children with these advantages although there's limited evidence that all this effort has value.

We do this because we believe that learning stems from instruction. By that logic the more avenues of adult-directed learning, the more children will benefit. But studies show that a child's innate drive to creatively solve problems is actually impeded when adults provide direct instruction.

This experience is repeated thousands of times a year in a child's life, **teaching her to look to authorities for** solutions, and is known to shape more linear, less innovative thinking.

Research also shows that a child's natural motivation tends to diminish in adult-led activities. Unless they've been raised on a steady diet of ready-made entertainment, children are naturally drawn to free play and discovery-based learning. They make up games, daydream, pretend, and launch their own projects—freely seeking out adults for resources and guidance when necessary. They are naturally drawn to achieve mastery.

My kids have shown me how motivated self-direction can kick into high gear in the teen years. They've earned their own money by shoveling stalls, which they spent to buy and restore a vintage car, go on a month-long backpacking trip, and build a bedroom-sized recording studio.

And they have stick-to-it-iveness—devoting years to pursuits like a bagpipe band, wildlife rehabilitation, farming, and their own intensive scholarship. **Homeschooling has helped us foster a young person's growing need for independence while providing useful guidance.**

4. I can't afford to provide a decent education.

Like many new homeschoolers, I thought I'd have to replicate everything from music class to chemistry lab. I knew I'd never have the time, energy, or money.

But we quickly discovered that the community around us is filled with people eager to impart skills and knowledge to the next generation, almost always for free.

They're found at ethnic centers, museums, libraries, colleges, churches, service organizations, plus clubs like those for rock hounds, ham radio enthusiasts, and astronomy buffs. My children's lives have been illuminated by spending time with biologists, potters, engineers, geologists, entrepreneurs, archaeologists, organic farmers, model railroaders, meteorologists—the list could take up this page.

People seem honored when asked to share a little of what they know. It's sad that young people are customarily segregated from adults doing fascinating things right in their own communities, especially in the teen years when they so desperately want role models.

We've also gotten together with fellow homeschoolers for countless field trips, enrichment programs, game days, clubs, and learning co-op classes.

My kids have re-enacted Shakespearean duels, toured factories, sheared sheep, raced sailboats, learned chemistry from a Ph.D chemist, debated Constitutional challenges, competed in robotics tournaments, built a hovercraft of their own design, calculated the position of the stars, played with world-class musicians, and spent an afternoon with an astronaut after winning a science contest. All free or practically free.

When certain subjects got really challenging we easily bartered with an expert or found a community college class to cover it. **And we've saved thousands by relying on the remarkable resources of our library system.**

Sure, I envy those homeschooling families who learn while bike riding in Ecuador or rambling through European castles. But I realize my kids haven't missed anything despite my penny pinching, **especially since studies indicate two-thirds of school kids say they're bored in class.**

Deep scholarship and hands-on learning are simply another homeschooling perk.

5. Homeschooling will deprive my kids of friends.

I realized the school day isn't really set up for socializing, although we'd come to rely on school as a source of same-age friendship.

Sadly, according to *Beyond the Classroom* by Laurence Steinberg, less than five percent of school kids belong to peer groups that value academic achievement—while pressure from prevailing peers steer young people toward underachievement.

And it turns out studies show homeschooled children have better social skills and fewer behavior problems than their demographically matched schooled peers.

Homeschooling families also tend to be more active in the community. Initially it took me a while to get used to homeschool gatherings where kids hung out with a wide range of ages and abilities. Sure, they're kids and not beacons of perfection, but I was pleased to see so much overall good cheer.

As for friends, my kids kept many of their school friends. They also made more as we widened our circle of acquaintances. **Many of their new friends were around the same age but some were decades older, bringing perspectives shaped by widely varying experiences.** They offered my children a route to maturity they couldn't have found in school amongst kids similar to themselves.

Their friends include a Scottish gentleman in his 70's, a group of automotive restoration enthusiasts, a wildlife rehabilitator in her 60's, fellow backpackers, people with differing physical challenges, Christians, Buddhists, atheists, Wiccans—well, you get the idea.

These friendships happened because they had the time to stretch in all sorts of interesting directions.

6. Homeschooling is an experiment.

Like any other parent, I'm driven to provide my children with the essential ingredients that lead to lifelong happiness and success. **Late at night, unable to sleep, I've entertained my share of doubts.**

What if homeschooling will limit their chances? I finally realized I was looking at it from too narrow a perspective.

Schooling is the experiment. **For 99 percent of all our time on earth, the human race never conceived of this institution.**

Our species nurtured children close to extended family, within the rich educational milieu of the community, trusting that young people would grow into responsible adulthood. Worked like a charm for eons.

Taking my kids out of school liberated them from the test-heavy approach of today's schools, one that actually has nothing to do with adult success.

Instead of spending over 1,200 hours each year in school, they could devote time to what more directly builds happiness as well as future success. Things like innovation, hands-on learning, and meaningful responsibility.

That doesn't mean I lost all my doubts. Some days *(all right, months)* I worried. It's hard to unlearn a mindset.

But now all four of my kids are in college or launched into careers.

I sat at a recent dinner with my family, appreciating our closeness. My kids take on challenges with grace, react with droll wit even under pressure, and haven't lost their zest for learning. We laughed as their lively conversation covered Norse mythology, caddisfly pheromones, zeppelin history, and lines from new movies.

I'm not sure how much I can credit to homeschooling, but I know it's given my kids freedom to explore their own possibilities.

And that's more than enough.

Websites Referenced in this Article

www.wired.com/geekmom/2012/12/school-violence-home schooling/

http://www.cato.org/sites/cato.org/files/serials/files/policy-report/2001/7/education.pdf

http://www.amazon.com/gp/product/0345472322/ref=as_li_qf_sp_asin_tl?ie=UTF8&camp=1789&creative=9325&creativeASIN=0345472322&linkCode=as2&tag=simplehomeschoolnet-20

http://lauragraceweldon.com/2012/08/28/observe-the-goldilocks-effect-in-action/

http://www.psychologytoday.com/blog/freedom-learn/201002/children-teach-themselves-read

http://www.nytimes.com/2011/08/13/your-money/childrens-activities-no-guarantee-of-later-success.html?_r=4&

http://www.creativitypost.com/psychology/the_educational_value_of_creative_disobedience

http://www.parentingscience.com/benefits-of-play.html

http://lauragraceweldon.com/2012/05/24/successful-teen-homeschooling-two-vital-factors/

http://www.wired.com/geekmom/2013/01/find-learn-from-experts/

http://www.livescience.com/1308-students-bored-school.html

http://www.amazon.com/gp/product/0684835754/ref=as_li_tf_tl?ie=UTF8&camp=1789&creative=9325&creativeASIN=0684835754&linkCode=as2&tag=simplehomeschoolnet-20

http://myplace.frontier.com/~thomas.smedley/smedleys.htm

http://lauragraceweldon.com/2012/01/30/better-test-scores-dont-lead-to-success/

http://lauragraceweldon.com/2012/01/10/how-the-10000-hour-rule-can-benefit-any-child/

LAURA GRACE WELDON is the author of *Free Range Learning: How Homeschooling Changes Everything*. She lives on a small farm with her family and is slow at work on her next book, *Subversive Cooking*. Connect with her at www.lauragraceweldon.com/blog-2. References available upon request.

Dana Goldstein

 **NO**

Liberals, Don't Homeschool Your Kids:
Why Teaching Children at Home
Violates Progressive Values

As a child growing up in Arizona and Georgia college towns during the 1980s and 1990s, the filmmaker Astra Taylor was "unschooled" by her lefty, countercultural parents. "My siblings and I slept late and never knew what day of the week it was," Taylor writes in a new essay in the literary journal *N+1*. "We were never tested, graded, or told to memorize dates, facts, or figures. . . . Some days we read books, made music, painted, or drew. Other days we argued and fought over the computer. Endless hours were spent watching reruns of 'The Simpsons' on videotape, though we had every episode memorized. When we weren't inspired—which was often—we simply did nothing at all."

Over the past year, there has been a resurgence of interest in homeschooling—not just the religious fundamentalist variety practiced by Michele Bachman and Rick Santorum, but also in secular, liberal homeschooling like Taylor's. Think no textbooks, history lessons about progressive social movements, and college-level math for precocious 13-year-olds. Some families implement this vision on their own, while others join cooperatives of like-minded, super-involved parents.

Homeschooling is so unevenly regulated from state to state that it is impossible to know exactly how many homeschoolers there are. Estimates range from about 1 million to 2 million children, and the number is growing. It is unclear how many homeschooling families are secular, but the political scientist Rob Reich has written that there is little doubt the homeschooling population has diversified in recent years. Yet whether liberal or conservative, "[o]ne article of faith unites all homeschoolers: that homeschooling should be unregulated," Reich writes. "Homeschoolers of all stripes believe that they alone should decide how their children are educated."

Could such a go-it-alone ideology ever be truly progressive—by which I mean, does homeschooling serve the interests not just of those who are doing it, but of society as a whole?

In her *N+1* piece, Taylor struggles to answer this question in the affirmative. Drawing upon her own upbringing, as well as on the traditions of the radical private school the Albany Free School, Taylor calls on parents and students to "empty the schools," which force students to endure "irrational authority six and a half hours a day, five days a week, in a series of cinder-block holding cells," she caricatures.

This overheated hostility toward public schools runs throughout the new literature on liberal homeschooling, and reveals what is so fundamentally illiberal about the trend: It is rooted in distrust of the public sphere, in class privilege, and in the dated presumption that children hail from two-parent families, in which at least one parent can afford (and wants) to take significant time away from paid work in order to manage a process—education—that most parents entrust to the community at-large.

Take, for instance, Sonia Songha's *New York Times* account of forming a preschool cooperative with six other brownstone-Brooklyn mothers, all of whom "said our children had basically never left our sides." Indeed, in a recent *Newsweek* report, the education journalist Linda Perlstein noted a significant number of secular homeschoolers are also adherents of attachment parenting, the perennially controversial ideology defined by practices such as co-sleeping with one's child and breast-feeding for far longer than typical, sometimes well beyond toddlerhood. Meanwhile, in suburban New Jersey, one "hippy" homeschooler told the local paper she feared exposing her kids to the presumably negative influences of teachers and peers. "I didn't want my child being raised by someone else for eight hours out of the day," she said.

Recent reports of teachers and teachers' aides in Los Angeles and New York molesting children only flame the fans of such fears. But these stories make news exactly because they are so rare; there's something creepy about giving in totally to the terrors of the outside world harming one's child. In a country increasingly separated by cultural chasms—Christian conservatives vs. secular humanists; Tea Partiers vs. Occupiers—should we really encourage children to trust only their parents or those hand-selected by them, and to mistrust civic life and public institutions?

Moreover, being your child's everything—her parent, teacher, baby-sitter, and afterschool program coordinator—requires a massive outlay of labor. Songha's pre-K cooperative hired a teacher, but parents ended up putting in 10 to 12 hours of work per week administrating the program. Astra Taylor's father was a college professor, while her mother supervised the four children's "unschooling."

What goes unmentioned is what made this lifestyle possible: the fact that Taylor's mother could afford to stay home with her kids. Yet Taylor bristles against the suggestion that there was anything unique about the ability of her upper-middle class, uber-intellectual parents to effectively "unschool" their children while still helping them grow into educated adults with satisfying professional lives. This critique "implies that most people are not gifted, and that they need to be guided, molded, tested, and inspected," Taylor complains. "What makes us so sure most people couldn't handle self-education?"

What makes us so sure? Reality. More than 70 percent of mothers with children under the age of 18 are in the workforce. One-third of all children and one-half of low-income children are being raised by a single parent. Fewer than one-half of young children, and only about one-third of low-income kids, are read to daily by an adult. Surely, this isn't the picture of a nation ready to "self-educate" its kids.

Nor can we allow homeschoolers to believe their choice impacts only their own offspring. Although the national school-reform debate is fixated on standardized testing and "teacher quality"—indeed, the uptick in secular homeschooling may be, in part, a backlash against this narrow education agenda—a growing body of research suggests "peer effects" have a large impact on student achievement. Low-income kids earn higher test scores when they attend school alongside middle-class kids, while the test scores of privileged children are impervious to the influence of less-privileged peers. So when college-educated parents pull their kids out of public schools, whether for private school or homeschooling, they make it harder for less-advantaged children to thrive.

Of course, no one wants to sacrifice his own child's education in order to better serve someone else's kid. But here's the great thing about attending racially and socio-economically integrated schools: It helps children become better grown-ups. Research by Columbia University soci-ologist Amy Stuart Wells found that adult graduates of integrated high schools shared a commitment to diversity, to understanding and bridging cultural differences, and to appreciating "the humanness of individuals across racial lines."

Taylor admits that "[m]any people, liberal and conservative alike, are deeply offended by critiques of compulsory schooling." I suppose I am one of them. I benefited from 13 years of public education in one of the most diverse and progressive school districts in the United States. My father, stepmother, stepfather, and grandfather are or were public school educators. As an education journalist, I've admired many public schools that use culturally relevant, high-standards curricula to engage even the most disadvantaged students. These schools are sustained by the talents of impossibly hard-working teachers who want to partner with parents and kids, not oppress them.

Despite our conflicting perspectives, I agree with Taylor that school ought to be more engaging, more intellectually challenging, and less obsessed with testing. But government is the only institution with the power and scale to intervene in the massive undertaking of better educating American children, 90 percent of whom currently attend public schools. (And it's worth remembering that schools provide not just education, but basic child care while parents are at work.) Lefty homeschoolers might be preaching sound social values to their children, but they aren't practicing them. If progressives want to improve schools, we shouldn't empty them out. We ought to flood them with our kids, and then debate vociferously what they ought to be doing.

DANA GOLDSTEIN is a Brooklyn-based journalist, a Schwartz Fellow at the New America Foundation, and a Puffin Fellow at the Nation Institute.

EXPLORING THE ISSUE

Is Homeschooling Kids in Their Best Interest and Ours?

Critical Thinking and Reflection

1. What are some arguments made in each side with which you agree or disagree?
2. What are the strengths and weaknesses of the two positions made in this chapter?
3. Pick the side with which you most agree. What are some additional arguments you would make to strengthen the case for or against homeschooling?
4. Think more broadly of the issue of homeschooling. What sort of support network do families need when they homeschool their children, and what can public schools do to create a more welcoming school environment for all students?

Is There Common Ground?

One of the challenges—as well as one of the wonderful qualities—of public schools is that they are a place in American society that bring diverse individuals and families together. Our courts have interpreted the First Amendment to keep schools from establishing religion, which means that teachers cannot place one religion over another or even put religion above non-religion.

However, students have lots of rights to freely express their own religion at schools as long as that expression does not adversely interfere with the schools educational mission. What are some ways we can ensure greater understanding of students' rights to freely express their religion in school? How can we ensure that parents better understand the different criteria for a school estab-lishing a religion versus students' freely exercising their religion? Additionally, how can homeschooled students get involved with a school's extra-curricular activities?

Create Central

www.mhhe.com/createcentral

Additional Resources

Arndt, Erica, *Homeschooling 101: A Guide to Getting Started* (Kindle, 2013)

Cook, Sandra, *Overcoming Your Fear of Homeschooling with Insider Information* (2013)

Weldon, Laura Grace, *Free Range Learning: How Homeschooling Changes Everything* (2010)

Internet References . . .

Home School Legal Defense Association

www.hslda.org

Homeschool World

www.home-school.com/

Online Schooling

www.k12.com/

Selected, Edited, and with Issue Framing Material by:
David M. Hall, Ph.D., *Delaware Valley College*

ISSUE

Should Pharmacists Be Able to Deny Emergency Contraception to Potentially Pregnant Women?

YES: Justice James A. Knecht, from *Morr-Fitz v. Pat Quinn*, Judgment of the Court (September 20, 2012).

NO: Susan A. Cohen, from "Objections, Confusion Among Pharmacists Threaten Access to Emergency Contraception." *The Guttmacher Report on Public Policy* (June 1999).

Learning Outcomes

After reading this issue, you will be able to:

- Summarize competing arguments related to pharmacists' obligations related to emergency contraception.
- Compare and contrast the political rights of women seeking emergency contraception and the moral rights of pharmacists.
- Evaluate the impact of laws allowing pharmacists to follow their conscience on health care in our communities.

ISSUE SUMMARY

YES: Justice Knecht argues that pharmacists have a right for conscious-based objections for dispensing emergency contraception.

NO: Susan A. Cohen argues that allowing pharmacists to deny emergency contraception is not their right and creates a slippery slope with giving people other necessary medications.

What happens if your job requires you to do things with which you morally disagree? Say your faith expects you to actively work to save the non-believers, but you are a public school teacher and are unable to do that with taxpayer dollars? Or say your faith requires that you cover your hair in public, but you are a police officer and are not allowed to wear a head covering. Or you are the Governor of a state that has the death penalty though your religious convictions are against it. Yet criminals are sentenced to death, and you are expected to sign death warrants.

The examples above largely deal with individuals managing their conscience and how their faith impacts their profession. When someone's religious convictions can impact the health care of the general public, the issue then raises more complicated scenarios.

Do you believe that emergency contraception is a right for women? Do you feel a religious exemption in the right of the pharmacist? How is a society supposed to balance to competing rights? How do we honor both religious convictions and a woman's right to reproductive freedom?

Emergency contraception operates something like a huge dose of oral contraception, which is often referred to as *the pill*. It is different from what is often called the *abortion pill*. Emergency contraception makes it more difficult for sperm to fertilize an egg. If the egg has fertilized the sperm, emergency contraception makes it less likely that the egg will attach to the top-third of the uterus. In contrast, the abortion pill stops a pregnancy once a fertilized egg has attached to the top-third of the uterus.

Nonetheless, emergency contraception gets caught between different definitions of where life begins. If you believe that a fertilized egg is a sacred life—and if that belief is anchored in your religious convictions—providing people with emergency contraception violates the very purpose for which you believe God placed you on Earth. Those pharmacists would argue that they don't have to fill that prescription, and you can find someone else to fill your script. These pharmacists are not saying that you cannot have emergency contraception. They are just saying that they shouldn't have to fill it themselves.

In contrast, others believe that women having access to emergency contraception is a fundamental right. They argue that women cannot be free if they cannot have reproductive freedom. While a woman denied can go to another pharmacist, they would argue that this creates a variety of problems. First, some women may be embarrassed and discouraged and not seek another pharmacist. Second, those who live in a more rural area may not have another place in which they can go to have another pharmacist fill their prescription. Most importantly, with emergency contraception, the closer it is taken to coitus, the more effective it is in preventing pregnancy. As a result, the delay in getting the prescription filled increases the chances of a viable, unwanted pregnancy.

Those who support the pharmacist exception believe that you cannot compel medical care providers to do something which they feel is immoral. For example, many Catholic hospitals do not provide emergency contraception to rape victims. If a rape victim attends a public hospital, it is likely that she will be provided with emergency contraception. Does a ruling like this impact what Catholic hospitals can do?

Both sides in this debate feel that they are protecting a fundamental right: religious convictions and reproductive freedom. Compromise is possible but not without consequences for one or both parties.

YES

James A. Knecht

Morr-Fitz v. Pat Quinn

Plaintiffs, two pharmacists and three corporations that own and operate pharmacies, filed suit seeking declaratory and injunctive relief against certain public officials who seek to enforce an administrative rule that requires pharmacies to dispense or aid in the dispensing of emergency contraception. The individual plaintiffs believe life begins at conception, emergency contraception may act as an abortifacient, and the dispensing of such medication is against their religious beliefs. The corporate plaintiffs have ethical guidelines that prevent the pharmacies they own and operate from dispensing emergency contraception.

The administrative rule at issue (Current Rule) does not specifically identify "emergency contraception" but applies to all medication approved by the United States Food and Drug Administration (FDA). Plaintiffs' third amended complaint alleges the Current Rule is invalid as it violates the Illinois Health Care Right of Conscience Act, the Illinois Religious Freedom Restoration Act, and the first amendment's free-exercise clause (U.S. Const., amend. I).

The circuit court found plaintiffs had sincere religious beliefs preventing them from dispensing emergency contraceptives. The court found the Current Rule unconstitutional and invalid under the Conscience Act and the Religious Freedom Act and issued a permanent injunction, enjoining defendants from enforcing the Current Rule. Defendants appeal, arguing (1) the injunction is overly broad in that it prohibits defendants from enforcing the Current Rule on other FDA-approved medications and against non-objecting pharmacies; and (2) the Current Rule is constitutional and does not violate either the Conscience Act or the Religious Freedom Act. We agree the injunction is overly broad but find the Conscience Act prohibits enforcement of the Current Rule on the issue of emergency contraceptives against these plaintiffs.

We affirm in part as modified and reverse in part.

Background

"Plan B" or "Emergency Contraceptives"

In their opening brief, defendants identified four products marketed in the United States and approved for sale by pharmacies: Plan B One-Step, ella, Next Choice, and levonorgestrel tablets. Each of these products is used to prevent "pregnancy in the few days after sex." The parties refer to these medications collectively as "Plan B" or "emergency contraceptives." Plaintiffs' exhibits, including product labeling approved by the FDA, show emergency contraception may curtail pregnancy by preventing the release of an egg, preventing fertilization, or preventing a fertilized egg from attaching. The FDA's official Web site acknowledges Plan B may prevent a fertilized egg from attaching. These contraceptives will not work if a fertilized egg is implanted.

Parties in the Litigation

Plaintiffs in this litigation include two individual pharmacists and corporations that own "community pharmacies." The plaintiff individuals are Luke Vander Bleek and Glen Kosirog, licensed Illinois pharmacists. Vander Bleek, a lifelong Roman Catholic, has been a pharmacist for over 20 years. Kosirog, a Christian since age 17, has been a pharmacist for over 25 years. Both Vander Bleek and Kosirog have religious-based objections to participating in any way in dispensing emergency contraceptives due to their beliefs these contraceptives may prevent a fertilized egg from attaching to a woman's uterus. The individual plaintiffs were added to the case with the first amended complaint.

The Litigation

In September 2005, plaintiffs Morr-Fitz, Inc., and Kosirog Pharmacy, Inc., filed a complaint for declaratory and injunctive relief against defendants. Plaintiffs, maintaining emergency contraceptives act as abortifacients, asked the court to enjoin defendants from enforcing the Permanent Rule, arguing the rule conflicts with Illinois law. Plaintiffs maintained the rule was void under the Conscience Act and the Religious Freedom. After the circuit court denied plaintiffs' request for a temporary restraining order on grounds of standing and ripeness, plaintiffs sought leave in October 2005 to amend the complaint.

In the proposed first amended complaint, plaintiffs added a claim the Permanent Rule substantially burdened plaintiffs' first-amendment rights to free exercise of religion. Plaintiffs maintained the Permanent Rule forced them to participate in abortions to which they were religiously and conscientiously opposed.

In November 2005, the circuit court granted plaintiffs leave to amend, as well as defendants' motion to dismiss

Knecht, James A. From *Appellate Court of Illinois*, 2012 IL App (4th) 110398, September 20, 2012.

on grounds of ripeness, lack of standing, and failure to exhaust administrative remedies. Plaintiffs appealed. By majority, this court, in *Morr-Fitz, Inc. v. Blagojevich* (2007), determined the issue was not ripe and affirmed the judgment. The majority concluded the plaintiffs had not pleaded facts establishing they felt the effects of the rule in a concrete way and would suffer a substantial hardship if they were not allowed to pursue their claim. The majority further concluded neither the Conscience Act nor the Religious Freedom Act made the claim ripe. Justice Turner dissented, finding plaintiffs' claims ripe and compelling under the Conscience Act and the Religious Freedom Act. Plaintiffs appealed.

While plaintiffs' petition for appeal to the Supreme Court of Illinois was pending, the Permanent Rule espoused in subsection (j) was amended. The Department added "several, more onerous provisions pertaining specifically to 'emergency contraception.'" The Second Permanent Rule mandated retail pharmacies use their "best efforts to maintain adequate stock of emergency contraception to the extent that it continues to sell contraception." It further mandated if a pharmacist objected to the dispensing of emergency contraception and no non-objecting pharmacist was present at the pharmacy, the "dispensing pharmacy" must sell the emergency contraceptive through "remote medication order processing," which involved having a non-objecting pharmacist at another location authorize a non-pharmacist employee at the dispensing pharmacy to dispense the drug. The Second Permanent Rule further required retail pharmacies ensure a non-objecting pharmacist was scheduled when the pharmacy was open or a licensed pharmacist was available to perform the remote-medication order-processing procedure when no non-objecting pharmacist was available at the dispensing pharmacy.

In December 2008, the Supreme Court of Illinois reversed the majority's decision in *Morr-Fitz*, finding plaintiffs' claims ripe. The court further determined plaintiffs were not required to exhaust administrative remedies and remanded the cause for a hearing on plaintiffs' motion for a preliminary injunction and further amendments to the complaint.

In August 2009, the circuit court granted plaintiffs a preliminary injunction, prohibiting defendants from enforcing the Second Permanent Rule against plaintiffs.

In April 2010, defendants issued the Current Rule, entitled "Community Pharmacy Services," which replaced the Second Permanent Rule. Emergency contraceptives are not mentioned in the Current Rule. Section (e), however, mandates "Pharmacies have a duty to deliver lawfully prescribed drugs to patients and to distribute nonprescription drugs approved by the [FDA] for restricted distribution by pharmacies, or to substitute a generic drug *** in a timely manner, or to contact the prescriber to obtain authorization to dispense a different drug that produces a similar clinical effect in a timely manner" (2010). The Current Rule includes exceptions to this requirement, but it does not list conscience- or religious-based objections. The listed exceptions include matters of professional judgment, such as when drug-drug interactions or drug-food interactions are indicated (2010) and when emergencies affect drug availability (2010). Section (g) mandates if a lawfully prescribed drug or nonprescription drug is not in stock or is otherwise unavailable, the pharmacy must provide the patient a timely alternative for appropriate therapy, which may include obtaining the drug. Suggested alternatives include, if the patient requests it, transmitting the prescription information to a pharmacy that will fill the prescription. A pharmacy that fails to comply with the Current Rule is subject to disciplinary action "or other enforcement" (2010).

In May 2010, plaintiffs filed a third amended complaint and a summary-judgment motion seeking relief against the Current Rule. In their third amended complaint, plaintiffs maintained the Current Rule violated the Conscience Act, the Religious Freedom Act, and the first amendment. Before trial, the circuit court granted the parties' joint motion in which defendants agreed not to pursue disciplinary action for violations of the previous rules and plaintiffs agreed to voluntarily dismiss claims made under Title VII of the Civil Rights Act of 1964 and the Illinois Human Rights Act.

In March 2011, a trial was held. Plaintiffs Vander Bleek and Kosirog testified for plaintiffs; Dr. Warren Wallace and Secretary Adams testified for defendants.

Plaintiff Vander Bleek, a pharmacist who resides in Morrison, testified he had been a pharmacist since 1986. He owned three pharmacies, with locations in Morrison, Sycamore, and Genoa. Vander Bleek is Roman Catholic and regularly attended church.

Vander Bleek testified he was aware of emergency contraceptives. He believed his faith prevented him from participating in the sale of emergency contraception because it has the potential for terminating human life. Vander Bleek believed human life begins at conception, and the FDA-approved product literature on the Plan B products indicates such medication may prevent pregnancy after fertilization. Vander Bleek testified his faith prevented him from selling emergency contraception and also from permitting his stores to stock the drugs or participating in a system through which he would transfer the prescription to another store to be filled.

According to Vander Bleek, his pharmacies had guidelines concerning emergency contraception. In May 2005, by letter, he informed his staff of this policy. Vander Bleek asked any pharmacist who worked for him to sign the policy. Since 2005 approximately three or four women had asked for emergency contraception in his Morrison store. About the same number had asked for those drugs in his other two stores combined.

Vander Bleek testified, upon hearing Governor Blagojevich's comments about the change in the law, he felt like he would have to choose between violating the law or his conscience. Vander Bleek watched an interview of Governor Blagojevich on television, when the governor said pharmacists unwilling to dispense emergency contraception should find a new job.

Vander Bleek testified the nearest location to his Morrison store where a woman could obtain emergency contraception was approximately 3½ blocks away. This location was an inpatient pharmacy at a public hospital, which stocked Plan B in the emergency room. The nearest pharmacy, however, was approximately 14 miles away. More than 12 pharmacies were within a 15-minute drive of the Morrison location. Regarding the Sycamore and Genoa locations, Vander Bleek testified a Walgreen's was approximately 10 minutes from his Genoa pharmacy and 5 minutes from his Sycamore store. Prescription emergency contraception was also available on the Internet.

Glenn Kosirog, a registered pharmacist for over 25 years and a resident of Wheaton, testified he was the sole shareholder in a corporation that owns Kosirog Pharmacy, a pharmacy that had been in his family over 50 years. Kosirog testified he had been a Christian since he was 17 years old. Kosirog believed emergency contraceptives to be "abortion pills," as emergency contraception taken after unprotected sex could destroy an embryo. Kosirog believed life begins at conception. Kosirog, because of his faith, could not have anything to do with emergency contraceptives.

Kosirog testified his store, since 2006 or 2007, had an "abortion pill policy." This policy requires a pharmacist, if presented with a prescription for emergency contraception, to return the prescription. Kosirog testified one or two women each month entered his store seeking emergency contraception. Over 12 pharmacies were within three or four miles of his Chicago pharmacy.

When Kosirog first learned of the requirement to sell emergency contraception, he felt coerced and frightened. He was concerned the government might close his pharmacy because of his beliefs. Because of the uncertainty surrounding the rules, he did not expand his business.

Warren Henry Wallace, a physician at Northwestern University Medical School, testified as an expert witness for defendants. Dr. Wallace testified he practiced medicine for 35 years. When he prescribed a medication for a patient, he expected the prescription would be filled and the patient would take it. Dr. Wallace would not inform a pharmacist of the reasons for the prescription and described situations where a woman's life and health would be endangered by a pregnancy. Dr. Wallace testified the failure to take emergency contraceptives in a timely manner "may lead to increased risk that it will be ineffective." When asked about the optimal time frame for taking emergency contraceptives, Dr. Wallace testified they were most effective when taken immediately after unprotected intercourse and "become progressively less effective over the course of the next several days."

Dr. Wallace testified he heard the term "dispensary" used to refer to a pharmacy. He agreed physicians were free to refuse to enter into physician-patient relationships for conscience-based reasons and pharmacists should have

that same right. Dr. Wallace testified until April 2010 there had not been a rule requiring every pharmacy to sell every drug. In his own personal experience, he was not aware of any instance in which a religious refusal to sell emergency contraceptives resulted in the woman's failure to obtain the drug.

Brent Adams, the secretary of financial professional regulation for the State of Illinois, testified he had been with the Department since July 2006. In October 2009, he was confirmed as secretary. In his role as secretary, Secretary Adams helped determine the Department's policy initiatives and directives.

Secretary Adams testified he drafted the Current Rule. Secretary Adams explained the prior rules were repealed as part of "a comprehensive rewrite of the rules in the context of amendments to the Pharmacy Practice Act." Upon learning of the Ninth Circuit's decision in the *Stormans, Inc. v. Selecky*, 586 F.3d 1109 (9th Cir. 2009), in which rules broadly expanding access to medications survived constitutional scrutiny, he decided to move in the same direction. The Current Rule was drafted "to promote the health and well-being of residents" and "to establish a regulatory framework that would protect access to medications for all Illinois residents." Secretary Adams testified his concern was with access to medication in general, but matters of Plan B contraception were also discussed, as were matters of post-exposure prophylaxis for human immunodeficiency virus (HIV) infection and psychotropic medications. Secretary Adams was not aware of any particular instance when a patient was denied emergency contraceptives because of a religious-based objection, but he "was aware of general controversy." His "concern was that at some future point, a patient in need of timely access to one of those remedies would be denied and the complaint process via the Department would not redress that concern in an adequate time frame."

Secretary Adams testified the duty to deliver applies to the pharmacy, not to pharmacists. The Department would learn of violations through consumer complaints. After a consumer filed a complaint, the Department would conduct an investigation and make a report to the prosecution if necessary. Pharmacies were responsible for drug delivery because they were the frontline deliverers of necessary medication. Pharmacists, individually, were not covered under the rule to address religious objections. Secretary Adams was unaware of any customer complaints under the previous rules regarding religious-based refusals to dispense emergency contraceptives.

Secretary Adams testified the Current Rule did not require doctors to write prescriptions for drugs. He acknowledged access to medication could be denied if a doctor refused to write a prescription. Secretary Adams testified his Department had a variance procedure that allowed him to make individualized assessments for parties seeking a variance. He could not foresee a situation in which he would give a variance for a religious objection.

Secretary Adams, in the process of drafting the Current Rule, met with the Retail Merchants Foundation, at least one pharmacist association, and Planned Parenthood. Secretary Adams did not meet with religious objectors. Secretary Adams testified he kept all of the materials related to the Current Rule in a file under the heading "Plan B." Secretary Adams could envision a health issue in which a patient is in need of medication and arrives at a pharmacy and is denied access. Secretary Adams agreed his rule did not require the pharmacy to stock the drug. He agreed timely therapeutic equivalent in some instances might mean the same day, but timeliness would depend on the circumstances. Secretary Adams would not agree the public hospital's selling the drug three blocks away was an alternative for Vander Bleek's refusal to sell emergency contraception at his pharmacy: "I find it unreasonable to expect a patient who is denied access at a pharmacy to think to go to the emergency room."

The circuit court found plaintiffs Vander Bleek and Kosirog had sincere religious- and conscience-based objections to participating in the distribution of the Plan B contraceptives. The court concluded the Current Rule is invalid on its face and as applied under the Conscience Act, the Religious Freedom Act, and the first amendment. The court entered judgment for plaintiffs on counts I, IV, and VI of the third amended complaint and permanently enjoined defendants and "those acting in concert" with them from enforcing the Current Rule. The court found no just reason for delaying the appeal. The court further issued a stay on the enforcement of the judgment but found the preliminary injunction that had been previously issued remained in effect until the matter is fully litigated on appeal.

This appeal followed.

Analysis

Conscience Act

In their opening brief, defendants next ask the court to find the Current Rule does not violate the free-exercise clause of the first amendment. Defendants argue the Current Rule is facially neutral, applies generally, and easily survives rational-basis review. In the alternative, defendants contend the Current Rule survives a strict-scrutiny test because the State has a compelling interest in establishing a uniform system of efficient local drug distribution and the Current Rule is narrowly tailored to satisfy that interest.

We decline defendants' invitation to begin with this constitutional issue. We should avoid constitutional questions when the case may be decided on other grounds. We begin with the question of whether the Current Rule violates statutory law, starting with our consideration of the Conscience Act.

In 1977, the General Assembly enacted the Conscience Act. In so doing, the General Assembly declared,

"It is the public policy of the State of Illinois to respect and protect the right of conscience of all persons who refuse to obtain, receive or accept, or who are engaged in, the delivery of, arrangement for, or payment of health care services and medical care whether acting individually, corporately, or in association with other persons."

Consistent with this policy, the General Assembly, in the Conscience Act, determined "[n]o physician or health care personnel shall be civilly or criminally liable to any person, estate, public or private entity or public official by reason of his or her refusal to perform, assist, counsel, suggest, recommend, refer or participate in any way in any particular form of health care service which is contrary to the conscience of such physician or health care personnel." The General Assembly further made it unlawful for public officials to discriminate against any person, in any manner, in licensing "because of such person's conscientious refusal to receive, obtain, accept, perform, assist, counsel, suggest, recommend, refer or participate in any way in any particular form of health care services contrary to his or her conscience." "Conscience" is defined as "a sincerely held set of moral convictions arising from belief in and relation to God, or which, though not so derived, arises from a place in the life of its possessor parallel to that filled by God among adherents to religious faiths."

The American Civil Liberties Union (ACLU) of Illinois, in its *amicus* brief, urges this court to interpret and apply the Conscience Act according to the parameters of the Religious Freedom Act. ACLU reasons the Religious Freedom Act was enacted after the Conscience Act and is more specific and the Conscience Act provides no guidelines that permit the allowance of competing interests.

We find these arguments unconvincing. Section 15 of the Religious Freedom Act provides the State "may not substantially *burden* a person's exercise of religion, even if the burden results from a rule of general applicability, unless it demonstrates that application of the burden to the person (i) is in furtherance of a compelling governmental interest and (ii) is the least restrictive means of furthering that compelling governmental interest." It does not apply here. The General Assembly, in enacting the Conscience Act, did "not substantially burden a person's exercise of religion," but instead bolstered it, by offering protections to those who seek not to act in the health-care setting due to religious convictions. The Conscience Act is more specific than the Religious Freedom Act because the Conscience Act deals specifically with the issue of health care, while the Religious Freedom Act would apply to any governmental action that "substantially burden[s] a person's exercise of religion."

ACLU of Illinois contends, however, the State must be permitted to weigh the interests of women who seek emergency contraceptives against those of pharmacists whom the State should be able to command to dispense medications at the woman's or physician's request. We agree the State as a whole has this authority. However, we do not agree defendants, as part of the executive branch of the State, necessarily have this authority here. This is not a case where the "State" has made *one* decision on the issue, but where the "State" has made *two* decisions. The executive branch decided to make Plan B available over any pharmacist's religious concerns, while the legislative branch decided to protect health-care personnel and health-care facilities from having to provide health care against their conscience or religious beliefs. We must decide whether the two decisions (*i.e.,* the Current Rule and the Conscience Act) act in harmony. If not, the Conscience Act prevails.

"Whenever an administrative rule conflicts with a statute, the rule will be held invalid and the statute followed."

The Conscience Act Applies to the Practice of Pharmacy

Defendants argue the Conscience Act does not apply in this case because pharmacists and pharmacies are not protected by its provisions. Defendants maintain the words "pharmacy" and "pharmacist" do not appear in the statute and the Act defines "health care" as treatment rendered only by "physicians, nurses, paraprofessionals or [a] health care facility." Defendants contend the issue of whether pharmacists are paraprofessionals is ambiguous and urges this court to examine the legislative history to resolve the ambiguity. While the terms "pharmacy" and "pharmacist" do not appear in the text, plaintiffs contend the plain language of the Conscience Act establishes it applies to them and there is no ambiguity.

The main "goal of statutory interpretation is to ascertain and give effect to the legislature's intent." The statutory language itself, given its plain and ordinary meaning, is the best indication of legislative intent. When the statutory language is clear, we will give it effect without resorting to other aids of construction.

Section 3 of the Conscience Act defines "health care" as follows:

> "Health care' means any phase of patient care, including but not limited to, testing; diagnosis; prognosis; ancillary research; instructions; family planning, counseling, referrals, or any other advice in connection with the use or procurement of contraceptives and sterilization or abortion procedures; medication; or surgery or other care or treatment rendered by a physician or physicians, nurses, paraprofessionals or health care facility, intended for the physical, emotional, and mental well-being of persons[.]" (West 2010)

A federal district court, in *Vandersand v. Wal-Mart Stores, Inc.,* rejected the same argument made by defendants. In *Vandersand*, the plaintiff, a licensed pharmacist in Illinois, argued his employer, Wal-Mart, wrongfully terminated his employment after he refused to dispense an emergency contraceptive based on his understanding the drug acted "with a significant abortifacient mechanism" and his religious beliefs did not permit him to dispense the drug. *Vandersand*. The plaintiff filed a complaint alleging, in part, his termination violated the Conscience Act. *Vandersand*. Wal-Mart moved to dismiss plaintiff's complaint, arguing, as defendants do here, the Conscience Act only protects treatment provided by physicians, nurses, paraprofessionals, or health-care facilities. The district court rejected this argument upon concluding Wal-Mart took the limiting language from the last clause of the "health care" definition in section 3 and that clause refers only to "surgery or other care or treatment," and not to the entire list of "health care" services appearing before it. The district court found such language did not apply to "family planning" and "medication" and anyone who refused to participate in providing medication because of his conscience is protected by the Conscience Act.

We agree with the analysis in *Vandersand*. The statutory language is clear and the limiting language upon which defendants rely does not apply to "medication." Section 5 of the Conscience Act prohibits discrimination in licensing against anyone "because of such person's conscientious refusal to receive, obtain, accept, perform, assist, counsel, suggest, recommend, refer or participate in any way in any particular form of health care [(*i.e.,* medication)] services contrary to his or her conscience."

We further find section 4 of the Conscience Act bars civil or criminal actions against plaintiffs for their refusal to dispense Plan B medication. Section 4, quoted above, protects "health care personnel" from civil and criminal liability when such personnel refuse to act according to their conscience. Section 3(c) of the Conscience Act defines "health care personnel" as "any nurse, nurses' aide, medical school student, professional, paraprofessional or *any other person who furnishes, or assists in the furnishing of, health care services.*" A pharmacist is a person who furnishes or assists in furnishing health-care services, *i.e.,* the provision of medication.

Finding the statutory language clearly applies to the provision of "medication" services, we need not attempt to interpret the term "paraprofessionals." We note defendants, in arguing the statute is ambiguous toward pharmacists, urged this court to find persuasive the comments of one representative on the floor of the House of Representatives, who stated pharmacists and pharmacies were specifically excluded, on their own request, from the Conscience Act. Such statements might be minimally persuasive if we found this provision of the Conscience Act ambiguous and if the statements were not made approximately *20 years after* the Conscience Act was enacted.

Plaintiffs next argue sections 9 and 10 of the Conscience Act similarly protect the corporate plaintiffs, who manage "health care facilities" from government action under the Current Rule. Plaintiffs maintain pharmacies fall within the definition of "health care facilities" as they are "dispensaries" or, in the alternative, "location[s] wherein health care services are provided to any person." Defendants maintain the term "dispensaries" refers to an part of a larger institution, such as a school, hospital, or factory. Defendants further maintain there is ambiguity in the term "health care facilities" and urges this court to follow the same legislative history cited above.

Section 9 provides, in part, no person or corporation that owns or operates a "health care facility" shall be liable to any public entity by reason of the health-care facility's refusal to provide any particular form of health-care service that violates the facility's conscience as set forth in its ethical guidelines or other governing documents. Section 10, in part, makes it unlawful for a public official to discriminate against any corporation who operates "an existing health care facility" in any way, including in licensing, because the corporation refused to permit "any particular form of health care service which violates the health care facility's conscience as documented in its existing or proposed ethical guidelines" or other governing documents.

Section 3(d) of the Conscience Act defines "health care facility" as follows:

> "any public or private hospital, clinic, center, medical school, medical training institution, laboratory or diagnostic facility, physician's office, infirmary, dispensary, ambulatory surgical treatment center or other institution or location wherein health care services are provided to any person, including physician organizations and associations, networks, joint ventures, and all other combinations of those organizations."

Defendants cite two definitions for "dispensary" to support their argument dispensaries generally refer to areas part of a larger institution. The first is from Webster's Third New International Dictionary 653 (1993): "a place where medicines or medical or dental aid are dispensed to ambulant patients (a [dispensary] in an industrial plant)." The second definition comes from American Heritage Dictionary: "[a]n office in a hospital, school, or other institution from which medical supplies and preparations are dispensed."

Plaintiffs emphasize the definitions for "dispensary" and "pharmacy" prove the terms are synonymous. Plaintiffs, citing Webster's Third New International Dictionary 653 and 1694 (1971), contend "dispensary" is defined as "a place where medicines are dispensed" and "pharmacy" is defined as "a place where medicines are dispensed." Plaintiffs point to defendants' expert witness's testimony, in which Dr. Wallace acknowledged he heard the term "dispensary" used in reference to a pharmacy. Plaintiffs further cite section 3 of the Pharmacy Practice Act, which defines "pharmacy" as a place where pharmacist care is provided and where medicines are dispensed or where a sign is affixed using words such as "Pharmacist," "Pharmacy," or "Dispensary."

We find a "pharmacy" is a "dispensary." A dispensary is "a place where medicine or medical or dental treatment is dispensed."

A pharmacy is "a place where medicines are compounded or dispensed."

Given the language of the Conscience Act, the General Assembly plainly intended to protect those institutions or organizations which dispense medication from having to act against their consciences. It would be a tortured interpretation to conclude individuals who dispense medicines inside a hospital or school are protected while individuals who dispense medicines outside the hospital or school are not. Pharmacies and pharmacists fall within the protections of the Conscience Act.

We further find convincing the argument a pharmacy is a "location wherein health care services are provided to any person." As we determined above, the definition of "health care" includes "medication." Because a pharmacy is a location where medication services are provided, it is a "health care facility" as defined in the Conscience Act.

The Provision of "Emergency Contraceptives" Is Not "Emergency Medical Care" Contemplated by the Conscience Act

Defendants argue, even if the Conscience Act applies to pharmacies and pharmacists, it does not permit them to refuse to provide emergency-contraceptive care. Defendants emphasize the Conscience Act specifically states in sections 6 and 9, "Nothing in this Act shall be construed so as to relieve a physician or other health care personnel from obligations under the law of providing emergency medical care." Defendants contend, because "every hour counts" in the effectiveness of Plan B contraceptives, the provision of emergency contraceptives falls within this exception.

Plaintiffs contend the language in sections 6 and 9 does not permit the Current Rule to stand. Plaintiffs contend the provisions mean the Conscience Act will not excuse health-care personnel from any independent legal obligation they may otherwise have to provide medical care and defendants have failed to identify any independent legal obligation on pharmacies or pharmacists to provide such care. Plaintiffs further contend a patient's need to maximize the drug's effectiveness within 72 hours is not proof of emergency medical care.

We disagree with plaintiffs' first contention. The Current Rule itself, if the provision of emergency contraceptives is "emergency medical care," would create its own "obligation[] under the law of providing emergency medical care." The issue thus turns on whether "emergency" contraceptives fall within the term "emergency medical care."

The Conscience Act does not define the term "emergency" in the context of "emergency medical care." Recently, however, the Supreme Court of Illinois defined "emergency" as "an unforeseen circumstance involving imminent danger to a person or property requiring an urgent response." The court arrived at this "plain and ordinary meaning of the term" when considering its context in section 10(b) of the Public Safety Employee Benefits Act (West 2006). Section 10(b) sets forth the eligibility requirements for firefighters, among others, to have their employer pay their health-insurance premiums. One situation in which a firefighter's health-insurance premiums will be paid is when an injury or death occurred when the firefighter responded "to what is reasonably believed to be an emergency." (Emphasis omitted.) (Internal quotation marks omitted.) In considering the term's meaning, the *Gaffney* court quoted Webster's Third New International Dictionary definition of the term: "a sudden bodily alteration such as is likely to require immediate medical attention (as a ruptured appendix or surgical shock)." "The *Gaffney* court found the term included "an element of urgency and the need for immediate action."

We find the plain and ordinary meaning of the term "emergency," as defined by our supreme court in *Gaffney*, is the meaning the General Assembly intended when it included the term in sections 6 and 9. Emergency medical care is medical care with "an element of urgency and the need for immediate action," such as "a ruptured appendix or surgical shock."

Applying this definition to the term, we find "emergency contraceptives" do not fall within the plain and ordinary meaning of the term "emergency." The Web site defendants cite for proof "every hour counts" indicates if "Plan B One-Step®" is "taken as directed within 72 hours (3 days), it can significantly decrease the chance that you will become pregnant."

The next line says "[a]bout seven out of every eight women who would have gotten pregnant will not become pregnant," without making any distinction based on whether the emergency contraceptive is taken in the first hour or the seventy-first hour. In addition, while Dr. Wallace testified emergency contraceptives become progressively less effective over the course of "several days," he also testified the effectiveness "*may* lead to increased risk that it will be ineffective" if a woman fails to take emergency contraceptives in a timely manner. Given the 72-hour window, even though the window may become narrower in that time frame, unprotected sex does not place a woman in imminent danger requiring an urgent response.

Our interpretation and application of the term "emergency" may not be the same definition that would be applied by a woman seeking the emergency contraceptive. However, the evidence here does not show there would be an imminent danger to the patient or the need for immediate attention as contemplated by the Conscience Act.

Conclusion

We affirm the circuit court's findings the Current Rule cannot be enforced against plaintiffs without violating the Conscience Act. We reverse the court's granting of a permanent injunction against defendants' enforcement of the Current Rule. We modify the injunction so it enjoins defendants from enforcing the Current Rule against these plaintiffs, who have conscience-based objections to the Current Rule.

Justice James A. Knecht is an Illinois district judge. He has been a judge since 1975 and is the chair of the Appellate Court Administrative Committee.

Susan A. Cohen

 **NO**

Objections, Confusion Among Pharmacists Threaten Access To Emergency Contraception

Emergency contraception—which basically amounts to taking a high dose of "regular" oral contraceptives very shortly after unprotected intercourse—is now widely acknowledged as capable of making a dramatic contribution toward reducing unintended pregnancies and, therefore, abortions. However, it is equally clear that a concerted public education effort is necessary for this medical technology, which has long been used in other countries, to live up to its full public health potential in the United States.

Over the past several years, such a campaign has been under way in the United States. According to a 1997 survey by the Kaiser Family Foundation, educational efforts directed at physicians and women about the existence and efficacy of emergency contraception have resulted in a marked increase in knowledge, and use, of the method nationwide. These efforts undoubtedly were bolstered by last year's approval by the Food and Drug Adminstration (FDA), for the first time, of an oral contraception regimen to be packaged and marketed in the United States specifically for postcoital use.

However, on a variety of fronts, there remain significant obstacles to widespread knowledge about and access to emergency contraception. Among them is a new, largely unanticipated hurdle concerning pharmacists. In isolated cases nationwide, individual pharmacists have refused to fill prescriptions for these emergency contraceptive pills (ECPs), presumably on the grounds that to do so is to facilitate abortion. Initially, these were considered fluke occurrences, but the problem has received increasing attention following a recent decision by Wal-Mart, one of the nation's largest drug retailers, to not sell ECPs.

These actions are largely based on confusion over what emergency contraception is and how it works—specifically, on the widespread misperception that emergency contraception is actually a method of abortion. This confusion has impeded not only the availability of ECPs vis-à-vis pharmacies but also the formulation of responsible public policy to address issues of pharmacist "conscience." Clearly, the situation calls for an immediate expansion of public education efforts around emergency contraception targeted specifically at pharmacists. A simultaneous challenge is ensuring that the development of public policy around this issue strikes an appropriate balance between any legitimate conscience claims of individual pharmacists and the ability of women to purchase legal contraceptive drugs in order to avoid unintended pregnancy.

Contraception, Not Abortion

In September 1998, FDA gave its long-awaited final approval to an emergency contraception "kit"—marketed under the name Preven—containing four oral contraceptive pills and a pregnancy test. Preven remains the only kit specifically packaged and marketed for emergency contraception in the United States, but 11 other regimens of oral contraceptives have been declared by FDA safe and effective for postcoital use. Since those regimens are not specifically *labeled* for that purpose, however, they are prescribed by providers as regular oral contraceptives, with special instructions on how to take the pills. Indeed, ECPs have been prescribed this way—"off label" and without special packaging—for decades.

Traditionally known as the "morning-after pill," ECPs actually can prevent pregnancy if taken within 72 hours of intercourse where there was known or suspected contraceptive failure or where no birth control was used. The regimen usually involves taking two or four oral contraceptive pills at first, followed by two or four more 12 hours later. Whether oral contraceptive pills are taken on a daily basis as an ongoing method of pregnancy prevention or in a concentrated dose in an "emergency" situation after unprotected intercourse, their potential modes of action remain the same. The best scientific evidence suggests that ECPs most often work by suppressing ovulation. But depending on the timing of intercourse in relation to a woman's hormonal cycle, they—as is the case with all hormonal contraceptive methods—also may prevent pregnancy either by preventing fertilization or by preventing implantation of a fertilized egg in the uterus (*TGR*, Vol. 1, No. 5, October 1998).

In the media and in political debates, ECPs are often confused with mifepristone, commonly known as RU-486. However, mifepristone—as currently being reviewed for approval by FDA—is clearly a method of abortion. Unlike mifepristone, ECPs cannot disrupt an established pregnancy and, therefore, cannot, under any circumstances, cause an abortion.

Time Is of the Essence

Having had unprotected sex and fearing the possibility of becoming pregnant, a woman—who must know that there is something she can still do to avoid becoming pregnant—has 72 hours in which to obtain and begin taking ECPs. First, she must contact a health care provider who is knowledgeable enough and willing to write her a prescription for the contraceptive. Then, she must find a pharmacist to fill her prescription. (It is in light of the inherent challenge to complete these steps within the narrow window of opportunity that moves are under way in some states to allow pharmacists themselves to directly *prescribe* as well as dispense ECPs—see box.)

By the time a woman connects with a medical provider and obtains a prescription for ECPs, she may have only a few hours to actually acquire and take them. In an urban area, a woman encountering a pharmacist who refuses to fill her prescription may well be able, within the time constraints, to find either another pharmacist at that drugstore or one at another drugstore who would be willing to do so.

Encountering a refusing pharmacist may present more significant access barriers, however, in a small town or rural area in which the number of pharmacists within reach may be very small.

Similarly, the problems are compounded when an entire drugstore chain will not provide them. This case arose recently when, shortly after FDA approved Preven last fall, Wal-Mart made a "business" decision, never publicly announced, not to provide the contraceptive.

Planned Parenthood of New York City, which learned of the decision through a survey it conducted of pharmacists in the New York City area, recently urged Wal-Mart to reconsider its policy, asking it to take into account the "significant health and social consequences" of effectively blocking access to this pregnancy prevention method even when it might be needed by a woman who has been raped. Wal-Mart issued a curt reply on April 30, stating that it remains firm in its position, but adding that "in the interest of serving and meeting the needs of our customers, our pharmacists will refer any request for the drug to a pharmacy that does carry it."

Clearly, where there are a variety of pharmacists and pharmacies, willingness to refer a woman seeking ECPs to another individual or store is critical. At the same time, even with a referral, an objection to dispensing ECPs in the best-case scenario creates hassle, and in the worst case may be tantamount to access denied altogether.

Policy Responses

Pharmacists are regulated by state boards of pharmacy, which have long-standing policies that in general, a pharmacist is obligated to dispense all medications for

---

IN SOME STATES, MEANWHILE, PHARMACISTS ARE ACTIVELY WORKING TO FACILITATE ECP ACCESS

Even as women's ability to obtain emergency contraceptive pills (ECPs) is being hampered by the refusal of some pharmacists to provide them, in other cases, pharmacists are actively working with women's health proponents to facilitate access to ECPs. In 1997, pharmacists in Washington State became the first in the country to secure the authority to prescribe ECPs as well as dispense them to women.

In Washington, as in 21 other states, existing law authorizes pharmacists to prescribe and dispense certain drug therapies on the basis of a set of protocols and the development of "collaborative agreements" between pharmacists and physicians or nurse practitioners. Prior to their application to emergency contraception, these laws were used to allow pharmacists to provide patients with, for example, immunizations and critical pain-relief therapy.

In July 1997, a group of organizations in Washington—including the State Board of Pharmacy, the State Pharmacy Association, family planning organizations and a public relations firm—began an innovative effort to make emergency contraception more widely available. The effort, which targeted the Puget Sound area, included educating pharmacists about ECPs, facilitating links between pharmacists and practitioners, and educating women in the state about emergency contraception. A major goal of the campaign was to spawn the development of collaborative agreements, which must be approved by the Washington State Board of Pharmacy. By August 1998, 117 such agreements had been submitted for review by the board.

The success of the Washington program has inspired other states to follow suit. Paving the way for a pharmacist-dispensation initiative in its state, the Oregon Medical Association House of Delegates in April reportedly passed a resolution backing the prescription of ECPs by pharmacists. Meanwhile, in California, the legislature currently is considering legislation that specifically would allow pharmacists to prescribe and dispense ECPs.

---

which he or she is licensed. There are only two significant exceptions to this rule: either when a pharmacist has sufficient reason to doubt that a prescription is valid or when use of the drug being prescribed could be against the patient's best interests, generally because it could provoke a harmful interaction with another drug the patient is taking.

The increasing popularity of ECPs, however—coupled with pharmacists' concerns over their potential obligations in legal assisted-suicide situations—appears to be spurring some pharmacists around the country to take issue with this obligation. This, in turn, is creating the perceived need to adjust both industry policies and state laws.

For example, the American Pharmaceutical Association (APhA), the professional association of pharmacists, adopted a policy last year that seeks to achieve balance between the rights of individual pharmacists to abide by their personal moral convictions and patients' needs for legal medications. Under the new policy, APhA "recognizes the individual pharmacist's right to exercise conscientious refusal *and* supports the establishment of systems to ensure patient access to legally prescribed therapy without compromising the pharmacist's right of conscientious refusal" (emphasis added).

Some state associations, in implementing this policy, are recommending that such "systems" ensure that at least one pharmacist in a given store be willing to dispense the medication. At a minimum, they call for the pharmacy, if not the individual pharmacist, to refer to another store that is known to provide full services.

Bills recently introduced in state legislatures, however, do not follow the APhA lead. For example, a 1998 South Dakota law permits any pharmacist to refuse to dispense medication if there is reason to believe it would be used to "destroy an unborn child"—which, under state law, is defined to include a fertilized egg even if it has not yet implanted in the uterus. As a result, in South Dakota, not only are ECPs available only at the option of individual pharmacists but so are all other methods that may act to prevent implantation of a fertilized egg—that is, all other hormonal contraceptive methods and the IUD. Furthermore, the South Dakota law does not address the access needs of the patients who are seeking legal medical therapy to which a pharmacist may object.

Pharmacist "conscience" legislation has been introduced this legislative session in Indiana, Kansas, Louisiana, Oregon and Wisconsin. Some of the measures are generic, allowing pharmacists to decline to provide any medication on conscience grounds, while others apply only to so-called abortion-inducing drugs—variously defined. The bill in Oregon is the broadest, applying to all drugs and to pharmacists as well as drugstore owners and operators.

A Question of Balance

While these measures were largely triggered by increasing use by American women of emergency *contraception*—and, specifically, by FDA approval of Preven—the impetus for them largely arises from some pharmacists' objections to participating in or facilitating *abortion*. It is logical to assume, then, that if pharmacists understood that ECPs are contraception and not abortion, much of the perceived need for changes in public policy would dissipate. After all, oral contraceptives and other hormonal methods—all of which are scientifically indistinguishable in their modes of action from ECPs—have been around for many years, and the overwhelming majority of pharmacists evidently have not objected to filling these prescriptions. To bring about this clarification will require a concerted education effort specifically targeting pharmacists.

At the same time, in crafting any policies that may be deemed necessary to address the conscience claims of pharmacists—in relation to ECPs or any other legal pharmaceuticals for that matter—policymakers would do well to heed the policy statement of pharmacists' national professional association. And that means any pharmacist conscience provision must also provide for the "establishment of *systems* to ensure patient access to legally prescribed therapy" (emphasis added). As some state pharmacist associations are coming to realize, implementation of the national policy may require—at a minimum—that at least one pharmacist in any given pharmacy be willing to dispense the medication in question or that the pharmacy itself be willing to refer the patient to a pharmacy that will.

Susan A. Cohen has been with the Guttmacher Institute since 1978 and is currently the Acting Vice President for Public Policy.

EXPLORING THE ISSUE

Should Pharmacists Be Able to Deny Emergency Contraception to Potentially Pregnant Women?

Critical Thinking and Reflection

1. What are some arguments made in each side with which you agree or disagree?
2. What are the strengths and weaknesses of the two positions made in this chapter?
3. Pick the side with which you most agree. What are some additional arguments you would make to strengthen the case for or against marriage equality?
4. Think more broadly about emergency contraception, women's right, and religious liberty. How would you balance these issues when it comes to emergency contraception?

Is There Common Ground?

Emergency contraception is arising as a new controversial issue in our society today. It raises some other questions about contraceptive bills and other techniques to avoid pregnancy. For example, birth control pills and breast-feeding are also hormonal methods that some couples use to avoid pregnancy. What sort of universal policies can we create to approach, from a legal perspective, when life begins? Otherwise, we continue to see these fights in a myriad of ways through not just emergency contraception but also work health care plans that include contraception.

Create Central

www.mhhe.com/createcentral

Additional Resources

Foster, Angela and L.L. Wynn, *Emergency Contraception: The Story of a Global Reproductive Health Technology* (2012).

Prescott, Heather Munro, *The Morning After: A History of Emergency Contraception in the United States* (2011).

Tone, Andrea, *Devices & Desires: A History of Contraceptives in America* (2002).

Internet References . . .

Contraception: an international reproductive health journal

www.contraceptionjournal.org

Emergency Contraception Website

www.ec.princeton.edu

WebMD: Emergency Contraception

www.webmd.com/sex-relationships/guide/emergency-contraception

Unit 2

UNIT

Parental Control and Children's Rights

*M*ost people can recall at one time or another being a child, and wanting to do something their parent didn't want them to do. When they asked their parent, "Why not?" the answer that came back was, "Because I said so." Parents have an enormous amount of social control over children, from a very young age. This power extends, however, beyond decisions about who a child can play with, how long she or he can stay up at night, or whether she or he can watch television for 10 more minutes. These decisions extend into areas that can affect a child for the rest of her or his life, including health and education. How much say should parents have in these types of decisions? How much say should a young child have, and also a teenager? This section examines particularly challenging parental decisions.

Selected, Edited, and with Issue Framing Material by:
David M. Hall, Ph.D., *Delaware Valley College*

ISSUE

Should Illegal Immigrant Families Be Able to Send Their Children to Public Schools?

YES: William Brennan, from Majority Opinion, *Plyler v. Doe* (1982)

NO: Warren Burger, from Dissenting Opinion, *Plyler v. Doe* (1982)

Learning Outcomes
After reading this issue, you will be able to: • Identify legal criteria such as the due process clause, the equal protection clause, and fundamental rights.   • Compare and contrast whether the U.S. Constitution protects undocumented immigrant children who reside in the United States.   • Evaluate the impact of this Supreme Court decision on illegal U.S. border crossings.

ISSUE SUMMARY

YES: William Brennan is regarded as one of the greatest intellectual leaders of the twentieth-century Supreme Court. He was regarded for writing extraordinarily forward-thinking opinions, especially regarding civil rights and civil liberties. This case proves no exception, as he captures an issue that seems even more pertinent today than when the Supreme Court addressed it. Brennan believes that children who are in the country and undocumented have a constitutional right to a public education.

NO: Warren Burger was the Chief Justice of the Supreme Court during a time in which it was slowly moving in a more conservative direction. He was an instrumental voice in many cases before the Supreme Court that had a more conservative outcome. Burger believes that undocumented immigrant children have no constitutional right to an education.

Although the percentage of the U.S. population that is foreign born has not increased significantly, there is a significant change in the country of origin from decades past. According to the Census Bureau, during 1960, 75 percent of those who were foreign born were from Europe. By 2009, over 80 percent of those who are foreign born are from Latin American and Asian countries (53.1 percent from Latin America, 27.7 percent from Asia, 12.7 percent from Europe, 3.9 percent from Africa, and 2.7 percent from other regions).

When looking at the data from specific countries, Mexico was the largest, accounting for almost 30 percent of foreign-born population, totaling approximately 11.5 million. The second-largest country of birth was China, representing just over 5 percent of the foreign-born population.

In 1960, the foreign born settled in traditional gateway states: New York, California, Texas, Florida, and Illinois. Today, foreign-born residents are increasingly likely to settle in states and communities that may not have a history of having large populations of foreign-born residents. Despite this, half of all foreign-born residents today live in California, New York, Texas, and Florida. According to public opinion polling, Gallup regularly asks a random sample of Americans the following question, "In your view, should immigration be kept at its present level, increased, or decreased?" In 2011, 43 percent of respondents, a plurality, argued that it should be decreased, 35 percent felt it should remain at its present level, and 18 percent of respondents felt it should be increased. How do these numbers compare and contrast with the general public's views at other periods in American history? According to their polling, there were periods of time in which larger numbers of Americans wanted to see decreased immigration, such as after 9/11 (58 percent) and during the mid-1990s (65 percent), when California voters supported reporting undocumented immigrant students to the Immigration and Naturalization Service. The poll's 18 percent support for increased immigration is tied for the highest percentage that response has ever received: in 1965, the first year that Gallup asked that question. Most Americans view immigration as a good thing for the country (57 percent) versus a bad thing (37 percent). The face of immigration has changed in the United States over recent decades. While in the previous decades it was largely European, more recently it is largely Hispanic and African. It is also found in more varied places than the traditional states associated with immigration. While in the mid-1990s the backlash to immigration was seen in California, today the backlash often occurs from untraditional places, sometimes rural and fairly distant from the U.S.-Mexican border.

Views about immigration are not necessarily the same as views about illegal immigration. For example, the state of Arizona passed a highly restrictive law targeting undocumented immigrants, and the United States filed suit, saying that the law is unconstitutional. However, 50 percent of Americans oppose the U.S. lawsuit while only 33 percent support it. When divided by political ideology, support for the lawsuit varies significantly: 56 percent of Democrats, 27 percent of Independents, and 11 percent of Republicans support the lawsuit. The concern that many states have is over undocumented immigration. In some cases, undocumented immigrants can comprise a sizable number of students. In challenging economic times when many districts are laying off teachers, a number of U.S.-born citizens voicing dismay and even anger at the public resources that are directed toward undocumented immigrants. There are school districts across the United States that were accustomed to having a small population of students who speak English as a second language. Today, many districts are seeing a steady increase in the number of speakers of English as a second language. Sometimes a backlash ensues, and visitors are looking for ways to adjust their instruction to correspond with this need. A case like this raises critical questions about the role of education and the role of the Constitution regarding education:

- What is the purpose and function of education in the United States today?
- What is the cost of sending undocumented immigrants to public schools?
- What is the value of sending undocumented immigrants to public schools?
- What is the cost of keeping undocumented immigrants out of public schools?
- What is the value of keeping undocumented immigrants out of public schools?

Immigration has played a critical role throughout American history, as has education. Public education has historically allowed many generations to improve their economic situation compared to that of their parents. Many children who are here illegally, and may have been here since they were infants, want the same opportunities as everyone else. At the same time, there are limited resources directed to public education. Adding more students, and in many cases adding more specialized teachers, creates additional expenses that the public education system would otherwise not need to assume. Also, allowing undocumented immigrants access to public schooling arguably proves to be a compelling incentive to come to the country illegally. The U.S. Constitution provides a wide array of protections. This case raises important questions not just about public education, but also constitutional rights:

- Do those rights and protections in the U.S. Constitution apply to everyone within the U.S. borders?
- Do the rights and protections in the U.S. Constitution apply only to U.S. citizens?
- Do constitutional protections vary depending on whether or not something is a fundamental right?

The U.S. Constitution applies certain rights regardless of popular opinion. In fact, the entire point of having rights enumerated in the Constitution is to keep certain rights from being at the whim of the majority. When the Constitution was written, there was not the sort of formal process for immigration that exists today.

Another perspective to view this from is one of safety and security. For example, proponents of the rights of undocumented immigrants will often say that it is dangerous to leave children on the streets all day. Having them behaving productively in schools will keep them engaged in ways that are beneficial to the larger society. Opponents of the rights of undocumented immigrants argue that such a system encourages dangerous and violent people to come to the United States, and that they use our laws to take advantage of U.S. citizens. Last, analyze the role of race and how that affects views about immigration:

- What role do you feel that race plays in views about immigration today?
- How are the changing demographics of American society influencing views about immigration and public education?
- How would you compare and contrast social problems and immigration (e.g., violence caused by immigrants) between generations past and today?
- How would you compare and contrast ingenuity and immigration between generations past and today?

Race has often played a significant role in American society, and definitions of whiteness and racial minorities have been reconstructed throughout American history. Immigration today, both documented and undocumented, is having a clear impact on American demographics and American culture. The relationship between race and immigration is a topic that merits close examination. This chapter contains excerpts from a Supreme Court opinion about whether undocumented immigrants have a right to attend public schools. This court case is not a recent one, yet the topic remains a priority and a major concern for a large number of Americans. What do we learn from the fact that such an issue remains divisive within our society for decades? When examining the articles in this chapter, apply them to the Legal Framework overview in the Introduction. Do your beliefs in this case fit more under Originalism or Living Document? Consider the larger implications of these decisions.

YES ↩

William Brennan

Majority Opinion, *Plyler v. Doe*

Justice Brennan delivered the opinion of the Court.

The question presented by these cases is whether, consistent with the Equal Protection Clause of the Fourteenth Amendment, Texas may deny to undocumented school-age children the free public education that it provides to children who are citizens of the United States or legally admitted aliens. . . .

I

In May, 1975, the Texas Legislature revised its education laws to withhold from local school districts any state funds for the education of children who were not "legally admitted" into the United States. The 1975 revision also authorized local school districts to deny enrollment in their public schools to children not "legally admitted" to the country. These cases involve constitutional challenges to those provisions.

This is a class action, filed in the United States District Court for the Eastern District of Texas in September, 1977, on behalf of certain school-age children of Mexican origin residing in Smith County, Tex., who could not establish that they had been legally admitted into the United States. The action complained of the exclusion of plaintiff children from the public schools of the Tyler Independent School District. . . . The State of Texas intervened as a party-defendant. After certifying a class consisting of all undocumented school-age children of Mexican origin residing within the School District, the District Court preliminarily enjoined defendants from denying a free education to members of the plaintiff class. In December, 1977, the court conducted an extensive hearing on plaintiffs' motion for permanent injunctive relief. . . .

II

The Fourteenth Amendment provides that

[n]o State shall . . . deprive any person of life, liberty, or property, without due process of law; nor deny to *any person within its jurisdiction* the equal protection of the laws.

(emphasis added.) Appellants argue at the outset that undocumented aliens, because of their immigration status, are not "persons within the jurisdiction" of the State of Texas, and that they therefore have no right to the equal protection of Texas law. We reject this argument. Whatever his status under the immigration laws, an alien is surely a "person" in any ordinary sense of that term. Aliens, even aliens whose presence in this country is unlawful, have long been recognized as "persons" guaranteed due process of law by the Fifth and Fourteenth Amendments. Indeed, we have clearly held that the Fifth Amendment protects aliens whose presence in this country is unlawful from invidious discrimination by the Federal Government. . . .

The Fourteenth Amendment to the Constitution is not confined to the protection of citizens. It says:

Nor shall any state deprive any person of life, liberty, or property without due process of law; nor deny to any person within its jurisdiction the equal protection of the laws.

These provisions are universal in their application, to all persons within the territorial jurisdiction, without regard to any differences of race, of color, or of nationality, and the protection of the laws is a pledge of the protection of equal laws.

In concluding that "all persons within the territory of the United States," including aliens unlawfully present, may invoke the Fifth and Sixth Amendments to challenge actions of the Federal Government, we reasoned from the understanding that the Fourteenth Amendment was designed to afford its protection to all within the boundaries of a State. Our cases applying the Equal Protection Clause reflect the same territorial theme:

Manifestly, the obligation of the State to give the protection of equal laws can be performed only where its laws operate, that is, within its own jurisdiction. It is there that the equality of legal right must be maintained. That obligation is imposed by the Constitution upon the States severally as governmental entities, each responsible for its own laws establishing the rights and duties of persons within its borders. . . .

Is it not essential to the unity of the people that the citizens of each State shall be entitled to all the privileges and immunities of citizens in the several States? Is it not essential to the unity of the Government and the unity of the people that all persons, *whether citizens or strangers, within this land,* shall have equal protection in every State in this Union in the rights of life and liberty and property?

Senator Howard, also a member of the Joint Committee of Fifteen, and the floor manager of the Amendment in the Senate, was no less explicit about the broad objectives of the Amendment, and the intention to make its provisions applicable to all who "may happen to be" within the jurisdiction of a State:

The last two clauses of the first section of the amendment disable a State from depriving not merely a citizen

Supreme Court of the United States, 1982.

of the United States, but *any person, whoever he may be,* of life, liberty, or property without due process of law, or from denying to him the equal protection of the laws of the State. This abolishes all class legislation in the States and does away with the injustice of subjecting one caste of persons to a code not applicable to another. . . . It will, if adopted by the States, forever disable every one of them from passing laws trenching upon those fundamental rights and privileges which pertain to citizens of the United States, *and to all persons who may happen to be within their jurisdiction.* . . .

Our conclusion that the illegal aliens who are plaintiffs in these cases may claim the benefit of the Fourteenth Amendment's guarantee of equal protection only begins the inquiry. The more difficult question is whether the Equal Protection Clause has been violated by the refusal of the State of Texas to reimburse local school boards for the education of children who cannot demonstrate that their presence within the United States is lawful, or by the imposition by those school boards of the burden of tuition on those children. It is to this question that we now turn. . . .

III

A

Sheer incapability or lax enforcement of the laws barring entry into this country, coupled with the failure to establish an effective bar to the employment of undocumented aliens, has resulted in the creation of a substantial "shadow population" of illegal migrants—numbering in the millions—within our borders. This situation raises the specter of a permanent caste of undocumented resident aliens, encouraged by some to remain here as a source of cheap labor, but nevertheless denied the benefits that our society makes available to citizens and lawful residents. The existence of such an underclass presents most difficult problems for a Nation that prides itself on adherence to principles of equality under law.

The children who are plaintiffs in these cases are special members of this underclass. Persuasive arguments support the view that a State may withhold its beneficence from those whose very presence within the United States is the product of their own unlawful conduct. These arguments do not apply with the same force to classifications imposing disabilities on the minor children of such illegal entrants. At the least, those who elect to enter our territory by stealth and in violation of our law should be prepared to bear the consequences, including, but not limited to, deportation. But the children of those illegal entrants are not comparably situated. Their "parents have the ability to conform their conduct to societal norms," and presumably the ability to remove themselves from the State's jurisdiction; but the children who are plaintiffs in these cases "can affect neither their parents' conduct nor their own status." Even if the State found it expedient to control the conduct of adults by acting against their children, legislation directing the onus of a parent's misconduct

against his children does not comport with fundamental conceptions of justice.

[V]isiting . . . condemnation on the head of an infant is illogical and unjust. Moreover, imposing disabilities on the . . . child is contrary to the basic concept of our system that legal burdens should bear some relationship to individual responsibility or wrongdoing. Obviously, no child is responsible for his birth, and penalizing the . . . child is an ineffectual—as well as unjust—way of deterring the parent.

Of course, undocumented status is not irrelevant to any proper legislative goal. Nor is undocumented status an absolutely immutable characteristic, since it is the product of conscious, indeed unlawful, action. But [the Texas law] is directed against children, and imposes its discriminatory burden on the basis of a legal characteristic over which children can have little control. It is thus difficult to conceive of a rational justification for penalizing these children for their presence within the United States. Yet that appears to be precisely the effect of [the Texas law].

Public education is not a "right" granted to individuals by the Constitution. But neither is it merely some governmental "benefit" indistinguishable from other forms of social welfare legislation. Both the importance of education in maintaining our basic institutions and the lasting impact of its deprivation on the life of the child mark the distinction. The "American people have always regarded education and [the] acquisition of knowledge as matters of supreme importance." But neither is it merely some governmental "benefit" indistinguishable from other forms of social welfare legislation. Both the importance of education in maintaining our basic institutions and the lasting impact of its deprivation on the life of the child mark the distinction. The "American people have always regarded education and [the] acquisition of knowledge as matters of supreme importance." We have recognized "the public schools as a most vital civic institution for the preservation of a democratic system of government." We have recognized "the public schools as a most vital civic institution for the preservation of a democratic system of government," and as the primary vehicle for transmitting "the values on which our society rests" (BRENNAN, J., concurring), and as the primary vehicle for transmitting "the values on which our society rests."

[A]s . . . pointed out early in our history, . . . some degree of education is necessary to prepare citizens to participate effectively and intelligently in our open political system if we are to preserve freedom and independence.

And these historic perceptions of the public schools as inculcating fundamental values necessary to the maintenance of a democratic political system have been confirmed by the observations of social scientists.

In addition, education provides the basic tools by which individuals might lead economically productive lives to the benefit of us all. In sum, education has a fundamental role in maintaining the fabric of our society. We cannot ignore the significant social costs borne by our

Nation when select groups are denied the means to absorb the values and skills upon which our social order rests.

In addition to the pivotal role of education in sustaining our political and cultural heritage, denial of education to some isolated group of children poses an affront to one of the goals of the Equal Protection Clause: the abolition of governmental barriers presenting unreasonable obstacles to advancement on the basis of individual merit. Paradoxically, by depriving the children of any disfavored group of an education, we foreclose the means by which that group might raise the level of esteem in which it is held by the majority. But more directly, "education prepares individuals to be self-reliant and self-sufficient participants in society." Illiteracy is an enduring disability. The inability to read and write will handicap the individual deprived of a basic education each and every day of his life. The inestimable toll of that deprivation on the social, economic, intellectual, and psychological wellbeing of the individual, and the obstacle it poses to individual achievement, make it most difficult to reconcile the cost or the principle of a status based denial of basic education with the framework of equality embodied in the Equal Protection Clause. What we said 28 years ago in 221. Illiteracy is an enduring disability. The inability to read and write will handicap the individual deprived of a basic education each and every day of his life. The inestimable toll of that deprivation on the social, economic, intellectual, and psychological wellbeing of the individual, and the obstacle it poses to individual achievement, make it most difficult to reconcile the cost or the principle of a status-based denial of basic education with the framework of equality embodied in the Equal Protection Clause. What we said 28 years ago in *Brown v. Board of Education* (1954) still holds true:

Today, education is perhaps the most important function of state and local governments. Compulsory school attendance laws and the great expenditures for education both demonstrate our recognition of the importance of education to our democratic society. It is required in the performance of our most basic public responsibilities, even service in the armed forces. It is the very foundation of good citizenship. Today it is a principal instrument in awakening the child to cultural values, in preparing him for later professional training, and in helping him to adjust normally to his environment. In these days, it is doubtful that any child may reasonably be expected to succeed in life if he is denied the opportunity of an education. Such an opportunity, where the state has undertaken to provide it, is a right which must be made available to all on equal terms.

B

These well-settled principles allow us to determine the proper level of deference to be afforded [the Texas law]. Undocumented aliens cannot be treated as a suspect class, because their presence in this country in violation of federal law is not a "constitutional irrelevancy." Nor is education a fundamental right; a State need not justify by compelling necessity every variation in the manner in which education is provided to its population. But more is involved in these cases than the abstract question whether [the Texas law] discriminates against a suspect class, or whether education is a fundamental right. [The Texas law] imposes a lifetime hardship on a discrete class of children not accountable for their disabling status. The stigma of illiteracy will mark them for the rest of their lives. By denying these children a basic education, we deny them the ability to live within the structure of our civic institutions, and foreclose any realistic possibility that they will contribute in even the smallest way to the progress of our Nation. In determining the rationality of [the Texas law], we may appropriately take into account its costs to the Nation and to the innocent children who are its victims. In light of these countervailing costs, the discrimination contained in [the Texas law] can hardly be considered rational unless it furthers some substantial goal of the State. . . .

IV

As we recognized in *De Canas v. Bica* (1976), the States do have some authority to act with respect to illegal aliens, at least where such action mirrors federal objectives and furthers a legitimate state goal. In *De Canas*, the State's program reflected Congress' intention to bar from employment all aliens except those possessing a grant of permission to work in this country. *Id.* at 361. In contrast, there is no indication that the disability imposed by [the Texas law] corresponds to any identifiable congressional policy. The State does not claim that the conservation of state educational resources was ever a congressional concern in restricting immigration. More importantly, the classification reflected in [the Texas law] does not operate harmoniously within the federal program.

To be sure, like all persons who have entered the United States unlawfully, these children are subject to deportation. But there is no assurance that a child subject to deportation will ever be deported. An illegal entrant might be granted federal permission to continue to reside in this country, or even to become a citizen. In light of the discretionary federal power to grant relief from deportation, a State cannot realistically determine that any particular undocumented child will in fact be deported until after deportation proceedings have been completed. It would, of course, be most difficult for the State to justify a denial of education to a child enjoying an inchoate federal permission to remain. . . .

V

First, appellants appear to suggest that the State may seek to protect itself from an influx of illegal immigrants. While a State might have an interest in mitigating the potentially harsh economic effects of sudden shifts in population, [the Texas law] hardly offers an effective method of dealing with an urgent demographic or economic problem. There is no evidence in the record suggesting that illegal entrants impose any significant burden on the State's economy. To the contrary, the available evidence suggests that illegal aliens underutilize public services, while contributing their labor to the local economy and tax money to the state. The dominant incentive for illegal entry into the State of Texas is the availability of employment; few if any illegal immigrants come to this country, or presumably to the State of Texas, in order to avail themselves of a free education. Thus, even making the doubtful assumption that the net impact of illegal aliens on the economy of the State is negative, we think it clear that "[c]harging tuition to undocumented children constitutes a ludicrously ineffectual attempt to stem the tide of illegal immigration," at least when compared with the alternative of prohibiting the employment of illegal aliens.

Second, while it is apparent that a State may "not . . . reduce expenditures for education by barring [some arbitrarily chosen class of] children from its schools," appellants suggest that undocumented children are appropriately singled out for exclusion because of the special burdens they impose on the State's ability to provide high-quality public education. But the record in no way supports the claim that exclusion of undocumented children is likely to improve the overall quality of education in the State. . . .

Finally, appellants suggest that undocumented children are appropriately singled out because their unlawful presence within the United States renders them less likely than other children to remain within the boundaries of the State, and to put their education to productive social or political use within the State. Even assuming that such an interest is legitimate, it is an interest that is most difficult to quantify. The State has no assurance that any child, citizen or not, will employ the education provided by the State within the confines of the State's borders. In any event, the record is clear that many of the undocumented children disabled by this classification will remain in this country indefinitely, and that some will become lawful residents or citizens of the United States. It is difficult to understand precisely what the State hopes to achieve by promoting the creation and perpetuation of a subclass of illiterates within our boundaries, surely adding to the problems and costs of unemployment, welfare, and crime. It is thus clear that whatever savings might be achieved by denying these children an education, they are wholly insubstantial in light of the costs involved to these children, the State, and the Nation.

VI

If the State is to deny a discrete group of innocent children the free public education that it offers to other children residing within its borders, that denial must be justified by a showing that it furthers some substantial state interest. No such showing was made here. Accordingly, the judgment of the Court of Appeals in each of these cases is

Affirmed.

 * Together with No. 80-1934, Texas et al. v. Certain Named and Unnamed Undocumented Alien Children et al., also on appeal from the same court.

WILLIAM BRENNAN is regarded as one of the greatest intellectual leaders of the twentieth-century Supreme Court. He was regarded for writing extraordinarily forward-thinking opinions, especially regarding civil rights and civil liberties. This case proves no exception as he captures an issue that seems even more pertinent today than when the Supreme Court addressed this issue. Brennan believes that children who are in the country and undocumented have a constitutional right to public education.

Warren Burger  **NO**

Dissenting Opinion, *Plyler v. Doe*

Chief Justice Burger, with whom Justice White, Justice Rehnquist, and Justice O'Connor join, dissenting.

Were it our business to set the Nation's social policy, I would agree without hesitation that it is senseless for an enlightened society to deprive any children—including illegal aliens—of an elementary education. I fully agree that it would be folly—and wrong—to tolerate creation of a segment of society made up of illiterate persons, many having a limited or no command of our language. However, the Constitution does not constitute us as "Platonic Guardians," nor does it vest in this Court the authority to strike down laws because they do not meet our standards of desirable social policy, "wisdom," or "common sense." We trespass on the assigned function of the political branches under our structure of limited and separated powers when we assume policymaking role as the Court does today.

The Court makes no attempt to disguise that it is acting to make up for Congress' lack of "effective leadership" in dealing with the serious national problems caused by the influx of uncountable millions of illegal aliens across our borders. The failure of enforcement of the immigration laws over more than a decade and the inherent difficulty and expense of sealing our vast borders have combined to create a grave socioeconomic dilemma. It is a dilemma that has not yet even been fully assessed, let alone addressed. However, it is not the function of the Judiciary to provide "effective leadership" simply because the political branches of government fail to do so.

The Court's holding today manifests the justly criticized judicial tendency to attempt speedy and wholesale formulation of "remedies" for the failures—or simply the laggard pace—of the political processes of our system of government. The Court employs, and, in my view, abuses, the Fourteenth Amendment in an effort to become an omnipotent and omniscient problem solver. That the motives for doing so are noble and compassionate does not alter the fact that the Court distorts our constitutional function to make amends for the defaults of others.

I

In a sense, the Court's opinion rests on such a unique confluence of theories and rationales that it will likely stand for little beyond the results in these particular cases. Yet the extent to which the Court departs from principled constitutional adjudication is nonetheless disturbing. I have no quarrel with the conclusion that the Equal Protection Clause of the Fourteenth Amendment *applies* to aliens who, after their illegal entry into this country, are indeed physically "within the jurisdiction" of a state. However, as the Court concedes, this "only begins the inquiry." The Equal Protection Clause does not mandate identical treatment of different categories of persons.

The dispositive issue in these cases, simply put, is whether, for purposes of allocating its finite resources, a state has a legitimate reason to differentiate between persons who are lawfully within the state and those who are unlawfully there. The distinction the State of Texas has drawn—based not only upon its own legitimate interests but on classifications established by the Federal Government in its immigration laws and policies—is not unconstitutional.

A

The Court acknowledges that, except in those cases when state classifications disadvantage a "suspect class" or impinge upon a "fundamental right," the Equal Protection Clause permits a state "substantial latitude" in distinguishing between different groups of persons. Moreover, the Court expressly—and correctly—rejects any suggestion that illegal aliens are a suspect class or that education is a fundamental right. Yet by patching together bits and pieces of what might be termed quasi-suspect-class and quasi-fundamental-rights analysis, the Court spins out a theory custom-tailored to the facts of these cases.

In the end, we are told little more than that the level of scrutiny employed to strike down the Texas law applies only when illegal alien children are deprived of a public education. If ever a court was guilty of an unabashedly result-oriented approach, this case is a prime example.

(1)

The Court first suggests that these illegal alien children, although not a suspect class, are entitled to special solicitude under the Equal Protection Clause because they lack "control" over or "responsibility" for their unlawful entry into this country. Similarly, the Court appears to take the position that [the Texas law] is presumptively "irrational" because it has the effect of imposing "penalties" on "innocent" children. However, the Equal Protection Clause does not preclude legislators from classifying among persons on the basis of factors and characteristics over which individuals may be said to lack "control."

Supreme Court of the United States, 1982.

Indeed, in some circumstances, persons generally, and children in particular, may have little control over or responsibility for such things as their ill health, need for public assistance, or place of residence. Yet a state legislature is not barred from considering, for example, relevant differences between the mentally healthy and the mentally ill, or between the residents of different counties simply because these may be factors unrelated to individual choice or to any "wrongdoing." The Equal Protection Clause protects against arbitrary and irrational classifications, and against invidious discrimination stemming from prejudice and hostility; it is not an all-encompassing "equalizer" designed to eradicate every distinction for which persons are not "responsible."

The Court does not presume to suggest that appellees' purported lack of culpability for their illegal status prevents them from being deported or otherwise "penalized" under federal law. Yet would deportation be any less a "penalty" than denial of privileges provided to legal residents? Illegality of presence in the United States does not—and need not—depend on some amorphous concept of "guilt" or "innocence" concerning an alien's entry. Similarly, a state's use of federal immigration status as a basis for legislative classification is not necessarily rendered suspect for its failure to take such factors into account.

The Court's analogy to cases involving discrimination against illegitimate children is grossly misleading. The State has not thrust any disabilities upon appellees due to their "status of birth." Rather, appellees' status is predicated upon the circumstances of their concededly illegal presence in this country, and is a direct result of Congress' obviously valid exercise of its "broad constitutional powers" in the field of immigration and naturalization. This Court has recognized that, in allocating governmental benefits to a given class of aliens, one "may take into account the character of the relationship between the alien and this country." When that "relationship" is a federally prohibited one, there can, of course, be no presumption that a state has a constitutional duty to include illegal aliens among the recipients of its governmental benefits.

(2)

The second strand of the Court's analysis rests on the premise that, although public education is not a constitutionally guaranteed right, "neither is it merely some governmental 'benefit' indistinguishable from other forms of social welfare legislation." Whatever meaning or relevance this opaque observation might have in some other context it simply has no bearing on the issues at hand. Indeed, it is never made clear what the Court's opinion means on this score.

The importance of education is beyond dispute. Yet we have held repeatedly that the importance of a governmental service does not elevate it to the status of a "fundamental right" for purposes of equal protection analysis. In *San Antonio Independent School Dist.*, JUSTICE POWELL, speaking for the Court, expressly rejected the proposition

that state laws dealing with public education are subject to special scrutiny under the Equal Protection Clause. Moreover, the Court points to no meaningful way to distinguish between education and other governmental benefits in this context. Is the Court suggesting that education is more "fundamental" than food, shelter, or medical care?

The Equal Protection Clause guarantees similar treatment of similarly situated persons, but it does not mandate a constitutional hierarchy of governmental services. JUSTICE POWELL, speaking for the Court in *San Antonio Independent School Dist.* put it well in stating that, to the extent this Court raises or lowers the degree of "judicial scrutiny" in equal protection cases according to a transient Court majority's view of the societal importance of the interest affected, we "assum[e] a legislative role, and one for which the Court lacks both authority and competence." Yet that is precisely what the Court does today.

The central question in these cases, as in every equal protection case not involving truly fundamental rights "explicitly or implicitly guaranteed by the Constitution," *San Antonio Independent School Dist.* is whether there is some legitimate basis for a legislative distinction between different classes of persons. The fact that the distinction is drawn in legislation affecting access to public education—as opposed to legislation allocating other important governmental benefits, such as public assistance, health care, or housing—cannot make a difference in the level of scrutiny applied.

B

Once it is conceded—as the Court does—that illegal aliens are not a suspect class, and that education is not a fundamental right, our inquiry should focus on and be limited to whether the legislative classification at issue bears a rational relationship to a legitimate state purpose.

The State contends primarily that [the Texas law] serves to prevent undue depletion of its limited revenues available for education, and to preserve the fiscal integrity of the State's school-financing system against an ever-increasing flood of illegal aliens—aliens over whose entry or continued presence it has no control. Of course such fiscal concerns alone could not justify discrimination against a suspect class or an arbitrary and irrational denial of benefits to a particular group of persons. Yet I assume no Member of this Court would argue that prudent conservation of finite state revenues is, *per se*, an illegitimate goal. Indeed, the numerous classifications this Court has sustained in social welfare legislation were invariably related to the limited amount of revenues available to spend on any given program or set of programs. The significant question here is whether the requirement of tuition from illegal aliens who attend the public schools—as well as from residents of other states, for example—is a rational and reasonable means of furthering the State's legitimate fiscal ends.

Without laboring what will undoubtedly seem obvious to many, it simply is not "irrational" for a state to conclude that it does not have the same responsibility to provide benefits for persons whose very presence in the state and this country is illegal as it does to provide for persons lawfully present. By definition, illegal aliens have no right whatever to be here, and the state may reasonably, and constitutionally, elect not to provide them with governmental services at the expense of those who are lawfully in the state. In *De Canas v. Bica* (1976), we held that a State may protect its fiscal interests and lawfully resident labor force from the deleterious effects on its economy resulting from the employment of illegal aliens.

And, only recently, this Court made clear that a State has a legitimate interest in protecting and preserving the quality of its schools and "the right of its own *bona fide residents* to attend such institutions on a preferential tuition basis." The Court has failed to offer even a plausible explanation why illegality of residence in this country is not a factor that may legitimately bear upon the bona fides of state residence and entitlement to the benefits of lawful residence.

It is significant that the Federal Government has seen fit to exclude illegal aliens from numerous social welfare programs, such as the food stamp program, the old-age assistance, aid to families with dependent children, aid to the blind, aid to the permanently and totally disabled, and supplemental security income programs, the Medicare hospital insurance benefits program, and the Medicaid hospital insurance benefits for the aged and disabled program. Although these exclusions do not conclusively demonstrate the constitutionality of the State's use of the same classification for comparable purposes, at the very least they tend to support the rationality of excluding illegal alien residents of a state from such programs so as to preserve the state's finite revenues for the benefit of lawful residents.

The Court maintains—as if this were the issue—that "barring undocumented children from local schools would not necessarily improve the quality of education provided in those schools." However, the legitimacy of barring illegal aliens from programs such as Medicare or Medicaid does not depend on a showing that the barrier would "improve the quality" of medical care given to persons lawfully entitled to participate in such programs. Modern education, like medical care, is enormously expensive, and there can be no doubt that very large added costs will fall on the State or its local school districts as a result of the inclusion of illegal aliens in the tuition-free public schools. The State may, in its discretion, use any savings resulting from its tuition requirement to "improve the quality of education" in the public school system, or to enhance the funds available for other social programs, or to reduce the tax burden placed on its residents; each of these ends is 'legitimate.'" The State need not show, as the Court implies, that the incremental cost of educating illegal aliens will send it into bankruptcy, or have a "'grave impact on the quality of education;'" that is not dispositive under a "rational basis" scrutiny. In the absence of a constitutional imperative to provide for the education of illegal aliens, the State may "rationally" choose to take advantage of whatever savings will accrue from limiting access to the tuition-free public schools to its own lawful residents, excluding even citizens of neighboring States.

Denying a free education to illegal alien children is not a choice I would make were I a legislator. Apart from compassionate considerations, the long-range costs of excluding any children from the public schools may well outweigh the costs of educating them. But that is not the issue; the fact that there are sound policy arguments against the Texas Legislature's choice does not render that choice an unconstitutional one.

II

The Constitution does not provide a cure for every social ill, nor does it vest judges with a mandate to try to remedy every social problem. Moreover, when this Court rushes in to remedy what it perceives to be the failings of the political processes, it deprives those processes of an opportunity to function. When the political institutions are not forced to exercise constitutionally allocated powers and responsibilities, those powers, like muscles not used, tend to atrophy. Today's cases, I regret to say, present yet another example of unwarranted judicial action which, in the long run, tends to contribute to the weakening of our political processes.

Congress, "vested by the Constitution with the responsibility of protecting our borders and legislating with respect to aliens" bears primary responsibility for addressing the problems occasioned by the millions of illegal aliens flooding across our southern border. Similarly, it is for Congress, and not this Court, to assess the "social costs borne by our Nation when select groups are denied the means to absorb the values and skills upon which our social order rests." While the "specter of a permanent caste" of illegal Mexican residents of the United States is indeed a disturbing one, it is but one segment of a larger problem, which is for the political branches to solve. I find it difficult to believe that Congress would long tolerate such a self-destructive result—that it would fail to deport these illegal alien families or to provide for the education of their children. Yet instead of allowing the political processes to run their course—albeit with some delay—the Court seeks to do Congress' job for it, compensating for congressional inaction. It is not unreasonable to think that this encourages the political branches to pass their problems to the Judiciary.

The solution to this seemingly intractable problem is to defer to the political processes, unpalatable as that may be to some.

1. It does not follow, however, that a state should bear the costs of educating children whose illegal presence in this country results from the default of the political branches of the Federal Government. A state has no power to prevent unlawful

immigration, and no power to deport illegal aliens; those powers are reserved exclusively to Congress and the Executive. If the Federal Government, properly chargeable with deporting illegal aliens, fails to do so, it should bear the burdens of their presence here. Surely if illegal alien children can be identified for purposes of this litigation, their parents can be identified for purposes of prompt deportation.

2. The Department of Justice recently estimated the number of illegal aliens within the United States at between 3 and 6 million.

3. The Court implies, for example, that the Fourteenth Amendment would not require a state to provide welfare benefits to illegal aliens.

4. Both the opinion of the Court and JUSTICE POWELL's concurrence imply that appellees are being "penalized" because their parents are illegal entrants. However, Texas has classified appellees on the basis of their own illegal status, not that of their parents. Children born in this country to illegal alien parents, including some of appellees' siblings, are not excluded from the Texas schools. Nor does Texas discriminate against appellees because of their Mexican origin or citizenship. Texas provides a free public education to countless thousands of Mexican immigrants who are lawfully in this country.

5. Appellees "lack control" over their illegal residence in this country in the same sense as lawfully resident children lack control over the school district in which their parents reside. Yet in *San Antonio Independent School Dist. v. Rodriguez* we declined to review under "heightened scrutiny" a claim that a State discriminated against residents of less wealthy school districts in its provision of educational benefits. There was no suggestion in that case that a child's "lack of responsibility" for his residence in a particular school district had any relevance to the proper standard of review of his claims. The result was that children lawfully here but residing in different counties received different treatment.

6. Indeed, even children of illegal alien parents born in the United States can be said to be "penalized" when their parents are deported.

7. It is true that the Constitution imposes lesser constraints on the Federal Government than on the states with regard to discrimination against lawfully admitted aliens. This is because "Congress and the President have broad power over immigration and naturalization which the States do not possess," Hampton, supra, at 95, and because state discrimination against legally resident aliens conflicts with and alters the conditions lawfully imposed by Congress upon admission, naturalization, and residence of aliens in the United States or the several states. However, the same cannot be said when Congress has decreed that certain aliens should not be admitted to the United States at all.

8. In support of this conclusion, the Court's opinion strings together quotations drawn from cases addressing such diverse matters as the right of individuals under the Due Process Clause to learn a foreign language; the First Amendment prohibition against state-mandated religious exercises in the public schools; the First Amendment prohibition against state-mandated religious exercises in the public schools; and state impingements upon the free exercise of religion; and state impingements upon the free exercise of religion. However, not every isolated utterance of this Court retains force when wrested from the context in which it was made. . . .

10. The Texas law might also be justified as a means of deterring unlawful immigration. While regulation of immigration is an exclusively federal function, a state may take steps, consistent with federal immigration policy, to protect its economy and ability to provide governmental services from the "deleterious effects" of a massive influx of illegal immigrants. The Court maintains that denying illegal aliens a free public education is an "ineffectual" means of deterring unlawful immigration, at least when compared to a prohibition against the employment of illegal aliens. Perhaps that is correct, but it is not dispositive; the Equal Protection Clause does not mandate that a state choose either the most effective and all-encompassing means of addressing a problem or none at all. Texas might rationally conclude that more significant "demographic or economic problem[s]" are engendered by the illegal entry into the State of entire families of aliens for indefinite periods than by the periodic sojourns of single adults who intend to leave the State after short-term or seasonal employment. It blinks reality to maintain that the availability of governmental services such as education plays no role in an alien family's decision to enter, or remain in, this country; certainly, the availability of a free bilingual public education might well influence an alien to bring his children, rather than travel alone for better job opportunities.

11. The Court suggests that the State's classification is improper because "[a]n illegal entrant might be granted federal permission to continue to reside in this country, or even to become a citizen." However, once an illegal alien is given federal permission to remain, he is no longer subject to exclusion from the tuition-free public schools under [the Texas law]. The Court acknowledges that the Tyler Independent School District provides a free public education to any alien who has obtained, or is in the process of obtaining, documentation from the United States Immigration and Naturalization Service. Thus, Texas has not taken it upon itself to determine which aliens are or are not entitled to United States residence. JUSTICE BLACKMUN's assertion that the Texas [law] will be applied to aliens "who

may well be entitled to . . . remain in the United States," is wholly without foundation.

12. The Court's opinion is disingenuous when it suggests that the State has merely picked a "disfavored group" and arbitrarily defined its members as nonresidents. Appellees' "disfavored status" stems from the very fact that federal law explicitly prohibits them from being in this country. Moreover, the analogies to Virginians or legally admitted Mexican citizens entering Texas are spurious. A Virginian's right to migrate to Texas, without penalty, is protected by the Constitution; and a lawfully admitted alien's right to enter the State is likewise protected by federal law.

13. The District Court so concluded primarily because the State would decrease its funding to local school districts in proportion to the exclusion of illegal alien children. 458 F.Supp. at 577.

14. I assume no Member of the Court would challenge Texas' right to charge tuition to students residing across the border in Louisiana who seek to attend the nearest school in Texas.

15. Professor Bickel noted that judicial review can have a "tendency over time seriously to weaken the democratic process." He reiterated James Bradley Thayer's observation that

"the exercise of [the power of judicial review], even when unavoidable, is always attended with a serious evil, namely, that the correction of legislative mistakes comes from the outside, and the people thus lose the political experience, and the moral education and stimulus that comes from fighting the question out in the ordinary way, and correcting their own errors. The tendency of a common and easy resort to this great function, now lamentably too common, is to dwarf the political capacity of the people, and to deaden its sense of moral responsibility."

WARREN BURGER was the Chief Justice of the Supreme Court during a time in which it was slowly moving into a more conservative direction. He was an instrumental voice in many cases before the Supreme Court that had a more conservative outcome. Burger believes that undocumented immigrant children have no constitutional right to education.

EXPLORING THE ISSUE

Should Illegal Immigrant Families Be Able to Send Their Children to Public Schools?

Critical Thinking and Reflection

1. What are some arguments made by each side with which you agree or disagree?
2. What are the strengths and weaknesses of the two positions made in this chapter?
3. This issue focuses on what is constitutional. In some cases, a person's morals may be in contradiction to the law. How do constitutional rights in this case relate to what you feel is morally right or morally wrong?
4. Think more broadly about the role of immigration, both documented and undocumented, in the United States today. Considering the ruling in this case, what remedies would be best for the creation of an immigration system that is in the best interest of the United States?

Is There Common Ground?

There are clear and distinct differences in this case regarding what should occur related to undocumented immigrant rights and public schooling. However, there is little disagreement that there are a substantial number of undocumented immigrants in the United States today. Some estimates say that the number of undocumented immigrants meets or exceeds 11 million. Many of these undocumented immigrants are children in public schools. The result is that some children are not U.S. citizens but will spend their entire childhood in this country, therefore feeling little different about their place in the United States than that of those who are citizens. Most would agree that immigration has historically had a positive impact on American society. Whether one agrees with the current system that is in place, everyone has a vested interest in fostering a system of immigration that is in the best interest of America's future. How should this affect acceptance, financial aid, and state tuition rates for colleges and universities? What are the implications on this ruling for future citizenship of undocumented immigrants?

Additional Resources

The American Civil Liberties Union on immigrant rights:

www.aclu.org/immigrants-rights

Taking action on immigration reform through Change.org:

http://immigration.change.org/

The National Network for Immigration and Refugee Rights:

www.nnirr.org/

End Illegal Immigration works to stop undocumented immigration:

www.endillegalimmigration.com/

Conservative USA calls to stop illegal immigration immediately:

www.conservativeusa.org/immigration.htm

Create Central

www.mhhe.com/createcentral

Internet References . . .

Immigrant Solidarity Network

www.immigrantsolidarity.org/

National Council of La Raza

www.nclr.org/

US Immigration Support

www.usimmigrationsupport.org/

Selected, Edited, and with Issue Framing Material by:
David M. Hall, Ph.D., *Delaware Valley College*

ISSUE

Should Parents Be Able to Choose Their Baby's Sex?

YES: Ellen Painter Dollar, from "Why Allowing Parents to Choose Their Baby's Gender Is Wrong," Patheos (& Other) Peeps, *Patheos.com* (September 24, 2012)

NO: Angela M. Long, from "Why Criminalizing Sex Selection Techniques Is Unjust: An Argument Challenging Conventional Wisdom," *Health Law Journal* (Annual 2006)

Learning Outcomes
After reading this issue, you will be able to:
• Summarize competing arguments related to choosing a baby's sex.
• Evaluate the ethical implications of where this can lead not just for gender discrimination but also beyond.
• Evaluate the rights of parents to identify the reasons for which sex selection should be permissible.

ISSUE SUMMARY

YES: Ellen Dollar argues that it is morally wrong to choose a baby's sex. She argues that this invites sexism and creates a slippery slope.

NO: Angela Long argues that denying sex selection can be overly restrictive as well as too punitive. Furthermore, some laws fail to stop all methods of sex selection.

Some parents care little about the sex of their child. When asked if they are hoping for a boy or a girl, they might say, "As long as it's healthy." Others care deeply. Some have always seen themselves raising a boy or a girl. Others are trying to keep a family name. Others have a number of male or female children and are hoping to have one child who is the opposite sex.

How much can we permit parents to choose the sex of their baby? Could institutional sexism result in a gender imbalance? After all, nature knows that more males die (both as fetuses and as humans) than girls, so nature creates more male pregnancies to create balance. Should humans be able to interfere with nature's selection?

This was always an issue in society—but only through issues of infanticide. Today, science has given us the power to make this decision *in utero* and *in vitro* (in a petri dish). In fact, society today can already go beyond mere sex selection—which is what opponents of sex selection have most feared: the slippery slope.

This conversation held a different level of controversy when sex selection had to be done *in utero* (in the uterus) versus *in vitro* (in a petri dish). A larger number of people object to sex selection of a fetus than of an embryo. There was a time when this was of little concern. In earlier parts of history, gender could not be determined until birth. Then scientific advances allowed us to determine sex *in utero*. What if we can determine sex even earlier?

A reproductive fertility doctor was recently giving a speech about a couple. They could both hear, and they had a deaf child. They loved their child, but when the mother became pregnant again, the amniocentesis revealed that their next child would also be deaf. They chose to get an abortion. They then sought out this fertility doctor. They decided to have a child with the plan that this doctor would figure out which embryos carried the deaf genes and which didn't. This doctor was able to do that, and today this family has a hearing child.

This previous paragraph can be chilling for many to read. If that technology existed when we were born, then perhaps some of us wouldn't be here today. How far are we willing to go in having designer babies?

There are other medical interventions *in utero* that are less controversial. What if they removed the gene that can lead to a type of cancer or another life threatening disease? Few people have a problem with this. Many would consider it a great disadvantage in life to have a disease that is life threatening.

What other advantages exist? Research shows that height can influence how much a man earns. Should parents be able to choose the tall gene when having a child? His or her hair color?

Sex selection *in utero* leads us down this path, a path that generations before us have not had to travel (at least not exactly, but there are some compelling parallels with the eugenics movement and other moments in history). We need to create criteria for what we will allow and what we will not.

Beyond that, right now you can only get the "tall gene" if you already have it. It cannot be injected into an embryo. But that's only right now. Researchers have tried to do this, but their results have been controversial and highly problematic. Many can imagine, however, that it is only a matter of time before this changes.

Where does this conversation begin? It begins with whether we will allow sex selection. Allowing sex selection also creates an important discussion about sexism. How many parents prefer they have boys? A recent Gallup poll showed that parents prefer sons over daughters by a rate of 40 percent to 28 percent. This preference isn't impacting birth rates because (a) perhaps many feel differently when a pregnancy has begun or a daughter is born and (b) most parents don't go through *in vitro* fertilization.

What if more parents go through *in vitro* fertilization. Parents have already told the doctor what life threatening illnesses they want to avoid. They have asked the doctor to locate the deaf gene. At that point, is there anything wrong with choosing the male or female gene?

We live in a time of great scientific advancement. How do we strike the right balance between what we are able to do and what we morally should do?

Ellen Painter Dollar

Why Allowing Parents to Choose Their Baby's Gender Is Wrong

When I write and speak about the ethical questions raised by reproductive technologies, I do not argue that reproductive technologies are all good or all bad, or that using these technologies is clearly right or clearly wrong. **My agenda, rather, is to encourage more robust and informed conversations around these technologies,** because the science has developed faster than our cultural conversations around their promise and pitfalls.

But as I've researched and discussed the fraught questions around reproductive technologies, I have, of course, developed opinions, one of which is that **it is unethical for fertility clinics to offer gender-selection services for nonmedical purposes.**

In the U.S., unregulated fertility clinics are largely allowed to do whatever technology allows them to do, so long as clients are willing and able to pay for it. **Anecdotal evidence and clinical data indicate that a growing number of prospective parents are willing to pay to have a baby of their desired gender.**

There are two different techniques whereby couples can attempt gender selection: Microsort, a sperm-sorting technique, allows clinicians to sort X-bearing and Y-bearing sperm, and then use the sperm with the desired chromosome to inseminate the mother-to-be. A more accurate, but also more invasive and expensive technique for gender selection is preimplantation genetic diagnosis (PGD). PGD was developed as a way to screen for fatal or debilitating genetic disorders at the embryonic stage; my own experience with reproductive technology involved using PGD to try to avoid passing my genetic bone disorder on to my children. **Many American clinics, however, now offer PGD as a way for couples to choose their baby's gender by choosing only fertilized eggs of the desired gender for implantation in the mother's uterus.**

The United Kingdom, Canada, and Australia all ban the use of PGD for gender selection for nonmedical purposes. PGD for gender selection is only justified if a couple's family history includes a particular sex-linked genetic disorder; that is, a disorder that predominantly or exclusively affects babies of one gender.

In the U.S., the growing use of technology to bear a child of a particular gender is driven by two different populations. **Immigrant families from countries such as India and China use the technology to ensure the birth of the much-wanted boy child.** Some U.S. fertility clinics have a history of advertising gender-selection services in foreign language newspapers targeting patriarchal cultures. There is also anecdotal evidence that couples of Indian, Chinese, and African background come to the U.S. from other countries to access gender-selection services.

The other population utilizing gender-selection technology are couples with one or more sons, in which the wife has an intense longing for a daughter. Jasmeet Sidhu, in her *Slate* article "How to Buy a Daughter," profiled Megan Simpson, who used PGD to have a girl after having three boys: "[Simpson] had grown up in a family of four sisters. She liked sewing, baking, and doing hair and makeup. She hoped one day to share these interests with a little girl whom she could dress in pink." Simpson uses highly emotional language in telling her story. After initially using sperm-sorting to become pregnant with her third baby, she "lay in bed and cried for weeks" upon discovering that she was pregnant with another boy. She ultimately decided not to abort her son and turned to PGD to ensure that her fourth child would be a girl.

I have no doubt that Simpson's anguish was real. But that anguish does not justify use of PGD for gender selection.

Gender Selection Is Bad for Women

Cultural preferences for male children stem from ancient, deep-seated ideals of what makes for stable families and communities. In cultures in which boys are more likely to be educated and employed in stable jobs that earn enough to support a family, families hope for boy children who will eventually contribute to the family's well-being and care for aging parents. Girls, on the other hand, are perceived as liabilities rather than assets, as they will not have the same possibilities for education and lucrative employment, and might even cost their family money in the form of marriage dowries.

The assumptions behind these ideals no longer hold water in our 21st century global culture. We know, of course, that girls and women are just as capable of succeeding in education and the workplace if given opportunities. Furthermore, a body of research indicates that empowering women in poor communities, such as with microloans for starting small businesses, doesn't just help individual women, but helps to raise entire families and communities out of poverty. **Recognizing that girls and women have the same educational, economic, and cultural potential as boys and men, we cannot justify providing gender-selection services that support false and outdated patriarchal ideals.**

Furthermore, a woman who comes to a clinic for help conceiving a boy is likely under pressure from her own and/or her husband's families, and possibly her husband himself, to do her duty by providing a male heir. In the name of "reproductive choice," we have allowed unregulated fertility clinics to provide gender-selection services that may, in very concrete ways, undermine individual women's ability to make childbearing decisions free of coercion.

Gender Selection Reinforces Constricting and False Gender Roles

Simpson (the woman profiled in Sidhu's *Slate* article) dreams of baking and sharing make-up secrets with her daughter. Liza Mundy, in researching her book on reproductive technology titled *Everything Conceivable*, noted that, "in the sex-selection chat rooms I looked at, there were lots of women looking forward to dressing little girls in pink outfits and putting pretty bows in their hair." And as Sidhu noted in researching her article:

> Interviews with several women from the forums at in-gender.com and genderdreaming.com yielded the same stories: a yearning for female bonding. Relationships with their own mothers that defined what kind of mother they wanted to be to a daughter. A desire to engage in stereotypical female activities that they thought would be impossible with a baby boy.

The problem, of course, is that little girls don't always love pink and baking and girl talk and make-up, just as little boys don't always love dirt and trucks and dinosaurs and football. The relationship between children's gender and their preferences is not exact, unchanging, or predictable. Why is pink a feminine color and blue a masculine color? Because we say so (at least for today). **Do we really want to allow parents in thrall to gender stereotypes to engineer their children for the sole purpose of meeting ephemeral and superficial cultural norms?**

I have a daughter who prefers "boyish" colors and toys and clothes, and a boy who prefers "girlish" colors and toys and clothes. I have seen firsthand that non-gender-conforming children's journeys through the judgment-laden landscape of childhood and adolescence is hard enough even if they have parents who don't give a hoot whether or not they are interested in mother/daughter manicure sessions. How much harder will this journey be for a little girl who hates baking and make-up and the color pink, but who was conceived for the stated reason of giving her mother a companion in these pursuits?

From my experience with two non-gender-conforming kids, I also know that girls who veer toward boyish things have an easier time than boys who veer toward girlish things. So I'd like to think that all those moms who equate their longed-for daughters with bows and sparkles would rise to the occasion if they ended up with a scabby-kneed, jeans-wearing, Star Wars-loving girl instead. **But I'd rather we encourage parents to prepare to embrace whatever child they receive *before* that child is conceived, rather than down the road when that child becomes capable of expressing her preferences.**

The Justifications for Gender Selection Are Almost Purely Parent-Focused

Why do I accept the use of PGD to screen for genetic disorders, under some circumstances, but not for gender?

Most of the time, when parents consider using PGD because of a genetic disorder in their family, **they consider the needs of *everyone* who will be affected by that decision, including themselves, their other children, and the child-to-be.** In contrast, when parents consider PGD to have a baby boy or girl for nonmedical reasons, **they primarily consider their own desires.**

For example, when my husband and I contemplated using PGD to have a baby free of my genetic bone disorder, we thought about how having a second child with this disorder (our first child, conceived naturally, had already inherited it) would affect us, our daughter, and our as-yet-unconceived second child. All-too-aware of the particular types of suffering that our bone disorder leads to, we considered whether we had an obligation to protect future children from that suffering. We thought about dozens of other factors, some of which were focused primarily on our needs and desires as parents, and many of which were focused on the needs and desires of our children.

When PGD is used for gender selection, in contrast, the primary needs and desires considered are those of the parents, and perhaps other family members. The essential questions are things like, "What gender child will make our family more secure?" "What gender child will I relate to better?" "What gender child will make me feel that I've fulfilled my destiny as a parent?" "What gender child will make my in-laws happiest?" The child's needs and desires, as an autonomous being who will one day make his or her way in the world outside the nuclear family, are nowhere to be seen.

No one approaches childbearing from a purely selfless standpoint. We all bring our own needs, desires, and hopes to our childbearing, some of which are noble and uplifting, and some of which are self-serving and petty. This is human nature. And, as Huffington Post columnist Lisa Belkin pointed out in a column on gender selection last week, we must be careful not to cut off fruitful conversation by dismissing anyone who considers using reproductive technology as a selfish monsters. The availability of so many reproductive choices can have the beneficial effect of helping us, as individuals and as a culture, to be more thoughtful about the choices we end up making.

As I said in the opening to this post, I have no doubt that Megan Simpson's tears and anguish over having only boys when she longed for a girl were genuine and heartfelt. This is part of what makes adulthood so painful—we must repeatedly learn to accept that our younger selves' vision for what our life would be like, and our actual life, often differ in profound, sometimes profoundly difficult, ways.

There is nothing wrong or monstrously selfish about grieving the lack of a longed-for daughter or son. **There is much that's wrong, however, with using ethically, emotionally, medically, and financially fraught technologies in an attempt to fill the hole that such grief leaves behind.**

Ellen Painter Dollar focuses her writing on faith, family, disability, and ethics. She identifies as a Christian theological conservative and also socially liberal.

Angela M. Long

Why Criminalizing Sex Selection Techniques Is Unjust: An Argument Challenging Conventional Wisdom

Introduction

The issue of sex selection is one that often invokes a great deal of controversy. In a society where we value equality between men and women should one be able to choose the sex of one's offspring? Would males be chosen over females, thus promoting continued inequality between the sexes? What about those whose culture and/or religion prefers that women bear a child of one sex over the other? What about those who just want an evenly balanced complement of children? . . .

Ethical Considerations

The use of sex selection techniques raises a host of ethical concerns. As noted there are concerns about whether the use of sex selection promotes inequality. In addition, there are concerns that continued use of the practice will negatively impact the population, in that the sex ratio will be skewed in favour of males. However, it is now generally acknowledged, at least in the context of Western society, that such a concern is overstated, as most people in Western countries would use sex selection mainly as a method of achieving a balanced family. There are also concerns about the use of sex selection techniques being a gateway for more problematic types of genetic selection, such as selection for certain physical criteria, such as height, eye/hair colour or physical prowess, or other desirable traits, such as intelligence. Many authors have noted that this is a "slippery slope" argument, and that eugenic fears about the use of sex selection techniques are vastly overstated. David McCarthy states:

> (a') selecting sex is not enhancing ability; (b') the child won't be able to complain that it wasn't made the opposite sex because had its parents selected the opposite sex it would not exist; (c') boys and girls are approximately equally valued, and the evidence is that most sex selection would be to achieve a balanced family.

While all of the medical techniques for selecting a child based on sex have the same goal, to have a child of one sex as opposed to the other, some of the techniques used are more ethically problematic than others, as was noted by the RCNRT in its Final Report. The use of PND and abortion for reasons of sex selection was found to be unethical, as it offends the principle of respect for human life and dignity by deliberately terminating a pregnancy already in progress that, except for reasons of sex, likely would have resulted in the birth of a child. At the time of the Commission's report, the practice amongst geneticists and obstetrician/gynaecologists in Canada was to not perform PND for the sole purposes of determining the sex of the fetus and this practice remains in place today. Such a stance is justified by the RCNRT as sex is not a disease.

> . . . the use of PND to determine fetal sex contradicts the very purpose and role of these procedures within the health care system—namely, to determine whether serious genetic diseases or congenital anomalies are present. Sex is not a disease, so the sex of the fetus is not medically relevant except in cases where a disease or anomaly is sex-linked.

Further, the RCNRT was against the provision of PND to women from cultures where sons are valued over daughters, as respect for human life and dignity, protection of the vulnerable and sexual equality were found to be more pressing issues. As a result, the RCNRT affirmed the Society of Obstetricians and Gynaecologists of Canada's [SOGC] practice guideline against PND for determination of sex. It further recommended that all practitioners who subsequently provide any sort of PND be licensed by the (yet to be formed) National Reproductive Technologies Commission, that adherence to the SOGC guideline against PND be adhered to as part of such a license and that information about fetal sex not be made available to patients prior to the third trimester. This step was taken as it was seen as inevitable that PND would soon be available in other forms and the Commission wanted to ensure that such practices would be monitored so that their use would not proliferate outside of the medical profession proper. It is interesting to note that the RCNRT here focused solely on the PND aspect of this sex selection

Long, Angela M. From *Health Law Journal*, vol. 14, 2006, pp. 69, 78–84, 85–89, 92–94, 103–104. Copyright © 2006 by Health Law Institute/University of Alberta. Used with permission.

technique and not on the abortion part of the technique, even though it found that abortion of a fetus solely on the basis of its sex is an unethical practice. This is likely due to the strong abortion rights that women possess in Canada since the decision of R. v. Morgentaler in 1988. A woman's right to obtain an abortion is constitutionally protected, therefore forcing the RCNRT and legislators to focus on regulating the PND of the fetus rather than on the abortion procedure itself.

The Commission also noted ethical difficulties with the second medical sex selection technique, PGD and IVF, as it is both an expensive and a very invasive process when used for the sole purpose of selecting a child for reasons of sex. First, it noted that using PGD and IVF for sex selection purposes is a misuse of resources. As noted above, IVF is a very expensive treatment. Second, the RCNRT noted that the procedure is risky for the women who undergo it. Women must be treated with potent fertility drugs and undergo the invasive egg retrieval process. In the case of using PGD and IVF for the sole purpose of sex selection, the risks to the woman were seen to outweigh the potential benefits. Third, PGD and IVF was seen to be disrespectful of the zygotes involved in the process.

> As we discuss in Chapter 22, zygotes do not have the same moral status as embryos or fetuses; they do not have a fixed and individual identity or a central nervous system, and the probability that they will result in a live born individual is low—perhaps one in five in those situations where both partners are likely to be fertile. Nonetheless, zygotes are not just human tissue; the potential they embody means that refusing to transfer a zygote solely on the basis of its sex is inconsistent with the respect owed to it.

As a result, the RCNRT recommended that the use of PGD and IVF be prohibited for sex selection purposes.

The last medical technique, sex selective insemination or sperm sorting, was found to be different, ethically speaking. As the technique is used prior to fertilization, the RCNRT notes that it does not raise issues about respect for human life, as there is no abortion of a fetus or discarding of a zygote that is already in existence. However, the RCNRT found that sex selective insemination raises the larger issue of sexual equality in some cases.

> For reasons discussed earlier, [the] Commissioners find it unacceptable for sex-selective insemination to be used in a way that undermines or jeopardizes equality—that is, to select first born sons, to select families with more sons than daughters, or to perpetuate the cultural devaluation of women.

However, as discussed below, in the Canadian context, sex selection insemination is unlikely to be used in such a manner, but rather as a mechanism to achieve family balancing, meaning having at least one child of each sex, with no general preference for boys or girls. In fact, the RCNRT found that when used in this manner, that sex selective insemination does not impede sexual equality. Despite this evidence, the RCNRT found that it could not endorse the use of sex selective insemination, even in cases of family balancing, as it would promote the idea that there is an "ideal" family prototype, in which there are children of both sexes, which would have the effect of diminishing the value of those families in which there were children of only one sex. As a result, the Commission recommended that sex selective insemination be used only in cases where there is a clear sex linked medical disorder underlying the request, but did not recommend that the its use be criminalized outright, as it has been in the AHRA.

Why People Want to Select for Sex in Canada

As discussed above, in Canada, the use of sex selection technologies to ensure the birth of one sex (male) over the other (female) is unlikely. If the technologies were to be used, they would be used overwhelmingly by those who want to balance their families by having at least one child of each sex. In addition, the studies have shown that most people would only use sex selection technologies where they already had at least one child of the opposite sex that they were seeking. This is not to say, however, that sex selection technologies could not be used in Canada in cases where prospective parents desire a son and do not want a daughter for either religious and/or cultural reasons, as we live in a multicultural society. In fact, one of the concerns to be addressed in this paper is the situation of those women who may wish to utilize sex selection techniques for religious and/or cultural purposes, as the current state of the law burdens these women more than women who may not feel the same pressure to employ sex selection techniques. As will be shown below, the current state of the law makes sex selection more dangerous for women than ever before.

Analysis

The Prohibition of Sex Selection Fails to Prohibit All Sex Selection Methods

The AHRA provision prohibiting sex selection does not explicitly define which procedures it attempts to limit. It states:

> 5. (1) No person shall knowingly
>
> (e) for the purpose of creating a human being, perform any procedure or provide, prescribe or administer any thing that would ensure or increase the probability that an embryo will be of a particular sex, or that would identify the sex of an in vitro embryo, except to prevent, diagnose or treat a sex-linked disorder or disease;

Upon reading this section it is clear that any kind of in vitro sex determination and subsequent implantation would be prohibited. In addition, techniques that involve the sorting of sperm to determine which were carriers of the X chromosome (for a female) and which were carriers of the Y chromosome (for a male) and then artificially inseminating only those sperm that were carriers of the desired chromosome would be caught by the provision. Both of these techniques would be procedures that would ensure or at least increase the chances that an embryo would be of a certain sex as mandated by the provision.

What is clearly not prohibited by this provision, however, is the most common form of sex selection technique, PND of the sex of the fetus and abortion of a fetus of the undesired sex. Looking closely at the prohibition, it is clear that only those techniques that would ensure or increase the chances that an embryo was of a certain sex, or that would identify the sex of an embryo in vitro are prohibited. Embryo is defined by the AHRA as:

> . . . a human organism during the first 56 days of its development following fertilization or creation, excluding any time during which its development has been suspended, and includes any cell derived from such an organism that is used for the purpose of creating a human being.

This means that identifying the sex of a human organism that is past the embryonic stage (into the fetal stage, past the 56th day) or an embryo that is not in vitro is permitted. In other words, the "traditional" sex selection technique (i.e. used before IVF and/or sperm sorting techniques came into existence), PND and abortion has been left out and can, thus, be considered legal. This lack of regulation is perhaps not too surprising, given the fact that the government could not legally deny a woman's right to abortion in Canada. It is surprising, though, that they failed to consider, or perhaps even ignored, the negative effect that banning pre-implantation sex selection techniques could have on the number of abortions being performed in Canada and that, conversely, other regulations may make it very difficult to actually utilize this so-called "legal" procedure. At the very least, as Julian Savulescu notes, the legislation creates an inconsistency that ". . . provide[s] couples with information from prenatal testing which allows them to select sex and not allow them to select sex by means which are more acceptable to them."

Leaving PND and abortion as the sole way to legally select a child on the basis of sex could result in many negative effects, arguably more than if there was no restriction at all. First, it could have the effect of increasing or at least stagnating the number of abortions for reasons of sex selection, when there are much less invasive means, both physically, mentally and ethically, that could be used to produce the same result; namely sperm sorting. As discussed above, sperm sorting is less ethically problematic as it is a pre-conception technique, which does not engage the sanctity of life or human dignity concerns that PND and abortion do. There is also considerable physical risk for the woman if PND and abortion is used when a safer method, i.e. sperm sorting, is medically available. Abortion is a surgical procedure, and as with any surgical procedure, it has inherent risks. Although properly performed abortions are safe, complications can occur. Some of the complications associated with abortion are hemorrhage, perforation of the uterus and infection.

If a woman will not consider an abortion and still wishes to have a child of a particular sex or to have a balanced family, she must endure multiple pregnancies and the inherent risks that go along with them. Even though Canada has an excellent obstetrical care system, complications in pregnancy are still common. Cook, Dickens and Fathalla note that approximately 15% of women worldwide will need some kind of medical care in order to avoid death or disability during their pregnancy. In addition, if women endure pregnancy and childbirth until a child of the desired sex is born, this will create an additional financial burden upon the family, as there could be more children to care for. When the technology exists to help women in their quest to have a child of one sex over the other in a relatively risk free manner, it does not make sense to prohibit its use, especially when the only legal alternatives could potentially be more harmful to the health and well-being of the mother and her family.

Despite the purported legality of PND and abortion, many women who wish to use this avenue may find it very difficult to do so. While women, by law, may obtain abortions freely in Canada, there are a host of policies and guidelines that can affect how free such access is in actuality. There is no clear policy across Canada on the time limit with respect to obtaining an abortion, meaning that time limits will vary from clinic to clinic and from place to place. For example, in Alberta, the time limit varies from up to 12 weeks to up to 20 weeks. In Saskatchewan, it varies from up to 12 weeks to up to 14 weeks. In Ontario, five clinics will perform abortions over 20 weeks, but only in cases of severe fetal abnormality. New Brunswick will provide only first trimester abortions, while Nova Scotia will provide them up to 16 weeks. In the Northwest Territories, abortions will only be performed up to 13 weeks and in the Yukon, they will only be performed up to 12 weeks. In addition to these limits on the gestational age of the fetus, there are also often long waiting periods, which can complicate matters, for example, in Manitoba there is often a six week waiting list to obtain an abortion. . . .

Prohibiting Sex Selection Through Criminal Sanction Is Regressive Policy

Rebecca Cook, Bernard Dickens and Mahmoud Fathalla in their book *Reproductive Health and Human Rights* have noted a general evolutionary trend in reproductive and sexual health law. They state that there are three stages: first, a state of morality, where criminal law governs areas of reproductive health and sexuality; second, a shift to health and welfare; and third, a shift from health and welfare to human rights. In speaking of the shift between these three stages they state: "[m]ovements in legal systems in this direction occur at different paces, but movement in the reverse direction is an international anomaly." In this case, Canada is certainly in the international minority and can be said to fit within this definition of 'anomaly' in its reversion to a stance of morality-based regulation rooted within the criminal law in the case of sex selection. While Cook, Dickens and Fathalla note a trend of increasing recognition for human rights in laws surrounding reproductive and sexual health law, that includes increased protection for principles of privacy and freedom of choice of whether to employ reproductive technologies or not, with the severe criminal limits on the use of sex selection techniques, Canada has indeed reversed directions.

It should be noted generally that not all movements towards the criminal law will negatively impact upon the reproductive and sexual health rights of individuals. Indeed, the use of criminal law may sometimes be required in order to protect reproductive and sexual health rights that would otherwise be harmed by the status quo. For example, it is arguable from a feminist perspective (although not necessarily agreed with) that the provision of the AHRA that criminalizes payment for surrogacy is one that protects the reproductive rights of women against commodification. If commercial surrogacy agreements were legal, there would be potential for women to sell their reproductive capacity for profit. Usually, so the theory goes, marginalized women would be most affected by such commodification, as they would have a higher economic need than those who are economically better off. In addition, from an equality perspective, the law criminalizing commercial surrogacy agreements promotes the general equal position of women in society, in that they are people and not merely wombs for hire. However, this is not the case with the prohibition on the use of sex selection techniques.

In legislating criminal prohibitions in the area of reproductive technologies, Parliament has included a wide gamut of activities, from sex selection, to cloning (both reproductive and therapeutic), to the creation of chimeras and the creation of human-animal hybrids. It is arguable, from various different perspectives, that a number of the prohibitions in the AHRA should in fact be regulated through criminal sanctions, such as commercial surrogacy and the creation of chimeras and human-animal hybrids. Certainly, the creation of such entities would have a negligible impact on the reproductive or sexual health of individuals, and as stated above, commercial surrogacy agreements could be viewed as hindering a human rights approach to reproductive and sexual health generally. But this cannot be said for all of the sections of the AHRA, most notably for the purposes of this paper, the provision prohibiting sex selection techniques under the threat of criminal sanction. Part of the problem may be that the

AHRA attempts to address too many different issues that affect different rights in just one piece of legislation. But this attempt to justify the criminal prohibition of all of these activities with one broad brush-stroke is erroneous and must be deconstructed to see if the justifications for the use of prohibitions and criminal sanctions as the preferred method of regulation in the Act as a whole can justify the prohibition and criminal sanction of sex selection techniques on its own.

The choice made by Parliament to prohibit sex selection and sanction a violation of such a prohibition through the criminal law, along with other reproductive technologies, as opposed to choosing a different kind of regulatory option, such as an effective ban through the licensing of clinics that offer sex selection services without the attendant criminal sanctions for violation, is significant. The predecessor to the Law Commission of Canada, the Law Reform Commission of Canada, in its seminal work entitled *Our Criminal Law* stated: "criminal law must be an instrument of last resort. It must be used as little as possible." As noted by Angela Campbell in the specific context of reproductive technologies, when enacting criminal legislation, Parliament must ensure that it has justified its use of criminal legislation as a last resort by ensuring that the targeted activity is both wrongful and causes harm to others. Specifically, she notes that the harm must be "serious in both nature and degree and if that harm is best dealt with through the mechanism of criminal law."

In the context of reproductive technologies generally, most would likely agree that there is much potential for harm to be had from the use of these technologies, including, perhaps, sex selection itself. What is at issue for many commentators, however, is whether the harm that could result through misuse of reproductive technologies is best dealt with through the use of the criminal law as opposed to other regulatory options and how Parliament ultimately justifies its use of the criminal law in regulating reproductive technologies. There are other regulatory options available, other than prohibition through criminalization, which could be equally effective in curbing the use of these technologies, including sex selection. Although there have been several incarnations of the AHRA, the justification that Parliament has provided for the need for such prohibitions and harsh criminal sanctions in the area of reproductive technologies has been that there is broad social consensus on the need for both. In fact, the government stated in its discussion paper on Bill C-47:

> . . . since there is widespread agreement among Canadians about prohibiting those aspects of NRGTs that are the most problematic, the government has moved quickly to legislate in this area.

However, as legal commentators were quick to point out, this social consensus did not in fact exist.

In several influential papers, Timothy Caulfield has criticized Parliament for employing criminal sanctions as the basis for its legislative scheme in all of its attempts to legislate in this area. One of the main justifications employed by Parliament in upholding the strong criminal sanctions with respect to reproductive technologies is that of a general social consensus against their use. Caulfield forcefully argues that such a social consensus does not exist, at least in some areas, such as against the use of embryonic stem cells and therapeutic cloning, and therefore, the criminal sanctions are not justified. He states:

> [d]espite evidence to the contrary, social consensus remains one of the primary justifications for the use of criminal bans . . . But is there evidence that therapeutic cloning is a grave concern to Canadians? On the contrary, available data suggests that the public supports the idea of therapeutic cloning.

Caulfield's criticism of the justification of the use of criminal sanctions in the AHRA applies with equal, if not more, force to the sex selection issue. In dealing with the issue of social consensus on the use of sex selection techniques, the RCNRT focused most of its energy on PND and abortion, citing that there is a broad social consensus that the practice is unacceptable to Canadians. The public was not even asked whether or not sperm sorting was acceptable or not. Under the heading "Views of Canadians" in the chapter on non-medical sex selection, on the topic of sperm sorting, all that the RCNRT stated was:

> There was less discussion of the other two methods of sex selection—sperm treatment methods and sex-selective zygote transfer—perhaps because there is much less public awareness of them.

If the views of the Canadian public were not even canvassed, there can hardly be said to be any social consensus on the issue of sperm sorting. In fact, the RCNRT did not even recommend prohibition of sex selection methods through the use of criminal sanctions, even after comprehensively studying the issue. This, along with the rate with which science progresses, re-ascertaining the views of Canadians would appear to be essential so that the criminal sanctions attached to sex selection techniques on the basis of social consensus could continue to be justified. Recall that the RCNRT's study began in 1989, more than fifteen years ago. For these reasons then, the government's justification for the prohibition of sex selection techniques through the use of criminal sanctions, which as noted in part one of this paper are only sperm sorting and PGD and implantation, falls flat.

Alison Harvison-Young and Angela Wasunna are equally critical of the existence of such a consensus in the area of reproductive technology. And while they contest whether the matters on which the government has stated that there is social consensus about actually exist, they also draw attention to two other issues regarding consensus. First, they argue that the areas in which there is consensus have been framed too broadly, allowing the government the ability to legislate too widely. They state:

> It is one thing to suggest that there is a broad social consensus opposing the commodification of reproduction. It is quite another to suggest, for example, that Canadians are generally opposed to the compensation of sperm donors, a practice that has been ongoing and uncontroversial in this country for many years. Yet that is one of the inferences that flows from the inclusion of the prohibition of such compensation in Bill C-47, and the reference to 'widespread agreement among Canadians' noted above.

In other words, is there actual consensus on each of the precise issues on which the government has legislated? Although there may be consensus that we should prohibit the commodification of life generally, as Harvison-Young and Wasunna point out, the same explanation can hardly be a justification for prohibiting the compensation of sperm donors through criminal sanction, as they involve substantially different things. . . .

In addition to requiting that activities that are the subject of criminal prohibitions be contrary to either social views or values and cause harm, Patrick Healy points out that there is another requirement that must be considered, whether criminal law is in fact the best method by which to regulate the activity:

> While these rationales might be sufficient for the enactment of criminal law in general terms, it does not necessarily follow that either is sufficient for the enactment of the specific offences proposed by the Commission. Of equal importance, moreover, given the crude bluntness of the criminal law as an instrument of social control, is the principle of restraint.

As the criminal law is a blunt instrument that engages the most basic liberty interests of those it governs, it must be considered to be necessary to deploy it in the circumstances of the situation. It must also be judged to be an effective tool by which to regulate the activity in question. In judging whether the use of the criminal law is the best regulatory avenue to follow, Healy notes that the magnitude of the harm must be taken into account:

> The criminal law should be used only when the magnitude of the threatened harm justifies firm repression and when no other, and lesser, form of legal control can adequately achieve the same result.

On the basis of the principle of restraint as outlined by Healy above, it is difficult to imagine that the criminal prohibition of sex selection techniques could he justified. The magnitude of harm is not substantial. As discussed above, the RCNRT recognized that the number of people who would use sex selection techniques in Canada would be small. This conclusion is further bolstered by the studies presented by Dahl in the first section of this paper. Clearly, then, the magnitude of harm, in terms of the number of people who are being deterred by the prohibition is not significant. In addition, it is not clear that other forms of regulation would not have been effective in attempting to curb the use of sex selection techniques. In fact, in the case of sex selection, it appears that Parliament did not even consider other forms of regulation.

Other systems of regulation, besides criminal prohibition, are in fact in place in other countries; systems of regulation that effectively prohibit sex selection techniques without making such activities subject to criminal sanctions. For example, in the United Kingdom, prohibition of the use of sex selection techniques has been achieved through the licensing of clinics that offer new reproductive technologies. The Human Fertilisation and Embryology Act 1990 [HFE Act] was enacted by the UK Parliament in 1990. The legislation set up a regulatory body, the Human Fertilisation and Embryology Authority to, among other things, license and monitor clinics that offer reproductive services such as IVF and PGD. Any clinics that wish to offer services covered by the legislation must be licensed by the HFEA. The HFEA is able to stipulate conditions in licensing, and in 1993, it stated that it would not grant licenses for the use of PGD or sex selection for non-medical purposes. This approach has the same effect of prohibiting certain kinds of sex selection techniques for non-medical purposes, but does so without the threat of criminal penalties. Clearly, this type of regulatory system, involving the licensing of clinics offering certain services could be as effective as a criminal prohibition in curbing sex selection from taking place. Indeed, Knoppers and Isasi, in the context of PGD, note that:

> . . . even more than civil status or mandatory counseling, the imposition of accreditation through licensing as a condition of operation is the one procedural mechanism with the greatest impact on reproductive genetic testing. Such an oversight mechanism with its traditional requirements of certification, quality assurance, standard operating procedures, reporting procedures and ethics approval of the introduction of technologies or for research can effectively curtail the availability of reproductive genetic testing.

Parliament should have considered such an option when deliberating on how to prohibit sex selection techniques before opting for a criminal prohibition.

Criminalization of activities may often be justified, however, Parliament must be careful not to be too quick to criminalize when the activity is not such that it conflicts with social views and/or values and other regulatory options that can have the same effect could be utilized. It is clear that in the case of sex selection that there is in fact no conflict with social views and/or values. It is even clearer that, even if sex selection did conflict with social views and/or values, that other, less punitive, regulatory options could have been used to achieve the same result. And by invoking a criminal prohibition on sex selection for non-medical purposes, then, Parliament is regressing with respect to its commitment to sexual and reproductive rights, as it focuses on the moral view of sex selection rather than on protecting the health and welfare of those who choose, for whatever reason, to use sex selection. The criminalization of sex selection forces women to subject themselves to more risk than necessary and it also imposes an ethnocentric morality upon those who choose to select for sex. . . .

Conclusion

While widespread use of sex selection techniques is most likely not something that we as Canadians would promote widely, at least to the extent that one sex would be consistently preferred over the other, it is a practice that does have validity in certain circumstances. In prohibiting certain methods of sex selection through the use of the criminal law, however, the Canadian Parliament has gone too far in their attempt to put an end to the practice in Canada. As has been demonstrated above, leaving the only legal method of sex selection as PND and abortion, which is the most ethically problematic, invasive and risky is a stark inconsistency that cannot be reconciled with the legislation. It is also questionable as to whether a criminal prohibition under these circumstances is warranted, as there is no consensus on either social views or values and it is clear that less insidious methods of regulation, such as the system currently employed by the U.K., could have been employed to achieve the same result. What is more is that given that it has been clearly demonstrated that there is not an equality problem in Canada with respect to sex preference, it is doubtful that any form of regulation of sex selection practices would ever stand in light of the Charter, especially if the Supreme Court makes clear that there is a right to reproductive autonomy under s. 7. Instead, Parliament should rethink the criminal prohibition, as well as any general prohibition of sex selection methods altogether.

ANGELA M. LONG wrote this as a doctor of law candidate at the University of Ottawa.

EXPLORING THE ISSUE

Should Parents Be Able to Choose Their Baby's Sex?

Critical Thinking and Reflection

1. What are some arguments made in each side with which you agree or disagree?
2. What are the strengths and weaknesses of the two positions made in this chapter?
3. Pick the side with which you most agree. What are some additional arguments you would make to strengthen the case for or against sex selection?
4. Think more broadly about sex selection, parents' right, gender equality, and your own personal morality. How would you balance these issues when it comes to choosing a baby's gender *in utero*?

Is There Common Ground?

This introduction creates some larger ethical questions about where this debate might lead. Beyond the discussion of sex selection, there might be more room for common ground over whether we are going to allow *in vitro* used for height selection, eye color, or other characteristics. What is the impact on future generations if we have an era of designer babies? This discussion leaves us with unresolved issues of sex selection, but it allows us to find common ground over the slippery slope issues involved.

Create Central

www.mhhe.com/createcentral

Additional Resources

Daniels, Ashley, *How to Choose the Sex of Your Baby: Amazingly Accurate Baby Gender Selection Techniques* (2012).

Green, Ronald M., *Babies by Design: The Ethics of Genetic Choice* (2008).

Purewal, Navtej, *Son Preference: Sex Selection, Gender and Culture in South Asia* (2010).

Internet References . . .

Embryo Project

embryo.asu.edu/pages/ethics-designer-babies

How Stuff Works

science.howstuffworks.com/life/genetic/designer-children.htm

World Health Organization—Preventing Gender-Biased Sex Selection

www.unfpa.org/webdav/site/global/shared/documents/publications/2011/Preventing_gender-biased_sex_selection.pdf

Selected, Edited, and with Issue Framing Material by:
David M. Hall, Ph.D., *Delaware Valley College*

ISSUE

Should Grandparents Have Visitation Rights for Their Grandchildren?

YES: Jennifer Russell, from "Grandparents Play an Essential Role in the Lives of Their Grandchildren," written for *Taking Sides: Family and Personal Relationships* (2011)

NO: Sandra Day O'Connor, from Plurality Opinion, *Troxel v. Granville* (2000)

Learning Outcomes
After reading this issue, you will be able to:
• Identify the agreed-upon rights and responsibilities associated with both parents and grandparents.
• Compare and contrast the arguments made for parents' rights versus those made for grandparents' rights.
• Evaluate the impact of the Supreme Court on states and how they might enact different laws and policies.

ISSUE SUMMARY

YES: Jennifer Russell is an attorney at SeniorLAW Center. She provides legal services to grandparents and other seniors raising relative children. Russell contends that grandparent custody and visitation statutes should be upheld, and argues that grandparents often play an essential role in their grandchildren's lives, especially during times of family turmoil.

NO: Sandra Day O'Connor was the first woman appointed to the United States Supreme Court. For much of her time on the court, she was the justice most likely to wind up in the majority opinion. O'Connor argues that the rights of parents trumps grandparents. As a result, grandparents would not have the right to see their grandchildren.

There are many ways in which families are changing, and one of those ways is the roles that grandparents play in their children's lives. While sometimes grandparents go so far as to raise children, there are other critical ways in which a wide array of grandparents contribute to their grandchildren's upbringing. What rights to grandparents have to see their own grandchildren? While they play a critical role, they are rarely the primary caregivers.

In recognition of this friction, many states have enacted laws to more clearly enumerate what rights grandparents should have regarding their grandchildren. This issue will look at arguments for both sides, using a case from the U.S. Supreme Court to argue that it is a parent's right to determine what is the best for his or her child, while a case from the Pennsylvania Supreme Court is used to argue that grandparent rights must be protected.

Grandparent visitation rights and partial custody statutes are rooted in recognition of the vital role grand-

parents play in a child's development. Although the relationship between a parent and a child is primary, legislatures have determined that grandparents' rights must be protected under the law, especially in situations where the link between the grandparent and the parent has been interfered with through the parent's illness, divorce, or even death. The traditional image of the happy grandparent holding the bouncing grandchild while the parent looks lovingly on the scene is an image that often conflicts with the reality of modern life, which finds many stresses on the family affecting these multigenerational relationships. Yet it is precisely in these highly stressed situations that the admittedly vital role of the grandparent needs to be weighed against the primary rights of the parent to decide what is best for the child. All states must ensure compliance with the spirit of *parens patriae*, the public policy doctrine that allows states to intervene in a family's affairs to the extent necessary to protect a child in need. But absent a showing that the child will be harmed significantly by a parent's choice to limit or end contact with a grandparent, a parent's decision should not be interfered with by government action. It is crucial to defend a parent's rights, especially in times of family flux and turmoil. Whatever benefit a grandparent may provide a grandchild, no one is better situated to determine what is in the best interests of a child than the parent.

Included in this issue is language from *Troxel v. Granville*, 530 U.S. 57 (2000), hereinafter "*Troxel*." In *Troxel*, a plurality of the U.S. Supreme Court ruled against a grandparent's visitation rights and affirmed the trial court's decision to invalidate a Washington State third-party visitation statute on constitutional grounds. The Washington statute was found to be overly broad because it allowed any third party to petition for custody at any time. The statute also failed to allow fit parents the presumption that they were acting in their child's best interests when, for example, they chose to eliminate contact with the child by a third party. The main question in *Troxel* was whether the Washington statute, which allows any person to petition for a court-ordered right to see a child over a custodial parent's objection if such visitation is found to be in the child's best interest, unconstitutionally interfere with the fundamental right of parents to rear their children? The Court concluded, in a 6–3 decision delivered by Justice

Sandra Day O'Connor, that the Washington statute violated the right of parents, under the due process clause of the Constitution's Fourteenth Amendment, to make decisions concerning the care, custody, and control of their children. Justice O'Connor wrote for the Court that "[t]he liberty interest at issue in this case—the interest of parents in the care, custody, and control of their children—is perhaps the oldest of the fundamental liberty interests recognized by this Court." Because the Court rested its decision on the sweeping breadth of *the Washington law* and the application of that broad, unlimited power in this case, it did not consider the primary constitutional question of this case—whether the Due Process Clause requires all non-parental visitation statutes to include a showing of harm or potential harm to the child as a condition precedent to granting visitation. Clearly, though, this case highlights that the constitutionality of any standard for awarding visitation turns on the specific manner in which that standard is applied and that the constitutional protections in this area are best "elaborated with care." The following language outlines the arguments that can be made to support a parent's right to choose for his or her child what relationship that child will have with his or her grandparent.

YES

Jennifer Russell

Grandparents Play an Essential Role in the Lives of Their Grandchildren

Grandparents play an essential and unique role in today's diverse family structures, one which deserves special recognition and protection. Many children live in homes where grandparents have assumed a variety of critical roles, greatly influencing a child's emotional, physical, and mental development and well-being. The 2000 U.S. Census revealed that 5.8 million grandparents lived with their minor grandchildren, 2.4 million of whom had the primary responsibility for these grandchildren. These numbers are growing. In 2008, the U.S. Census reported that 6.4 million grandparents had minor grandchildren living with them. Recognizing the reality of a significant grandparent role in American families and the benefits children derive from relationships with their grandparents, all fifty states have enacted statutes over the past half century granting grandparents the ability to seek visitation or partial custody of their grandchildren.

All states must ensure compliance with the spirit of *parens patriae*, the public policy doctrine that allows states to intervene in a family's affairs to the extent necessary to protect a child in need. It is crucial to defend grandparent visitation and custody rights under this doctrine because grandparents often provide a vital source of stabilization for children during times of family flux and turmoil and play an essential role in a child's development and well-being. For example, after the loss of a parent, arbitrary termination of a child's supportive and nurturing relationship with a grandparent by the surviving parent can be very detrimental to the child. States have an interest in seeing that children in disrupted families are not arbitrarily deprived of the benefit of these relationships. This article will discuss *Hiller v. Fausey*, 588 Pa. 342 (2006), hereinafter "*Hiller*," the Pennsylvania Supreme Court case that upheld a grandparent visitation and partial custody statute in Pennsylvania. The purpose of this article is to advocate for the continued rights of grandparents to seek visitation and partial custody, especially during times of crisis in a child's life.

The Pennsylvania statute at issue in *Hiller*, 23 Pa.C.S. §5311, hereinafter called "the Pennsylvania law," allowed a grandparent or great-grandparent to seek visitation or partial custody of an unmarried grandchild (or great-

grandchild) upon the death of the parent who was related to the petitioner. However, before an award of visitation or partial custody, the court must find that it will be in the child's best interests, and that it will not interfere with the relationship between the child and surviving parent. The statute also required courts to consider the amount of previous contact between the grandparent or great-grandparent petitioner and child.

In *Hiller*, a maternal grandmother was arbitrarily denied visitation with the child in question, her grandson, by the child's father after the death of the child's mother. The grandmother shared a close relationship with her grandson before his mother's death, and the denial of contact by the father eventually caused her to seek partial custody of the child over the father's objections. This case highlights the conflict between parents' rights to rear their children and the government's interest in protecting children from harm. Parents have a constitutionally protected right to make decisions concerning the care, custody, and control of their children. States, however, have a compelling interest in protecting the health and emotional welfare of children. The *Hiller* case advanced to the Pennsylvania Supreme Court, where the court sided with the grandmother and affirmed the award of partial custody to the child's grandmother. The court held that the compelling interest of the state and best interests of the child outweighed the father's decision to cut off the grandmother's nurturing relationship with her grandson.

The paramount concern in all custody disputes is the "best interests of the child."[1] The goal is to "foster those relationships which will be meaningful for the child, while protecting the child from situations which would have a harmful effect."[2] A best interest analysis requires courts to consider all factors relevant to the physical, intellectual, emotional, and spiritual well-being of a child.[3] In *Hiller*, the child and his grandmother shared a close relationship, seeing each other on an almost daily basis during the last two years of his mother's life as she was battling cancer. After his mother's death, the grandmother made repeated attempts to maintain contact with her grandson but was denied any contact by her grandson's father. At trial, the grandmother was able to rebut the presumption afforded to the father that his decision to deny contact was in the child's best interests. She was able to prove instead that partial custody was in her grandson's best interests, and also that it would not interfere with the parent–child relationship, as required by the statute. The trial court awarded her partial custody for one weekend per month and one week per summer.

The child's father appealed the trial court's decision to the Pennsylvania Superior Court, the mid-level Pennsylvania court that reviews such decisions, asserting that application of the Pennsylvania statute violated his due process rights under the Fourteenth Amendment of the U.S. Constitution. The Due Process Clause of the Fourteenth Amendment protects the fundamental right of parents to make decisions concerning the care, custody, and control of their children.[4] When a party raises an infringement of a fundamental right under the Fourteenth Amendment, the court typically applies a "strict scrutiny analysis." This analysis asks if the infringement of the individual's right by the state law or action is necessary to promote a compelling state interest, and also whether it is narrowly tailored to further that compelling state interest.

The Pennsylvania Superior Court began its analysis by comparing the Pennsylvania statute, which allowed the grandmother to seek partial custody, with a Washington State statute that the U.S. Supreme Court found unconstitutional in *Troxel v. Granville*, 530 U.S. 57 (2000), hereinafter "*Troxel*." In *Troxel*, the U.S. Supreme Court affirmed the Washington Supreme Court's decision to invalidate a Washington non-parental visitation statute on constitutional grounds. The Washington statute at issue allowed *any third party* to seek visitation of a child *at any time* and permitted the court to authorize visitation if it served the child's best interests. The Court found the statute to be overly broad because it allowed any third party to seek visitation of a child at any time. The statute also failed to allow fit parents the presumption that they were acting in their child's best interests when, for example, they chose to eliminate contact with the child by a third party. Finding the statute had violated a parent's constitutional right to make decisions concerning the care, custody, and control of their child, the Court affirmed the lower court's decision to invalidate the statute.

The Pennsylvania Superior Court in *Hiller* found the Pennsylvania statute was distinguishable from the Washington statute that the U.S. Supreme Court found unconstitutional. It found the Pennsylvania statute did not violate the father's rights under the Fourteenth Amendment, and it upheld the trial court's application of the Pennsylvania statute and the award of partial custody to the *Hiller* grandmother. It concluded that although the trial court presumed that the father, as a fit parent, was acting in his child's best interests, the grandmother overcame this presumption by demonstrating that granting her partial custody was in the child's best interests, due in part to the loving and supportive relationship she provided to her grandson as he worked

through his grief. The grandmother also demonstrated that partial custody would not interfere with the parent–child relationship.

Unsatisfied with the Superior Court's decision, the father then appealed to the Pennsylvania Supreme Court, arguing that a grandparent should be required to show compelling circumstances, such as harm to the child resulting from denial of visitation, before a court can interfere with a parent's constitutional right to make decisions concerning the care, custody, and control of the child. The Pennsylvania Supreme Court granted review to determine whether the trial court's application of the Pennsylvania law violated the father's rights under the Fourteenth Amendment.

The Pennsylvania Supreme Court first discussed *Troxel* and found all of the U.S. Supreme Court justices, with the exception of one, "recognized the existence of a constitutionally protected right of parents to make decisions concerning the care, custody, and control of their children, which includes determining which third parties may visit with their children and to what extent."[5] A majority of the U.S. Supreme Court also agreed that "fit parents are entitled to a presumption that they act in the best interests of their children."[6]

In light of the U.S. Supreme Court's findings in *Troxel*, the father in *Hiller* requested the Pennsylvania Supreme Court find the lower courts erred in concluding that application of the Pennsylvania statute was constitutional in his case. He maintained that the lower courts did not afford his decision to deny contact with the child's grandmother the special weight it deserved. He asserted that grandparents should be required to show "compelling circumstances such as unfitness of the parent or significant harm to the child resulting from denial of visitation or partial custody" before courts can interfere with parental decisions regarding the child.[7] The grandmother rejected the father's assertion that the Constitution requires she first demonstrate parental unfitness or harm to the child before allowing her partial custody. In *Troxel*, the U.S. Supreme Court did not determine whether this was required.

The grandmother distinguished the Washington statute at issue in *Troxel* from the Pennsylvania statute at issue in *Hiller*. She argued the Pennsylvania statute was a perfect balance between protecting parents' fundamental rights and the state's interest in protecting the best interests and welfare of a child who had lost a parent and is at risk of losing the relationship with a grandparent. She believed the trial court properly applied the Pennsylvania statute and weighed all factors necessary to render a decision that both promoted the child's best interests and protected the parent's due process rights. The trial court made detailed findings with regard to the child's best interests, found partial custody would not interfere with the parent–child relationship, and found the father would not provide contact for the grandmother with the child absent a court order.

The Pennsylvania Supreme Court analyzed the constitutionality of the Pennsylvania law and found little merit in the father's attempt to diminish the importance in the clear differences between the Pennsylvania statute and the Washington statute invalidated by the U.S. Supreme Court. The court acknowledged that the right to make decisions regarding the care, custody, and control of one's child is one of the oldest fundamental rights protected by the Due Process Clause of the Fourteenth Amendment. The Pennsylvania Supreme Court then applied a strict scrutiny analysis of this infringement on the father's fundamental right, first analyzing whether the infringement was supported by a compelling state interest and then whether the infringement was narrowly tailored to effectuate that interest.

The court acknowledged and confirmed that the state has a longstanding interest in protecting the health and emotional welfare of children. The court also confirmed that the state can apply the *parens patriae* doctrine to intervene in a family's private affairs to the extent necessary to protect a child's health and welfare. This is allowed over the objections of a parent, thus infringing on that parent's fundamental right regarding the child. Recognizing that the state's compelling interest in protecting children's welfare can be the basis for infringing on a parent's fundamental right, the court then asked whether the infringement premised upon this interest was narrowly tailored to effectuate the interest. The court found the infringement was narrowly tailored because the Pennsylvania statute at issue was limited to a grandparent (or great-grandparent) whose deceased child (or grandchild) was the parent of the child for whom custody was sought. This was in stark contrast with the overly broad Washington statute invalidated by the U.S. Supreme Court in *Troxel* that allowed *any third party* to petition for visitation of a child *at any time*.

The Pennsylvania Supreme Court also found the statute properly protected parents' fundamental rights in that Pennsylvania courts are not only required to ensure that visitation or partial custody will serve the best interests of the child, but also that it *will not interfere* with the parent–child relationship. Additionally, courts must consider the amount of previous contact between the child and petitioner, allowing for an assessment of their prior relationship. Moreover, Pennsylvania precedent requires courts to provide a presumption in favor of a fit parent's decision, which is exactly what the U.S. Supreme Court faulted the trial court in *Troxel* for failing to do. Pennsylvania precedent already gives special weight and deference to the parent–child relationship, properly tipping controversies with third parties in the parent's favor.

The U.S. Supreme Court in *Troxel* did not decide whether the Due Process Clause requires all non-parental visitation statutes to include a showing of harm or potential harm as a condition precedent to granting visitation or partial custody to a third party. In declining to make this determination, the Court left the decision to individual states. The Pennsylvania Supreme Court in *Hiller* disagreed with the father's argument that the Pennsylvania statute should require a showing of harm, concluding this requirement would vitiate the purpose of the statute as well as Pennsylvania's policy of assuring "continuing contact of the child or children with the grandparent when the parent is deceased, divorced, or separated."[8] While the parent–child relationship must be given special weight and deference, and should not typically be disturbed unless there is a showing of harm, the court found that it can be disturbed without a showing of harm if circumstances "clearly indicate the appropriateness of awarding custody to a non-parent."[9]

The Pennsylvania Supreme Court held the stringent requirements of the Pennsylvania law, combined with the presumption in Pennsylvania legal precedent that fit parents act in their children's best interests, sufficiently protects parents' fundamental rights. The court found that a grandparent or great-grandparent did not have to demonstrate parental unfitness or a showing of harm when seeking visitation or partial custody. The Pennsylvania statute thus survived its constitutional challenge. The statute's application in *Hiller* was upheld because it was properly applied by the lower courts, and the child was able to continue his beneficial and nurturing relationship with his maternal grandmother following the tragic death of his mother.

In *Troxel*, the U.S. Supreme Court reaffirms its view that the Due Process Clause of the Fourteenth Amendment protects parents' interest in the care, custody, and control of their children. However, the Court also made clear that non-parental visitation statutes are constitutional, provided they are carefully tailored, contain procedures and/or provisions that are respectful of the parent–child relationship, further a compelling state interest, and protect the best interests of the child. All the justices in *Troxel*, except one, agreed on a state's interest in establishing non-parental visitation and partial custody laws, clearly recognizing the changing reality of the American family and the crucial role that grandparents and other third parties play in children's lives.

In *Hiller*, the Pennsylvania Supreme Court recognized that the Pennsylvania law met all requirements set forth by the U.S. Supreme Court for a constitutional non-parental visitation statute. The statute is narrowly drawn to limit the class of third persons to parents or grandparents of the deceased parent, requires any award of visitation or partial custody to be in the child's best interests and mandates it not interfere with the parent–child relationship. The statute also requires courts to consider the amount of prior contact between the petitioner and child. For a court to override a parent's decision to deny contact, a grandparent petitioner must provide evidence that their request is truly in the child's best interests.

By enacting this law, the Pennsylvania legislature acknowledged that children who have experienced the death of a parent may need protection against unilateral terminations of the child's relationships with kin of the deceased parent. Without this statute, a child would have no recourse against this additional loss, thus compounding his tragedy. The Pennsylvania law carefully balances the rights of parents against the state's compelling interest. It protects the welfare of children who have experienced the death of a parent while promoting a beneficial relationship between grandparents and grandchildren, crucial in our increasingly intergenerational and interconnected society.

As *Hiller* highlights, grandparents can play an essential role in the protection of a child's development and welfare in today's families. Pennsylvania has recognized that this role deserves special recognition and protection and allows grandparents to petition for custody and/or supervised physical custody (visitation) in a variety of circumstances. So many children are raised in single-parent, intergenerational, and kinship care homes, where relatives such as grandparents have primary responsibility for the children, that the conventional nuclear family is no longer America's norm. Children that are raised in environments with a great deal of family flux can suffer detrimental effects on their development and well-being. The stabilizing relationship and various forms of support and security that many grandparents provide are critical to ensuring a grandchild's mental, physical, and emotional development.

This source of stability and support from a grandparent with whom the child has a close relationship is even more crucial when that child has suffered the tragic loss of a parent. Loss of a parent can lead to depression and other emotional disturbances; severing another deep family attachment can exacerbate a child's pain and cause additional harm to the child. It is not in a child's best interests to arbitrarily be denied contact with that nurturing grandparent after the loss of a parent, particularly when the child has had a longstanding relationship with the grandparent. The fundamental right of parents to the custody of their children, which includes the ability to deny third-party relationships, must be balanced with and restricted by the state's interest, which includes the emotional development and well-being of a grieving child.

Hiller focused on the Pennsylvania statute allowing grandparents and great-grandparents to seek partial custody or visitation upon the death of a parent. Pennsylvania grandparents can also seek custody or visitation in other circumstances. Although much of the substance of custody law remains the same since *Hiller* was decided in 2006, changes were made to Pennsylvania's custody laws in January 2011. Grandparents and great-grandparents continue to have the right to petition for partial physical and supervised physical custody (previously, "visitation") when the parent of the child who is related to the petitioner is deceased, when the parents are separated for at least six months or have commenced divorce proceedings,

or when the child has resided with the grandparent or great-grandparent for one year and is then subsequently removed from the home by the parents.[10] The Pennsylvania law at issue in *Hiller* now falls under the revised custody laws.[11]

Grandparents in Pennsylvania can petition for *any* form of physical or legal custody if 1) their relationship with the child began with the consent of a parent or under court order, 2) they have assumed or are willing to assume responsibility for the child, and 3) the child has been determined to be a dependent child under state law, or is substantially at risk due to parental abuse, neglect, drug or alcohol abuse or incapacity, or was living with that grandparent for one year and is then removed from the home by the parents.[12] The variety of circumstances under which a grandparent can seek "visitation" or custody of their grandchild in Pennsylvania is a strong testament to, and acknowledgment by the legislature of, the role that grandparents play in the development and well-being of children, especially in families suffering from disruption, loss, and broken relationships.

Many grandparents are *in loco parentis* to their grandchildren, meaning they have assumed all of the parental rights and duties of, and obligations for, the child, and are acting as the child's parent, but are doing so without a court order in place. This is problematic because caregivers cannot obtain necessary medical or mental health care for a child without the necessary legal decision-making authority. Under Pennsylvania's current custody law, individuals who are *in loco parentis* now have a statutorily-conferred right to petition for any form of physical or legal custody of that child, providing many grandparent caregivers with the relief they need.[13]

A child's best interest is the guiding force by which custody determinations are made. However, custody law continues to evolve and develop in light of our changing society. While parents have constitutionally protected parental rights, grandparents are increasingly afforded greater authority, rights and liberties in light of their crucial role and the support they provide to children and families across the United States.

In *Hiller,* the Pennsylvania Supreme Court found the grandmother had a nurturing and loving relationship with her grandson that was highly beneficial for the child. Recognizing that this relationship was in the "best interests of the child," the court affirmed the grandmother's legal right to continue her involvement in her grandson's life. This landmark decision highlights the vital role grandparents play in the lives of many children, especially in times of crisis. As states continue to seek ways to protect the health and welfare of children, the evolution of grandparent visitation and partial custody statutes reflects the recognition of the vital role grandparents play in maintaining the well-being of children and families alike.

Notes

1. *Douglas v. Wright,* 801 A.2d 586, 591 (2002)
2. *Id.*
3. *Id.*
4. *Troxel v. Granville,* 530 U.S. 57, 66 (2000)
5. *Hiller v. Fausey,* 904 A.2d 875, 883 (2006)
6. *Id.*
7. *Id.* at 884.
8. 23 Pa.C.S. §5301
9. *Id.* at 889–90.
10. 23 Pa.C.S. §5325

11. 23 Pa.C.S. §5325(1)
12. 23 Pa.C.S. §5324(3)
13. 23 Pa.C.S. §5324(2)

JENNIFER RUSSELL, Esq., is an attorney at SeniorLAW Center and addresses the legal concerns of senior relatives. Russell argues that grandparents are an essential part of their grandchildren's lives and have a right to see and participate in their lives.

Sandra Day O'Connor

 **NO**

Plurality Opinion

Justice O'Connor announced the judgment of the Court and delivered an opinion, in which the Chief Justice, Justice Ginsburg, and Justice Breyer join.

Section 26.10.160(3) of the Revised Code of Washington *(editor's note—hereinafter called "the Washington law")* permits "[a]ny person" to petition a superior court for visitation rights "at any time," and authorizes that court to grant such visitation rights whenever "visitation may serve the best interest of the child." Petitioners Jenifer and Gary Troxel petitioned a Washington Superior Court for the right to visit their grandchildren, Isabelle and Natalie Troxel. Respondent Tommie Granville, the mother of Isabelle and Natalie, opposed the petition. The case ultimately reached the Washington Supreme Court, which held *the Washington law* unconstitutionally interferes with the fundamental right of parents to rear their children.

The demographic changes of the past century make it difficult to speak of an average American family. The composition of families varies greatly from household to household. While many children may have two married parents and grandparents who visit regularly, many other children are raised in single-parent households. Understandably, in these single-parent households, persons outside the nuclear family are called upon with increasing frequency to assist in the everyday tasks of child rearing. In many cases, grandparents play an important role.

The nationwide enactment of nonparental visitation statutes is assuredly due, in some part, to the States' recognition of these changing realities of the American family. Because grandparents and other relatives undertake duties of a parental nature in many households, States have sought to ensure the welfare of the children therein by protecting the relationships those children form with such third parties. The States' nonparental visitation statutes are further supported by a recognition, which varies from State to State, that children should have the opportunity to benefit from relationships with statutorily specified persons—for example, their grandparents. The extension of statutory rights in this area to persons other than a child's parents, however, comes with an obvious cost. For example, the State's recognition of an independent third-party interest in a child can place a substantial burden on the traditional parent–child relationship.

The Washington law permits "any person" to petition a superior court for visitation rights "at any time," and authorizes that court to grant such visitation rights whenever "visitation may serve the best interest of the child." Petitioners Jenifer and Gary Troxel petitioned a Washington Superior Court for the right to visit their grandchildren, Isabelle and Natalie Troxel. Respondent Tommie Granville, the mother of Isabelle and Natalie, opposed the petition. The case ultimately reached the Washington Supreme Court, which held that *the Washington law* unconstitutionally interferes with the fundamental right of parents to rear their children.

Tommie Granville and Brad Troxel shared a relationship that ended in June 1991. The two never married, but they had two daughters, Isabelle and Natalie. Jenifer and Gary Troxel are Brad's parents, and thus the paternal grandparents of Isabelle and Natalie. After Tommie and Brad separated in 1991, Brad lived with his parents and regularly brought his daughters to his parents' home for weekend visitation. Brad committed suicide in May 1993. Although the Troxels at first continued to see Isabelle and Natalie on a regular basis after their son's death, Tommie Granville informed the Troxels in October 1993 that she wished to limit their visitation with her daughters to one short visit per month.

In December 1993, the Troxels commenced the present action by filing, in the Washington Superior Court for Skagit County, a petition to obtain visitation rights with Isabelle and Natalie. *The Washington law (under which they brought this action)* provides: "Any person may petition the court for visitation rights at any time including, but not limited to, custody proceedings. The court may order visitation rights for any person when visitation may serve the best interest of the child whether or not there has been any change of circumstances." At trial, the Troxels requested two weekends of overnight visitation per month and two weeks of visitation each summer. Granville did not oppose visitation altogether, but instead asked the court to order one day of visitation per month with no overnight stay. In 1995, the Superior Court issued an oral ruling and entered a visitation decree ordering visitation one weekend per month, one week during the summer, and four hours on both of the petitioning grandparents' birthdays.

Granville appealed, during which time she married Kelly Wynn. Before addressing the merits of Granville's appeal, the Washington Court of Appeals remanded the case to the Superior Court for entry of written findings

Supreme Court of the United States, 2000.

of fact and conclusions of law. On remand, the Superior Court found that visitation was in Isabelle and Natalie's best interests:

> "The Petitioners [the Troxels] are part of a large, central, loving family, all located in this area, and the Petitioners can provide opportunities for the children."
>
> ". . . The court took into consideration all factors regarding the best interest of the children and considered all the testimony before it. The children would be benefitted from spending quality time with the Petitioners, provided that that time is balanced with time with the childrens' [sic] nuclear family. The court finds that the childrens' [sic] best interests are served by spending time with their mother and stepfather's other six children."
>
> Approximately nine months after the Superior Court entered its order on remand, Granville's husband formally adopted Isabelle and Natalie.

The Washington Court of Appeals reversed the lower court's visitation order and dismissed the Troxels' petition for visitation, holding that nonparents lack standing to seek visitation unless a custody action is pending. In the Court of Appeals' view, that limitation on nonparental visitation actions was "consistent with the constitutional restrictions on state interference with parents' fundamental liberty interest in the care, custody, and management of their children." The Washington Supreme Court granted the Troxels' petition for review and, after consolidating their case with two other visitation cases, affirmed. The court disagreed with the Court of Appeals' decision on the statutory issue and found that *the Washington law* gave the Troxels standing to seek visitation, irrespective of whether a custody action was pending. The Washington Supreme Court nevertheless agreed with the Court of Appeals' ultimate conclusion that the Troxels could not obtain visitation of Isabelle and Natalie pursuant to *the Washington law*. The court rested its decision on the Federal Constitution, holding that *the Washington law* unconstitutionally infringes on the fundamental right of parents to rear their children. In the court's view, there were at least two problems with the nonparental visitation statute. First, according to the Washington Supreme Court, the Constitution permits a State to interfere with the right of parents to rear their children only to prevent harm or potential harm to a child. *The Washington law* fails that standard because it requires no threshold showing of harm. Second, by allowing "'any person' to petition for forced visitation of a child at 'any time' with the only requirement being that the visitation serve the best interest of the child," the Washington visitation statute sweeps too broadly. "It is not within the province of the state to make significant decisions concerning the custody of children merely because it could make a 'better' decision." The Washington Supreme Court held that "parents have a right to limit visitation of their children with third

persons," and that between parents and judges, "the parents should be the ones to choose whether to expose their children to certain people or ideas."

The demographic changes of the past century make it difficult to speak of an average American family. The composition of families varies greatly from household to household. While many children may have two married parents and grandparents who visit regularly, many other children are raised in single-parent households. The nationwide enactment of nonparental visitation statutes is assuredly due, in some part, to the States' recognition of these changing realities of the American family. Because grandparents and other relatives undertake duties of a parental nature in many households, States have sought to ensure the welfare of the children therein by protecting the relationships those children form with such third parties. The States' nonparental visitation statutes are further supported by a recognition, which varies from State to State, that children should have the opportunity to benefit from relationships with statutorily specified persons—for example, their grandparents. The extension of statutory rights in this area to persons other than a child's parents, however, comes with an obvious cost. For example, the State's recognition of an independent third-party interest in a child can place a substantial burden on the traditional parent–child relationship.

The Fourteenth Amendment provides that no State shall "deprive any person of life, liberty, or property, without due process of law." We have long recognized that the Amendment's Due Process Clause, like its Fifth Amendment counterpart, "guarantees more than fair process." The Clause also includes a substantive component that "provides heightened protection against government interference with certain fundamental rights and liberty interests."

The liberty interest at issue in this case—the interest of parents in the care, custody, and control of their children—is perhaps the oldest of the fundamental liberty interests recognized by this Court. More than 75 years ago, in *Meyer v. Nebraska*, 262 U.S. 390 (1923), we held that the "liberty" protected by the Due Process Clause includes the right of parents to "establish a home and bring up children" and "to control the education of their own." Two years later, in *Pierce v. Society of Sisters*, 268 U.S. 510 (1925), we again held that the "liberty of parents and guardians" includes the right "to direct the upbringing and education of children under their control." We explained in *Pierce* that "the child is not the mere creature of the State; those who nurture him and direct his destiny have the right, coupled with the high duty, to recognize and prepare him for additional obligations."

In subsequent cases also, we have recognized the fundamental right of parents to make decisions concerning the care, custody, and control of their children. See, e.g., *Stanley v. Illinois*, 405 U.S. 645 (1972) ("It is plain that the interest of a parent in the companionship, care, custody, and management of his or her children 'comes to this Court with a momentum for respect lacking when appeal is made to liberties which derive merely from shifting economic arrangements'"); *Wisconsin v. Yoder,* 406 U.S. 205(1972) ("The history and culture of Western civilization reflect a strong tradition of parental concern for the nurture and upbringing of their children. This primary role of the parents in the upbringing of their children is now established beyond debate as an enduring American tradition".) In light of this extensive precedent, it cannot now be doubted that the Due Process Clause of the Fourteenth Amendment protects the fundamental right of parents to make decisions concerning the care, custody, and control of their children.

The Washington law, as applied to Granville and her family in this case, unconstitutionally infringes on that fundamental parental right. The Washington nonparental visitation statute is breathtakingly broad. According to the statute's text, "*any person* may petition the court for visitation rights *at any time,*" and the court may grant such visitation rights whenever "visitation may serve *the best interest of the child.*" That language effectively permits any third party seeking visitation to subject any decision by a parent concerning visitation of the parent's children to state-court review. Once the visitation petition has been filed in court and the matter is placed before a judge, a parent's decision that visitation would not be in the child's best interest is accorded no deference. *The Washington law* contains no requirement that a court accord the parent's decision any presumption of validity or any weight whatsoever. Instead, the Washington statute places the best-interest determination solely in the hands of the judge. Should the judge disagree with the parent's estimation of the child's best interests, the judge's view necessarily prevails. Thus, in practical effect, in the State of Washington, a court can disregard and overturn *any* decision by a fit custodial parent concerning visitation whenever a third party affected by the decision files a visitation petition, based solely on the judge's determination of the child's best interests.

Turning to the facts of this case, the record reveals that the Superior Court's order was based on precisely the type of mere disagreement we have just described and nothing more. The Superior Court's order was not founded on any special factors that might justify the State's interference with Granville's fundamental right to make decisions concerning the rearing of her two daughters. To be sure, this case involves a visitation petition filed by grandparents soon after the death of their son—the father of Isabelle and Natalie—but the combination of several factors here compels our conclusion that *the Washington law,* as applied, exceeded the bounds of the Due Process Clause.

First, the Troxels did not allege, and no court has found, that Granville was an unfit parent. That aspect of the case is important, for there is a presumption that fit parents act in the best interests of their children. As this Court explained in *Parham*:

> "Our constitutional system long ago rejected any notion that a child is the mere creature of the State and, on the contrary, asserted that parents generally have the right, coupled with the high duty, to recognize and prepare [their children] for additional obligations. . . . The law's concept of the family rests on a presumption that parents possess what a child lacks in maturity, experience, and capacity for judgment required for making life's difficult decisions. More important, historically it has recognized that natural bonds of affection lead parents to act in the best interests of their children."

Accordingly, so long as a parent adequately cares for his or her children (i.e., is fit), there will normally be no reason for the State to inject itself into the private realm of the family to further question the ability of that parent to make the best decisions concerning the rearing of that parent's children.

The problem here is not that the Washington Superior Court intervened, but that when it did so, it gave no special weight at all to Granville's determination of her daughters' best interests. More importantly, it appears that the Superior Court applied exactly the opposite presumption. In reciting its oral ruling after the conclusion of closing arguments, the Superior Court judge explained:

> "The burden is to show that it is in the best interest of the children to have some visitation and some quality time with their grandparents. I think in most situations a commonsensical approach [is that] it is normally in the best interest of the children to spend quality time with the grandparent, unless the grandparent, [sic] there are some issues or problems involved wherein the grandparents, their lifestyles are going to impact adversely upon the children. That certainly isn't the case here from what I can tell."

The judge's comments suggest that he presumed the grandparents' request should be granted unless the children would be "impacted adversely." In effect, the judge placed on Granville, the fit custodial parent, the burden of *disproving* that visitation would be in the best interest of her daughters. The judge reiterated moments later: "I think [visitation with the Troxels] would be in the best interest of the children and I haven't been shown it is not in [the] best interest of the children."

The decisional framework employed by the Superior Court directly contravened the traditional presumption that a fit parent will act in the best interest of his or her child. In that respect, the court's presumption failed to provide any protection for Granville's fundamental constitutional right to make decisions concerning the rearing of her own daughters. In an ideal world, parents might always seek to cultivate the bonds between grandparents and their grandchildren.

Needless to say, however, our world is far from perfect, and in it, the decision whether such an intergenerational relationship would be beneficial in any specific case is for the parent to make in the first instance. And, if a fit parent's decision of the kind at issue here becomes subject to judicial review, the court must accord at least some special weight to the parent's own determination. . . .

Considered together with the Superior Court's reasons for awarding visitation to the Troxels, the combination of these factors demonstrates that the visitation order in this case was an unconstitutional infringement on Granville's fundamental right to make decisions concerning the care, custody, and control of her two daughters. . . .

SANDRA DAY O'CONNOR was the first woman appointed to the United States Supreme Court. For much of her time on the court, she was the justice most likely to wind up in the majority opinion. O'Connor argues that the rights of parents trump grandparents. As a result, grandparents would not have the visitation right to see their grandchildren.

EXPLORING THE ISSUE

Should Grandparents Have Visitation Rights for Their Grandchildren?

Critical Thinking and Reflection

1. What are some arguments made by each side with which you agree or disagree?
2. What are the strengths and weaknesses of the two positions made in this chapter?
3. Compare and contrast the competing arguments made for parents' rights versus grandparents' rights. Which legal arguments are stronger? How does this fit with your views of what is morally right and morally wrong?
4. Think more broadly about the role of child visitation and custody rights. While this chapter focuses on the rights of parents versus the rights of grandparents, this chapter also raises an important question: what is in the best interest of children?

Is There Common Ground?

Many believe that parents should play the primary role in raising their children, while also acknowledging the critical role of extended family, particularly grandparents, in child rearing. How do we determine the right balance when there are disputes within families? Almost everyone would agree that they want to do what is best for the children, yet so often that can get lost in the competing needs and rights of parents and grandparents. While this chapter focuses on different court cases, most would agree that regardless of the verdict, everyone is harmed if we get to the point that we drag a family through court. What are some ways to find peace through this conflict without subjecting the family, and particularly the children, to a drawn-out court battle?

Create Central

www.mhhe.com/createcentral

Additional Resources

The following websites are resources for grandparents' rights:

www.grandparents.com/gp/content/expert-advice/
legal/article/
dograndparentshavetherightstheyshould.html

www.grandparentsrights.org/

www.caringgrandparents.com/

http://family-law.freeadvice.com/family-law/child_
custody/grandparents_visitation_rights.htm

Internet References . . .

AARP

www.aarp.org/

Grandparents.com: Rights State by State

www.grandparents.com/family-and-relationships/
grandparents-rights/grandparent-rights-united-states

SeniorLAW Center

http://seniorlawcenter.org/

Selected, Edited, and with Issue Framing Material by:
David M. Hall, Ph.D., *Delaware Valley College*

ISSUE

Should Courts Be Able to Discriminate Against Immigrant Fathers?

YES: Neal Kumar Katyal et al., from "On Writ of Certiorari: Brief for the United States," *Ruben Flores-Villar v. United States of America* (2010).

NO: Steven F. Hubachek et al., from "On Writ of Certiorari: Brief for Petitioner," *Ruben Flores-Villar v. United States of America* (2010).

Learning Outcomes
After reading this issue, you will be able to: • Identify basic arguments made for and against holding fathers to a different standard than mothers involving the citizenship of their children. • Compare and contrast the competing arguments regarding the role of gender equality when examining the citizenship of immigrants' children. • Evaluate the implications of this policy on immigrants and U.S. society.

ISSUE SUMMARY

YES: Neal Kumar Katyal served as Acting Solicitor General in the Obama administration at the time of this case. Katyal argues that Congress created legislation with a different standard of citizenship for biological fathers versus biological mothers and that this different standard served a rational interest and should be upheld.

NO: Steven Hubachek is the Counsel of Record for the Federal Defenders of San Diego, Inc. Hubachek argues that this law discriminates against men because it makes it more difficult for immigrant fathers to pass on their citizenship to their children than for immigrant mothers.

G enerally speaking, the law prohibits discrimination on the basis of a person's biological sex. Despite this fact, there are longstanding beliefs that women are more nurturing than men. Some people take an essentialist perspective and say that this is how women have always been for innate reasons. Others take a social constructionist perspective and argue that women are seen as more nurturing due to how females are raised and the social constructions of gender roles. Divorce courts traditionally have difficulty in determining child custody, and some argue that mothers are placed at an unfair advantage. In fact, many fathers' rights groups will strenuously argue that courts discriminate against fathers on a decision-by-decision basis. They argue that the anti-father bias in society and reflected in our courts is damaging not only to fathers but also to children. Of course, this view is not shared by all. Others argue that courts are looking for what is in the best interest of the children rather than what is in the best interest of the father.

The U.S. Constitution provides certain protections from being discriminated against due to a person's sex. As a result, many laws, including our court system in most divorce cases, are expected to approach the topic of divorce from a gender-neutral standpoint. The question of this issue, however, is what happens when contemporary views of sex and gender are interjected with views about immigration and naturalization. Does determining citizenship merit a different standard for immigrant citizens versus natural-born citizens? According to the U.S. government, the answer to that question is yes.

There are some cases in which treating people differently based on their biological sex is required by law. Specifically, courts are instructed to treat immigrant fathers differently from how they would treat immigrant mothers, with fathers held to a higher standard in order for their children to have U.S. citizenship when they are born outside the United States. For this reason, it is important to examine this issue not just from a perspective of biological sex, but also immigration.

According to the U.S. Census Bureau, during 2009 there were 38.5 million people living in the United States, which represents 12.5 percent of the population. Most of these foreign-born residents are here on legal visas or are naturalized citizens. Of the 38.5 million foreign-born population, it is estimated that approximately 12 million are neither naturalized citizens nor here on a valid visa, often referred to as undocumented immigrants or illegal immigrants. Immigration was at its height between the late 1800s and early 1900s, when foreign-born residents accounted for 13–15 percent of the entire U.S. population. The average American tends to believe in and expect equal treatment under the law for men and women alike. In the case of immigration and citizenship, many are surprised to learn that this is not the case. Indeed, citizenship is far more complex than many realize. The most simple rule of citizenship is the one with which people are most familiar: all persons born in the United States are citizens of the United States. What happens if your parent is a naturalized U.S. citizen, but you are born outside the United States and you are born out of wedlock? This is where the law particularly becomes more complicated and varied. If you are born out of wedlock to a mother who is a naturalized U.S. citizen, there is one criterion to meet: she must have resided in the United States for one year prior to the birth of the child. Today, if you are born out of wedlock to a father who is a naturalized U.S. citizen, the following must be proven:

- He lived in the United States for at least ten years prior to the birth of the child.
- Five of the ten years must have occurred after turning 14 years old.

Many fathers' rights groups and others complain that courts are systematically discriminatory toward men by assuming that women play a primary role in child rearing.

They argue that this occurs for fathers who are U.S.-born citizens. Although this is an area of debate in our society, here we have a statutory law that holds children of undocumented immigrants to a different standard depending on whether it is a father or a mother who is a U.S. citizen. When discussing immigration, are you surprised to see why there might be different criteria for fathers and mothers? What are some reasons that you think people might support different treatment based on gender? What are some reasons that you think people might oppose different treatment based on gender? This is a way in which U.S. law unequivocally creates a different standard for males than for females. Although the U.S. Constitution does not contain an Equal Rights Amendment that would prohibit discrimination based on biological sex, it does contain an Equal Protection Clause in the Fourteenth Amendment, which states that the government cannot "deny to any person within its jurisdiction equal protection under the law." This amendment was passed after the Civil War, so there is some debate about how it should be interpreted. Most would agree that it should provide equal protection if one is discriminated against due to race, as that was the intent when it was passed. If they are discriminated against due to their biological sex, however, there is less agreement. Generally speaking, the courts extend protection if discrimination is based on biological sex, but it is a lower level of protection than would be extended based on race. This issue contains excerpts from a court case on this matter. Here we see the U.S. government making its case for immigration policy, as well as those supportive of immigrant rights making the case for those adversely affected by this law. This raises questions regarding why there should be a different standard in the cases of immigrant parents. Is there a compelling state interest to hold different standards based on the biological sex of the parent? Or does this have more to do with immigration and border control?

YES

Neal Kumar Katyal et al.

On Writ of Certiorari: Brief for the United States

In order for a United States citizen who has a child abroad with a non–United States citizen to transmit his or her citizenship to the foreign-born child, the U.S. citizen parent must have been physically present in the United States for a particular period of time prior to the child's birth. The question presented is: Whether Congress's decision to impose a shorter physical-presence requirement on unwed citizen mothers of foreign-born children than on other parents of foreignborn children through [the law] (1970) violates the Fifth Amendment's guarantee of equal protection.

Article I of the United States Constitution assigns to Congress the "Power To establish an uniform Rule of Naturalization throughout the United States." [The] U.S. Const. Art. I. Pursuant to that authority, Congress has elected to confer United States citizenship by statute on certain persons born outside the United States through various provisions in the Immigration and Nationality Act (INA). At the time of petitioner's birth in 1974, a child born outside the United States to married parents, only one of whom was a U.S. citizen, could acquire citizenship through his or her U.S. citizen parent if, before the child's birth, the citizen parent had been physically present in the United States for a total of ten years, at least five of which were after the parent had turned fourteen years of age. The same physical-presence requirement applied if the child was born out of wedlock and the father was a U.S. citizen (and if the paternity was established through legitimation while the child was under age 21). If, however, the child was born out of wedlock outside the United States and only his mother was a U.S. citizen, [the law] transmits U.S. citizenship to the child if the mother was a citizen of the United States at the time of the child's birth and had been physically present in the United States before the child's birth for a continuous period of at least one year.

In 1974, petitioner was born in Tijuana, Mexico, to unmarried parents. His mother is a citizen and national of Mexico, and his father, who was 16 years old at the time of petitioner's birth, is a U.S. citizen who resided in the United States for much of his life. Although petitioner's father was a U.S. citizen from birth, petitioner's father did not obtain formal documentation of that fact until May 24, 1999 (almost 25 years after petitioner was born), when he was issued a certificate of citizenship upon his own application. Petitioner's father was confirmed as a citizen from birth based on the fact that his mother—petitioner's paternal grandmother—was a U.S. citizen by birth in the United States, and met the requirements of [the law] to transmit citizenship to her out-of-wedlock child (petitioner's father) at the time of his birth. It is not clear that petitioner's father was aware of his U.S. citizenship prior to adulthood.

When petitioner was two months old, his father and paternal grandmother brought him to the United States to receive medical treatment. After petitioner was released from the hospital, he lived with his father and grandmother in the San Diego area, where he grew up. Although petitioner's father is not listed on his birth certificate, in 1985 the father acknowledged petitioner as his son by filing an acknowledgment of paternity with the Civil Registry in Mexico.

On March 17, 1997, petitioner was convicted of importation of marijuana, in violation of [US law], and was sentenced to 24 months of imprisonment. After serving his sentence, petitioner was ordered removed from the United States, and he was removed on October 16, 1998. Petitioner repeatedly returned to the United States following removal, resulting in additional removal proceedings in 1999 (when he was twice deported) and again in 2002. In June 2003, following another illegal reentry, petitioner was convicted of two counts of illegal entry into the United States in violation of [the law], and was again removed in October 2003. Petitioner again reentered the United States illegally and was once again removed in March 2005, after which he yet again unlawfully returned to the United States.

On February 24, 2006, petitioner was arrested and charged with being a deported alien found in the United States after deportation, in violation of [U.S. law]. Petitioner has since served his sentence and been released under supervision and then deported. The completion of petitioner's sentence and his deportation do not, however, render the present proceeding moot. After his indictment, petitioner filed an application for a certificate of citizenship with the Department of Homeland Security (DHS). DHS denied petitioner's application (and his administrative appeal) because it was physically impossible for petitioner's father, who was 16 years old when petitioner was born, to have been present in the United States for five years after his fourteenth birthday, but prior to petitioner's birth, in order for him to transmit U.S. citizenship to petitioner.

Supreme Court of the United States, 2010.

The government filed a motion in limine in petitioner's illegal-reentry prosecution to exclude evidence of petitioner's purported citizenship because petitioner did not qualify for citizenship under the [law]. The district court granted the motion after concluding that no reasonable juror could find that petitioner's father satisfied the transmission-of-citizenship requirements of the [law]. The district court also rejected petitioner's equal protection challenge to application of the physical-presence requirements to his father. Following a bench trial on stipulated facts, petitioner was convicted of violating [US law] by illegally entering the United States without permission after having been removed. He was sentenced to 42 months of imprisonment.

On appeal, petitioner reasserted his contention that the versions of Sections 1401(a)(7) and 1409 applicable at the time of his birth violated the equal protection component of the Fifth Amendment's Due Process Clause because they required a U.S. citizen father of a child born abroad out of wedlock to have been physically present in the United States for a total of at least five years following his fourteenth birthday in order to transmit his citizenship to his child, while a U.S. citizen mother in such a situation need only have been physically present in the United States for a continuous period of one year. The court of appeals rejected petitioner's contention and affirmed his conviction. The court concluded that the answer to petitioner's equal protection argument "follows from the Supreme Court's opinion in *Nguyen v. INS.*" In *Nguyen*, this Court held that [the law] does not discriminate on the basis of gender in violation of equal protection principles by requiring a citizen father—but not a citizen mother—to take steps to establish his connection (through legitimation, adjudication, or acknowledgment) to a child born out of wedlock outside the United States before he can transmit U.S. citizenship to the child.

Assuming that intermediate scrutiny applies to petitioner's equal protection challenge, the court of appeals determined that, "[a]lthough the means at issue are different in this case—an additional residence requirement for the unwed citizen father—the government's interests are no less important, and the particular means no less substantially related to those objectives, than in *Nguyen.*" The court reasoned that applying different physical-presence requirements to unwed citizen mothers and fathers was substantially related to the important government interests in minimizing the risk of statelessness of foreign-born children and in "assuring a link between an unwed citizen father, and this country, to" the child. The court relied on its analysis in *Runnett v. Shultz*, (9th Cir. 1990), in which it observed that "illegitimate children are more likely to be 'stateless' at birth" because "if the U.S. citizen mother is not a dual national, and the illegitimate child is born in a country that does not recognize citizenship by *jus soli* (citizenship determined by place of birth), the child can acquire no citizenship other than his mother's at birth." The court found that concern about statelessness justified

a shorter physical-presence requirement for mothers of out-of-wedlock children to "insure that the child will have a nationality at birth." The Court acknowledged that the "fit" between the means and the objectives was "not perfect," but found it "sufficiently persuasive in light of the virtually plenary power that Congress has to legislate in the area of immigration and citizenship."

Summary of Argument

Pursuant to its authority under Article I of the Constitution, Congress has enacted comprehensive rules governing immigration and naturalization. One subset of those rules governs the acquisition of citizenship by children born abroad to U.S. citizen parents. When a U.S. citizen has a child abroad with a non-citizen, Congress requires that the U.S. citizen parent have satisfied a physical-presence requirement prior to the child's birth before the parent may transmit his or her citizenship to the child as of birth. That requirement applies to married fathers and married mothers—and it applies to unmarried fathers such as petitioner's. In an effort to reduce the number of children who may be born stateless, Congress has applied a shorter physical-presence requirement to unmarried U.S. citizen mothers who give birth abroad. Such physical-presence requirements on the U.S. citizen parents of children born abroad ensure that foreign-born children will have sufficient connections to the United States to merit citizenship, and this Court has long upheld Congress's decision to require such a connection.

Petitioner asserts an equal protection challenge to this statutory framework on behalf of his father. But petitioner's father has never asserted such a claim on his own behalf, and petitioner cannot demonstrate any hindrance to his father's having done so. Petitioner therefore lacks third-party standing to assert his father's equal protection claim.

Congress's choice of rules governing naturalization is entitled to deference by this Court and is subject to review under rational basis standards. But even if heightened review is applied to the equal protection challenge asserted here on behalf of petitioner's father, the statutory provisions are constitutional. There is no serious dispute that reducing the number of children born stateless is an important government objective. Congress chose to pursue that objective by applying a shorter physical-presence requirement to unwed U.S. citizen mothers of foreign-born children than to other U.S. citizen parents. That statutory scheme is constitutionally permissible because it is substantially related to the government's important interest.

As Congress knew, most countries apply *jus sanguinis* citizenship laws, pursuant to which a child's citizenship is determined at birth through his blood relationship to a parent rather than with reference to his place of birth. In most of those countries—as indeed in most *jus soli* countries such as the United States—the only parental relationship that is legally recognized or formalized at birth for a child born out of wedlock is usually that of his mother. Thus, at birth, the child's only means of taking citizenship is through his mother. Although such a child's father may subsequently take actions to establish a legally recognized parental relationship, there is no guarantee that he will ever do so. Because impediments to an unwed mother's ability to transmit her citizenship to a child at birth create a substantially higher risk that a child will be born stateless, Congress eased the requirements for acquisition of U.S. citizenship by the children of those mothers.

The fact that Congress did not eliminate the possibility that any foreign-born child of a U.S. citizen parent would be stateless, either at birth or at some point later in his life, does not render its chosen framework unconstitutional. No foreign-born person has a free-standing constitutional right to U.S. citizenship, and no U.S. citizen has a free-standing right to transmit his or her citizenship to a foreign-born child. Congress balances competing interests in enacting laws governing naturalization. The carefully measured rules Congress enacted serve the important governmental interest in ensuring that children born abroad have sufficient ties to this country to merit citizenship and the interest in reducing statelessness—and consequently do not violate equal protection.

Even if this Court were to determine that the differing physical-presence requirements in [the law] violated equal protection, petitioner is not entitled to the relief he seeks, namely a reversal of his criminal conviction based on a determination that he has been a citizen from birth. The fact that Congress chose to apply the more stringent physical-presence requirements in [the law] to a substantial majority of U.S. citizen parents of foreign-born children, the need to preserve necessary flexibility for Congress, as well as adherence to this Court's longstanding treatment of naturalization requirements lead to the conclusion that the proper way to cure any equal protection violation would be to apply the longer physical-presence requirements in [the law], on a prospective basis, to unwed citizen mothers. Petitioner's suggestions that the Court either extend the shorter physical-presence requirement in [the law] to unmarried fathers (but not to married parents of either gender) or retain the unequal treatment but reduce the length of the physical-presence requirement applicable to unmarried men make little sense and could foreclose future revision by Congress. Equalizing the treatment of all citizen parents of foreign-born children as suggested here would eliminate any equal protection problem and most faithfully preserve Congress's policy choices.

Argument

Petitioner Lacks Standing to Assert the Equal Protection Rights of his Father

Petitioner has not suffered any differential treatment by virtue of his own gender. Petitioner's equal protection complaint instead is that his father is treated less favorably than a U.S. citizen mother with respect to the ability to transmit U.S. citizenship to a child born abroad out of wedlock. That claim is properly raised by petitioner's father, who is the subject of the allegedly unconstitutional differential treatment.

This Court has held that a party ordinarily "cannot rest his claim to relief on the legal rights or interests of third parties." In such a case, a litigant may not assert the constitutional rights of an absent third party unless the litigant has a "close relation" to the party whose rights are asserted, and there is "some hindrance to the third party's ability to protect his or her own interests." Those restrictions "arise from the understanding that the third-party right holder may not, in fact, wish to assert the claim in question, as well as from the belief that 'third parties themselves usually will be the best proponents of their rights.'"

Although we may assume that petitioner has a close relationship with his father, petitioner cannot satisfy this Court's limits on *jus tertii* standing because, as the court of appeals found, "the record discloses no obstacle that would prevent [petitioner's father] from asserting his own constitutional rights." It is true that petitioner's father is not entitled to intervene in petitioner's criminal case in order to assert his equal protection challenge; but the inquiry is not whether a third party may assert his own rights in this particular case, but whether he may effectively assert them at all. Petitioner has not demonstrated any "daunting" or "considerable practical" barriers—or indeed, any barriers at all—to his father's protection of his own rights if he chose to do so.

Shortly after petitioner's birth in 1974, his father brought him to the United States to receive medical care. After his release from the hospital, petitioner lived with his father and paternal grandmother near San Diego. J.A. Although petitioner's father formally acknowledged his paternity in 1985 in Mexico, he took no steps to have petitioner declared a U.S. citizen. Petitioner's father did not, for example, apply for a certificate of citizenship on behalf of petitioner when petitioner was a minor. If that application was turned down, petitioner's father could have brought an action on petitioner's behalf challenging that denial under [the law], and raising the claim that his inability to transmit citizenship to petitioner violated his Fifth Amendment rights. Nor did petitioner's father ever apply to have petitioner naturalized when petitioner was a child (father initially filed suit with foreign-born child seeking such a declaration).

Petitioner offers no justification for his father's failure to assert his equal protection claim by bringing his own action. It is true that petitioner's father did not himself obtain a certificate of citizenship until 1999, when petitioner was already 24 years old. But petitioner's father was automatically a citizen at birth by virtue of his mother's citizenship, and his ignorance of that fact does not constitute the type of hindrance to assertion of his own rights that would confer on petitioner third-party standing to raise those rights.

Moreover, once petitioner became an adult, petitioner's father could have joined an equal protection claim a later suit by petitioner himself under [the law], following a denial of an application by petitioner for such a certificate (father asserted claim under the Fifth Amendment by participating in child's petition for judicial review of removal order). Petitioner is correct that a majority of the Court in *Miller* found that the petitioner in that case had third-party standing to assert her citizen father's equal protection rights. But that finding in *Miller* was based on the existence of an actual hindrance to the citizen father's demonstrated efforts to pursue his equal protection claim. In *Miller*, the petitioner and her father had together sought a declaration that the father's inability to transmit citizenship to his foreign born daughter violated the Fifth Amendment. At the government's urging, the district court had dismissed the petitioner's father from the suit and the father had failed to appeal that ruling. The Court concluded that, under those circumstances, the right-holder (the petitioner's father) faced a sufficient barrier to the actual assertion of his rights to confer third-party standing on his daughter.

That holding does not apply to petitioner in this case, however, because two crucial elements are missing: (1) unlike petitioner's father, the father in *Miller* had in fact taken steps to attempt to assert his equal protection rights; and (2) the father in *Miller* was prevented through dismissal from the suit from pursuing vindication of his rights, while no obstacle prevented petitioner's father from pursuing those rights in the proper manner. "Here, although we have an injured party before us, the party actually discriminated against is both best suited to challenging the statute and available to undertake that task." Petitioner has failed to demonstrate that his father is unable "to advance his own rights," because of a "genuine obstacle" that rises to the level of a hindrance.

NEAL KUMAR KATYAL served as Acting Solicitor General in the Obama administration at the time of this case. Katyal argues that Congress created legislation with a different standard of citizenship for biological fathers versus biological mothers and that this different standard served a rational interest and should be upheld.

Steven F. Hubachek et al.

 **NO**

On Writ of Certiorari: Brief for Petitioner

Petitioner, Ruben Flores-Villar, was born out of wedlock on October 7, 1974, in Tijuana, Mexico. His father, Ruben Trinidad Floresvillar, was then a 16-year-old U.S. citizen. Although he would have testified at trial that he resided in the United States for at least ten years before [his son's] birth, he was too young to have five years' presence after turning 14 as required for transmission of citizenship.

When two months old, [the] father and paternal grandmother brought him into the United States for medical treatment. Thereafter, the hospital sent, on Petitioner's father's behalf, a letter to border authorities requesting a permit for Petitioner to enter the United States. Petitioner's mother authorized his release from the hospital to his paternal grandmother for adoption planning. Although Petitioner was not adopted, his mother took no part in his upbringing.

Petitioner grew up in San Diego county with his father, attending local schools. Petitioner's father formally recognized him by filing a paternity acknowledgment in the Tijuana civil registry in 1985, when Petitioner was 11, and claimed Petitioner as his son on his United States income taxes.

In 2006, Petitioner was indicted for being a deported alien found in the United States, in violation of [U.S. law]. On September 22, 2006, Petitioner filed an application seeking a Certificate of Citizenship. Petitioner's father and paternal grandmother submitted supporting declarations. *Id.* 84-90. On December 14, 2006, his application was denied:

> The fact of your legitimation is not in question. . . .
> Since your father was only sixteen at the time of
> your birth, it is physically impossible for him to
> have [the] required physical presence necessary
> (five years after age fourteen) in order for you to
> acquire United States citizenship through him.

Petitioner nonetheless sought to defend by contending that he is a citizen. The government moved to preclude the defense. Petitioner responded that the statutory scheme in place at his birth violated the Fifth Amendment's equal protection guarantee. Petitioner sought a jury instruction applying the shorter physical presence requirement to his father. His father would have testified in Petitioner's defense, but the district court precluded the testimony. The district court found Petitioner guilty and sentenced him to 42 months' custody.

Since 1940, citizen fathers, but not citizen mothers, have been required to meet a lengthy residency requirement before transmitting citizenship to their foreign-born, non-marital children. The 1952 Act, effective at Petitioner's birth, perpetuated the discrimination, maintaining a physical presence requirement under which men below age 19 could not transmit citizenship. Age never prevented transmission of citizenship to a woman's non-marital child.

Because this statutory scheme discriminates against fathers of non-marital children based on gender, it denies equal protection. Intermediate scrutiny is warranted because of our Nation's history of sex discrimination in laws governing transmission of citizenship, and the significance of citizens' interest in transmitting citizenship to their children. The "plenary power" doctrine, which the Court has applied in the context of the entry of aliens into the United States, does not warrant some lesser standard of scrutiny, because acquisition of citizenship at birth is fundamentally different from the immigration or naturalization of an alien. Further, even if the plenary power doctrine applies, the classification of a congressional power as "plenary" does not exempt congressional action in that area from constitutional scrutiny.

Regardless, the discriminatory scheme at issue survives neither intermediate scrutiny nor rational basis review. While the government has consistently contended that Congress adopted the discriminatory, sex-based residence requirements to avoid statelessness of non-marital children of U.S. citizen mothers, it has not met its burden to demonstrate that avoiding statelessness was the actual purpose of the discriminatory residency requirements. Moreover, the risk of statelessness applies to the non-marital children of U.S. citizen mothers *and* fathers. The discriminatory scheme actually creates new risks of statelessness for non-marital children of U.S. fathers. Thus, the "statelessness" rationale cannot justify the discrimination under any standard.

Nguyen v. INS (2001) is not to the contrary. *Nguyen* approved distinctions that were biologically based: by delivering a child, a woman necessarily had strong evidence of parentage and at least an opportunity to form a relationship with the child. By requiring the father to take a formal act prior to the child's 18th birthday, the statutory scheme provided the evidence and opportunity that biology had guaranteed the mother. The residence requirements posed by the instant scheme have no biological basis: there is no reason to believe that mothers are more adept at forming ties to the United States than are fathers or that fathers' non-marital children experience statelessness in any different way.

The denial of equal protection effected by gender discrimination can and should be fully remedied by extension of the benefit offered by [the law]—the limited residence requirement—to both men and women. Extension of benefits is a traditional remedy for equal protection violations and is supported by the INA's severability provision.

Alternatively, severance of the application of former section 1401(g)'s requirement of 5 years' residence in the United States after age 14, which disables some younger men, but not younger women, from transmitting citizenship to their non-marital children, could partially remedy the discrimination against Petitioner's father such that Petitioner could at least offer evidence of his father's 10-year U.S. residence at trial. Even if the equal protection violation cannot be remedied by a grant of citizenship, the government nonetheless should be estopped from invoking that unconstitutional scheme to support a criminal conviction.

Finally, Petitioner meets the requirements of third-party standing to litigate the gender discrimination against his father in defending against this government-initiated prosecution.

The Statutory Scheme for Acquisition of Citizenship by Non-Marital, Foreign-Born Children Discriminates Based on Gender

Since 1940, citizen fathers, but not citizen mothers, have been required to meet a lengthy residency requirement before transmitting citizenship to their foreign-born, non-marital children. The 1940 Act required an unwed citizen father to demonstrate ten years' physical presence in the United States prior to the child's birth, five of which had to be after the age of sixteen. Fathers under age 21 could not transmit citizenship. Prior residence of any length was sufficient for women. The 1952 Act, in effect at Petitioner's birth, perpetuated the discrimination, maintaining the ten years' physical presence requirement, before the nonmarital child's birth, five of which had to be after age 14. Men under 19 were disabled from transmitting citizenship. For women, the law required only one year's residence prior to the non-marital child's birth. A woman's age never prevented transmission of citizenship to her non-marital child.

Petitioner was born out of wedlock, in Mexico, to a U.S. citizen father and an alien mother. Although his father legitimated and raised him in the United States from infancy, the district court precluded Petitioner's citizenship defense because his father's age at Petitioner's birth, 16, made it impossible to transmit citizenship. Because the statutory scheme discriminates against fathers of non-marital children by imposing a differential residence requirement based on gender, it denies equal protection.

The 1940 Act Allowed Women Freely to Transmit Citizenship to Non-Marital Children, but Created New Barriers to Transmission of Citizenship to Legitimated Children by Men

Explicitly addressing non-marital children for the first time, Congress adopted [the law], which provided that men could transmit citizenship after satisfying an age-calibrated, 10-year residence requirement and upon legitimation of the child during the child's minority. As to women, [the law] provided that, absent legitimation, her non-marital child would be a U.S. citizen if she "had the nationality of the United States at the time of the child's birth, and had previously resided in the United States or one of the outlying possessions." The framework established in the 1940 Act remains in place today, albeit with a less onerous residence requirement.

Commentary published before passage of the 1940 Act suggested the non-marital, foreign-born children of both men *and* women were at risk of statelessness. If Congress had sought to alleviate concerns that the non-marital children of female U.S. citizens would be stateless, it accomplished that by providing for U.S. nationality for the non-marital children of women subject to a modest pre-birth residence requirement, of any length, in the United States. Current law reduces the residence requirement applicable to men to 5 years and imposes a one-year requirement on women. The requirement of pre-birth residence vindicates a well-established Congressional goal of ensuring that citizenship not pass through generations of expatriate citizens living outside the United States for their entire lives.

But the 1940 Act's discriminatory residence requirements lead to very different results as to the children of U.S. citizen fathers, exposing many children of U.S. fathers to risks of statelessness and discouraging such fathers from legitimating their offspring. Congress would have been aware of a significant risk of statelessness on the part of the foreign-born, non-marital children of U.S. citizen fathers, as the Attorney General had suggested that such children were not citizens even when legitimated. "If, in these cases, the country of birth adhered strictly to the principle of *jus sanguinis* in determining nationality, these children had no effective citizenship, unless it was acquired through the mother."

In stark contrast to its solicitousness as to the children of U.S. citizen mothers, Congress's response to this grave risk was to limit severely the ability of fathers to transmit citizenship to non-marital children, requiring lengthy residence (10 years) in the United States for legitimated children and making no provision for non-legitimated children. The incongruity of this approach is illustrated by the study cited to Congress in support of the proposed legislation.

> [T]he Department of State has for a long time fol-lowed the rule that an illegitimate child follows the nationality of the mother, in the absence of legitimation according to law by the father. It is significant to observe that the same *lacuna* exists in the statutory law of about half the states studied.

"The majority rule with respect to legal recognition or legitimation is that the child takes the father's national-ity." Thus, as of 1940, many states attributed the mother's nationality to the non-marital child *unless* the father legit-imated the child. The legitimated, non-marital children of U.S. fathers therefore faced the prospect of being denied the nationalities of their mothers by virtue of legitimation, leaving them dependent upon their U.S. citizen fathers to provide nationality.

The State Department's witness at the hearings on the proposed code identified a number of countries in which legitimation deprived a child of her mother's national-ity. In Iraq, citizenship could not be acquired through the mother, although a child born in Iraq whose father was ordinarily resident in Iraq at the time of the child's birth could opt for Iraqi citizenship upon attaining his majority (provided the child had not already acquired the national-ity of a foreign country). In the Netherlands, a child could only acquire citizenship through the mother if "the child [was] born outside of wedlock [and] acknowledged only by the mother, provided that the mother, at the time of the birth, had the status of a Dutch national . . ." In other countries, such as Japan and Monaco, a child born out of wedlock would only obtain the mother's nationality if the mother acknowledged the child before the father (or in Japan, if the father was unknown or had no nationality). In Jordan, the risk of statelessness would exist regardless of legitimation because citizenship is derived only through the father.

The Congressional scheme, however, would often make it impossible for those fathers to fulfill that need.

By requiring 10 years of residence, Congress cre-ated a serious risk that non-marital, legitimated children of U.S. citizen fathers would be rendered stateless unless the father met a stringent residence requirement that no mother of a non-marital child was obliged to satisfy. More-over, Congress made it impossible, not merely difficult, for a non-marital, legitimated child born to a U.S. citizen father under age 21 to claim U.S. citizenship as of birth because at least 5 of the 10 years' residence in the United States must take place after age 16.

Indeed, a U.S. citizen father who could not meet the residence requirements would be forced to consider care-fully whether legitimation was in his child's interest, inas-much as formal legitimation—even marriage to the child's mother—might result in statelessness, because a claim to the mother's nationality could be extinguished while at the same time no claim to U.S. citizenship would be pos-sible. Children who were not legitimated, of course, would be able to claim the mother's nationality in approximately half the states that Sandifer surveyed. Thus, Congress both visited statelessness upon many legitimated children of U.S. citizen fathers and perversely gave U.S. citizens who fathered non-marital children strong incentives not to legitimate their children.

The government conceded that rules denying citi-zenship to many legitimated, non-marital children of U.S. citizen fathers create a grave risk of statelessness, acknowl-edging that, under the 1940 scheme, "[t]here would be a parallel problem of statelessness in the case of children who lost their mother's foreign citizenship due to legiti-mation by their United States citizen father." Indeed, the government conceded that the risk of statelessness per-sists today, acknowledging in 2000 that "it remains the case that children born out of wedlock generally are rec-ognized to have the citizenship of the mother *unless and until* legitimated or formally acknowledged by the father." Thus, even today, U.S. citizen fathers who responsibly fulfill their obligations to their non-marital children run the risk of rendering those children stateless if the father cannot meet a residence requirement that is not imposed upon mothers of non-marital children.

Even if statelessness concerns prompted differential residence requirements, concerns that the children of U.S. mothers might be stateless in no way justifies disabling a class of U.S. fathers—those under 21 under the 1940 Act and those under 19 under the 1952 Act—from transmit-ting citizenship to their legitimated children. No class of U.S. citizen mothers is so disabled from ensuring that her non-marital child has a nationality.

Thus, Congress in 1940 was faced with challenges to practices under which both the non-marital, foreign-born children of women and legitimated children of men had claims to U.S. citizenship. Congress codified the practice as to women bearing non-marital children, but adopted a discriminatory scheme that offered narrow protection to fathers. It exposed citizen-fathers' non-marital chil-dren to risks of statelessness if the fathers were younger, or could not meet a 10-year residence requirement, or had not legitimated their children. The 1940 Act therefore tol-erated substantial risks of statelessness as to non-marital children of men.

Steven F. Hubachek is the Counsel of Record for the Fed-eral Defenders of San Diego, Inc. Hubachek argues that this law discriminates against men as it makes it more dif-ficult for immigrant fathers to pass on their citizenship to their children than for immigrant mothers.

EXPLORING THE ISSUE

Should Courts Be Able to Discriminate Against Immigrant Fathers?

Critical Thinking and Reflection

1. What are some arguments made by each side with which you agree or disagree?
2. What are the strengths and weaknesses of the two positions made in this issue?
3. This issue focuses on what is legal. In some cases, a person's morals may be in contradiction to the law. How do legal rights in this case relate to what you feel is morally right or morally wrong?
4. Think more broadly about the role of immigration, both legal and illegal, in the United States today. Considering the ruling in this case, what remedies would be best for the creation of a policy for citizenship for immigrants' children that is in the best interest of the United States?

Is There Common Ground?

The vast majority of people would agree that children of U.S. citizens should themselves be citizens. Conversely, the vast majority would agree that the United States has a right and an obligation to create a system of immigration that is best for the nation's long-term goals. The challenges arise in determining how to balance these competing values and interests. In order to meet this challenge, the following questions must be addressed: What are the rights of naturalized immigrant fathers? What are the rights of naturalized immigrant mothers? What is necessary to ensure the best interest of the United States?

Create Central

www.mhhe.com/createcentral

Additional Resources

The American Civil Liberties Union on immigrant rights:

www.aclu.org/immigrants-rights

Taking action on immigration reform through Change.org:

http://immigration.change.org/

National Network for Immigration and Refugee Rights:

www.nnirr.org/

End Illegal Immigration works to stop undocumented immigration:

www.endillegalimmigration.com/

Conservative USA calls to stop illegal immigration immediately:

www.conservativeusa.org/immigration.htm

Internet References . . .

Family Legal Help: Fathers' Rights Philadelphia

http://familylegalhelp.org/unbundled-fathers-rights/city/philadelphia/?app_t=%2Bfather's%20%2Brights&gclid=CKqv1uubkLsCFYNxOgodQHYAAQ

Fathers' Rights Foundation

www.fathers-rights.com/

Fathers' Rights Advocate

http://dadsrights.com/

Selected, Edited, and with Issue Framing Material by:
David M. Hall, Ph.D., *Delaware Valley College*

ISSUE

Do Parents Have the Right to Deny Their Children Lifesaving Medical Care Due to Their Religious Convictions?

YES: Calvin P. Johnson, from "Closing Statement for Parents: In Re the Matter of the Welfare of the Child of Colleen and Anthony Hauser," Minnesota, District Court, Fifth Judicial District (2009)

NO: John R. Rodenberg, from "Opinion of the Court: In the Matter of the Welfare of the Child of Colleen and Anthony Hauser," Minnesota, District Court, Fifth Judicial District (2009)

Learning Outcomes

After reading this issue, you will be able to:

- Identify the major arguments made for and against parents denying their child lifesaving medical treatment.
- Compare and contrast the competing arguments made for and against parents denying their child lifesaving medical treatment in this issue.
- Evaluate the implications of parents denying their child life saving medical treatment on children's health as well as religious liberty.

ISSUE SUMMARY

YES: Calvin P. Johnson, Esq., is the attorney for the parents, Colleen and Anthony Hauser. Johnson argues that the government forcing medical care for the Hauser child violates his religious liberty and is abusive to this child.

NO: John R. Rodenberg is the District Court judge in this case. Rodenberg argues that all parties are acting out of convictions for the best interest of the child. He also argues that the state has a compelling interest to act against Hauser's religious views for medical care since the child is only thirteen years old.

The use of chemotherapy as a cancer treatment dates back to the early twentieth century. It was designed as the use of chemicals to treat disease. In 1935, the National Cancer Institute was set up and provided an organized system for screening drugs that treated cancer. However, the level of toxicity of the drugs proved to be a challenge for wider use of this treatment.

During World War II, it was noted that when troops were exposed to sulfur mustards due to an accidental spill, more purposeful research occurred to better understand the impact of these chemicals on things like cancer.

While initially highly controversial, attempts to treat cancer with chemotherapy would enjoy wide levels of support over the coming decades. Within the past couple of decades, it has become a highly regarded method for treating cancer.

Christian Scientists have received a considerable amount of attention for refusing medical care for themselves and their children, sometimes for even life-threatening illnesses such as cancer. Generally speaking, many Christian scientists are expected to heal themselves through prayer of minor sicknesses such as the cold and flu as well as life-threatening conditions such as cancer. However, if a child dies as a result of his or her parents denying their child life saving medical care, then the parents are sometimes charged and prosecuted.

Although Christian Scientists receive perhaps the highest profile for this belief, they are by no means the only religion that subscribes to such a belief. The Nemenhah and Indigenous Traditional Organization, also known as the Oklevueha Native American church of Nemenhah, was established by self-determination in 2002. They describe themselves as a "restoration of the Pre-Colonial and Pre-Conquest Nomadic Indigenous People which inhabited parts of Central America, North America, the Pacific Islands, Japan, Korea, China, and Tibet anciently." Their Web site states that they focus on "the Healing of the Body Physical, the Body Familial, the Body Societal and the Whole Earth." The Nemenhah are committed to natural healing.

The Nemenhah Constitution states the following:

- We believe in miracles, such as cures, healings, prophecies, visions . . . and that it is the right of all people to heal and be healed without restriction from any earthly government, for natural medicine and natural modalities of healing are gifts of the Creator.
- The Sacred Sahaptan Healing Way is that body of knowledge which is compiled into a uniform curriculum for the systematic training and education of the Medicine Men and Medicine Women of the Band. It is the criteria by which Band Adoption is entered into and the basis and foundation of this spiritual and physical ceremonies.
- Article Fifteen: The right of community members to choose their method and kind of medicine shall not be denied or abridged in any way and the councils shall not enact any counsel that shall place one profession or modality of medicine over any other, except when such professions or modalities tend to render a person unable to earn a living, or when they threaten to do so.

Clearly, this religion possesses the basic tenet that they have their own rights to determine the best course for healing when sick. That course includes a denial of intervention for modern Western remedies.

The First Amendment to the U.S. Constitution says, "Congress shall make no law respecting an establishment of religion, or prohibiting the free exercise thereof." The First Amendment provides us with this right, known as the Free Exercise Clause, as one that is so important that it is often referred to as a fundamental right.

What sort of limitations do we place on fundamental rights? Should we allow human sacrifice? Use of drugs? Wearing a weapon such as a knife, which also has strong religious significance in some cultures, in schools? Opting out of a class at school because a child feels that it violates his or her religious convictions?

In short, we are attempting to determine when there is a compelling state interest to intervene. In the case of the Hausers, which is explored in this chapter, the question is how do we protect a child with cancer. The Hausers argued in court that they should be free to intervene as

they wish with their son's cancer. Their son had Hodgkin's lymphoma. His story would generate national headlines.

Doctors argued that with proper medical treatment, Daniel had a 90% chance of survival. Without the treatment, he would have only a 5% chance of survival. The Hausers, who belong to the Nemenhah faith, believe that their son is a medicine man and can best determine his path in healing his body and spirit.

The judge ruled that Daniel had to get chemotherapy. As a result, Daniel's mother took him and fled.

Jeffrey Toobin, CNN senior legal analyst, says that the state must intervene: "Virtually all the time the court says that what this mother is doing, while we sympathize with her pain, this is child abuse. He is a minor. He is not qualified to make the decision for himself. This is what it means to be a minor: other people make your decisions for you. This is the same thing as if he got hit by a car, blocking the ambulance. If need be, they have to take the kid away, strap him down, and apply chemotherapy. . . . It's life or death."

After Daniel and his mother fled, Daniel was eventually returned after almost one week on the run. The parents consented to have their son undergo his chemotherapy treatment.

The doctors treating Daniel received mail from all over the country, ranging from those who believe in natural medicine to anti-abortion activists to conspiracy theorists. One opponent of the medical intervention created a Web site of a needle being injected into a monkey and said that doctors were "dripping poison into yet another child."

Daniel did not have a positive reaction to the chemotherapy, explained a family spokesman: "Danny has had a horrible day, he's felt terrible all day long. He's not happy. The doctor changed the number of chemotherapy drugs in the protocol submitted to the court. Danny is not tolerating the drugs well and has been vomiting all day. He is understandably angry and depressed about being forced to go through the ravages of chemotherapy again."

Daniel Hauser's lymphoma went into remission after his radiation treatment. Although his doctors credit the radiation, the Hausers credit Daniel's good diet.

In this issue, you have excerpts from the primary sources from the court case, representing both sides. You can determine the reasoning of the Hausers, as well as the court, in informing your decision.

YES

Calvin P. Johnson

Closing Statement for Parents: In Re the Matter of the Welfare of the Child of Colleen and Anthony Hauser

Respondents, Colleen and Anthony Hauser, submit this legal memorandum in support of their closing arguments in this matter.

Thank you to all, with your words of encouragement. And thank you to those on the other side, for genuinely believing in their position.

Most importantly, I thank Danny Hauser, a true Medicine man. This thirteen-year-old young man has turned this community upside down and inside out. A world is listening.

I respectfully submit that he is one of the more powerful medicine men around.

Danny is a Medicine man by virtue of his ranking as a male in the family. That is contained in the Nemenhah Constitution that you could not understand. It is written in clear language.

This Court has always held, from day one, to the steadfast principle of protecting our children. We do not harm our children. We do not torture our children.

Yet the path advocated by the State is one of torture and criminal action.

There is a reason why 91% of the oncologists on staff at McGill Cancer Centre in Montreal do not take chemotherapy or allow their family members to take it for cancer treatment. It's too toxic, and not effective. This is exactly as the standard of medical care advocated and pronounced by Dr. Shealy.

This matter has been pummeled to death with the percentage of a 90% cure rate. And yet we come to find that a cure rate can be defined as "tumor shrinkage" but not the elimination of cancer, at all. In fact, given the statistics as provided to this Court, and demonstrated by a reputable, peer-reviewed, journal (*Clinical Oncology*, 2004; 16:549–560.), the real rate of survival hovers around 35–40%.

Apparently, if a study predicts a 6% success rate, and they achieve 12%, the cancer industry reports that as a 50% increase in their success rates. It is unconscionable that the absolute numbers were not given to the Hausers in this particular matter. It is unconscionable that the cancer industry would perpetrate a number that does not stand up to actual fact. And it is unconscionable that we

had to enter into an emotional issue when the true issue is the care of a thirteen-year-old young man, and the ability of that young man and his parents to realistically assess their best survival rates from reputable, peer-reviewed medical journals, before making their decision.

To condense the posture of this case, it looks like this:

A doctor went to a state official and said we have a 90% chance that this young man is going to die if he does not use my product.

By legal definition, if you use the product, it constitutes felony assault, and may very well constitute torture, when you force the use of the product against the will of the victim.

It will seriously damage the largest component of this young man's body: his immune system.

It may kill him.

Without question, it will cause serious disfigurement, including the fact that there will probably be no progeny of this thirteen-year-old young man.

It will cost $92,900 just for the first round of chemotherapeutic agents and initial testing, and we will apply it five to six more times.

We cannot tell you the manner in which we can do this against the will of the child.

When we promise a 90% cure rate, that really only amounts to 40.3%, as measured by the best statistics available from our very own peer-reviewed medical journals.

We will not rebut a very prominent surgeon's opinion that chemotherapy constitutes torture.

We will make this application five or six more times, over the course of six months.

If the young man is still alive after that time, we will apply radiation to him.

We will do this against his religious beliefs, and we will try to convince the Court that his religion is not his.

Further, we will make sure that you cannot consider any other modes or options for health treatment, because they are not approved by a "standard of care" that does nothing to address this soul's individual consciousness.

If I brought a client in front of this Court and asked for permission to do this, you would look at me and ask that I be locked up, not just my client. If we would make a proposal to exercise torture on any of the detainees at

United States District Court, Minnesota, Fifth Judicial District, 2009.

Guantanamo, in the same measure as advocated by the doctors in this case, our country's reputation would be in a shambles. It is too easy to fall prey to that 90% number. This is a real case, involving real issues, and involving freedom of consciousness.

The Hausers . . . have integrated a process of pH-balanced therapy that is and has been accepted in much of the world. This water machine that Danny told the Court (Kangen water) is found in practically every major hospital in Japan.

We have long known the history of the pH balance. After World War II, the only survivors of Hiroshima and Nagasaki were the Japanese monks who focused on a diet of miso soup and short-grained brown rice, a pH-balanced diet. They lived. The others died horrible deaths.

It is entirely fitting that Japan would be a leader in this "standard of care." It would be a shame to preclude a modality of healing for a thirteen-year-old because we determined it is more fitting to torture and to assault the juvenile, with poisons he does not want.

The point is simple: the Hausers have elected forms of alternative healthcare that they believe to be more effective and more beneficial than those recommended by the cancer industry.

This trial is the act of two loving parents who will go to any length to save their child from assault and torture.

This Court has a long and strong history of protecting children. Now is the time to do so, according to the dictates of Danny and his family's consciousness and spiritual being. The fact remains, that there are an abundance of scientifically proven, medical therapies available for Danny. If this Court wants to intervene, consistent with their conscious and religious beliefs, It must follow the reasonable path of healing as articulated by our evidence.

The Guardian Ad Litem takes no consideration of the spiritual path chosen by the parties. Nor does she give any power of the parents to help with the spiritual education of their son.

What is without question is the verification of Danny's status as a member of the Nemenhah band. This has not been refuted.

What is without question is that we, even the Guardian Ad Litem, must allow Danny's conscience to worship God as he sees fit. His conscience shall not be infringed. She cannot infringe upon it now. Nor shall she control or interfere with his right of conscience. Nor can the State. The State is attempting to do so, by their act.

We qualify our "liberty of conscience" in that we cannot exercise acts of licentiousness or justify practices inconsistent with the peace or safety of the State. We do not assault our children. We do not torture the juveniles of this state. We are a bright and shining beacon for freedom and justice for the rest of the world.

We come to understand that healing is more than just a physical act of the administration of drugs or chemicals. It begins at the deep level of Soul, and continues through the mind, emotional and physicals bodies.

The confidence of healing is of paramount concern. Danny holds this confidence, and is self-sufficient in his understanding of healing. He is self-actualized, and not in that group of 99.2% of those people who will die in the next fifteen years, from their beliefs.

What has happened is, by his very acts and deeds, Danny has become a torch bearer of an important message: the people of this state have the right to chose their own reasonable medical modality. We have the ability to go beyond those standards established by the courts, and the medical "religion," and to go beyond the "standard of care" advocated and compelled upon all doctors in this state.

We heard the testimony of Dr. Bostrom, who indicated that Danny could be part of a study.

It is entirely reasonable for parents to reject experimentation upon their son, especially when his life is on the line.

It is ironic that the parents have to fight for their right not to have radiation on Danny, and yet, by the flip of a coin, if Danny is selected in one of the factions of the study group, he won't get radiation.

Finally, before you get to the heart of my legal argument, I would ask the court to consider the definition of a medicine man. Again, like all these computer people, I go to Wikipedia for a first review.

Medicine man, Role in Native Society:

"The primary function of these 'medicine elders' is to secure the health of the spiritual world, including the Great Spirit, for the benefit of the entire community. Sometimes the help sought may be for the sake of healing disease, sometimes it may be for the sake of healing the psyche, sometimes the goal is to promote harmony between human groups or between humans and nature."

I realize that Ms. Oliver doesn't know what a Medicine man looks like. In seeing and understanding the changes brought about by this thirteen-year-old young man, we are coming to understand what a Medicine man does.

We are moving into a new arena of consciousness. We are rejecting a modality of treatment that is assaultive and torturous. We are relying upon our bodies to do what the good Lord intended: to heal.

Legal Argument as Applied from the Facts

The Guardian Ad Litem's Testimony Constitutes an Impermissible Imposition of a Religious Test

Religious freedoms are constitutionally protected by both the United States Bill of Rights, as well as by our Minnesota Constitution. Specifically, these documents state:

U.S. Bill of Rights: Amendment I

Congress shall make no law respecting an establishment of religion, or prohibiting the free exercise thereof; or abridging the freedom of speech, or of the press; or the right of the people peaceably to assemble, and to petition the Government for a redress of grievances.

Minnesota State Constitution: Article I, Bill of Rights

Sec. 16. Freedom of conscience; no preference to be given to any religious establishment or mode of worship. The enumeration of rights in this constitution shall not deny or impair others retained by and inherent in the people. The right of every man to worship God according to the dictates of his own conscience shall never be infringed; nor shall any man be compelled to attend, erect or support any place of worship, or to maintain any religious or ecclesiastical ministry, against his consent; nor shall any control of or interference with the rights of conscience be permitted, or any preference be given by law to any religious establishment or mode of worship; but the liberty of conscience hereby secured shall not be so construed as to excuse acts of licentiousness or justify practices inconsistent with the peace or safety of the state, nor shall any money be drawn from the treasury for the benefit of any religious societies or religious or theological seminaries.

    Sec. 17. Religious tests and property qualifications prohibited. No religious test or amount of property shall be required as a qualification for any office of public trust in the state. No religious test or amount of property shall be required as a qualification of any voter at any election in this state; nor shall any person be rendered incompetent to give evidence in any court of law or equity in consequence of his opinion upon the subject of religion.

"Religious liberty is a precious right," *State v. Hershberger* (Minn. 1990). The people of this state have always cherished religious liberty, and the high importance of protecting this right is demonstrated by its treatment in our constitution, where it appears even before any reference to the formation of a government. *State by Cooper v. French* (Minn. 1990). The Minnesota Supreme Court has consistently held that article I, section 16 of the Minnesota Constitution affords greater protection against governmental action affecting religious liberties than the First Amendment of the federal constitution. "Whereas the first amendment establishes a limit on government action at the point of *prohibiting* the exercise of religion, section 16 precludes even an *infringement* on or an *interference* with religious freedom," *Hershberger*. Thus, government action that is permissible under the federal constitution because it does not prohibit religious practices but merely infringes on or interferes with religious practices may nonetheless violate the Minnesota Constitution.

Minnesota courts employ a heightened "compelling state interest balancing test" when determining whether a challenged law infringes on or interferes with religious practices. The test has four prongs: (1) whether the objector's beliefs are sincerely held; (2) whether the state regulation burdens the exercise of religious beliefs; (3) whether the state interest in the regulation is overriding or compelling; and (4) whether the state regulation uses the least restrictive means.

As the Court will recall, the Guardian Ad Litem had stipulated to the genuineness of both the parents' and Daniel's religious beliefs. However, during trial, the Guardian Ad Litem broke her word when said she was now challenging the agreed-upon Pre-Trial Stipulation. Mr. and Mrs. Hauser have been prejudiced, because they were not adequately informed that this would be an issue for trial. In fact, they were told the opposite.

As argued in Respondents' previous Memorandum, parents have a significant interest in establishing a spiritual path for their child. The State may not come in and qualify that path. To do so violates State and Federal Constitutional Protections.

The qualification by the Guardian Ad Litem is limited in this situation. While she indicated that she read the Constitution of the Nemenhah Spiritual Path, she testified that she did not understand it. She further testified that she did not see any of the principals embodied in the way of life of the Hausers. She could not tell the Court why Danny is a medicine man.

On the contrary, the Hausers have demonstrated an ability to walk their path in all aspects of their lives. They will do no harm. They eat food from the land, not polluted by pesticides and herbicides. They use oils, herbs, and other remedies to promote and maintain healthy bodies. They act as a harmonious family together.

In the present case, Danny's Guardian Ad Litem has attempted to qualify his membership and beliefs in the Nemenhah spiritual path. Her doing so constitutes an impermissible religious test, in violation of both the Federal and Minnesota Constitutions. There is no evidence contradicting Danny's beliefs in the Nemenhah faith or its spiritual path, or that these beliefs are anything but sincere. Certainly, the interference that is being advocated in this case, that of forcing Danny to undergo chemotherapy when such treatment is in direct violation of these religious beliefs burdens Danny's exercise of his religious beliefs. The state has failed to demonstrate a compelling interest in this matter that would justify imposition of the propounded medical treatment in violation of Danny's religious beliefs.

CALVIN P. JOHNSON, ESQ., of the Calvin P. Johnson Law Firm, is the attorney for the parents, Colleen and Anthony Hauser. Johnson argues that the government forcing medical care for Hauser violates his religious liberty and is abusive to this child.

John R. Rodenberg

 **NO**

Opinion of the Court: In the Matter of the Welfare of the Child of Colleen and Anthony Hauser

The Court is today determining that the Petition alleging Daniel Hauser to be a child in need of protection or services has been proven by clear and convincing evidence. The Court is also concluding that the State of Minnesota, through Brown County Family Services ("BCFS"), has demonstrated a compelling state interest in the life and welfare of Daniel sufficient to override the fundamental constitutional rights of both the parents and Daniel to the free exercise of religion and the due process right of the parents to direct the religious and other upbringing of their child.

This much is certain and the Court so finds: All of the actions of the parties which bring this matter before the Court have been done in good faith. The parents, Daniel, the treating doctors, the child welfare agency, the Brown County Attorney and the Guardian ad Litem have at all times acted in good faith herein.

. . .

Daniel Hauser is currently 13 years of age. He has been diagnosed as suffering from nodular sclerosing Hodgkin's disease, stage IIB. The Hauser family's local family practice doctor, Dr. Joyce, correctly identified on January 21, 2009 that "lymphoma certainly seems likely" when Daniel presented with a persistent cough, fatigue, swollen lymph nodes and other symptoms. Dr. Joyce made a referral to oncology specialists at Children's Hospitals. The diagnosis was made there and it was determined that the cancer was readily treatable by therapies including chemotherapy.

Daniel's mother consented to the administration of the recommended chemotherapy beginning on February 5, 2009. The gravity and imminence of Daniel's situation limited the available options. Mrs. Hauser effectively consented to the initiation of chemotherapy after being adequately informed of her rights as Daniel's parent.

Daniel's lymphoma responded well to the initial round of chemotherapy.

Unfortunately Daniel also had adverse side effects to the administration of chemotherapy. While this was not unusual, both Daniel and his parents were justifiably quite concerned. The parents, acting in absolute parental good faith, chose to seek out a second opinion and consulted with Mayo Clinic. Mayo Clinic doctors concurred with the earlier medical advice. The parents, again in complete good faith, sought a third medical opinion, this time from the University of Minnesota Hospitals. Again, the recommendation was that the additional course of chemotherapy should be undertaken.

The doctors at these facilities, which are among the finest available in this part of the country, agree that Daniel has a very good chance of a complete recovery with additional chemotherapy and possibly radiation. Estimates of complete 5-year remission with this course range from 80% to 95%. These doctors are also in agreement that Daniel has very little chance of surviving 5 years without the prescribed course of treatment. If the mediastinal tumor were to increase in size and become resistant to chemotherapy, as all of these doctors opine that it will without the prescribed treatment, the long-term prospects for Daniel decrease significantly, even if the chemotherapy is resumed in the future.

The family has also consulted with Dr. Kotulski, an osteopathic physician practicing in Mankato, Minnesota. Dr. Kotulski agrees with the recommended chemotherapy. The Hauser family's local doctor, Dr. Joyce, also agrees with the recommendations of the oncologists.

In short, five (5) different medical doctors, three (3) of whom specialize in pediatric oncology, have all agreed upon the necessary medical care for Daniel.

There were several experts testifying at trial who believe in alternatives to chemotherapy for treatment of some cancers in some instances. However, there was absolutely no evidence presented at trial from any health care practitioner who has examined Daniel and who recommends any course of treatment different than that prescribed by the oncologists and medical doctors. The evidence is uncontroverted that Hodgkin's lymphoma, stage IIB, is best treated by chemotherapy and possible later radiation.

The family has a genuine and strong belief in the benefits of holistic medicine and, specifically, in Nemenhah. Nemenhah is based upon Native American healing practices. Daniel is deemed to be a "medicine man" by Nemenhah and does not wish to receive any additional chemotherapy.

United States District Court, Minnesota, Fifth Judicial District, 2009.

Daniel Hauser is an extremely polite and pleasant young man. While he is 13 years of age, Daniel is unable to read. He does not know what the term "elder" means, although he claims to be one. He knows he is a medicine man under Nemenhah teachings, but is unable to identify how he became a medicine man or what teachings he has had to master to become one. He believes in the principle of "do no harm" and attributes his belief to Nemenhah teachings. He lacks the ability to give informed consent to medical procedures.

The doctors who have filed reports with Brown County concerning Daniel and who testified in this case have acted in conformity with their duties under well-established Minnesota statutory law. Brown County has properly brought this matter before the Court for determination and has filed a Petition with the Court as it is authorized to do by [law]. The parents and Daniel have properly asserted their positions in the matter in a very orderly and respectful fashion, with the capable assistance of counsel. The Guardian ad Litem, whose role it is to advocate for the best interests of a child claimed to be in need of protection or services, has carefully considered the matter and has expressed her opinions as to the child's best interests consistent with her obligation to the Court.

There are sharp differences in the positions of the parties.

The Hauser family members have a constitutional right to freedom of belief. The parents also have a right to parent their child that is based in the Due Process Clause of the United States Constitution. These constitutional freedoms can be overcome only upon a showing of a compelling state interest.

Correspondingly, there can scarcely be imagined a governmental interest more compelling than protecting the life of a child.

Minnesota has a long-standing statutory requirement that parents must provide "necessary medical care" for a child and providing that "complementary and alternative health care" is not sufficient. Multiple Minnesota statutes so provide. The legislature has also mandated by statute that both medical providers and "complementary and alternative practitioners" must report to child welfare authorities any situation in which a child is not being provided with "necessary medical care."

As applied to this case, Minnesota's statutory provisions have an effect upon the religious practices of the Hauser family. The mother asserts that a core tenet of Nemenhah is "first do no harm." The mother asserts that God intends that the body should be healed the natural way and that chemotherapy and radiation are poisons. Daniel also professes to the primacy of the "do no harm" tenet.

Under the relevant authorities and as applied to the facts in this case, Brown County has demonstrated a compelling state interest in seeing to it that Daniel's prospects for life are maximized by his being found in need to protection or services. The parents are free to provide Daniel with complementary or alternative therapies, but under Minnesota law, as applied here consistent with both federal and state constitutions, the parents must provide "necessary medical care" to Daniel.

As set forth below, the Court is intending to leave Daniel in the custody of his parents and to allow the parents the maximum legally-permissible range of choices for treatment of Daniel. Daniel loves his parents and they love him. He should remain with them as long as he receives treatment complying with the minimum standards of parental care provided by Minnesota law.

The issue in this case is not whether the State of Minnesota should have enacted the law as it did. The Court is obligated to apply the law as it is written unless to do so would violate a constitutional right. Settled state and federal case law establish that the State of Minnesota may constitutionally intervene in the present matter.

Surely many will think that the law should be different. With issues as sensitive as these, there are bound to be strong feelings both ways about what the law should be. To the extent that the parties involved in this case and members of the public in general believe that [the Minnesota law] or any other statute should be revisited, those arguments are properly made to the Minnesota Legislature. The Court is resolving this matter solely with reference to the relevant legal authorities, and not based upon the Court's personal opinion with regard to what Minnesota substantive law should be. The only personal observation the Court makes is this: If the Minnesota Legislature ever reconsiders the relevant statutes, I am confident that I join all of the others involved in this matter in hoping, and indeed in praying, that Daniel Hauser lives to testify at that hearing.

. . .

Conclusions of Law

- Daniel Hauser is a child in need of protection or services within the meaning of [Minnesota law].
- The parents and Daniel have made their arguments with respect to the free exercise clause of the First Amendment to the United States Constitution. "Congress shall make no law respecting an establishment of religion, or prohibiting the free exercise thereof; or abridging the freedom of speech, or of the press; or the right of the people peaceably to assemble, and to petition the Government for a redress of grievances." The Minnesota Constitution also contains a provision relating to religious liberty. "The right of every man to worship God according to the dictates of his own conscience shall never be infringed . . . nor shall any control of or interference with the rights of conscience be permitted. . . ." This provision of the Minnesota Constitution affords greater protection for religious liberties against governmental action than the first amendment of the federal constitution. The Court is analyzing the free exercise claim under both provisions. In that that state

constitution affords greater protection to the free exercise of religion and imposes a higher standard in order to justify any state action the impinges upon the free exercise of religion and conscience, it follows that if Brown County is able to satisfy the requirements of the Minnesota Constitution in this matter, then it will also have satisfied the requirements of the federal constitution.

. . .

- The State of Minnesota has legislatively determined that ensuring that children receive necessary medical care is very important state interest. This state interest is also reflected in the requirement imposed upon both medical doctors and practitioners of complimentary or alternative therapies to report to child welfare agencies any failure to provide "necessary medical care."

- The law does not condone the injury of children, nor will it accommodate danger for children. The welfare of children is a matter of paramount concern. The power of the courts to protect children is now exercised by the state as an attribute of its sovereignty. The state as *parens patriae* has authority to assume parental authority over a child who because of misfortune or helplessness is unable to properly care for himself.

- *Wisconsin v. Yoder* (1972) involved Amish parents who refused to send their children to school past the 8th grade. The Amish claimed that the compulsory attendance statute encroached on their rights and the rights of their children to the free exercise of the religious beliefs they and their forbears had adhered to for almost three centuries. The U.S. Supreme Court wrote that: "In evaluating those claims we must be careful to determine whether the Amish religious faith and their mode of life are, as they claim, inseparable and interdependent. A way of life, however virtuous and admirable, may not be interposed as a barrier to reasonable state regulation of education if it is based on purely secular considerations; to have the protection of the Religion Clauses, the claims must be rooted in religious belief." Wisconsin argued that its interest in its system of compulsory education was compelling, such that even the established religious practices of the Amish needed to give way. Wisconsin argued that its system of compulsory education prepared children to participate in our political system so as to preserve freedom and independence and also that education prepares individuals to be self-reliant and self-sufficient participants in society. The U.S. Supreme Court accepted those propositions but determined that the State had not made a sufficient showing to justify the severe interference with religious freedom entailed by compulsory education, in light of evidence that the Amish were a successful, though nonconventional, society in America. Wisconsin also asserted a *parens patriae* interest in the well-being and educational opportunities of Amish children. The Supreme Court wrote that: "if the State

is empowered, as *parens patriae* to 'save' a child from himself or his Amish parents by requiring an additional two years of compulsory formal high school education, the State will in large measure influence, if not determine, the religious future of the child. When the interests of parenthood are combined with a free exercise claim of the nature revealed by this record, more than merely a 'reasonable relation to some purpose within the competency of the State' is required to sustain the validity of the State's requirement under the First Amendment. To be sure, the power of the parent, even when linked to a free exercise claim, may be subject to limitation . . . if it appears that parental decisions will jeopardize the health or safety of the children, or have a potential for significant social burdens." (bolding added). The Supreme Court determined that "the record strongly indicated that accommodating the religious objections of the Amish by forgoing one, or at most two, additional years of compulsory education will not impair the physical or mental health of the child. . . ."

- Minnesota courts have enunciated and applied a balancing test, balancing the state's interest in cases such as this against the actor's free-exercise interest in religious-based conduct. Where it is undisputed that the religious belief is sincerely held and that the religious belief would be burdened by the proposed regulation, the balancing test requires proof of a compelling state interest. Minnesota has a compelling interest in protecting the welfare of children. A parent may exercise genuinely held religious beliefs; but the resulting conduct, though motivated by religious belief, must yield when—judged by accepted medical practice—it jeopardizes the life of a child. Religious practices must bend to the state's interest in protecting the welfare of a child whenever the child might die without the intervention of conventional medicine. This is settled Minnesota law.

- In *Hofbauer v. Saratoga County Department of Social Services* (N.Y. App. 1979), a case similar to this matter, a county filed a petition to have an eight-year-old child, who was suffering from Hodgkin's Disease, adjudged to be a child neglected by his parents. The parents were not following the treating physician's recommendations for radiation and chemotherapy, but instead entrusted the child to the care of a duly licensed physician advocating nutritional or metabolic therapies, including laetrile injections. The New York appellate court held that the decision as to whether the parents were providing adequate medical care must be "whether the parents, once having sought accredited medical assistance and having been made aware of the seriousness of their child's affliction and the possibility of cure if a certain mode of treatment is undertaken, have provided for their child a treatment which is recommended by their physician and which has not been totally rejected by all responsible medical authority."

- The present situation is *unlike* that in the Hoffbauer case. There, a medical authority was monitoring the treatment. If there were to be a medically approved way to treat Daniel's Hodgkin's lymphoma different than what the five different medical/osteopathic doctors have thus far opined, then the parents here would be free to pursue such an option under the statute. Where there is unanimity of medical opinion and where the matter is an important one of life and death, the State has a compelling State interest sufficient to overcome the parents' Free Exercise and Due Process rights.

- The Court's resolution of the issue presented is limited to the specific factual situation present. What is not before the Court in this matter is the issue of whether there would ever be the case of an older or particularly mature minor who expresses a position opposed to medical treatment and who might therefore have a constitutional right to direct his or her own treatment contrary to what is "medically necessary." This matter, as more fully described above, involves a 13-year-old child who has only a rudimentary understanding at best of the risks and benefits of chemotherapy. He genuinely opposes the imposition of chemotherapy. However, he does not believe he is ill currently. The fact is that he is very ill currently. He has Hodgkin's lymphoma which is apparently not in remission from the available evidence. In this case, the state has a compelling state interest sufficient to override the minor's genuine opposition. . . .

JOHN R. RODENBERG is the District Court Judge in this case. Rodenberg argues that all parties are acting out of convictions for the best interest of the child. He also argues that the state has a compelling interest to act against Hauser's religious views for medical care since the child is only 13 years old.

EXPLORING THE ISSUE

Do Parents Have the Right to Deny Their Children Lifesaving Medical Care Due to Their Religious Convictions?

Critical Thinking and Reflection

1. What are some arguments made by each side with which you agree or disagree?
2. What are the strengths and weaknesses of the two positions made in this issue?
3. Pick the side with which you most agree. What are some additional arguments you would make to strengthen the case for or against parents denying their children lifesaving medical treatment?
4. Think more broadly of the issue of religious liberty and the medical care of children.
5. How do you balance a fundamental right with science and an adolescent's life?

Is There Common Ground?

Even the judge in this case acknowledged that everyone involved was looking out for the best interest of Daniel Hauser. The right to express our religion is a fundamental right that enjoys wide protection in our society. At the same time, protecting the health and welfare of children is critical in any caring society. How much power should be ceded to medical professionals? Although the state did not support the position of Daniel's parents, what might have caused a different outcome? What if Daniel's illness were not fatal? In what circumstances, if any, would you let parents' decision-making rights supersede the states decision based on the testimony of medical professionals?

Create Central

www.mhhe.com/createcentral

Additional Resources

Nemenah and Traditional Indigenous Organization:

www.nemenhah.org/

Christian Science:

http://christianscience.com/

Washington Post article about prayer and healing:

www.washingtonpost.com/wp-dyn/content/ article/2006/03/23/AR2006032302177.html

Healing Scripture:

http://healingscripture.com/

Religious tolerance and medical care:

www.religioustolerance.org/medical1.htm

Internet References . . .

American Bar Association: Rights of Children Regarding Medical Treatment

www.americanbar.org/newsletter/publications/ gp_solo_magazine_home/gp_solo_magazine_index/ medicaltreatment.html

Attorney Supporting Parents' Rights

www.robertslaw.org/refuse-medical-treatment.htm

University of Illinois Chicago School of Medicine: Ethics in Clerkships

www.uic.edu/depts/mcam/ethics/refusal.htm

Unit 3

UNIT

Non-Traditional Families and Relationships

*T*he American family today is decidedly different than during the Leave it to Beaver *era. Children grow up in a wide array of families: two married parents, single parents, grandparents raising children, lesbian and gay parents, and many other family structures. As the composition of a family changes, it is critical to take a closer look at the twenty-first century family. What does a changing family mean for modern-day America?*

Selected, Edited, and with Issue Framing Material by:
David M. Hall, Ph.D., *Delaware Valley College*

ISSUE

Does the Federal Government Discriminate Against Same-Sex Couples If It Refuses to Recognize Their Marriage?

YES: Anthony Kennedy, from Majority Decision, *United States v. Windsor*, Supreme Court of the United States (2013)

NO: Antonin Scalia, from Dissenting Opinion, *United States v. Windsor*, Supreme Court of the United States (2013)

Learning Outcomes
After reading this issue, you will be able to: • Summarize competing arguments related to federal recognition of marriage based on sexual orientation.   • Apply concepts of originalism versus living document interpretations of the Constitution to same-sex couples.   • Evaluate the implications of federal interpretations of marriage on legal and social standing for lesbian and gay families.

ISSUE SUMMARY

YES: Anthony Kennedy argues that same-sex couples face unconstitutional discrimination from the federal government when their relationships are not recognized. Kennedy argues that the Defense of Marriage Act discriminates against and demeans same-sex couples.

NO: Antonin Scalia argues that the U.S. Constitution does not provide any specific protections for same-sex couples. In fact, he argues that the Court should not even be hearing this case. However, since they did hear the case, he argues that the Court has no power to overturn the Defense of Marriage Act.

The first written law related to marriage is found in the Code of Hammurabi. Since then, there has been a wide array of written laws throughout the world related to marriages and relationships. In American history, the definition of marriage has been reconstructed many times.

Early in American history, women were regarded as the property of their husbands. Their husbands were, in effect, their voices, whether she agreed or disagreed. In fact, women often could not serve on juries or vote. Over time, women earned further political rights and, eventually, social rights.

By the mid-twentieth century, women found wide access to contraception. An older friend of mine recalls the days when the birth control pill first came out. Her doctor would only give her a prescription for it with the permission of her husband. Once the Supreme Court ruled that women could have access to contraception, women had power over their reproductive decisions, and the role

of gender in a marriage was reconstructed. While childbearing played a critical role for many families, work and economic opportunity began to play an additional role for women in their relationships.

At the same time, life span has lengthened significantly over the course of American history. Widowed men and women were getting married long after their reproductive years had passed.

In contemporary America, sex in marriage no longer had to lead to procreation. In marriages, sex for recreation rather than procreation became a right for everyone. When gay and lesbian couples sought the right to marry, their argument for their rights had to be reconciled with this fact.

Additionally, the Supreme Court had ruled that interracial marriages were a fundamental right (had President Obama's parents tried to marry when he was born in the state of Virginia, they would have been guilty of a crime punishable by time in prison). The Court specifically ruled that marriage is a fundamental relationship right, and the government cannot discriminate based on race.

As this case reached the Court, it did not ask a specific question on the right to marry. However, it asked about whether the federal government could ignore same-sex couples. By now, the Courts have ruled that marriage is a fundamental relationship right and that procreation is not a necessary part of a marriage. What does this mean when we discuss same-sex couples?

The Constitution does not say anything about sexual orientation. However, a previous Court decision referred to sexual orientation as immutable. If that is true, are same-sex couples entitled to constitutional protections? How does the concept of Originalism apply? Living Constitution?

While this case may very well be a landmark case one day, it does not address whether or not same-sex couples have the right to marry. At the time of writing, no Supreme Court case has addressed this question. However, this case is likely, if not certain, to play a major role in a future Supreme Court case that evaluates whether there is a constitutional right to marriage equality for same-sex couples.

YES ↵

Anthony Kennedy

Majority Decision, *United States v. Windsor*

Justice Kennedy delivered the opinion of the Court.

Two women then resident in New York were married in a lawful ceremony in Ontario, Canada, in 2007. Edith Windsor and Thea Spyer returned to their home in New York City. When Spyer died in 2009, she left her entire estate to Windsor. Windsor sought to claim the estate tax exemption for surviving spouses. She was barred from doing so, however, by a federal law, the Defense of Marriage Act, which excludes a same-sex partner from the definition of "spouse" as that term is used in federal statutes. Windsor paid the taxes but filed suit to challenge the constitutionality of this provision. The United States District Court and the Court of Appeals ruled that this portion of the statute is unconstitutional and ordered the United States to pay Windsor a refund. This Court granted certiorari and now affirms the judgment in Windsor's favor.

I

In 1996, as some States were beginning to consider the concept of same-sex marriage, see, e.g., Baehr v. Lewin (1993), and before any State had acted to permit it, Congress enacted the Defense of Marriage Act (DOMA). DOMA contains two operative sections: Section 2, which has not been challenged here, allows States to refuse to recognize same-sex marriages performed under the laws of other States.

Section 3 is at issue here. It amends the Dictionary Act in Title 1, §7, of the United States Code to provide a federal definition of "marriage" and "spouse." Section 3 of DOMA provides as follows:

> "In determining the meaning of any Act of Congress, or of any ruling, regulation, or interpretation of the various administrative bureaus and agencies of the United States, the word 'marriage' means only a legal union between one man and one woman as husband and wife, and the word 'spouse' refers only to a person of the opposite sex who is a husband or a wife."

The definitional provision does not by its terms forbid States from enacting laws permitting same-sex marriages or civil unions or providing state benefits to residents in that status. The enactment's comprehensive definition of marriage for purposes of all federal statutes and other regulations or directives covered by its terms, however, does control over 1,000 federal laws in which marital or spousal status is addressed as a matter of federal law.

Edith Windsor and Thea Spyer met in New York City in 1963 and began a long-term relationship. Windsor and Spyer registered as domestic partners when New York City gave that right to same-sex couples in 1993. Concerned about Spyer's health, the couple made the 2007 trip to Canada for their marriage, but they continued to reside in New York City. The State of New York deems their Ontario marriage to be a valid one.

Spyer died in February 2009, and left her entire estate to Windsor. Because DOMA denies federal recognition to same-sex spouses, Windsor did not qualify for the marital exemption from the federal estate tax, which excludes from taxation "any interest in property which passes or has passed from the decedent to his surviving spouse." Windsor paid $363,053 in estate taxes and sought a refund. The Internal Revenue Service denied the refund, concluding that, under DOMA, Windsor was not a "surviving spouse." Windsor commenced this refund suit in the United States District Court for the Southern District of New York. She contended that DOMA violates the guarantee of equal protection, as applied to the Federal Government through the Fifth Amendment.

While the tax refund suit was pending, the Attorney General of the United States notified the Speaker of the House of Representatives, that the Department of Justice would no longer defend the constitutionality of DOMA's §3. Noting that "the Department has previously defended DOMA against . . . challenges involving legally married same-sex couples," App. 184, the Attorney General informed Congress that "the President has concluded that given a number of factors, including a documented history of discrimination, classifications based on sexual orientation should be subject to a heightened standard of scrutiny." The Department of Justice has submitted many §530D letters over the years refusing to defend laws it deems unconstitutional, when, for instance, a federal court has rejected the Government's defense of a statute and has issued a judgment against it. This case is unusual, however, because the §530D letter was not preceded by an adverse judgment. The letter instead reflected the Executive's own conclusion, relying on a definition still being debated and considered in the courts, that heightened equal protection scrutiny should apply to laws that classify on the basis of sexual orientation.

Supreme Court of the United States, June 26, 2013.

Although "the President . . . instructed the Department not to defend the statute in Windsor," he also decided "that Section 3 will continue to be enforced by the Executive Branch" and that the United States had an "interest in providing Congress a full and fair opportunity to participate in the litigation of those cases." Id., at 191–193. The stated rationale for this dual-track procedure (determination of unconstitutionality coupled with ongoing enforcement) was to "recogniz[e] the judiciary as the final arbiter of the constitutional claims raised."

In response to the notice from the Attorney General, the Bipartisan Legal Advisory Group (BLAG) of the House of Representatives voted to intervene in the litigation to defend the constitutionality of §3 of DOMA. The Department of Justice did not oppose limited intervention by BLAG. The District Court denied BLAG's motion to enter the suit as of right, on the rationale that the United States already was represented by the Department of Justice. The District Court, however, did grant intervention by BLAG as an interested party.

On the merits of the tax refund suit, the District Court ruled against the United States. It held that §3 of DOMA is unconstitutional and ordered the Treasury to refund the tax with interest. Both the Justice Department and BLAG filed notices of appeal, and the Solicitor General filed a petition for certiorari before judgment. Before this Court acted on the petition, the Court of Appeals for the Second Circuit affirmed the District Court's judgment. It applied heightened scrutiny to classifications based on sexual orientation, as both the Department and Windsor had urged. The United States has not complied with the judgment. Windsor has not received her refund, and the Executive Branch continues to enforce §3 of DOMA.

In granting certiorari on the question of the constitutionality of §3 of DOMA, the Court requested argument on two additional questions: whether the United States' agreement with Windsor's legal position precludes further review and whether BLAG has standing to appeal the case. All parties agree that the Court has jurisdiction to decide this case; and, with the case in that framework, the Court appointed Professor Vicki Jackson as amicus curiae to argue the position that the Court lacks jurisdiction to hear the dispute.

II

It is appropriate to begin by addressing whether either the Government or BLAG, or both of them, were entitled to appeal to the Court of Appeals and later to seek certiorari and appear as parties here.

There is no dispute that when this case was in the District Court it presented a concrete disagreement between opposing parties, a dispute suitable for judicial resolution. "[A] taxpayer has standing to challenge the collection of a specific tax assessment as unconstitutional; being forced to pay such a tax causes a real and immediate economic injury to the individual taxpayer." Hein v. Freedom From Religion Foundation, Inc. (2007) (plurality opinion). Windsor suffered a redressable injury when she was required to pay estate taxes from which, in her view, she was exempt but for the alleged invalidity of §3 of DOMA.

The decision of the Executive not to defend the constitutionality of §3 in court while continuing to deny refunds and to assess deficiencies does introduce a complication. Even though the Executive's current position was announced before the District Court entered its judgment, the Government's agreement with Windsor's position would not have deprived the District Court of jurisdiction to entertain and resolve the refund suit; for her injury (failure to obtain a refund allegedly required by law) was concrete, persisting, and unredressed. The Government's position—agreeing with Windsor's legal contention but refusing to give it effect—meant that there was a justiciable controversy between the parties, despite what the claimant would find to be an inconsistency in that stance. Windsor, the Government, BLAG, and the amicus appear to agree upon that point. The disagreement is over the standing of the parties, or aspiring parties, to take an appeal in the Court of Appeals and to appear as parties in further proceedings in this Court.

The amicus' position is that, given the Government's concession that §3 is unconstitutional, once the District Court ordered the refund the case should have ended; and the amicus argues the Court of Appeals should have dismissed the appeal. The amicus submits that once the President agreed with Windsor's legal position and the District Court issued its judgment, the parties were no longer adverse. From this standpoint the United States was a prevailing party below, just as Windsor was. Accordingly, the amicus reasons, it is inappropriate for this Court to grant certiorari and proceed to rule on the merits; for the United States seeks no redress from the judgment entered against it.

This position, however, elides the distinction between two principles: the jurisdictional requirements of Article III and the prudential limits on its exercise. See Warth v. Seldin (1975). The latter are "essentially matters of judicial self-governance." The Court has kept these two strands separate: "Article III standing, which enforces the Constitution's case-or-controversy requirement, see Lujan v. Defenders of Wildlife; and prudential standing, which embodies 'judicially self-imposed limits on the exercise of federal jurisdiction.'"

The requirements of Article III standing are familiar:

"First, the plaintiff must have suffered an 'injury in fact'—an invasion of a legally protected interest which is (a) concrete and particularized, and (b) 'actual or imminent, not "conjectural or hypothetical."' Second, there must be a causal connection between the injury and the conduct complained of—the injury has to be 'fairly . . . trace[able] to the challenged action of the defendant, and not . . . th[e] result [of] the independent action of some third party not before the court.' Third, it must be 'likely,' as opposed to merely 'speculative,' that the injury will be 'redressed by a favorable decision.'"

Rules of prudential standing, by contrast, are more flexible "rule[s] . . . of federal appellate practice," Deposit Guaranty Nat. Bank v. Roper (1980), designed to protect the courts from "decid[ing] abstract questions of wide public significance even [when] other governmental institutions may be more competent to address the questions and even though judicial intervention may be unnecessary to protect individual rights."

In this case the United States retains a stake sufficient to support Article III jurisdiction on appeal and in proceedings before this Court. The judgment in question orders the United States to pay Windsor the refund she seeks. An order directing the Treasury to pay money is "a real and immediate economic injury," indeed as real and immediate as an order directing an individual to pay a tax. That the Executive may welcome this order to pay the refund if it is accompanied by the constitutional ruling it wants does not eliminate the injury to the national Treasury if payment is made, or to the taxpayer if it is not. The judgment orders the United States to pay money that it would not disburse but for the court's order. The Government of the United States has a valid legal argument that it is injured even if the Executive disagrees with §3 of DOMA, which results in Windsor's liability for the tax. Windsor's ongoing claim for funds that the United States refuses to pay thus establishes a controversy sufficient for Article III jurisdiction. It would be a different case if the Executive had taken the further step of paying Windsor the refund to which she was entitled under the District Court's ruling.

The Court's conclusion that this petition may be heard on the merits does not imply that no difficulties would ensue if this were a common practice in ordinary cases. The Executive's failure to defend the constitutionality of an Act of Congress based on a constitutional theory not yet established in judicial decisions has created a procedural dilemma. On the one hand, as noted, the Government's agreement with Windsor raises questions about the propriety of entertaining a suit in which it seeks affirmance of an order invalidating a federal law and ordering the United States to pay money. On the other hand, if the Executive's agreement with a plaintiff that a law is unconstitutional is enough to preclude judicial review, then the Supreme Court's primary role in determining the constitutionality of a law that has inflicted real injury on a plaintiff who has brought a justiciable legal claim would become only secondary to the President's. This would undermine the clear dictate of the separation-of-powers principle that "when an Act of Congress is alleged to conflict with the Constitution, '[i]t is emphatically the province and duty of the judicial department to say what the law is.'" Zivotofsky

v. Clinton (2012). Similarly, with respect to the legislative power, when Congress has passed a statute and a President has signed it, it poses grave challenges to the separation of powers for the Executive at a particular moment to be able to nullify Congress' enactment solely on its own initiative and without any determination from the Court.

The Court's jurisdictional holding, it must be underscored, does not mean the arguments for dismissing this dispute on prudential grounds lack substance. Yet the difficulty the Executive faces should be acknowledged. When the Executive makes a principled determination that a statute is unconstitutional, it faces a difficult choice. Still, there is no suggestion here that it is appropriate for the Executive as a matter of course to challenge statutes in the judicial forum rather than making the case to Congress for their amendment or repeal. The integrity of the political process would be at risk if difficult constitutional issues were simply referred to the Court as a routine exercise. But this case is not routine. And the capable defense of the law by BLAG ensures that these prudential issues do not cloud the merits question, which is one of immediate importance to the Federal Government and to hundreds of thousands of persons. These circumstances support the Court's decision to proceed to the merits.

III

When at first Windsor and Spyer longed to marry, neither New York nor any other State granted them that right. After waiting some years, in 2007 they traveled to Ontario to be married there. It seems fair to conclude that, until recent years, many citizens had not even considered the possibility that two persons of the same sex might aspire to occupy the same status and dignity as that of a man and woman in lawful marriage. For marriage between a man and a woman no doubt had been thought of by most people as essential to the very definition of that term and to its role and function throughout the history of civilization. That belief, for many who long have held it, became even more urgent, more cherished when challenged. For others, however, came the beginnings of a new perspective, a new insight. Accordingly some States concluded that same-sex marriage ought to be given recognition and validity in the law for those same-sex couples who wish to define themselves by their commitment to each other. The limitation of lawful marriage to heterosexual couples, which for centuries had been deemed both necessary and fundamental, came to be seen in New York and certain other States as an unjust exclusion.

Slowly at first and then in rapid course, the laws of New York came to acknowledge the urgency of this issue for same-sex couples who wanted to affirm their commitment to one another before their children, their family, their friends, and their community. And so New York recognized same-sex marriages performed elsewhere; and then it later amended its own marriage laws to permit same-sex marriage. New York, in common with, as of this writing, 11 other States and the District of Columbia, decided that same-sex couples should have the right to marry and so live with pride in themselves and their union and in a status of equality with all other married persons. After a statewide deliberative process that enabled its citizens to discuss and weigh arguments for and against same-sex marriage, New York acted to enlarge the definition of marriage to correct what its citizens and elected representatives perceived to be an injustice that they had not earlier known or understood.

Against this background of lawful same-sex marriage in some States, the design, purpose, and effect of DOMA should be considered as the beginning point in deciding whether it is valid under the Constitution. By history and tradition the definition and regulation of marriage, as will be discussed in more detail, has been treated as being within the authority and realm of the separate States. Yet it is further established that Congress, in enacting discrete statutes, can make determinations that bear on marital rights and privileges. Just this Term the Court upheld the authority of the Congress to preempt state laws, allowing a former spouse to retain life insurance proceeds under a federal program that gave her priority, because of formal beneficiary designation rules, over the wife by a second marriage who survived the husband. Hillman v. Maretta (2013); see also Ridgway v. Ridgway (1981); Wissner v. Wissner (1950). This is one example of the general principle that when the Federal Government acts in the exercise of its own proper authority, it has a wide choice of the mechanisms and means to adopt. Congress has the power both to ensure efficiency in the administration of its programs and to choose what larger goals and policies to pursue.

Other precedents involving congressional statutes which affect marriages and family status further illustrate this point. In addressing the interaction of state domestic relations and federal immigration law Congress determined that marriages "entered into for the purpose of procuring an alien's admission [to the United States] as an immigrant" will not qualify the noncitizen for that status, even if the noncitizen's marriage is valid and proper for state-law purposes. And in establishing income-based criteria for Social Security benefits, Congress decided that although state law would determine in general who qualifies as an applicant's spouse, common-law marriages also should be recognized, regardless of any particular State's view on these relationships.

Though these discrete examples establish the constitutionality of limited federal laws that regulate the meaning of marriage in order to further federal policy, DOMA has a far greater reach; for it enacts a directive applicable to over 1,000 federal statutes and the whole realm of federal regulations. And its operation is directed to a class of persons that the laws of New York, and of 11 other States, have sought to protect.

In order to assess the validity of that intervention it is necessary to discuss the extent of the state power and authority over marriage as a matter of history and tradition. State laws defining and regulating marriage, of course, must respect the constitutional rights of persons, see, e.g., Loving v. Virginia (1967); but, subject to those guarantees, "regulation of domestic relations" is "an area that has long been regarded as a virtually exclusive province of the States."

The recognition of civil marriages is central to state domestic relations law applicable to its residents and citizens. See Williams v. North Carolina (1942) ("Each state as a sovereign has a rightful and legitimate concern in the marital status of persons domiciled within its borders"). The definition of marriage is the foundation of the State's broader authority to regulate the subject of domestic relations with respect to the "[p]rotection of offspring, property interests, and the enforcement of marital responsibilities." Ibid. "[T]he states, at the time of the adoption of the Constitution, possessed full power over the subject of marriage and divorce . . . [and] the Constitution delegated no authority to the Government of the United States on the subject of marriage and divorce." Haddock v. Haddock (1906).

Consistent with this allocation of authority, the Federal Government, through our history, has deferred to state-law policy decisions with respect to domestic relations. In De Sylva v. Ballentine (1956), for example, the Court held that, "[t]o decide who is the widow or widower of a deceased author, or who are his executors or next of kin," under the Copyright Act "requires a reference to the law of the State which created those legal relationships" because "there is no federal law of domestic relations." In order to respect this principle, the federal courts, as a general rule, do not adjudicate issues of marital status even when there might otherwise be a basis for federal jurisdiction. Federal courts will not hear divorce and custody cases even if they arise in diversity because of "the virtually exclusive primacy . . . of the States in the regulation of domestic relations."

The significance of state responsibilities for the definition and regulation of marriage dates to the Nation's beginning; for "when the Constitution was adopted the common understanding was that the domestic relations of husband and wife and parent and child were matters reserved to the States." Marriage laws vary in some respects from State to State. For example, the required minimum age is 16 in Vermont, but only 13 in New Hampshire. Likewise the permissible degree of consanguinity can vary (most States permit first cousins to marry, but a handful—such as Iowa and Washington—prohibit the practice). But these rules are in every event consistent within each State.

Against this background DOMA rejects the long-established precept that the incidents, benefits, and obligations of marriage are uniform for all married couples within each State, though they may vary, subject to constitutional guarantees, from one State to the next. Despite these considerations, it is unnecessary to decide whether this federal intrusion on state power is a violation of the Constitution because it disrupts the federal balance. The State's power in defining the marital relation is of central relevance in this case quite apart from principles of federalism. Here the State's decision to give this class of persons the right to marry conferred upon them a dignity and status of immense import. When the State used its historic and essential authority to define the marital relation in this way, its role and its power in making the decision enhanced the recognition, dignity, and protection of the class in their own community. DOMA, because of its reach and extent, departs from this history and tradition of reliance on state law to define marriage. "[D]iscriminations of an unusual character especially suggest careful consideration to determine whether they are obnoxious to the constitutional provision."

The Federal Government uses this state-defined class for the opposite purpose—to impose restrictions and disabilities. That result requires this Court now to address whether the resulting injury and indignity is a deprivation of an essential part of the liberty protected by the Fifth Amendment. What the State of New York treats as alike the federal law deems unlike by a law designed to injure the same class the State seeks to protect.

In acting first to recognize and then to allow same-sex marriages, New York was responding "to the initiative of those who [sought] a voice in shaping the destiny of their own times." These actions were without doubt a proper exercise of its sovereign authority within our federal system, all in the way that the Framers of the Constitution intended. The dynamics of state government in the federal system are to allow the formation of consensus respecting the way the members of a discrete community treat each other in their daily contact and constant interaction with each other.

The States' interest in defining and regulating the marital relation, subject to constitutional guarantees, stems from the understanding that marriage is more than a routine classification for purposes of certain statutory benefits. Private, consensual sexual intimacy between two adult persons of the same sex may not be punished by the State, and it can form "but one element in a personal bond that is more enduring." Lawrence v. Texas (2003). By its recognition of the validity of same-sex marriages performed in other jurisdictions and then by authorizing same-sex unions and same-sex marriages, New York sought to give further protection and dignity to that bond. For same-sex couples who wished to be married, the State acted to give their lawful conduct a lawful status. This status is a far-reaching legal acknowledgment of the intimate relationship between two people, a relationship deemed by the State worthy of dignity in the community equal with all other marriages. It reflects both the community's considered perspective on the historical roots of the institution of marriage and its evolving understanding of the meaning of equality.

IV

DOMA seeks to injure the very class New York seeks to protect. By doing so it violates basic due process and equal protection principles applicable to the Federal Government. The Constitution's guarantee of equality "must at the very least mean that a bare congressional desire to harm a politically unpopular group cannot" justify disparate treatment of that group. Department of Agriculture v. Moreno (1973). In determining whether a law is motived by an improper animus or purpose, "[d]iscriminations of an unusual character" especially require careful consideration. DOMA cannot survive under these principles. The responsibility of the States for the regulation of domestic relations is an important indicator of the substantial societal impact the State's classifications have in the daily lives and customs of its people. DOMA's unusual deviation from the usual tradition of recognizing and accepting state definitions of marriage here operates to deprive same-sex couples of the benefits and responsibilities that come with the federal recognition of their marriages. This is strong evidence of a law having the purpose and effect of disapproval of that class. The avowed purpose and practical effect of the law here in question are to impose a disadvantage, a separate status, and so a stigma upon all who enter into same-sex marriages made lawful by the unquestioned authority of the States.

The history of DOMA's enactment and its own text demonstrate that interference with the equal dignity of same-sex marriages, a dignity conferred by the States in the exercise of their sovereign power, was more than an incidental effect of the federal statute. It was its essence. The House Report announced its conclusion that "it is both appropriate and necessary for Congress to do what it can to defend the institution of traditional heterosexual marriage. ... H. R. 3396 is appropriately entitled the 'Defense of Marriage Act.' The effort to redefine 'marriage' to extend to homosexual couples is a truly radical proposal that would fundamentally alter the institution of marriage." H. R. Rep. No. 104–664, pp. 12–13 (1996). The House concluded that DOMA expresses "both moral disapproval of homosexuality, and a moral conviction that heterosexuality better comports with traditional (especially Judeo-Christian) morality." The stated purpose of the law was to promote an "interest in protecting the traditional moral teachings reflected in heterosexual-only marriage laws." Ibid. Were there any doubt of this far-reaching purpose, the title of the Act confirms it: The Defense of Marriage.

The arguments put forward by BLAG are just as candid about the congressional purpose to influence or interfere with state sovereign choices about who may be married. As the title and dynamics of the bill indicate, its purpose is to discourage enactment of state same-sex marriage laws and to restrict the freedom and choice of couples married under those laws if they are enacted. The congressional goal was "to put a thumb on the scales and influence a state's decision as to how to shape its own marriage laws." Massachusetts, 682 F. 3d, at 12–13. The Act's demonstrated purpose is to ensure that if any State decides to recognize same-sex marriages, those unions will be treated as second-class marriages for purposes of federal law. This raises a most serious question under the Constitution's Fifth Amendment.

DOMA's operation in practice confirms this purpose. When New York adopted a law to permit same-sex marriage, it sought to eliminate inequality; but DOMA frustrates that objective through a system-wide enactment with no identified connection to any particular area of federal law. DOMA writes inequality into the entire United States Code. The particular case at hand concerns the estate tax, but DOMA is more than a simple determination of what should or should not be allowed as an estate tax refund. Among the over 1,000 statutes and numerous federal regulations that DOMA controls are laws pertaining to Social Security, housing, taxes, criminal sanctions, copyright, and veterans' benefits.

DOMA's principal effect is to identify a subset of state-sanctioned marriages and make them unequal. The principal purpose is to impose inequality, not for other reasons like governmental efficiency. Responsibilities, as well as rights, enhance the dignity and integrity of the person. And DOMA contrives to deprive some couples married under the laws of their State, but not other couples, of both rights and responsibilities. By creating two contradictory marriage regimes within the same State, DOMA forces same-sex couples to live as married for the purpose of state law but unmarried for the purpose of federal law, thus diminishing the stability and predictability of basic personal relations the State has found it proper to acknowledge and protect. By this dynamic DOMA undermines both the public and private significance of state-sanctioned same-sex marriages; for it tells those couples, and all the world, that their otherwise valid marriages are unworthy of federal recognition. This places same-sex couples in an unstable position of being in a second-tier marriage. The differentiation demeans the couple, whose moral and sexual choices the Constitution protects, see Lawrence, and whose relationship the State has sought to dignify. And it humiliates tens of thousands of children now being raised by same-sex couples. The law in question makes it even more difficult for the children to understand the integrity and closeness of their own family and its concord with other families in their community and in their daily lives.

Under DOMA, same-sex married couples have their lives burdened, by reason of government decree, in visible and public ways. By its great reach, DOMA touches many aspects of married and family life, from the mundane to the profound. It prevents same-sex married couples from obtaining government healthcare benefits they would otherwise receive. It deprives them of the Bankruptcy Code's special protections for domestic-support obligations. It forces them to follow a complicated procedure to file their state and federal taxes jointly. It prohibits them from being buried together in veterans' cemeteries.

For certain married couples, DOMA's unequal effects are even more serious. The federal penal code makes it a crime to "assaul[t], kidna[p], or murde[r] . . . a member of the immediate family" of "a United States official, a United States judge, [or] a Federal law enforcement officer," with the intent to influence or retaliate against that official, §115(a)(1). Although a "spouse" qualifies as a member of the officer's "immediate family," §115(c)(2), DOMA makes this protection inapplicable to same-sex spouses.

DOMA also brings financial harm to children of same-sex couples. It raises the cost of health care for families by taxing health benefits provided by employers to their workers' same-sex spouses. And it denies or reduces benefits allowed to families upon the loss of a spouse and parent, benefits that are an integral part of family security. See Social Security Administration, Social Security Survivors Benefits 5 (2012) (benefits available to a surviving spouse caring for the couple's child), online at http://www.ssa.gov/pubs/EN-05-10084.pdf.

DOMA divests married same-sex couples of the duties and responsibilities that are an essential part of married life and that they in most cases would be honored to accept were DOMA not in force. For instance, because it is expected that spouses will support each other as they pursue educational opportunities, federal law takes into consideration a spouse's income in calculating a student's federal financial aid eligibility. Same-sex married couples are exempt from this requirement. The same is true with respect to federal ethics rules. Federal executive and agency officials are prohibited from "participat[ing] personally and substantially" in matters as to which they or their spouses have a financial interest. A similar statute prohibits Senators, Senate employees, and their spouses from accepting high-value gifts from certain sources, and another mandates detailed financial disclosures by numerous high-ranking officials and their spouses. Under DOMA, however, these Government-integrity rules do not apply to same-sex spouses.

* * *

The power the Constitution grants it also restrains. And though Congress has great authority to design laws to fit its own conception of sound national policy, it cannot deny the liberty protected by the Due Process Clause of the Fifth Amendment.

What has been explained to this point should more than suffice to establish that the principal purpose and the necessary effect of this law are to demean those persons who are in a lawful same-sex marriage. This requires the Court to hold, as it now does, that DOMA is unconstitutional as a deprivation of the liberty of the person protected by the Fifth Amendment of the Constitution.

The liberty protected by the Fifth Amendment's Due Process Clause contains within it the prohibition against denying to any person the equal protection of the laws. While the Fifth Amendment itself withdraws from Government the power to degrade or demean in the way this law does, the equal protection guarantee of the Fourteenth Amendment makes that Fifth Amendment right all the more specific and all the better understood and preserved.

The class to which DOMA directs its restrictions and restraints are those persons who are joined in same-sex marriages made lawful by the State. DOMA singles out a class of persons deemed by a State entitled to recognition and protection to enhance their own liberty. It imposes a disability on the class by refusing to acknowledge a status the State finds to be dignified and proper. DOMA instructs all federal officials, and indeed all persons with whom same-sex couples interact, including their own children, that their marriage is less worthy than the marriages of others. The federal statute is invalid, for no legitimate purpose overcomes the purpose and effect to disparage and to injure those whom the State, by its marriage laws, sought to protect in personhood and dignity. By seeking to displace this protection and treating those persons as living in marriages less respected than others, the federal statute is in violation of the Fifth Amendment. This opinion and its holding are confined to those lawful marriages.

The judgment of the Court of Appeals for the Second Circuit is affirmed.

It is so ordered.

ANTHONY KENNEDY is a Supreme Court justice. He is often referred to as the swing vote on the Supreme Court. His legacy may largely be for expanding the constitutional rights for lesbian and gay couples.

Antonin Scalia

Dissenting Opinion, *United States v. Windsor*

Justice Scalia, with whom Justice Thomas joins, and with whom The Chief Justice joins as to Part I, dissenting.

This case is about power in several respects. It is about the power of our people to govern themselves, and the power of this Court to pronounce the law. Today's opinion aggrandizes the latter, with the predictable consequence of diminishing the former. We have no power to decide this case. And even if we did, we have no power under the Constitution to invalidate this democratically adopted legislation. The Court's errors on both points spring forth from the same diseased root: an exalted conception of the role of this institution in America.

I

A

The Court is eager—hungry—to tell everyone its view of the legal question at the heart of this case. Standing in the way is an obstacle, a technicality of little interest to anyone but the people of We the People, who created it as a barrier against judges' intrusion into their lives. They gave judges, in Article III, only the "judicial Power," a power to decide not abstract questions but real, concrete "Cases" and "Controversies." Yet the plaintiff and the Government agree entirely on what should happen in this lawsuit. They agree that the court below got it right; and they agreed in the court below that the court below that one got it right as well. What, then, are we doing here?

The answer lies at the heart of the jurisdictional portion of today's opinion, where a single sentence lays bare the majority's vision of our role. The Court says that we have the power to decide this case because if we did not, then our "primary role in determining the constitutionality of a law" (at least one that "has inflicted real injury on a plaintiff") would "become only secondary to the President's." But wait, the reader wonders—Windsor won below, and so cured her injury, and the President was glad to see it. True, says the majority, but judicial review must march on regardless, lest we "undermine the clear dictate of the separation-of-powers principle that when an Act of Congress is alleged to conflict with the Constitution, it is emphatically the province and duty of the judicial department to say what the law is."

That is jaw-dropping. It is an assertion of judicial supremacy over the people's Representatives in Congress and the Executive. It envisions a Supreme Court standing (or rather enthroned) at the apex of government, empowered to decide all constitutional questions, always and everywhere "primary" in its role.

This image of the Court would have been unrecognizable to those who wrote and ratified our national charter. They knew well the dangers of "primary" power, and so created branches of government that would be "perfectly coordinate by the terms of their common commission," none of which branches could "pretend to an exclusive or superior right of settling the boundaries between their respective powers." The Federalist, No. 49 (J. Madison). The people did this to protect themselves. They did it to guard their right to self-rule against the black-robed supremacy that today's majority finds so attractive. So it was that Madison could confidently state, with no fear of contradiction, that there was nothing of "greater intrinsic value" or "stamped with the authority of more enlightened patrons of liberty" than a government of separate and coordinate powers.

For this reason we are quite forbidden to say what the law is whenever (as today's opinion asserts) "an Act of Congress is alleged to conflict with the Constitution." We can do so only when that allegation will determine the outcome of a lawsuit, and is contradicted by the other party. The "judicial Power" is not, as the majority believes, the power "to say what the law is," ibid., giving the Supreme Court the "primary role in determining the constitutionality of laws." The majority must have in mind one of the foreign constitutions that pronounces such primacy for its constitutional court and allows that primacy to be exercised in contexts other than a lawsuit. The judicial power as Americans have understood it (and their English ancestors before them) is the power to adjudicate, with conclusive effect, disputed government claims (civil or criminal) against private persons, and disputed claims by private persons against the government or other private persons. Sometimes (though not always) the parties before the court disagree not with regard to the facts of their case (or not only with regard to the facts) but with regard to the applicable law—in which event (and only in which event) it becomes the "province and duty of the judicial department to say what the law is."

Supreme Court of the United States, June 26, 2013.

In other words, declaring the compatibility of state or federal laws with the Constitution is not only not the "primary role" of this Court, it is not a separate, free-standing role at all. We perform that role incidentally—by accident, as it were—when that is necessary to resolve the dispute before us. Then, and only then, does it become "the province and duty of the judicial department to say what the law is." That is why, in 1793, we politely declined the Washington Administration's request to "say what the law is" on a particular treaty matter that was not the subject of a concrete legal controversy. 3 Correspondence and Public Papers of John Jay 486–489 (H. Johnston ed. 1893). And that is why, as our opinions have said, some questions of law will never be presented to this Court, because there will never be anyone with standing to bring a lawsuit. As Justice Brandeis put it, we cannot "pass upon the constitutionality of legislation in a friendly, non-adversary, proceeding"; absent a "real, earnest and vital controversy between individuals," we have neither any work to do nor any power to do it. Our authority begins and ends with the need to adjudge the rights of an injured party who stands before us seeking redress. Lujan v. Defenders of Wildlife (1992).

That is completely absent here. Windsor's injury was cured by the judgment in her favor. And while, in ordinary circumstances, the United States is injured by a directive to pay a tax refund, this suit is far from ordinary. Whatever injury the United States has suffered will surely not be redressed by the action that it, as a litigant, asks us to take. The final sentence of the Solicitor General's brief on the merits reads: "For the foregoing reasons, the judgment of the court of appeals should be affirmed." Brief for United States (merits) 54 (emphasis added). That will not cure the Government's injury, but carve it into stone. One could spend many fruitless afternoons ransacking our library for any other petitioner's brief seeking an affirmance of the judgment against it. What the petitioner United States asks us to do in the case before us is exactly what the respondent Windsor asks us to do: not to provide relief from the judgment below but to say that that judgment was correct. And the same was true in the Court of Appeals: Neither party sought to undo the judgment for Windsor, and so that court should have dismissed the appeal (just as we should dismiss) for lack of jurisdiction. Since both parties agreed with the judgment of the District Court for the Southern District of New York, the suit should have ended there. The further proceedings have been a contrivance, having no object in mind except to elevate a District Court judgment that has no precedential effect in other courts, to one that has precedential effect throughout the Second Circuit, and then (in this Court) precedential effect throughout the United States.

We have never before agreed to speak—to "say what the law is"—where there is no controversy before us. In the more than two centuries that this Court has existed as an institution, we have never suggested that we have the power to decide a question when every party agrees with both its nominal opponent and the court below on that question's answer. The United States reluctantly conceded that at oral argument. See Tr. of Oral Arg. 19–20.

The majority's discussion of the requirements of Article III bears no resemblance to our jurisprudence. It accuses the amicus (appointed to argue against our jurisdiction) of "elid[ing] the distinction between . . . the jurisdictional requirements of Article III and the prudential limits on its exercise." Ante, at 6. It then proceeds to call the requirement of adverseness a "prudential" aspect of standing. Of standing. That is incomprehensible. A plaintiff (or appellant) can have all the standing in the world—satisfying all three standing requirements of Lujan that the majority so carefully quotes, ante, at 7—and yet no Article III controversy may be before the court. Article III requires not just a plaintiff (or appellant) who has standing to complain but an opposing party who denies the validity of the complaint. It is not the amicus that has done the eliding of distinctions, but the majority, calling the quite separate Article III requirement of adverseness between the parties an element (which it then pronounces a "prudential" element) of standing. The question here is not whether, as the majority puts it, "the United States retains a stake sufficient to support Article III jurisdiction," ibid. the question is whether there is any controversy (which requires contradiction) between the United States and Ms. Windsor. There is not.

I find it wryly amusing that the majority seeks to dismiss the requirement of party-adverseness as nothing more than a "prudential" aspect of the sole Article III requirement of standing. (Relegating a jurisdictional requirement to "prudential" status is a wondrous device, enabling courts to ignore the requirement whenever they believe it "prudent"—which is to say, a good idea.) Half a century ago, a Court similarly bent upon announcing its view regarding the constitutionality of a federal statute achieved that goal by effecting a remarkably similar but completely opposite distortion of the principles limiting our jurisdiction. The Court's notorious opinion in Flast v. Cohen (1968), held that standing was merely an element (which it pronounced to be a "prudential" element) of the sole Article III requirement of adverseness. We have been living with the chaos created by that power-grabbing decision ever since, see Hein v. Freedom From Religion Foundation, Inc. (2007), as we will have to live with the chaos created by this one.

The authorities the majority cites fall miles short of supporting the counterintuitive notion that an Article III "controversy" can exist without disagreement between the parties. In Deposit Guaranty Nat. Bank v. Roper (1980), the District Court had entered judgment in the individual plaintiff's favor based on the defendant bank's offer to pay the full amount claimed. The plaintiff, however, sought to appeal the District Court's denial of class certification under Federal Rule of Civil Procedure 23. There was a continuing dispute between the parties concerning the issue raised on appeal. The same is true of the other case cited by the majority, Camreta v. Greene, (2011). There the District Court found that the defendant state officers had violated the Fourth Amendment, but rendered judgment in their favor because they were entitled to official immunity, application of the Fourth Amendment to their conduct not having been clear at the time of violation. The officers sought to appeal the holding of Fourth Amendment violation, which would circumscribe their future conduct; the plaintiff continued to insist that a Fourth Amendment violation had occurred. The "prudential" discretion to which both those cases refer was the discretion to deny an appeal even when a live controversy exists—not the discretion to grant one when it does not. The majority can cite no case in which this Court entertained an appeal in which both parties urged us to affirm the judgment below. And that is because the existence of a controversy is not a "prudential" requirement that we have invented, but an essential element of an Article III case or controversy. The majority's notion that a case between friendly parties can be entertained so long as "adversarial presentation of the issues is assured by the participation of amici curiae prepared to defend with vigor" the other side of the issue, ante, at 10, effects a breathtaking revolution in our Article III jurisprudence.

It may be argued that if what we say is true some Presidential determinations that statutes are unconstitutional will not be subject to our review. That is as it should be, when both the President and the plaintiff agree that the statute is unconstitutional. Where the Executive is enforcing an unconstitutional law, suit will of course lie; but if, in that suit, the Executive admits the unconstitutionality of the law, the litigation should end in an order or a consent decree enjoining enforcement. This suit saw the light of day only because the President enforced the Act (and thus gave Windsor standing to sue) even though he believed it unconstitutional. He could have equally chosen (more appropriately, some would say) neither to enforce nor to defend the statute he believed to be unconstitutional, see Presidential Authority to Decline to Execute Unconstitutional Statutes (Nov. 2, 1994)—in which event Windsor would not have been injured, the District Court could not have refereed this friendly scrimmage, and the Executive's determination of unconstitutionality would have escaped this Court's desire to blurt out its view of the law. The matter would have been left, as so many matters ought to be left, to a tug of war between the President and the Congress, which has innumerable means (up to and including impeachment) of compelling the President to enforce the laws it has written. Or the President could have evaded presentation of the constitutional issue to this Court simply by declining to appeal the District Court and Court of Appeals dispositions he agreed with. Be sure of this much: If a President wants to insulate his judgment of unconstitutionality from our review, he can. What the views urged in this dissent produce is not insulation from judicial review but insulation from Executive contrivance.

The majority brandishes the famous sentence from Marbury v. Madison (1803) that "[i]t is emphatically the province and duty of the judicial department to say what the law is." Ante, at 12 (internal quotation marks omitted). But that sentence neither says nor implies that it is always the province and duty of the Court to say what the law is—much less that its responsibility in that regard is a "primary" one. The very next sentence of Chief Justice Marshall's opinion makes the crucial qualification that today's majority ignores: "Those who apply the rule to particular cases, must of necessity expound and interpret that rule." Only when a "particular case" is before us—that is, a controversy that it is our business to resolve under Article III— do we have the province and duty to pronounce the law. For the views of our early Court more precisely addressing the question before us here, the majority ought instead to have consulted the opinion of Chief Justice Taney in Lord v. Veazie (1850):

> "The objection in the case before us is . . . that the plaintiff and defendant have the same interest, and that interest adverse and in conflict with the interest of third persons, whose rights would be seriously affected if the question of law was decided in the manner that both of the parties to this suit desire it to be.

"A judgment entered under such circumstances, and for such purposes, is a mere form. The whole proceeding was in contempt of the court, and highly reprehensible . . . . A judgment in form, thus procured, in the eye of the law is no judgment of the court. It is a nullity, and no writ of error will lie upon it. This writ is, therefore, dismissed." Id., at 255–256.

There is, in the words of Marbury, no "necessity [to] expound and interpret" the law in this case; just a desire to place this Court at the center of the Nation's life. 1 Cranch, at 177.

II

For the reasons above, I think that this Court has, and the Court of Appeals had, no power to decide this suit. We should vacate the decision below and remand to the Court of Appeals for the Second Circuit, with instructions to dismiss the appeal. Given that the majority has volunteered its view of the merits, however, I proceed to discuss that as well.

A

There are many remarkable things about the majority's merits holding. The first is how rootless and shifting its justifications are. For example, the opinion starts with seven full pages about the traditional power of States to define domestic relations—initially fooling many readers, I am sure, into thinking that this is a federalism opinion.

But we are eventually told that "it is unnecessary to decide whether this federal intrusion on state power is a violation of the Constitution," and that "[t]he State's power in defining the marital relation is of central relevance in this case quite apart from principles of federalism" because "the State's decision to give this class of persons the right to marry conferred upon them a dignity and status of immense import." Ante, at 18. But no one questions the power of the States to define marriage (with the concomitant conferral of dignity and status), so what is the point of devoting seven pages to describing how long and well established that power is? Even after the opinion has formally disclaimed reliance upon principles of federalism, mentions of "the usual tradition of recognizing and accepting state definitions of marriage" continue. What to make of this? The opinion never explains. My guess is that the majority, while reluctant to suggest that defining the meaning of "marriage" in federal statutes is unsupported by any of the Federal Government's enumerated powers, nonetheless needs some rhetorical basis to support its pretense that today's prohibition of laws excluding same-sex marriage is confined to the Federal Government (leaving the second, state-law shoe to be dropped later, maybe next Term). But I am only guessing.

Equally perplexing are the opinion's references to "the Constitution's guarantee of equality." Ibid. Near the end of the opinion, we are told that although the "equal protection guarantee of the Fourteenth Amendment makes [the] Fifth Amendment [due process] right all the more specific and all the better understood and preserved"—what can that mean?—"the Fifth Amendment itself withdraws from Government the power to degrade or demean in the way this law does." The only possible interpretation of this statement is that the Equal Protection Clause, even the Equal Protection Clause as incorporated in the Due Process Clause, is not the basis for today's holding. But the portion of the majority opinion that explains why DOMA is unconstitutional (Part IV) begins by citing Bolling v. Sharpe (1954), Department of Agriculture v. Moreno (1973), and Romer v. Evans (1996)—all of which are equal-protection cases. And those three cases are the only authorities that the Court cites in Part IV about the Constitution's meaning, except for its citation of Lawrence v. Texas (2003) (not an equal-protection case) to support its passing assertion that the Constitution protects the "moral and sexual choices" of same-sex couples.

Moreover, if this is meant to be an equal-protection opinion, it is a confusing one. The opinion does not resolve and indeed does not even mention what had been the central question in this litigation: whether, under the Equal Protection Clause, laws restricting marriage to a man and a woman are reviewed for more than mere rationality. That is the issue that divided the parties and the court below. In accord with my previously expressed skepticism about the Court's "tiers of scrutiny" approach, I would review this classification only for its rationality. See

United States v. Virginia (1996) (Scalia, J., dissenting). As nearly as I can tell, the Court agrees with that; its opinion does not apply strict scrutiny, and its central propositions are taken from rational-basis cases like Moreno. But the Court certainly does not apply anything that resembles that deferential framework.

The majority opinion need not get into the strict-vs.-rational-basis scrutiny question, and need not justify its holding under either, because it says that DOMA is unconstitutional as "a deprivation of the liberty of the person protected by the Fifth Amendment of the Constitution"; that it violates "basic due process" principles; and that it inflicts an "injury and indignity" of a kind that denies "an essential part of the liberty protected by the Fifth Amendment." The majority never utters the dread words "substantive due process," perhaps sensing the disrepute into which that doctrine has fallen, but that is what those statements mean. Yet the opinion does not argue that same-sex marriage is "deeply rooted in this Nation's history and tradition," Washington v. Glucksberg (1997), a claim that would of course be quite absurd. So would the further suggestion (also necessary, under our substantive-due-process precedents) that a world in which DOMA exists is one bereft of "ordered liberty."

Some might conclude that this loaf could have used a while longer in the oven. But that would be wrong; it is already overcooked. The most expert care in preparation cannot redeem a bad recipe. The sum of all the Court's nonspecific hand-waving is that this law is invalid (maybe on equal-protection grounds, maybe on substantive-due-process grounds, and perhaps with some amorphous federalism component playing a role) because it is motivated by a "bare . . . desire to harm" couples in same-sex marriages. It is this proposition with which I will therefore engage.

B

As I have observed before, the Constitution does not forbid the government to enforce traditional moral and sexual norms. See Lawrence v. Texas, (2003) (Scalia, J., dissenting). I will not swell the U. S. Reports with restatements of that point. It is enough to say that the Constitution neither requires nor forbids our society to approve of same-sex marriage, much as it neither requires nor forbids us to approve of no-fault divorce, polygamy, or the consumption of alcohol.

However, even setting aside traditional moral disapproval of same-sex marriage (or indeed same-sex sex), there are many perfectly valid—indeed, downright boring—justifying rationales for this legislation. Their existence ought to be the end of this case. For they give the lie to the Court's conclusion that only those with hateful hearts could have voted "aye" on this Act. And more importantly, they serve to make the contents of the legislators' hearts quite irrelevant: "It is a familiar principle of constitutional law that this Court will not strike down an otherwise constitutional statute on the basis of an alleged illicit legislative motive." United States v. O'Brien, (1968). Or at least it was a familiar principle. By holding to the contrary, the majority has declared open season on any law that (in the opinion of the law's opponents and any panel of like-minded federal judges) can be characterized as mean-spirited.

The majority concludes that the only motive for this Act was the "bare . . . desire to harm a politically unpopular group." Bear in mind that the object of this condemnation is not the legislature of some once-Confederate Southern state (familiar objects of the Court's scorn, see, e.g., Edwards v. Aguillard, 1987)), but our respected coordinate branches, the Congress and Presidency of the United States. Laying such a charge against them should require the most extraordinary evidence, and I would have thought that every attempt would be made to indulge a more anodyne explanation for the statute. The majority does the opposite—affirmatively concealing from the reader the arguments that exist in justification. It makes only a passing mention of the "arguments put forward" by the Act's defenders, and does not even trouble to paraphrase or describe them. I imagine that this is because it is harder to maintain the illusion of the Act's supporters as unhinged members of a wild-eyed lynch mob when one first describes their views as they see them.

To choose just one of these defenders' arguments, DOMA avoids difficult choice-of-law issues that will now arise absent a uniform federal definition of marriage. Imagine a pair of women who marry in Albany and then move to Alabama, which does not "recognize as valid any marriage of parties of the same sex." Ala. Code §30–1–19(e) (2011). When the couple files their next federal tax return, may it be a joint one? Which State's law controls, for federal-law purposes: their State of celebration (which recognizes the marriage) or their State of domicile (which does not)? (Does the answer depend on whether they were just visiting in Albany?) Are these questions to be answered as a matter of federal common law, or perhaps by borrowing a State's choice-of-law rules? If so, which State's? And what about States where the status of an out-of-state same-sex marriage is an unsettled question under local law? DOMA avoided all of this uncertainty by specifying which marriages would be recognized for federal purposes. That is a classic purpose for a definitional provision.

Further, DOMA preserves the intended effects of prior legislation against then-unforeseen changes in circumstance. When Congress provided (for example) that a special estate-tax exemption would exist for spouses, this exemption reached only opposite-sex spouses—those being the only sort that were recognized in any State at the time of DOMA's passage. When it became clear that changes in state law might one day alter that balance, DOMA's definitional section was enacted to ensure that state-level experimentation did not automatically alter the basic operation of federal law, unless and until Congress

made the further judgment to do so on its own. That is not animus—just stabilizing prudence. Congress has hardly demonstrated itself unwilling to make such further, revising judgments upon due deliberation. See, e.g., Don't Ask, Don't Tell Repeal Act of 2010.

The Court mentions none of this. Instead, it accuses the Congress that enacted this law and the President who signed it of something much worse than, for example, having acted in excess of enumerated federal powers—or even having drawn distinctions that prove to be irrational. Those legal errors may be made in good faith, errors though they are. But the majority says that the supporters of this Act acted with malice—with the "purpose" (ante, at 25) "to disparage and to injure" same-sex couples. It says that the motivation for DOMA was to "demean,"; to "impose inequality,"; to "impose . . . a stigma,"; to deny people "equal dignity," ibid.; to brand gay people as "unworthy," ante, at 23; and to "humiliat[e]" their children, ibid. (emphasis added).

I am sure these accusations are quite untrue. To be sure (as the majority points out), the legislation is called the Defense of Marriage Act. But to defend traditional marriage is not to condemn, demean, or humiliate those who would prefer other arrangements, any more than to defend the Constitution of the United States is to condemn, demean, or humiliate other constitutions. To hurl such accusations so casually demeans this institution. In the majority's judgment, any resistance to its holding is beyond the pale of reasoned disagreement. To question its high-handed invalidation of a presumptively valid statute is to act (the majority is sure) with the purpose to "disparage," "injure," "degrade," "demean," and "humiliate" our fellow human beings, our fellow citizens, who are homosexual. All that, simply for supporting an Act that did no more than codify an aspect of marriage that had been unquestioned in our society for most of its existence—indeed, had been unquestioned in virtually all societies for virtually all of human history. It is one thing for a society to elect change; it is another for a court of law to impose change by adjudging those who oppose it hostes humani generis, enemies of the human race.

*   *   *

The penultimate sentence of the majority's opinion is a naked declaration that "[t]his opinion and its holding are confined" to those couples "joined in same-sex marriages made lawful by the State." I have heard such "bald, unreasoned disclaimer[s]" before. When the Court declared a constitutional right to homosexual sodomy, we were assured that the case had nothing, nothing at all to do with "whether the government must give formal recognition to any relationship that homosexual persons seek to enter." Now we are told that DOMA is invalid because it "demeans the couple, whose moral and sexual choices the Constitution protects,"—with an accompanying citation of Lawrence. It takes real cheek for today's majority to assure us, as it is going out the door, that a constitutional requirement to give formal recognition to same-sex marriage is not at issue here—when what has preceded that assurance is a lecture on how superior the majority's moral judgment in favor of same-sex marriage is to the Congress's hateful moral judgment against it. I promise you this: The only thing that will "confine" the Court's holding is its sense of what it can get away with.

I do not mean to suggest disagreement with The Chief Justice's view, ante, pp. 2–4 (dissenting opinion), that lower federal courts and state courts can distinguish today's case when the issue before them is state denial of marital status to same-sex couples—or even that this Court could theoretically do so. Lord, an opinion with such scatter-shot rationales as this one (federalism noises among them) can be distinguished in many ways. And deserves to be. State and lower federal courts should take the Court at its word and distinguish away.

In my opinion, however, the view that this Court will take of state prohibition of same-sex marriage is indicated beyond mistaking by today's opinion. As I have said, the real rationale of today's opinion, whatever disappearing trail of its legalistic argle-bargle one chooses to follow, is that DOMA is motivated by "bare . . . desire to harm" couples in same-sex marriages. How easy it is, indeed how inevitable, to reach the same conclusion with regard to state laws denying same-sex couples marital status. Consider how easy (inevitable) it is to make the following substitutions in a passage from today's opinion:

> "DOMA's This state law's principal effect is to identify a subset of state-sanctioned marriages constitutionally protected sexual relationships, see Lawrence, and make them unequal. The principal purpose is to impose inequality, not for other reasons like governmental efficiency. Responsibilities, as well as rights, enhance the dignity and integrity of the person. And DOMA this state law contrives to deprive some couples married under the laws of their State enjoying constitutionally protected sexual relationships, but not other couples, of both rights and responsibilities."

Or try this passage:

> "[DOMA] This state law tells those couples, and all the world, that their otherwise valid marriages relationships are unworthy of federal state recognition. This places same-sex couples in an unstable position of being in a second-tier marriage relationship. The differentiation demeans the couple, whose moral and sexual choices the Constitution protects, see Lawrence, ..."

Or this—which does not even require alteration, except as to the invented number:

"And it humiliates tens of thousands of children now being raised by same-sex couples. The law in question makes it even more difficult for the children to under-

stand the integrity and closeness of their own family and its concord with other families in their community and in their daily lives."

Similarly transposable passages—deliberately transposable, I think—abound. In sum, that Court which finds it so horrific that Congress irrationally and hatefully robbed same-sex couples of the "personhood and dignity" which state legislatures conferred upon them, will of a certitude be similarly appalled by state legislatures' irrational and hateful failure to acknowledge that "personhood and dignity" in the first place. As far as this Court is concerned, no one should be fooled; it is just a matter of listening and waiting for the other shoe.

By formally declaring anyone opposed to same-sex marriage an enemy of human decency, the majority arms well every challenger to a state law restricting marriage to its traditional definition. Henceforth those challengers will lead with this Court's declaration that there is "no legitimate purpose" served by such a law, and will claim that the traditional definition has "the purpose and effect to disparage and to injure" the "personhood and dignity" of same-sex couples. The majority's limiting assurance will be meaningless in the face of language like that, as the majority well knows. That is why the language is there. The result will be a judicial distortion of our society's debate over marriage—a debate that can seem in need of our clumsy "help" only to a member of this institution.

As to that debate: Few public controversies touch an institution so central to the lives of so many, and few inspire such attendant passion by good people on all sides. Few public controversies will ever demonstrate so vividly the beauty of what our Framers gave us, a gift the Court pawns today to buy its stolen moment in the spotlight: a system of government that permits us to rule ourselves. Since DOMA's passage, citizens on all sides of the question have seen victories and they have seen defeats. There have been plebiscites, legislation, persuasion, and loud voices—in other words, democracy. Victories in one place for some, see North Carolina Const., Amdt. 1 (providing that "[m]arriage between one man and one woman is the only domestic legal union that shall be valid or recognized in this State") (approved by a popular vote, 61% to 39% on May 8, 2012), are offset by victories in other places for others, see Maryland Question 6 (establishing "that Maryland's civil marriage laws allow gay and lesbian couples to obtain a civil marriage license") (approved by a popular vote, 52% to 48%, on November 6, 2012). Even in a single State, the question has come out differently on different occasions. Compare Maine Question 1 (permitting "the State of Maine to issue marriage licenses to same-sex couples") (approved by a popular vote, 53% to 47%, on November 6, 2012) with Maine Question 1 (rejecting "the new law that lets same-sex couples marry") (approved by a popular vote, 53% to 47%, on November 3, 2009).

In the majority's telling, this story is black-and-white: Hate your neighbor or come along with us. The truth is more complicated. It is hard to admit that one's political opponents are not monsters, especially in a struggle like this one, and the challenge in the end proves more than today's Court can handle. Too bad. A reminder that disagreement over something so fundamental as marriage can still be politically legitimate would have been a fit task for what in earlier times was called the judicial temperament. We might have covered ourselves with honor today, by promising all sides of this debate that it was theirs to settle and that we would respect their resolution. We might have let the People decide.

But that the majority will not do. Some will rejoice in today's decision, and some will despair at it; that is the nature of a controversy that matters so much to so many. But the Court has cheated both sides, robbing the winners of an honest victory, and the losers of the peace that comes from a fair defeat. We owed both of them better. I dissent.

Antonin Scalia is a Supreme Court justice. He is often considered to be one of the intellectual heavyweights of the conservative block of justice on the Supreme Court.

EXPLORING THE ISSUE

Does the Federal Government Discriminate Against Same-Sex Couples If It Refuses to Recognize Their Marriage?

Critical Thinking and Reflection

1. What are some arguments made in each side with which you agree or disagree?
2. What are the strengths and weaknesses of the two positions made in this chapter?
3. Pick the side with which you most agree. What are some additional arguments you would make to strengthen the case for or against marriage equality?
4. Think more broadly about marriage equality. What is required to define the Constitution's role in whether or not marriage for same-sex couples is a fundamental right?

Is There Common Ground?

Both justices in this chapter are reading the same Constitution and the same case law. What are their primary differences about same-sex marriage? What arguments do they specifically make about same-sex relationships? Is there common ground about the role that the legislature can play? One issue not examined is civil unions, something that is often rejected by parties on both sides of this debate. Based on this ruling, couples in civil unions do not enjoy federal protections.

Additional Resources

Liptak, Adam, *To Love and Uphold* (2013)

Sullivan, Andrew, *Same-Sex Marriage: Pro and Con* (2004)

Robinson, Gene, *God Believes in Love: Straight Talk about Gay Marriage* (2013)

Create Central

www.mhhe.com/createcentral

Internet References . . .

American Center for Law and Justice

www.aclj.org/traditional-marriage

Gay Marriage Pro and Con

www.gaymarriage.procon.org

Marriage Equality USA

www.marriageequality.org

Selected, Edited, and with Issue Framing Material by:
David M. Hall, Ph.D., *Delaware Valley College*

ISSUE

Should Private Sexual Acts Between Gay Couples Be Illegal?

YES: Anthony Kennedy, from Majority Opinion, *Lawrence v. Texas*, U.S. Supreme Court (2003)

NO: Antonin Scalia, from Dissenting Opinion, *Lawrence v. Texas*, U.S. Supreme Court (2003)

Learning Outcomes
After reading this issue, you will be able to: • Identify the major arguments made for and against anti-sodomy laws. • Compare and contrast the competing arguments made for and against anti-sodomy laws in this issue. • Evaluate the implications of whether or not certain types of private, consensual sexual acts are legal or illegal.

ISSUE SUMMARY

YES: Anthony Kennedy, Associate Justice of the Supreme Court of the United States, was appointed to the Court by President Reagan in 1988. In this case, Kennedy is writing for a six-member majority that overturns a previous case, *Bowers v. Hardwick. Bowers* is overturned by Kennedy's opinion, therefore striking down state anti-sodomy laws.

NO: Antonin Scalia, Associate Justice of the Supreme Court of the United States, was appointed to the Court by President Reagan in 1986. Scalia writes that there are no constitutional protections from discrimination based on sexual orientation and that state sodomy laws should be upheld.

Anti-sodomy laws have been found throughout Western civilization dating back to the Middle Ages, a time during which the belief became common that non-procreative sex was immoral. The legacy of these morals is still evident in American society today. Throughout American history, homosexuality has been regarded as morally wrong and therefore has often been illegal. Many nineteenth- and twentieth-century religious readers and psychologists regarded homosexuality as a mental illness.

In 1948, Dr. Alfred Kinsey published the groundbreaking book *Sexual Behavior in the Human Male,* which was followed with the 1953 publication of another groundbreaking book, *Sexual Behavior in the Human Female.* In both texts, the longest chapters were specifically about homosexuality. Kinsey's work had a significant impact on challenging American sexual morality, and he was particularly concerned about the discrimination faced by those who were lesbian, gay, and bisexual, a population that at the time was largely regarded as sex criminals. His work, though widely read at the time, did not have an immediate widespread impact on public perceptions of those who were lesbian, gay, or bisexual. In fact, Kinsey's books were published at the onset of the Lavender Scare, a period in

which it was official U.S. policy to fire lesbian and gay federal employees.

The American Psychological Association removed homosexuality from its list of mental disorders in 1973. Coming out of the closet became increasingly common, and challenges to state anti-sodomy laws were practically inevitable. In 1986, the U.S. Supreme Court ruled in *Bowers v. Hardwick* to uphold state anti-sodomy laws.

In 2003, the Supreme Court heard a similar anti-sodomy case with *Lawrence v. Texas.* Prior to *Bowers* and *Lawrence,* the Supreme Court had three times ruled in favor of a non-procreative right to sex. In the 1965 case of *Griswold v. Connecticut,* the Supreme Court ruled that married couples have the right to have access to contraception. *Eisenstadt v. Baird* (1972) extended this same right to unmarried couples. In 1973, the Supreme Court ruled in *Roe v. Wade* that women have a constitutional right to obtain an abortion. This right has been upheld in subsequent Supreme Court cases. Although each of these cases deals with non-procreative sexual behaviors, they address neither sodomy nor homosexuality.

Lawrence v. Texas began when John Lawrence, who was not getting along with his neighbor, was engaged in consensual sex in his residence with another man, Tyron Garner. Lawrence's neighbor called the police with a false report of a burglary in Lawrence's residence. The police, having legal grounds to enter Lawrence's residence based on the phone call, entered and found Lawrence and Garner having sex. Lawrence and Garner were arrested, and the police charged them with violating Texas's antihomosexual conduct law. For having been caught engaging in consensual sex in a private residence, both men were found guilty, spent a night in prison, and were fined $200.

Lawrence and Garner appealed their conviction, claiming that their constitutional rights had been violated. Explicit in their argument was a challenge to the constitutional reasoning behind *Bowers v. Hardwick,* essentially arguing that *Bowers* had been wrongly decided and should be overturned. In 2003, *Lawrence v. Texas* reached the Supreme Court of the United States.

Review the legal framework section of the Introduction that examines Original Intent and Living Constitution. The opinions in this case are clear examples of these concepts. Try to identify which opinion is written from an Original Intent perspective and which is written from a Living Constitution perspective.

Lawrence and Garner won the case, and anti-sodomy laws were struck down in the remaining states that had them. Lawrence's neighbor was charged with making a false report to the police. *Lawrence v. Texas* is beginning to be regarded as a landmark Supreme Court case. Although this case was a significant victory for those who advocate for lesbian, gay, and bisexual rights, many students are stunned to find that, until recently, sodomy was illegal in many states. It may be interesting to research the history of anti-sodomy laws in your state.

How would you assess how the political climate has changed since 2003, when this decision was issued? In what ways was Justice Scalia correct and in what ways was he incorrect about the changes he said this decision could lead to?

A significant number of cases dealing with sexual orientation have been decided in state courts. In 2003, same-sex marriage was prohibited in all 50 states and the District of Columbia. As this book reaches publication, same-sex marriage is permitted in six states (Connecticut, Iowa, Massachusetts, New Hampshire, New York, and Vermont) and Washington, D.C. California has 18,000 same-sex married couples who wed during a brief period of legal recognition. Other states, such as California and Maryland, have active efforts to make same-sex marriage legal. In addition, there are states, such as New Jersey, California, and Rhode Island, that have active movements working to ensure that same-sex marriage rights are extended to their states.

In addition to states extending equal marital rights, many large corporations are instituting the equivalent in the workplace. According to the Human Rights Campaign's 2009 Corporate Equality Index, 259 companies employing more than 9 million employees prohibit discrimination based on sexual orientation and gender identity, while providing domestic partner benefits to their employees. These companies, when operating in states that deny lesbian and gay couples the right to marry, treat same-sex couples just as they treat married, heterosexual couples.

Some of the states that permit same-sex marriage have done so through state court order, while others have done so through legislative action. The case of *Lawrence v. Texas* did not serve as cited precedent in any of these state court decisions. However, this chapter demonstrates how quickly societal values have changed on this topic in, historically speaking, a relatively short period of time.

Based on what you learned from reading this chapter, what might be some topics for future Supreme Court cases at the federal level that will be related to sexual orientation? For what types of topics might *Lawrence v. Texas* be a particularly pertinent precedent?

YES ↩

Anthony Kennedy

Majority Opinion, *Lawrence v. Texas*

Liberty protects the person from unwarranted government intrusions into a dwelling or other private places. In our tradition, the State is not omnipresent in the home. And there are other spheres of our lives and existence, outside the home, where the State should not be a dominant presence. Freedom extends beyond spatial bounds. Liberty presumes an autonomy of self that includes freedom of thought, belief, expression, and certain intimate conduct. The instant case involves liberty of the person both in its spatial and more transcendent dimensions.

The question before the Court is the validity of a Texas statute making it a crime for two persons of the same sex to engage in certain intimate sexual conduct.

In Houston, Texas, officers of the Harris County Police Department were dispatched to a private residence in response to a reported weapons disturbance. They entered an apartment where one of the petitioners, John Geddes Lawrence, resided. The right of the police to enter does not seem to have been questioned. The officers observed Lawrence and another man, Tyron Garner, engaging in a sexual act. The two petitioners were arrested, held in custody overnight, and charged and convicted before a Justice of the Peace.

The complaints described their crime as "deviate sexual intercourse, namely anal sex, with a member of the same sex (man)." It provides: "A person commits an offense if he engages in deviate sexual intercourse with another individual of the same sex." The statute defines "[d]eviate sexual intercourse" as follows:

"(A) any contact between any part of the genitals of one person and the mouth or anus of another person; or

"(B) the penetration of the genitals or the anus of another person with an object."

We granted certiorari (2002) to consider three questions:

"1. Whether Petitioners' criminal convictions under the Texas 'Homosexual Conduct' law—which criminalizes sexual intimacy by same-sex couples, but not identical behavior by different-sex couples—violate the Fourteenth Amendment guarantee of equal protection of laws?

"2. Whether Petitioners' criminal convictions for adult consensual sexual intimacy in the home violate their vital interests in liberty and privacy protected by the Due Process Clause of the Fourteenth Amendment?

"3. Whether *Bowers* v. *Hardwick*, (1986), should be overruled?"

The petitioners were adults at the time of the alleged offense. Their conduct was in private and consensual.

We conclude the case should be resolved by determining whether the petitioners were free as adults to engage in the private conduct in the exercise of their liberty under the Due Process Clause of the Fourteenth Amendment to the Constitution. For this inquiry, we deem it necessary to reconsider the Court's holding in *Bowers*.

There are broad statements of the substantive reach of liberty under the Due Process Clause; but the most pertinent beginning point is our decision in *Griswold* v. *Connecticut* (1965).

In *Griswold,* the Court invalidated a state law prohibiting the use of drugs or devices of contraception and counseling or aiding and abetting the use of contraceptives. The Court described the protected interest as a right to privacy and placed emphasis on the marriage relation and the protected space of the marital bedroom.

"It is true that in *Griswold,* the right of privacy in question inhered in the marital relationship. . . . If the right of privacy means anything, it is the right of the *individual*, married or single, to be free from unwarranted governmental intrusion into matters so fundamentally affecting a person as the decision whether to bear or beget a child."

The opinions in *Griswold* and *Eisenstadt* were part of the background for the decision in *Roe* v. *Wade* (1973). As is well known, the case involved a challenge to the Texas law prohibiting abortions, but the laws of other States were affected as well. Although the Court held the woman's rights were not absolute, her right to elect an abortion did have real and substantial protection as an exercise of her liberty under the Due Process Clause. The Court cited cases that protect spatial freedom and cases that go well beyond it. *Roe* recognized the right of a woman to make certain fundamental decisions affecting her destiny and confirmed once more that the protection of liberty under the Due Process Clause has a substantive dimension of fundamental significance in defining the rights of the person.

In *Carey* v. *Population Services Int'l* (1977), the Court confronted a New York law forbidding sale or distribution of contraceptive devices to persons under 16 years of age. Although there was no single opinion for the Court, the law was invalidated. Both *Eisenstadt* and *Carey*, as well as the holding and rationale in *Roe*, confirmed that the reasoning of *Griswold* could not be confined to the protection of rights of married adults. This was the state of the law

---

Majority Opinion: *Lawrence v. Texas*, United States Supreme Court 539 U. S 558 (2003).

with respect to some of the most relevant cases when the Court considered *Bowers* v. *Hardwick.*

The facts in *Bowers* had some similarities to the instant case. A police officer, whose right to enter seems not to have been in question, observed Hardwick, in his own bedroom, engaging in intimate sexual conduct with another adult male. The conduct was in violation of a Georgia statute making it a criminal offense to engage in sodomy. One difference between the two cases is that the Georgia statute prohibited the conduct whether or not the participants were of the same sex, while the Texas statute, as we have seen, applies only to participants of the same sex. Hardwick was not prosecuted, but he brought an action in federal court to declare the state statute invalid. He alleged he was a practicing homosexual and that the criminal prohibition violated rights guaranteed to him by the Constitution. The Court, in an opinion by Justice White, sustained the Georgia law.

The Court began its substantive discussion in *Bowers* as follows: "The issue presented is whether the Federal Constitution confers a fundamental right upon homosexuals to engage in sodomy and hence invalidates the laws of the many States that still make such conduct illegal and have done so for a very long time." That statement, we now conclude, discloses the Court's own failure to appreciate the extent of the liberty at stake. To say that the issue in *Bowers* was simply the right to engage in certain sexual conduct demeans the claim the individual put forward, just as it would demean a married couple were it to be said marriage is simply about the right to have sexual intercourse. The laws involved in *Bowers* and here are, to be sure, statutes that purport to do no more than prohibit a particular sexual act. Their penalties and purposes, though, have more far-reaching consequences, touching upon the most private human conduct, sexual behavior, and in the most private of places, the home. The statutes do seek to control a personal relationship that, whether or not entitled to formal recognition in the law, is within the liberty of persons to choose without being punished as criminals.

This, as a general rule, should counsel against attempts by the State, or a court, to define the meaning of the relationship or to set its boundaries absent injury to a person or abuse of an institution the law protects. It suffices for us to acknowledge that adults may choose to enter upon this relationship in the confines of their homes and their own private lives and still retain their dignity as free persons. When sexuality finds overt expression in intimate conduct with another person, the conduct can be but one element in a personal bond that is more enduring. The liberty protected by the Constitution allows homosexual persons the right to make this choice.

Having misapprehended the claim of liberty there presented to it, and thus stating the claim to be whether there is a fundamental right to engage in consensual sodomy, the *Bowers* Court said: "Proscriptions against that conduct have ancient roots." In academic writings, and in many of the scholarly *amicus* briefs filed to assist the Court in this case, there are fundamental criticisms of the historical premises relied upon by the majority and concurring opinions in *Bowers*. We need not enter this debate in the attempt to reach a definitive historical judgment, but the following considerations counsel against adopting the definitive conclusions upon which *Bowers* placed such reliance.

At the outset, it should be noted that there is no longstanding history in this country of laws directed at homosexual conduct as a distinct matter. Beginning in colonial times, there were prohibitions of sodomy derived from the English criminal laws passed in the first instance by the Reformation Parliament of 1533. The English prohibition was understood to include relations between men and women as well as relations between men and men. Nineteenth-century commentators similarly read American sodomy, buggery, and crime-against-nature statutes as criminalizing certain relations between men and women and between men and men. The absence of legal prohibitions focusing on homosexual conduct may be explained in part by noting that, according to some scholars, the concept of the homosexual as a distinct category of person did not emerge until the late 19th century. Thus, early American sodomy laws were not directed at homosexuals as such, but instead sought to prohibit nonprocreative sexual activity more generally. This does not suggest approval of homosexual conduct. It does tend to show that this particular form of conduct was not thought of as a separate category from like conduct between heterosexual persons.

Laws prohibiting sodomy do not seem to have been enforced against consenting adults acting in private. A substantial number of sodomy prosecutions and convictions for which there are surviving records were for predatory acts against those who could not or did not consent, as in the case of a minor or the victim of an assault. As to these, one purpose for the prohibitions was to ensure there would be no lack of coverage if a predator committed a sexual assault that did not constitute rape as defined by the criminal law. Thus, the model sodomy indictments presented in a 19th-century treatise addressed the predatory acts of an adult man against a minor girl or minor boy. Instead of targeting relations between consenting adults in private, 19th-century sodomy prosecutions typically involved relations between men and minor girls or minor boys, relations between adults involving force, relations between adults implicating disparity in status, or relations between men and animals.

To the extent that there were any prosecutions for the acts in question, 19th-century evidence rules imposed a burden that would make a conviction more difficult to obtain, even taking into account the problems always inherent in prosecuting consensual acts committed in private. Under then-prevailing standards, a man could not be convicted of sodomy based upon testimony of a consenting partner, because the partner was considered an accomplice.

A partner's testimony, however, was admissible if he or she had not consented to the act or was a minor, and therefore incapable of consent. The rule may explain in part the infrequency of these prosecutions. In all events, that infrequency makes it difficult to say that society approved of a rigorous and systematic punishment of the consensual acts committed in private and by adults. The longstanding criminal prohibition of homosexual sodomy upon which the *Bowers* decision placed such reliance is as consistent with a general condemnation of nonprocreative sex as it is with an established tradition of prosecuting acts because of their homosexual character.

The policy of punishing consenting adults for private acts was not much discussed in the early legal literature. We can infer that one reason for this was the very private nature of the conduct. Despite the absence of prosecutions, there may have been periods in which there was public criticism of homosexuals as such and an insistence that the criminal laws be enforced to discourage their practices. But far from possessing "ancient roots," American laws targeting same-sex couples did not develop until the last third of the 20th century. The reported decisions concerning the prosecution of consensual, homosexual sodomy between adults for the years 1880–1995 are not always clear in the details, but a significant number involved conduct in a public place.

It was not until the 1970s that any State singled out same-sex relations for criminal prosecution, and only nine States have done so. Post-*Bowers*, even some of these States did not adhere to the policy of suppressing homosexual conduct. Over the course of the last decades, States with same-sex prohibitions have moved toward abolishing them.

In summary, the historical grounds relied upon in *Bowers* are more complex than the majority opinion and the concurring opinion by Chief Justice Burger indicate. Their historical premises are not without doubt and, at the very least, are overstated.

It must be acknowledged, of course, that the Court in *Bowers* was making the broader point that for centuries there have been powerful voices to condemn homosexual conduct as immoral. The condemnation has been shaped by religious beliefs, conceptions of right and acceptable behavior, and respect for the traditional family. For many persons, these are not trivial concerns but profound and deep convictions accepted as ethical and moral principles to which they aspire and which thus determine the course of their lives. These considerations do not answer the question before us, however. The issue is whether the majority may use the power of the State to enforce these views on the whole society through operation of the criminal law. "Our obligation is to define the liberty of all, not to mandate our own moral code." *Planned Parenthood of Southeastern Pa.* v. *Casey.*

Chief Justice Burger joined the opinion for the Court in *Bowers* and further explained his views as follows: "Decisions of individuals relating to homosexual conduct have been subject to state intervention throughout the history of Western civilization. Condemnation of those practices is firmly rooted in Judeo-Christian moral and ethical standards." As with Justice White's assumptions about history, scholarship casts some doubt on the sweeping nature of the statement by Chief Justice Burger as it pertains to private homosexual conduct between consenting adults. In all events, we think that our laws and traditions in the past half century are of most relevance here. These references show an emerging awareness that liberty gives substantial protection to adult persons in deciding how to conduct their private lives in matters pertaining to sex.

In 1955 the American Law Institute promulgated the Model Penal Code and made clear that it did not recommend or provide for "criminal penalties for consensual sexual relations conducted in private." It justified its decision on three grounds: (1) The prohibitions undermined respect for the law by penalizing conduct many people engaged in; (2) the statutes regulated private conduct not harmful to others; and (3) the laws were arbitrarily enforced and thus invited the danger of blackmail. Other States soon followed.

In *Bowers*, the Court referred to the fact that before 1961, all 50 States had outlawed sodomy, and that at the time of the Court's decision, 24 States and the District of Columbia had sodomy laws. Justice Powell pointed out that these prohibitions often were being ignored, however. Georgia, for instance, had not sought to enforce its law for decades.

The sweeping references by Chief Justice Burger to the history of Western civilization and to Judeo-Christian moral and ethical standards did not take account of other authorities pointing in an opposite direction. A committee advising the British Parliament recommended in 1957 repeal of laws punishing homosexual conduct. Parliament enacted the substance of those recommendations 10 years later.

Of even more importance, almost five years before *Bowers* was decided the European Court of Human Rights considered a case with parallels to *Bowers* and to today's case. An adult male resident in Northern Ireland alleged he was a practicing homosexual who desired to engage in consensual homosexual conduct. The laws of Northern Ireland forbade him that right. He alleged that he had been questioned, his home had been searched, and he feared criminal prosecution. The court held that the laws proscribing the conduct were invalid under the European Convention on Human Rights. Authoritative in all countries that are members of the Council of Europe (21 nations then, 45 nations now), the decision is at odds with the premise in *Bowers* that the claim put forward was insubstantial in our Western civilization.

In our own constitutional system, the deficiencies in *Bowers* became even more apparent in the years following its announcement. The 25 States with laws prohibiting the relevant conduct referenced in the *Bowers* decision are reduced now to 13, of which 4 enforce their laws only against homosexual conduct. In those States where sodomy is still proscribed, whether for same-sex or heterosexual conduct, there is a pattern of nonenforcement with respect to consenting adults acting in private. The State of Texas admitted in 1994 that as of that date, it had not prosecuted anyone under those circumstances.

Persons in a homosexual relationship may seek autonomy for these purposes, just as heterosexual persons do. The decision in *Bowers* would deny them this right.

The . . . post-*Bowers* case of principal relevance is *Romer* v. *Evans* (1996). There the Court struck down class-based legislation directed at homosexuals as a violation of the Equal Protection Clause. *Romer* invalidated an amendment to Colorado's constitution which named as a solitary class persons who were homosexuals, lesbians, or bisexual either by "orientation, conduct, practices, or relationships," and deprived them of protection under state antidiscrimination laws. We concluded that the provision was "born of animosity toward the class of persons affected" and, further, that it had no rational relation to a legitimate governmental purpose.

As an alternative argument in this case, counsel for the petitioners and some *amici* contend that *Romer* provides the basis for declaring the Texas statute invalid under the Equal Protection Clause. That is a tenable argument, but we conclude the instant case requires us to address whether *Bowers* itself has continuing validity. Were we to hold the statute invalid under the Equal Protection Clause, some might question whether a prohibition would be valid if drawn differently, say, to prohibit the conduct both between same-sex and different-sex participants.

Equality of treatment and the due process right to demand respect for conduct protected by the substantive guarantee of liberty are linked in important respects, and a decision on the latter point advances both interests. If protected conduct is made criminal and the law which does so remains unexamined for its substantive validity, its stigma might remain even if it were not enforceable as drawn for equal protection reasons. When homosexual conduct is made criminal by the law of the State, that declaration in and of itself is an invitation to subject homosexual persons to discrimination both in the public and in the private spheres. The central holding of *Bowers* has been brought in question by this case, and it should be addressed. Its continuance as precedent demeans the lives of homosexual persons.

The stigma this criminal statute imposes, moreover, is not trivial. The offense, to be sure, is but a class C misdemeanor, a minor offense in the Texas legal system. Still, it remains a criminal offense, with all that imports for the dignity of the persons charged. The petitioners will bear on their record the history of their criminal convictions. Just this Term, we rejected various challenges to state laws requiring the registration of sex offenders. We are advised that if Texas convicted an adult for private, consensual homosexual conduct under the statute here in question, the convicted person would come within the registration laws of a least four States were he or she to be subject

to their jurisdiction. This underscores the consequential nature of the punishment and the state-sponsored condemnation attendant to the criminal prohibition. Furthermore, the Texas criminal conviction carries with it the other collateral consequences always following a conviction, such as notations on job application forms, to mention but one example.

The foundations of *Bowers* have sustained serious erosion from our recent decisions in *Casey* and *Romer*. When our precedent has been thus weakened, criticism from other sources is of greater significance. In the United States criticism of *Bowers* has been substantial and continuing, disapproving of its reasoning in all respects, not just as to its historical assumptions. The courts of five different States have declined to follow it in interpreting provisions in their own state constitutions parallel to the Due Process Clause of the Fourteenth Amendment.

To the extent *Bowers* relied on values we share with a wider civilization, it should be noted that the reasoning and holding in *Bowers* have been rejected elsewhere. The European Court of Human Rights has followed not *Bowers* but its own decision in *Dudgeon* v. *United Kingdom*. Other nations, too, have taken action consistent with an affirmation of the protected right of homosexual adults to engage in intimate, consensual conduct. The right the petitioners seek in this case has been accepted as an integral part of human freedom in many other countries. There has been no showing that in this country, the governmental interest in circumscribing personal choice is somehow more legitimate or urgent.

The rationale of *Bowers* does not withstand careful analysis. In his dissenting opinion in *Bowers*, Justice Stevens came to these conclusions:

"Our prior cases make two propositions abundantly clear. First, the fact that the governing majority in a State has traditionally viewed a particular practice as immoral is not a sufficient reason for upholding a law prohibiting the practice; neither history nor tradition could save a law prohibiting miscegenation from constitutional attack. Second, individual decisions by married persons, concerning the intimacies of their physical relationship, even when not intended to produce offspring, are a form of "liberty" protected by the Due Process Clause of the Fourteenth Amendment. Moreover, this protection extends to intimate choices by unmarried as well as married persons."

Justice Stevens' analysis, in our view, should have been controlling in *Bowers* and should control here.

Bowers was not correct when it was decided, and it is not correct today. It ought not to remain binding precedent. *Bowers* v. *Hardwick* should be and now is overruled.

The present case does not involve minors. It does not involve persons who might be injured or coerced or who are situated in relationships where consent might not easily be refused. It does not involve public conduct or prostitution. It does not involve whether the government must give formal recognition to any relationship that homosexual persons seek to enter. The case does involve two adults who, with full and mutual consent from each other, engaged in sexual practices common to a homosexual lifestyle. The petitioners are entitled to respect for their private lives. The State cannot demean their existence or control their destiny by making their private sexual conduct a crime. Their right to liberty under the Due Process Clause gives them the full right to engage in their conduct without intervention of the government. "It is a promise of the Constitution that there is a realm of personal liberty which the government may not enter." The Texas statute furthers no legitimate state interest which can justify its intrusion into the personal and private life of the individual.

Had those who drew and ratified the Due Process Clauses of the Fifth Amendment or the Fourteenth Amendment known the components of liberty in its manifold possibilities, they might have been more specific. They did not presume to have this insight. They knew times can blind us to certain truths and later generations can see that laws once thought necessary and proper in fact serve only to oppress. As the Constitution endures, persons in every generation can invoke its principles in their own search for greater freedom.

The judgment of the Court of Appeals for the Texas Fourteenth District is reversed, and the case is remanded for further proceedings not inconsistent with this opinion.

It is so ordered.

ANTHONY KENNEDY is an Associate Justice of the Supreme Court of the United States who was appointed by President Ronald Reagan in 1988. Since the retirement of Justice Sandra Day O'Connor in 2005, Justice Kennedy has been the most important swing vote on the Supreme Court, especially in constitutional litigation.

Antonin Scalia

Dissenting Opinion, *Lawrence v. Texas*

Most of the rest of today's opinion has no relevance to its actual holding—that the Texas statute "furthers no legitimate state interest which can justify" its application to petitioners under rational-basis review. Though there is discussion of "fundamental proposition[s]," and "fundamental decisions," *ibid.* nowhere does the Court's opinion declare that homosexual sodomy is a "fundamental right" under the Due Process Clause; nor does it subject the Texas law to the standard of review that would be appropriate (strict scrutiny) if homosexual sodomy *were* a "fundamental right." Thus, while overruling the *outcome* of *Bowers,* the Court leaves strangely untouched its central legal conclusion: "[R]espondent would have us announce . . . a fundamental right to engage in homosexual sodomy. This we are quite unwilling to do." Instead, the Court simply describes petitioners' conduct as "an exercise of their liberty"—which it undoubtedly is—and proceeds to apply an unheard-of form of rational-basis review that will have far-reaching implications beyond this case.

(1) A preliminary digressive observation with regard to the first factor: The Court's claim that *"Planned Parenthood* v. *Casey, supra,* "casts some doubt" upon the holding in *Bowers* (or any other case, for that matter) does not withstand analysis. As far as its holding is concerned, *Casey* provided a *less* expansive right to abortion than did *Roe, which was already on the books when Bowers was decided.* I have never heard of a law that attempted to restrict one's "right to define" certain concepts; and if the passage calls into question the government's power to regulate *actions based on* one's self-defined "concept of existence, etc.," it is the passage that ate the rule of law.

(2) Bowers, the Court says, has been subject to "substantial and continuing [criticism], disapproving of its reasoning in all respects, not just as to its historical assumptions." Exactly what those nonhistorical criticisms are, and whether the Court even agrees with them, are left unsaid, although the Court does cite two books. Of course, *Roe* too (and by extension *Casey)* had been (and still is) subject to unrelenting criticism, including criticism from the two commentators cited by the Court today.

(3) That leaves, to distinguish the rock-solid, unamendable disposition of *Roe* from the readily overrulable *Bowers,* only the third factor. "[T]here has been," the Court says, "no individual or societal reliance on *Bowers* of the sort that could counsel against overturning its holding. . . ." *Ante,* at 16. It seems to me that the "societal reliance" on the principles confirmed in *Bowers* and

discarded today has been overwhelming. Countless judicial decisions and legislative enactments have relied on the ancient proposition that a governing majority's belief that certain sexual behavior is "immoral and unacceptable" constitutes a rational basis for regulation. We ourselves relied extensively on *Bowers* when we concluded, in *Barnes* v. *Glen Theatre, Inc.* (1991), that Indiana's public indecency statute furthered "a substantial government interest in protecting order and morality." State laws against bigamy, same-sex marriage, adult incest, prostitution, masturbation, adultery, fornication, bestiality, and obscenity are likewise sustainable only in light of *Bowers'* validation of laws based on moral choices. Every single one of these laws is called into question by today's decision; the Court makes no effort to cabin the scope of its decision to exclude them from its holding. See *ante,* at 11 (noting "an emerging awareness that liberty gives substantial protection to adult persons in deciding how to conduct their private lives *in matters pertaining to sex*" (emphasis added)). The impossibility of distinguishing homosexuality from other traditional "morals" offenses is precisely why *Bowers* rejected the rational-basis challenge. "The law," it said, "is constantly based on notions of morality, and if all laws representing essentially moral choices are to be invalidated under the Due Process Clause, the courts will be very busy indeed."

Texas Penal Code (2003) undoubtedly imposes constraints on liberty. So do laws prohibiting prostitution, recreational use of heroin, and, for that matter, working more than 60 hours per week in a bakery. But there is no right to "liberty" under the Due Process Clause, though today's opinion repeatedly makes that claim. The Fourteenth Amendment *expressly allows* States to deprive their citizens of "liberty," so long as "due process of law" is provided:

"No state shall . . . deprive any person of life, liberty, or property, *without due process of law.*"

Our opinions applying the doctrine known as "substantive due process" hold that the Due Process Clause prohibits States from infringing *fundamental* liberty interests, unless the infringement is narrowly tailored to serve a compelling state interest. We have held repeatedly, in cases the Court today does not overrule, that *only* fundamental rights qualify for this so-called "heightened scrutiny" protection—that is, rights which are "'deeply rooted in this Nation's history and tradition.'" All other liberty interests may be abridged or abrogated pursuant to a validly enacted state law if that law is rationally related to a legitimate state interest.

Dissenting Opinion: *Lawrence v. Texas,* United States Supreme Court 539 U. S 558 (2003).

Bowers held, first, that criminal prohibitions of homosexual sodomy are not subject to heightened scrutiny because they do not implicate a "fundamental right" under the Due Process Clause. Noting that "[p]roscriptions against that conduct have ancient roots," *id.*, at 192, that "[s]odomy was a criminal offense at common law and was forbidden by the laws of the original 13 States when they ratified the Bill of Rights," and that many States had retained their bans on sodomy, *Bowers* concluded that a right to engage in homosexual sodomy was not "'deeply rooted in this Nation's history and tradition.'"

The Court today does not overrule this holding. Not once does it describe homosexual sodomy as a "fundamental right" or a "fundamental liberty interest," nor does it subject the Texas statute to strict scrutiny. Instead, having failed to establish that the right to homosexual sodomy is "'deeply rooted in this Nation's history and tradition,'" the Court concludes that the application of Texas's statute to petitioners' conduct fails the rational-basis test, and overrules *Bowers*' holding to the contrary, "The Texas statute furthers no legitimate state interest which can justify its intrusion into the personal and private life of the individual."

The Court's description of "the state of the law" at the time of *Bowers* only confirms that *Bowers* was right. The Court points to *Griswold* v. *Connecticut* (1965). But that case *expressly disclaimed* any reliance on the doctrine of "substantive due process," and grounded the so-called "right to privacy" in penumbras of constitutional provisions *other than* the Due Process Clause. *Eisenstadt* v. *Baird* (1972), likewise had nothing to do with "substantive due process"; it invalidated a Massachusetts law prohibiting the distribution of contraceptives to unmarried persons solely on the basis of the Equal Protection Clause. Of course *Eisenstadt* contains well known dictum relating to the "right to privacy," but this referred to the right recognized in *Griswold*—a right penumbral to the *specific* guarantees in the Bill of Rights, and not a "substantive due process" right.

Roe v. *Wade* recognized that the right to abort an unborn child was a "fundamental right" protected by the Due Process Clause. The *Roe* Court, however, made no attempt to establish that this right was "'deeply rooted in this Nation's history and tradition'"; instead, it based its conclusion that "the Fourteenth Amendment's concept of personal liberty . . . is broad enough to encompass a woman's decision whether or not to terminate her pregnancy" on its own normative judgment that anti-abortion laws were undesirable. We have since rejected *Roe*'s holding that regulations of abortion must be narrowly tailored to serve a compelling state interest.

After discussing the history of anti-sodomy laws, the Court proclaims that, "it should be noted that there is no longstanding history in this country of laws directed at homosexual conduct as a distinct matter." This observation in no way casts into doubt the "definitive [historical] conclusion" on which *Bowers* relied: that our Nation has a longstanding history of laws prohibiting *sodomy in general*—regardless of whether it was performed by same-sex or opposite-sex couples:

"It is obvious to us that neither of these formulations would extend a fundamental right to homosexuals to engage in acts of consensual sodomy. Proscriptions against that conduct have ancient roots. *Sodomy* was a criminal offense at common law and was forbidden by the laws of the original 13 States when they ratified the Bill of Rights. In 1868, when the Fourteenth Amendment was ratified, all but 5 of the 37 States in the Union had *criminal sodomy laws*. In fact, until 1961, all 50 States outlawed *sodomy*, and today, 24 States and the District of Columbia continue to provide criminal penalties for *sodomy* performed in private and between consenting adults. Against this background, to claim that a right to engage in such conduct is 'deeply rooted in this Nation's history and tradition' or 'implicit in the concept of ordered liberty' is, at best, facetious."

It is (as *Bowers* recognized) entirely irrelevant whether the laws in our long national tradition criminalizing homosexual sodomy were "directed at homosexual conduct as a distinct matter." Whether homosexual sodomy was prohibited by a law targeted at same-sex sexual relations or by a more general law prohibiting both homosexual and heterosexual sodomy, the only relevant point is that it *was* criminalized—which suffices to establish that homosexual sodomy is not a right "deeply rooted in our Nation's history and tradition." The Court today agrees that homosexual sodomy was criminalized and thus does not dispute the facts on which *Bowers actually* relied.

Next the Court makes the claim, again unsupported by any citations, that "[l]aws prohibiting sodomy do not seem to have been enforced against consenting adults acting in private." *Ante*, at 8. The key qualifier here is "acting in private"—since the Court admits that sodomy laws *were* enforced against consenting adults (although the Court contends that prosecutions were "infrequent"). I do not know what "acting in private" means; surely consensual sodomy, like heterosexual intercourse, is rarely performed on stage. If all the Court means by "acting in private" is "on private premises, with the doors closed and windows covered," it is entirely unsurprising that evidence of enforcement would be hard to come by. (Imagine the circumstances that would enable a search warrant to be obtained for a residence on the ground that there was probable cause to believe that consensual sodomy was then and there occurring.) Surely that lack of evidence would not sustain the proposition that consensual sodomy on private premises with the doors closed and windows covered was regarded as a "fundamental right," even though all other consensual sodomy was criminalized. There are 203 prosecutions for consensual, adult homosexual sodomy reported in the West Reporting system and official state reporters from the years 1880–1995. There are also records of 20 sodomy prosecutions and 4 executions during the colonial period. *Bowers*' conclusion that homosexual sodomy is not a fundamental right "deeply rooted in this Nation's history and tradition" is utterly unassailable.

Realizing that fact, the Court instead says: "[W]e think that our laws and traditions in the past half century are of most relevance here. These references show *an emerging awareness* that liberty gives substantial protection to adult persons in deciding how to conduct their private lives *in matters pertaining to sex*" (emphasis added). Apart from the fact that such an "emerging awareness" does not establish a "fundamental right," the statement is factually false. States continue to prosecute all sorts of crimes by adults "in matters pertaining to sex": prostitution, adult incest, adultery, obscenity, and child pornography. Sodomy laws, too, have been enforced "in the past half century," in which there have been 134 reported cases involving prosecutions for consensual, adult, homosexual sodomy. In relying, for evidence of an "emerging recognition," upon the American Law Institute's 1955 recommendation not to criminalize "'consensual sexual relations conducted in private,'" the Court ignores the fact that this recommendation was "a point of resistance in most of the states that considered adopting the Model Penal Code." Gaylaw 159.

In any event, an "emerging awareness" is by definition not "deeply rooted in this Nation's history and tradition[s]," as we have said "fundamental right" status requires. Constitutional entitlements do not spring into existence because some States choose to lessen or eliminate criminal sanctions on certain behavior. Much less do they spring into existence, as the Court seems to believe, because *foreign nations* decriminalize conduct. The *Bowers* majority opinion *never* relied on "values we share with a wider civilization," but rather rejected the claimed right to sodomy on the ground that such a right was not "'deeply rooted in *this Nation's* history and tradition'" (emphasis added). *Bowers'* rational-basis holding is likewise devoid of any reliance on the views of a "wider civilization." The Court's discussion of these foreign views (ignoring, of course, the many countries that have retained criminal prohibitions on sodomy) is therefore meaningless dicta. Dangerous dicta, however, since "this Court . . . should not impose foreign moods, fads, or fashions on Americans."

I turn now to the ground on which the Court squarely rests its holding: the contention that there is no rational basis for the law here under attack. This proposition is so out of accord with our jurisprudence—indeed, with the jurisprudence of *any* society we know—that it requires little discussion.

The Texas statute undeniably seeks to further the belief of its citizens that certain forms of sexual behavior are "immoral and unacceptable," *Bowers*—the same interest furthered by criminal laws against fornication, bigamy, adultery, adult incest, bestiality, and obscenity. *Bowers* held that this *was* a legitimate state interest. The Court today reaches the opposite conclusion. The Texas statute, it says, "furthers *no legitimate state interest* which can justify its intrusion into the personal and private life

of the individual" (emphasis addded). The Court embraces instead Justice Stevens' declaration in his *Bowers* dissent, that "the fact that the governing majority in a State has traditionally viewed a particular practice as immoral is not a sufficient reason for upholding a law prohibiting the practice." This effectively decrees the end of all morals legislation. If, as the Court asserts, the promotion of majoritarian sexual morality is not even a *legitimate* state interest, none of the above-mentioned laws can survive rational-basis review.

Finally, I turn to petitioners' equal-protection challenge, which no Member of the Court save Justice O'Connor, *ante*, at 1 (opinion concurring in judgment), embraces: On its face, §21.06(a) applies equally to all persons. Men and women, heterosexuals and homosexuals, are all subject to its prohibition of deviate sexual intercourse with someone of the same sex. To be sure, §21.06 does distinguish between the sexes insofar as concerns the partner with whom the sexual acts are performed: men can violate the law only with other men, and women only with other women. But this cannot itself be a denial of equal protection, since it is precisely the same distinction regarding partner that is drawn in state laws prohibiting marriage with someone of the same sex while permitting marriage with someone of the opposite sex.

The objection is made, however, that the antimiscegenation laws invalidated in *Loving* v. *Virginia* (1967), similarly were applicable to whites and blacks alike, and only distinguished between the races insofar as the *partner* was concerned. In *Loving*, however, we correctly applied heightened scrutiny, rather than the usual rational-basis review, because the Virginia statute was "designed to maintain White Supremacy." A racially discriminatory purpose is always sufficient to subject a law to strict scrutiny, even a facially neutral law that makes no mention of race. No purpose to discriminate against men or women as a class can be gleaned from the Texas law, so rational-basis review applies. That review is readily satisfied here by the same rational basis that satisfied it in *Bowers*—society's belief that certain forms of sexual behavior are "immoral and unacceptable." This is the same justification that supports many other laws regulating sexual behavior that make a distinction based upon the identity of the partner—for example, laws against adultery, fornication, and adult incest and laws refusing to recognize homosexual marriage.

Justice O'Connor argues that the discrimination in this law which must be justified is not its discrimination with regard to the sex of the partner but its discrimination with regard to the sexual proclivity of the principal actor.

"While it is true that the law applies only to conduct, the conduct targeted by this law is conduct that is closely correlated with being homosexual. Under such circumstances, Texas' sodomy law is targeted at more than conduct. It is instead directed toward gay persons as a class."

Of course, the same could be said of any law. A law against public nudity targets "the conduct that is closely correlated with being a nudist," and hence "is targeted at more than conduct"; it is "directed toward nudists as a class." But be that as it may. Even if the Texas law *does* deny equal protection to "homosexuals as a class," that denial *still* does not need to be justified by anything more than a rational basis, which our cases show is satisfied by the enforcement of traditional notions of sexual morality.

Justice O'Connor simply decrees application of "a more searching form of rational basis review" to the Texas statute. The cases she cites do not recognize such a standard, and reach their conclusions only after finding, as required by conventional rational-basis analysis, that no conceivable legitimate state interest supports the classification at issue. Nor does Justice O'Connor explain precisely what her "more searching form" of rational-basis review consists of. It must at least mean, however, that laws exhibiting "'a . . . desire to harm a politically unpopular group'" are invalid *even though* there may be a conceivable rational basis to support them.

This reasoning leaves on pretty shaky grounds state laws limiting marriage to opposite-sex couples. Justice O'Connor seeks to preserve them by the conclusory statement that "preserving the traditional institution of marriage" is a legitimate state interest. But "preserving the traditional institution of marriage" is just a kinder way of describing the State's *moral disapproval* of same-sex couples. Texas's interest in §21.06 could be recast in similarly euphemistic terms: "preserving the traditional sexual mores of our society." In the jurisprudence Justice O'Connor has seemingly created, judges can validate laws by characterizing them as "preserving the traditions of society" (good); or invalidate them by characterizing them as "expressing moral disapproval" (bad).

Today's opinion is the product of a Court, which is the product of a law-profession culture that has largely signed on to the so-called homosexual agenda, by which I mean the agenda promoted by some homosexual activists directed at eliminating the moral opprobrium that has traditionally attached to homosexual conduct. I noted in an earlier opinion the fact that the American Association of Law Schools (to which any reputable law school *must* seek to belong) excludes from membership any school that refuses to ban from its job-interview facilities a law firm (no matter how small) that does not wish to hire as a prospective partner a person who openly engages in homosexual conduct.

One of the most revealing statements in today's opinion is the Court's grim warning that the criminalization of homosexual conduct is "an invitation to subject homosexual persons to discrimination both in the public and in the private spheres." It is clear from this that the Court has taken sides in the culture war, departing from its role of assuring, as neutral observer, that the democratic rules of engagement are observed. Many Americans do not want persons who openly engage in homosexual conduct as partners in their business, as scoutmasters for their children, as teachers in their children's schools, or as boarders in their home. They view this as protecting themselves and their families from a lifestyle that they believe to be immoral and destructive. The Court views it as "discrimination" which it is the function of our judgments to deter. So imbued is the Court with the law profession's anti-anti-homosexual culture, that it is seemingly unaware that the attitudes of that culture are not obviously "mainstream"; that in most States, what the Court calls "discrimination" against those who engage in homosexual acts is perfectly legal; that proposals to ban such "discrimination" under Title VII have repeatedly been rejected by Congress.

Let me be clear that I have nothing against homosexuals, or any other group, promoting their agenda through normal democratic means. Social perceptions of sexual and other morality change over time, and every group has the right to persuade its fellow citizens that its view of such matters is the best. That homosexuals have achieved some success in that enterprise is attested to by the fact that Texas is one of the few remaining States that criminalize private, consensual homosexual acts. But persuading one's fellow citizens is one thing, and imposing one's views in absence of democratic majority will is something else. I would no more *require* a State to criminalize homosexual acts—or, for that matter, display *any* moral disapproval of them—than I would *forbid* it to do so. What Texas has chosen to do is well within the range of traditional democratic action, and its hand should not be stayed through the invention of a brand-new "constitutional right" by a Court that is impatient of democratic change. It is indeed true that "later generations can see that laws once thought necessary and proper in fact serve only to oppress," and when that happens, later generations can repeal those laws. But it is the premise of our system that those judgments are to be made by the people, and not imposed by a governing caste that knows best.

One of the benefits of leaving regulation of this matter to the people rather than to the courts is that the people, unlike judges, need not carry things to their logical conclusion. The people may feel that their disapprobation of homosexual conduct is strong enough to disallow homosexual marriage, but not strong enough to criminalize private homosexual acts—and may legislate accordingly. The Court today pretends that it possesses a similar freedom of action, so that that we need not fear judicial imposition of homosexual marriage, as has recently occurred in Canada (in a decision that the Canadian Government has chosen not to appeal). At the end of its opinion—after having laid waste the foundations of our rational-basis jurisprudence—the Court says that the present case "does not involve whether the government must give formal recognition to any relationship that homosexual persons seek to enter." Do not believe it. More illuminating than this bald, unreasoned disclaimer is the progression of thought displayed by an earlier passage in the Court's opinion, which notes the constitutional protections afforded to "personal decisions relating to *marriage*, procreation, contraception, family relationships, child rearing, and education," and then declares that "[p]ersons in a homosexual relationship may seek autonomy for these purposes, just as heterosexual persons do" (emphasis added). Today's opinion dismantles the structure of constitutional law that has permitted a distinction to be made between heterosexual and homosexual unions, insofar as formal recognition in marriage is concerned. If moral disapprobation of homosexual conduct is "no legitimate state interest" for purposes of proscribing that conduct, and if, as the Court coos (casting aside all pretense of neutrality), "[w]hen sexuality finds overt expression in intimate conduct with another person, the conduct can be but one element in a personal bond that is more enduring," what justification could there possibly be for denying the benefits of marriage to homosexual couples exercising "[t]he liberty protected by the Constitution," Surely not the encouragement of procreation, since the sterile and the elderly are allowed to marry. This case "does not involve" the issue of homosexual marriage only if one entertains the belief that principle and logic have nothing to do with the decisions of this Court. Many will hope that, as the Court comfortingly assures us, this is so.

The matters appropriate for this Court's resolution are only three: Texas's prohibition of sodomy neither infringes a "fundamental right" (which the Court does not dispute), nor is unsupported by a rational relation to what the Constitution considers a legitimate state interest, nor denies the equal protection of the laws. I dissent.

ANTONIN SCALIA is an Associate Justice of the Supreme Court of the United States who was appointed by President Ronald Reagan in 1986. Justice Scalia is the longest-serving justice currently on the Court and is the Senior Associate Justice.

EXPLORING THE ISSUE

Should Private Sexual Acts Between Gay Couples Be Illegal?

Critical Thinking and Reflection

1. What are some arguments made by each side with which you agree or disagree?
2. What are the strengths and weaknesses of the two positions made in this chapter?
3. Pick the side with which you most agree.
4. What are some additional arguments you would make to strengthen the case for or against anti-sodomy laws?
5. Think more broadly of the issue of anti-sodomy laws. This law inherently affects same-sex couples. What do the existence of such laws, or the absence of them, demonstrate about larger views about sexual orientation and power in American society?

Is There Common Ground?

While there might be differences in views regarding what laws should say regarding relationships, what about status related to discrimination? Are there those who would support anti-sodomy laws but also agree that no one should be fired due to their sexual orientation or gender identity/ expression? Are there those who oppose anti-sodomy laws but want to work to create a greater understanding about diversity and inclusion?

In addition, if we are going to uphold anti-sodomy laws, what does that mean about other rights? If sodomy can be illegal, can contraception become illegal? After all, is it any different for heterosexuals to have non-procreative sex versus those who are gay or lesbian? What are the implications (good and/or bad) of agreeing that there are no inherent rights to private, sexual behavior?

Create Central

www.mhhe.com/createcentral

Additional Resources

American Family Association:

www.afa.net

Focus on the Family:

www.focusonthefamily.com/

Human Rights Campaign:

www.hrc.org

Lambda Legal:

www.lambdalegal.org/

Internet References . . .

American Family Association

www.afa.net

Focus on the Family

www.focusonthefamily.com

Human Rights Campaign

www.hrc.org

Lambda Legal

www.lambdalegal.org

Selected, Edited, and with Issue Framing Material by:
David M. Hall, Ph.D., *Delaware Valley College*

ISSUE

Are Traditional Families Better Than Nontraditional Families?

YES: Allan C. Carlson and Paul T. Mero, excerpts from *The Natural Family: A Manifesto* (2005–2006)

NO: Mark Good, "Nontraditional Families and Childhood Progress through School," written for *Taking Sides: Family and Personal Relationships* (2012)

Learning Outcomes

After reading this issue, you will be able to:

- Identify the major arguments made for and against the traditional family.
- Compare and contrast the competing arguments made for and against the traditional family in this issue.
- Evaluate the implications of changing family structure on children and the larger American society.

ISSUE SUMMARY

YES: Allan Carlson is President of the Howard Center for Family, Religion & Society and Distinguished Fellow in Family Policy Studies at the Family Research Council in Washington, D.C. Paul Mero is President of the Sutherland Institute and a Trustee of the ALS Foundation. Carlson and Mero argue that America needs to return to a traditional family headed by a man and a woman.

NO: Mark Good is a Professor of Counselor Education at West Chester University and the President of Opn-Wyd, a diversity and communication company. Good argues that diversity in traditional and nontraditional families is healthy. In fact, he argues that it can be damaging to hold up the traditional family as the ideal familial structure.

Throughout most of American history, the concept of marriage and parenthood has seen a mild fluctuation. Ages for marriage may have changed a bit. Much has remained steady and intact, but over the past decades, we also have seen a fairly profound change in the nature of family.

Greater access to birth control, which was guaranteed to all married couples by the Supreme Court during the late 1960s, gave couples greater power over the timing of and frequency of child rearing. While women still face discrimination in terms of employment and wages, today's woman has more opportunities in the workplace than in generations past. Indeed, there was a time in American history when marriage was virtually the only way that women could secure their economic future. Today, women face different challenges than men, but millions manage to provide to support single mothers and their children. During times of economic distress, the discrepancy in wages can result in increased job secu-

rity for women. For example, while there certainly is discrimination based on wages, in 2010, more women were employed than men.

Economic opportunities for women are by no means the only issue reconstructing our definition of families. For example, same-sex marriage, something not recognized in any of the 50 states just one decade ago, is legal in six states and Washington, D.C., and is likely to spread to additional states over the coming years. Today, the number of adults who have never married remains much higher than it had been for generations past. This trend is not absent of having children, as there is also a rise in single parents raising children in the United States.

What do these changes mean? These days, are adult generations living in diverse family structures at the expense of and to the detriment of children? Or have we reached a more democratic, egalitarian family structure that comes closer to embracing our nation's true diversity? The answer divides a wide array of Americans.

Each political party has a different view of the value of traditional versus nontraditional families. The 2008 Republican National Platform states the following:

Preserving Traditional Marriage

Because our children's future is best preserved within the traditional understanding of marriage, we call for a constitutional amendment that fully protects marriage as a union of a man and a woman. . . .

Republicans recognize the importance of having in the home a father and a mother who are married. The two-parent family still provides the best environment of stability, discipline, responsibility, and character. Children in homes without fathers are more likely to commit a crime, drop out of school, become violent, become teen parents, use illegal drugs, become mired in poverty, or have emotional or behavioral problems. We support the courageous efforts of single-parent families to provide a stable home for their children. . . .

As the family is our basic unit of society, we oppose initiatives to erode parental rights.

On which side of this debate would one find the Republican Party? If we look back to the Political Ideology continuum at the start of the chapter, where would the aforementioned views fall along the continuum? While supporting the traditional family, there is an acknowledgment of the "courage" of single parents. Why is this, when they cite a two-parent family as the ideal?

What about examining the Republican position through a Lakoffian Nation as Family framework, also cited in the Introduction. Does this represent Strict Father Morality? Nurturant Parent Morality? What does the language itself tell you about the larger worldview of the Republican Party as stated in this section of their platform?

The Democratic National Committee released its own platform that mentions families without using the word *traditional*:

Children and Families

If we are to renew America, we must do a better job of investing in the next generation of Americans.

For parents, the first and most sacred responsibility is to support our children: setting an example of excellence, turning off the TV, and helping with the homework. But we must also support parents as they strive to raise their children in a new era. We must make it easier for working parents to spend time with their families when they need to. . . We also must recognize that caring for family members and managing a household is real and valuable work.

Fatherhood

Too many fathers are missing—missing from too many lives and too many homes. Children who grow up without a father are five times more likely to live in poverty and are more likely to commit crime, drop out of school, abuse drugs, and end up in prison. We need more fathers to realize that responsibility does not end at conception. We need them to understand that what makes a man is not the ability to have a child—it's the courage to raise one.

On which side of this debate would one find the Democratic Party? If we look back to the Political Ideology continuum at the start of the chapter, where would the aforementioned views fall along the continuum? While supporting the family, there is a listing of the qualities of good parents rather than a focus on the structure of the family. Why do Democrats avoid citing the structure of the ideal American family?

What about examining the Democratic position through a Lakoffian Nation as Family framework. Does this represent Strict Father Morality? Nurturant Parent Morality? What does the language itself tell you about the larger worldview of the Democratic Party, as stated in this section of their platform?

This issue contains two articles about whether the traditional family is the ideal family structure. *The Natural Family: A Manifesto* contains excerpts in this book intended to help the reader understand the case for the traditional (i.e., natural) family. The counterpoint by Professor Good argues that family diversity is itself a valuable goal in a pluralistic society.

YES ↵

**Allan C. Carlson
and Paul T. Mero**

The Natural Family: A Manifesto

What is the natural family? The answer comes to the woman and the man who take the risk of turning their love into promises of lifelong devotion.

In doing so, they will discover the story of the family, at once an ideal vision and a universal reality. In our time, they will also sense crisis, for malignant forces tear at the common source of freedom, order, virtue, and children. To set things right, they will need to look for clear principles, open goals, and a firm course of action. They also will need to reject false charges and weak compromise. Still, through these acts they shall come to know true liberty, a rekindled hearth, and a real homecoming, for themselves and for all humankind.

The Story of the Family

A young man and a young woman draw toward each other. They yearn to be as one. When they see the other, broad smiles appear. They sense the possibility of joy. Alone, they feel partial, incomplete. When together, they feel whole. The people among whom they live bless this bond in the celebration of marriage. The man and the woman exchange public vows with each other, and also with their kindred and neighbors, and the two become one flesh.

Over time, their joy and passion will be tested by the twists and surprises of life. They will cry together, sometimes in happiness, sometimes in sorrow. They will face sickness; they may know poverty; they could face dislocation or natural disaster; they might be torn apart by war. In times of despair or loss, they will find strength in each other. Facing death, they will feel the warm spiritual balm that heals the pain of physical separation. The conjugal bond built on fidelity, mutual duty, and respect allows both of them to emerge into their full potential; they become as their Creator intended, a being complete.

This marriage creates a new family, a home, the first and fundamental unit of human society. Here, husband and wife build a small economy. They share the work of provisioning, drawing on each one's interests, strengths, and skills. They craft a home which becomes a special place on earth. In centuries past, the small farm or the artisan's shop was the usual expression of this union between the sexual and the economic. Today, the urban townhouse, apartment, or suburban home are more common. Still, the small home economy remains the vital center of daily existence.

The wife and husband also build their home as a spiritual place. They learn that family and faith are, in fact, two sides of the same coin. The vital home rests on reverence, worship, and prayer.

From this same natural union flows new human life. Children are the first end, or purpose, of marriage. The couple watch with wonder as their first baby grows within the mother. Joy and awe drive away doubt and fear as they find their love transformed into a living child. Parts of their own beings have gone into the child's making, forming a new and unique person. The new father takes on the protection of the new mother in her time of vulnerability and dependence. A happiness follows the trial of childbirth as the new mother nurses her baby and as the father caresses his first born. Receiving a child through adoption sparks similar feelings. From such amazing moments, these parents are the child's first teachers; their home, the child's first, most vital school. They pass to the child the skills of living and introduce the satisfactions of talking, reading, reasoning, and exploring the world.

Inspired by love, the couple opens its union to additional children, filling their home, and filling the earth. These parents will know the delight of watching brothers and sisters grow together. They will watch with a mix of pride and worry as their children take their first steps, attempt their first chores, take on their first responsibilities. Among the children, there will be bruised knees, quarrels over toys, lost sport contests, tears, and laughter. As the children grow, they enter by steps a broader world. In all this, though, their parents stand as guides and guardians, and the home serves as a shelter and the focus of their common life.

Indeed, the natural family opens its home to other kin. The love and care which flow from parents to young children are mirrored in the care and love that adult children give to their aging parents. The truly rich family draws on the strengths of three or more generations. This family cares for its own. Each generation sees itself as a link in an unbroken chain, through which the family extends from and into the centuries.

A Time of Crisis

And yet, the natural family—*part of the created order, imprinted on our natures, the source of bountiful joy, the fountain of new life, the bulwark of ordered liberty*—stands reviled and threatened in the early 21st century. Foes have mounted attacks on all aspects of the natural family, from the bond of marriage to the birth of children to the true democracy of free homes. Ever more families show weaknesses and disorders. We see growing numbers of young adults rejecting the fullness and joy of marriage, choosing instead cheap substitutes or standing alone, where they are easy prey for the total state. Too many children are born outside of wedlock, ending as wards of that same state. Too few children are born inside married-couple homes, portending depopulation.

What has caused this alienation of humankind from its true nature and real home? Two basic assaults on the natural family have occurred, with their roots reaching back several hundred years: in brief, the challenge of industrialism and the assault of new, family-denying ideas.

On the one hand, the triumph of industrialism brought a "great disruption" or a "great transformation" in human affairs. The creation of wealth accelerated under the regime of industry. Yet this real gain rested on tearing productivity away from the hearth, on a disruption of the natural ecology of family life. The primal bond of home and work appeared to dissolve into air. Family-made goods and tasks became commodities, things to be bought and sold. Centralized factories, offices, and warehouses took over the tasks of the family workshop, garden, kitchen, and storeroom. Husbands, wives, and even children were enticed out of homes and organized in factories according to the principle of efficiency. Impersonal machines undermined the natural complementarity of the sexes in productive tasks. Children were left to fend for themselves, with the perception that their families no longer guided their futures; rather, the children now looked to faceless employers.

Politicians also embraced the industrial ideal and its claims to efficiency. New laws denied children a family-centered education and put them in mass state schools. Fertility tumbled, for "it . . . has yet to be [shown] . . . that any society can sustain stable high fertility beyond two generations of mass schooling." The state also invaded the home, seizing the protection of childhood from parents through the reform school movement and later schemes to "prevent child abuse." Family households, formerly function-rich beehives of useful, productive work and mutual support, tended to become merely functionless, overnight places of rest for persons whose active lives and loyalties lay elsewhere.

More critically, new ideas emerged over the same years that rejected the natural family. Some political thinkers held that the individual, standing alone, was the true cell of society; that family bonds—including those between husband and wife and between mother and child—showed merely the power of one selfish person over another. Other theorists argued that the isolated self, the lone actor in "the state of nature," was actually oppressed by institutions such as family and church. In this view, the central state was twisted into a supposed agent of liberation. It alone could free the enslaved individual from "the chains of tradition." From these premises emerged a

terrible cloud of ideologies that shared a common target: the natural family. These idea systems included socialism, feminism, communism, sexual hedonism, racial nationalism, and secular liberalism.

By the 1990's, their campaign was global. Cynically, they used the International Year of the Family, 1994, to launch a series of United Nations conferences designed to tear down the natural family in the developing nations, as well. Cairo, Beijing, Istanbul, and Copenhagen were the arenas where they tried to impose this "post-family" order.

In our time, the partisans of a "post-family" world are still the ones on the offensive. For example, our pro-family movement has failed to restore legal protection to marriage by rolling back the "no-fault" revolution. Instead, by 2005, we are in a desperate fight simply to keep the vital institution of marriage from being fitted to homosexuals. And our two movements have failed to slow the war of governments on human fertility, despite the new likelihood of a catastrophic depopulation of the developed *and* developing nations through the global "empty cradle."

A Vision

And so, we advance here a new vision and a fresh statement of principles and goals appropriate for the 21st century and the third millennium.

We see a world restored in line with the intent of its Creator. We envision a culture—found both locally and universally—that upholds the marriage of a woman to a man, and a man to a woman, as the central aspiration for the young. This culture affirms marriage as the best path to health, security, fulfillment, and joy. It casts the home built on marriage as the source of true political sovereignty, the fountain of democracy. It also holds the household framed by marriage to be the primal economic unit, a place marked by rich activity, material abundance, and broad self-reliance. This culture treasures private property in family hands as the rampart of independence and liberty. It celebrates the marital sexual union as the unique source of new human life. We see these homes as open to a full quiver of children, the source of family continuity and social growth. We envision young women growing into wives, homemakers, and mothers; and we see young men growing into husbands, homebuilders, and fathers.

We see true happiness as the product of persons enmeshed in vital bonds with spouses, children, parents, and kin. We look to a landscape of family homes, lawns, and gardens busy with useful tasks and ringing with the laughter of many children. We envision parents as the first educators of their children. We see homes that also embrace extended family members who need special care due to age or infirmity. We view neighborhoods, villages, and townships as the second locus of political sovereignty. We envision a freedom of commerce that respects and serves family integrity. And we look to nation-states that hold the protection of the natural family to be their first responsibility.

Our Principles

To advance this vision, we advocates for the natural family assert clear principles to guide our work in the new century and millennium.

- We affirm that the natural family, not the individual, is the fundamental unit of society.
- We affirm the natural family to be the union of a man and a woman through marriage for the purposes of sharing love and joy, propagating children, providing their moral education, building a vital home economy, offering security in times of trouble, and binding the generations.
- We affirm that the natural family is a fixed aspect of the created order, one ingrained in human nature. Distinct family systems may grow weaker or stronger. However, the natural family cannot change into some new shape; nor can it be re-defined by eager social engineers.
- We affirm that the natural family is the ideal, optimal, true family system. While we acknowledge varied living situations caused by circumstance or dysfunction, all other "family forms" are incomplete or are fabrications of the state.
- We affirm the marital union to be the authentic sexual bond, the only one open to the natural and responsible creation of new life.
- We affirm the sanctity of human life from conception to natural death; each newly conceived person holds rights to live, to grow, to be born, and to share a home with its natural parents bound by marriage.
- We affirm that the natural family is prior to the state and that legitimate governments exist to shelter and encourage the natural family.
- We affirm that the world is abundant in resources. The breakdown of the natural family and moral and political failure, not human "overpopulation," account for poverty, starvation, and environmental decay.
- We affirm that human depopulation is the true demographic danger facing the earth in this new century. Our societies need more people, not fewer.
- We affirm that women and men are equal in dignity and innate human rights, but different in function. Even if sometimes thwarted by events beyond the individual's control (or sometimes given up for a religious vocation), the calling of each boy is to become husband and father; the calling of each girl is to become wife and mother. Everything that a man does is mediated by his aptness for fatherhood. Everything that a woman does is mediated by her aptness for motherhood. Culture, law, and policy should take these differences into account.
- We affirm that the complementarity of the sexes is a source of strength. Men and women exhibit profound biological and psychological differences. When united in marriage, though, the whole becomes greater than the sum of the parts.

- We affirm that economic determinism is false. Ideas and religious faith can prevail over material forces. Even one as powerful as industrialization can be tamed by the exercise of human will.
- We affirm the "family wage" ideal of "equal pay for equal family responsibility." Compensation for work and taxation should reinforce natural family bonds.
- We affirm the necessary role of private property in land, dwelling, and productive capital as the foundation of familial independence and the guarantor of democracy. In a just and good society, all families will hold real property.
- And we affirm that lasting solutions to human problems rise out of families and small communities. They cannot be imposed by bureaucratic and judicial fiat. Nor can they be coerced by outside force.

Our Platform

From these principles, we draw out a simple, concrete platform for the new century and millennium. To the world, we say:

- We will build a new culture of marriage, where others would define marriage out of existence.
- We will welcome and celebrate more babies and larger families, where others would continue a war on human fertility.
- We will find ways to bring mothers, fathers, and children back home, where others would further divide parents from their children.
- And we will create true home economies, where others would subject families to the full control of big government and vast corporations.

To do these things, we must offer positive encouragements, and we must also correct the policy errors of the past. Specifically:

To Build a New Culture of Marriage . . .

- We will craft schooling that gives positive images of chastity, marriage, fidelity, motherhood, fatherhood, husbandry, and housewifery. We will end the corruption of children through state "sex education" programs.
- We will build legal and constitutional protections around marriage as the union of a man and a woman. We will end the war of the sexual hedonists on marriage.
- We will transform social insurance, welfare, and housing programs to reinforce marriage, especially the marriage of young adults. We will end state incentives to live outside of marriage.
- We will place the weight of the law on the side of spouses seeking to defend their marriages. We will end state preferences for easy divorce by repealing "no-fault" statutes.

- We will recognize marriage as a true and full economic partnership. We will end "marriage penalties" in taxation.
- We will allow private insurers to recognize the health advantages of marriage and family living, according to sound business principles. We will end legal discrimination against the married and child-rich.
- We will empower the legal and cultural guardians of marriage and public morality. We will end the coarsening of our culture.

To Welcome More Babies Within Marriage . . .

- We will praise churches and other groups that provide healthy and fertile models of family life to the young. We will end state programs that indoctrinate children, youth, and adults into the contraceptive mentality.
- We will restore respect for life. We will end the culture of abortion and the mass slaughter of the innocents.
- We will create private and public campaigns to reduce maternal and infant mortality and to improve family health. We will end government campaigns of population control.
- We will build special protections for families, motherhood, and childhood. We will end the terrible assault on these basic human rights.
- We will celebrate husbands and wives who hold open their sexual lives to new children. We will end the manipulation and abuse of new human life in the laboratories.
- We will craft generous tax deductions, exemptions, and credits that are tied to marriage and the number of children. We will end the oppressive taxation of family income, labor, property, and wealth.
- We will create credits against payroll taxes that reward the birth of children and that build true family patrimonies. We will end existing social insurance incentives toward childlessness.
- We will offer tax benefits to businesses that provide "natal gifts" and "child allowances" to their employees. We will end legal incentives that encourage business corporations to ignore families.

To Bring Mothers, and Fathers, Home . . .

- We will ensure that stay-at-home parents enjoy at least the same state benefits offered to day-care users. We will end all discriminations against stay-at-home parents.
- We will encourage new strategies and technologies that would allow home-based employment to blossom and prosper. We will end policies that unfairly favor large, centralized businesses and institutions.
- We will favor small property that reintegrates home and work. We will end taxes, financial incentives, subsidies, and zoning laws that discourage small farms and family-held businesses.

To Create a True Home Economy . . .

- We will allow men and women to live in harmony with their true natures. We will end the aggressive state promotion of androgyny.
- We will encourage employers to pay a "family wage" to heads of households. We will end laws that prohibit employers from recognizing and rewarding family responsibility.
- We will craft laws that protect home schools and other family-centered schools from state interference. We will give real control of state schools to small communities so that their focus might turn toward home and family. And we will create measures (such as educational tax credits) that recognize the exercise of parental responsibility. We will end discriminatory taxes and policies that favor mass state education of the young.
- We will hold up the primacy of parental rights and hold public officials accountable for abuses of their power. We will end abuse of the "child-abuse" laws.
- We will encourage self-sufficiency through broad property ownership, home enterprise, home gardens, and home workshops. We will end the culture of dependency found in the welfare state.
- We will celebrate homes that are centers of useful work. We will end state incentives for home building that assume, and so create, families without functions.

The Usual Charges

We know that certain charges will be leveled against us. Some will say that we want to turn back the clock, to restore a mythical American suburban world of the 1950's. Others will charge that we seek to subvert the rights of women or that we want to impose white, Western, Christian values on a pluralistic world. Still others will argue that we ignore science or reinforce patriarchal violence. Some will say that we block inevitable social evolution or threaten a sustainable world with too many children.

So, in anticipation, let us be clear:

We Look Forward with Hope, While Learning from the Past

It is true that we look with affection to earlier familial eras such as "1950's America." Indeed, for the first time in one hundred years, five things happened simultaneously in America (and in Australia and parts of Western Europe, as well) during this time: the marriage rate climbed; the divorce rate fell; marital fertility soared; the equality of households increased; and measures of child well-being and adult happiness rose. These were the social achievements of "the greatest generation." We look with delight on this record and aspire to recreate such results.

However, we also know that this specific development was a one-generation wonder. It did not last. Some children of the "baby boom" rebelled. Too often, this rebellion was foolish and destructive. Still, we find weaknesses in the family model of "1950's America." We see that it was largely confined to the white majority. Black families actually showed mounting stress in these years: a retreat from marriage; more out-of-wedlock births. Also, this new suburban model—featuring long commutes for fathers and tract homes without the central places such as parks and nearby shops where mothers and youth might have found healthy community bonds—proved incomplete. Finally, we see the "companionship marriage" ideal of this time, which embraced psychological tasks to the exclusion of material and religious functions, as fragile. We can, and we will, do better.

We Believe Wholeheartedly in Women's Rights

Above all, we believe in rights that recognize women's unique gifts of pregnancy, birthing, and breastfeeding. The goal of androgyny, the effort to eliminate real differences between women and men, does every bit as much violence to human nature and human rights as the old efforts by the communists to create "Soviet Man" and by the nazis to create "Aryan Man." We reject social engineering, attempts to corrupt girls and boys, to confuse women and men about their true identities. At the same time, nothing in our platform would prevent women from seeking and attaining as much education as they want. Nothing in our platform would prevent women from entering jobs and professions to which they aspire. We do object, however, to restrictions on the liberty of employers to recognize family relations and obligations and so reward indirectly those parents staying at home to care for their children. And we object to current attacks on the Universal Declaration of Human Rights, a document which proclaims fundamental rights to family autonomy, to a family wage for fathers, and to the special protection of mothers.

We Believe That the Natural Family Is Universal, an Attribute of All Humankind

We confess to holding Christian values regarding the family: the sanctity of marriage; the desire by the Creator that we be fruitful and multiply; Jesus' miracle at the wedding feast; His admonitions against adultery and divorce. And yet, we find similar views in the other great world faiths. Moreover, we even find recognition of the natural family in the marriage rituals of animists. Because it is imprinted on our natures as human beings, we know that the natural family can be grasped by all persons who open their minds to the evidence of their senses and their hearts to the promptings of their best instincts. Also, in the early

21st century, there is little that is "Western" about our views. The voices of the "post family" idea are actually today's would-be "Westernizers." They are the ones who largely rule in the child-poor, aging, dying lands of "the European West." It is they who seek to poison the rest of the world with a grim, wizened culture of death. Our best friends are actually to be found in the developing world, in the Third World, in the Middle East, Africa, South Asia, South America. Our staunchest allies tend not to be white, but rather people of color. Others seek a sterile, universal darkness. We seek to liberate the whole world—including dying Europa—for light and life, for children.

We Celebrate the Findings of Empirical Science

Science, honestly done and honestly reported, is the friend of the natural family. The record is clear from decades of work in sociology, psychology, anthropology, sociobiology, medicine, and social history: children do best when they are born into and raised by their two natural parents. Under *any* other setting—including one-parent, step-parent, homosexual, cohabitating, or communal households—children predictably do worse. Married, natural-parent homes bring health, learning, and success to the offspring reared therein. Science shows that these same homes give life, wealth, and joy to wives and husbands, as well. Disease, depression, and early death come to those who reject family life. This result should not really cause surprise. Science, after all, is the study of the natural order. And while the Creator forgives, nature never does.

We Seek to Reduce Domestic Violence

All families fall short of perfection and a few families fail. We, too, worry about domestic violence. We know that people can make bad choices, that they can fall prey to selfishness and their darker instincts. We also know that persons can live in places or times where they have few models of solid homes, few examples of good marriages. All the same, we also insist that the natural family is not the source of these human failures. The research here is clear. Women are safest physically when married and living with their husbands. Children are best sheltered from sexual, physical, and emotional abuse when they live with their married natural parents. In short, the natural family is the *answer* to abuse. We also know that all husbands and wives, all mothers and fathers, need to be nurtured toward and encouraged in their proper roles. These are the first tasks of all worthy social institutions.

We Believe That While Distinct Family Systems Change, the Design of the Natural Family Never Does

Regarding the natural family, we deny any such thing as social evolution. The changes we see are either decay away from or renewal toward the one true family model. From our very origin as a unique creature on earth, we humans have been defined by the long-term bonding of a woman and a man, by their free sharing of resources, by a complementary division of labor, and by a focus on the procreation, protection, and rearing of children in stable homes. History is replete with examples of distinct family systems that have grown strong and built great civilizations, only to fall to atomism, vice, and decay. Even in our Western Civilization, we can identify periods of family decline and disorder, followed by successful movements of renewal. It is true that the last forty years have been a time of great confusion and decay. We now sense a new summons to social rebirth.

We Seek a Sustainable Human Future

With sadness, we acknowledge that the new Malthusian impulse has succeeded in its war against children all too well. Fertility is tumbling around the globe. A majority of nations have already fallen into "the aging trap" of depopulation. As matters now stand, the predictable future is one of catastrophic population decline, economic contraction, and human tragedy. Our agenda actually represents the earth's best hope for a sustainable future.

Looking Forward

That large task requires new ways of thinking and acting. Our vision of the hearth looks forward, not to the past, for hope and purpose. We see the vital home reborn through startling new movements such as home schooling. We marvel at fresh inventions that portend novel bonds between home and work. We are inspired by a convergence of religious truth with the evidence of science around the vital role of the natural family. We see the prospect of a great civil alliance of religious orthodoxies, within nations and around the globe; not to compromise on doctrines held dear, but to defend our family systems from the common foe. With wonder, we find a shared happiness with people once distrusted or feared. We enjoy new friendships rooted in family ideals that cross ancient divides. We see the opportunity for an abundant world order built on the natural family.

We issue a special call to the young, those born over the last three to four decades. You are the children of a troubled age, a time of moral and social disorder. You were conceived into a culture of self-indulgence, of abortion, a culture embracing death. More than all generations before, you have known the divorce of parents. You have lived too often in places without fathers. You have been taught to deny your destinies as young women and young men. You have been forced to read books that mock marriage, motherhood, and fatherhood. Persons who should have protected you—teachers, judges, public officials— often left you as prey to moral and sexual predators. Many of you are in fact the victims of a kind of cultural rape: seduced into early sexual acts, then pushed into sterility.

And yet, you are also the ones with the power to make the world anew. Where some members of *our* generation helped to corrupt the world, you will be the builders. You have seen the darkness. The light now summons you. It is your time to lead, with the natural family as your standard and beacon. Banish the lies told to you. Claim your natural freedom to create true and fruitful marriages. Learn from the social renewal prompted by "the greatest generation" and call on them for special support. You have the chance to shape a world that welcomes and celebrates children. You have the ability to craft a true homecoming. Your generation holds the destiny of humankind in its hands. The hopes of all good and decent people lie with you.

The Call

A new spirit spreads in the world, the essence of the natural family. We call on all people of goodwill, whose hearts are open to the promptings of this spirit, to join in a great campaign. The time is close when the persecution of the natural family, when the war against children, when the assault on human nature shall end.

The enemies of the natural family grow worried. A triumph that, not so many years ago, they thought complete is no longer sure. Their fury grows. So do their attempts, ever more desperate, at coercion. Yet their mistakes also mount in number. They misread human nature. They misread the times.

We all are called to be the actors, the moral soldiers, in this drive to realize the life ordained for us by our Creator. Our foes are dying, of their own choice; we have a world to gain. Natural families of all races, nations, and creeds, let us unite.

"TO THE WORLD, WE SAY:
- We will build a new culture of marriage, where others would define marriage out of existence.
- We will welcome and celebrate more babies and larger families, where others would continue a war on human fertility.
- We will find ways to bring mothers, fathers, and children back home, where others would further divide parents from their children.
- And we will create true home economies, where others would subject families to the full control of big government and vast corporations."

ALLAN C. CARLSON is President of the Howard Center for Family, Religion & Society and Distinguished Fellow in Family Policy Studies at the Family Research Council in Washington, D.C. Paul T. Mero is President of the Sutherland Institute and a Trustee of the ALS Foundation. Carlson and Mero argue that American needs to return to a traditional family and is headed by a man and woman.

Mark Good

 **NO**

Nontraditional Families and Childhood Progress through School

What types of outcomes can be expected for children raised by same-sex couples, relative to children in other types of families? The answer is vitally important both for public policy relating to same-sex marriage and adoption (Eskridge 2002; Koppelman 2002), and for theories of how family structure matters. Supporters and opponents of same-sex marriage rights agree that the legal issue of same-sex marriage rights should revolve around the question of childhood outcomes for children raised by same-sex couples (Alvaré 2005; Patterson 2002). In this paper, I examine progress through school, i.e., normal progress versus grade retention, for children of same-sex couples compared to children of other family types, using data from the 2000 U.S. census.

The debate over same-sex unions and their children draws from and informs a more general literature concerning family structure's effect on children. The literature on family structure has generally focused on structural variations within heterosexual parented families, contrasting heterosexual married couples, heterosexual remarried couples, and (presumably heterosexual) single mothers (Cherlin 1992; McLanahan and Sandefur 1994). Even though same-sex couples are a small minority of all couples (1% of all couples in census 2000 were same-sex couples), the inclusion of same-sex couples can provide researchers with more leverage over the key question of how family structure matters in general.

Studies of family structure and children's outcomes nearly universally find at least a modest advantage for children raised by their married biological parents. The question which has bedeviled researchers, and which remains essentially unresolved, is *why* (Cherlin 1999). Some results have indicated that socioeconomic status explains most or all of the advantage of children raised by married couples (Biblarz and Raftery 1999; Gennetian 2005; Ginther and Pollak 2004), while other scholars find that family structure has an enduring effect on children net of all other factors (McLanahan and Sandefur 1994; Zill 1996). Married couples tend to be the most prosperous type of family unit, and this economic prosperity undoubtedly has certain advantages for children (but also see Mayer 1997).

Literature Review

Same-Sex Parenting

The modern reality of same-sex couples raising children long postdates the classical psychological theories of child development (for example, Freud [1905] 1975). Recent research on childhood socialization to gender roles has emphasized peer groups and genetics as much as direct parental influence (Harris 1998; Maccoby 1990). In-depth studies of the psychosocial development of children raised by lesbians or by same-sex couples has found that these children are normal and well adjusted (Chan, Raboy and Patterson 1998b; Flaks et al. 1995; Golombok et al. 2003), though as I discuss below, there are also critics of the small-N literature on same-sex couples and their children.

Same-sex couples become parents in three main ways. First, through one partner's (generally prior) heterosexual relationship; second, through adoption; third, through donor insemination or surrogate parenting (Stacey 2006). Same-sex couples cannot become parents through misuse or failure of birth control, the way heterosexual couples can. Parenthood is more difficult to achieve for same-sex couples than for heterosexual couples, which implies a stronger selection effect for same-sex parents. If gays and lesbians have to work harder to become parents, it could be the case that the gays and lesbians who do become parents are on average more dedicated to the hard work of parenting than their heterosexual peers, and this could be beneficial for their children.

In Judith Stacey's (2006 p. 39) discussion of gay adoption, she describes the gay men of Los Angeles as having to search through the state's ". . . overstocked warehouse of 'hard to place' children, the majority of whom . . . have been removed from families judged negligent, abusive, or incompetent. Most of the state's stockpiled children . . . are children of color, and disproportionately boys with 'special needs.'" If it is the case that same-sex couples who adopt mainly have access to 'special needs' children, the special needs of these children could exert a downward bias on the average outcomes for children of same-sex couples. Fortunately, the census distinguishes between the head of household's "own children," adopted children, stepchildren, and foster children.

Nearly all children of gay and lesbian parents attend schools and live in neighborhoods whose other children come overwhelmingly from families with heterosexual parents. In other words, children of same-sex couples share a common peer and school environment with children of heterosexual couples. To the extent that peer environment is a primary socializing environment for children (Harris 1998; Maccoby 1990; for a survey, see Rutter 2002), whatever differences sexual orientation of parents makes within the home may well be mediated and diffused by the common peer and school environments that children share regardless of the gender or sexual orientation of their parents.

How the Census Complements the Existing Literature

Our research lists 45 empirical studies of outcomes of children of same-sex couples, comprising all of the journal articles listed in Fiona Tasker's (2005) comprehensive survey which examined childhood outcomes, plus several more recent studies listed by Wald (2006), and all four studies listed by Meezan and Rauch (2005) as the highest quality studies in this field, and all the more recent studies which cite the earlier ones. None of the studies cited in our research find statistically significant disadvantages for children raised by gay and lesbian parents compared to other children.

The uniform finding of no significant disadvantage for children raised by gay or lesbian parents has been convincing to some scholars (Ball and Pea 1998; Meezan and Rauch 2005; Stacey and Biblarz 2001; Wald 2006), though others remain unconvinced (Lerner and Nagai 2001; Nock 2001; Wardle 1997). Several points are worth commenting upon. First, as the critics have noted, convenience sampling dominated this literature in the past (Nock 2001). More recent scholarship has answered this criticism by using nationally representative probability samples derived from the National Longitudinal Study of Adolescent Health (Add Health, see Wainright and Patterson 2006, 2008; Wainright et al. 2004), as well as studies constructed from a hybrid of probability sampling and convenience sampling (Golombok et al. 2003; Perry et al. 2004).

A second critique of the literature, that the sample sizes of the studies are too small to allow for statistically powerful tests, continues to be relevant. The mean number of children of gay or lesbian parents in these studies is 39, and the median is 37, and both numbers would be slightly lower if studies without comparison groups were excluded. The nationally representative studies in the series found only 44 children who were raised by lesbian couples in the Add Health survey. Golombok et al (2003) found only 18 lesbian mothers out of 14,000 mothers in the Avon Longitudinal Study of Parents and Children, which is why they supplemented this sample with snow-ball sampling and their own convenience sample. The universally small sample sizes of the studies in the existing literature has left room for several critiques, including the critique that small sample studies would not have the statistical power to identify the effects of homosexual parents on childhood outcomes, even if such effects did exist (Lerner and Nagai 2001; Nock 2001). A third potential weakness of this literature is the narrowness of family structures under study (Tasker 2005). Of the 45 studies listed, only seven examined the children of gay fathers, and only two of these seven studies had a more traditional family control group built into the study.

Among the convenience sample studies, several of the most important have been based on samples of women who became parents through assisted reproductive technology (ART-Brewaeys et al. 1997; Chan et al. 1998b; Flaks et al. 1995). Because individuals who become parents through assisted means can be identified through the reproductive clinic and are therefore easier to recruit than the general population of same-sex couple parents, the literature on same-sex couple parenting has tended to feature studies of the kind of women who can afford ART: white upper middle class women. Nationally representative data tends to paint a different picture: in the U.S. census, same-sex couple parents tend to be more working class and are much more likely to be racially nonwhite compared to heterosexual married couples.

The debate over same-sex marriage and gay and lesbian adoption rights revolves around many competing sets of assumptions with political, religious, and ideological axes which cannot be resolved or even fully addressed in this paper. To the extent the debate is an empirical debate, that is to the extent that disagreement remains over the meaning of the empirical literature on the development of children of same-sex couples, this paper offers a new perspective.

To supplement the existing small-scale studies, I offer a large sample study of children from the U.S. Census, including 3,502 children of same-sex couples who had been living with both parents for at least five years (2,030 children living with lesbian mothers and 1,472 children living with gay fathers, see our research), and more than 700,000 children in grades 1–8 from other family types. This sample size more than satisfies Nock's (2001) criteria of 800 as the minimum number of gay and lesbian couples required for statistically useful study.

The U.S. census has several major disadvantages: normal progress through school is the only available children's outcome, and even this outcome is measured with less precision than one would hope for. Although the census data have several important limitations for the research questions considered here, the strengths of the census data (large sample, national representativity, and a full array of family structures) address important lacunae in the literature, and as such, this study offers a potentially useful new perspective on how family structure matters to children. Although the census data are far from ideal for the subject under study here, better data are nowhere on the horizon.

Grade Retention

Grade retention (the opposite of normal progress through school) has been increasing in U.S. schools since President Bill Clinton proposed ending social promotion in schools in his State of the Union address in 1998 (Alexander, Entwisle and Dauber 2003:viii; Hauser 2001). Grade retention is an important childhood outcome because retention in the primary grades is a strong indicator of a lack of childhood readiness for school, and we know that effective parenting is a crucial ingredient in school readiness (Brooks-Gunn and Markman 2005). Brooks-Gunn and Markman argue that the lower school readiness of racial minority children is due, in part, to parenting practices which differ from the authoritative parenting style favored in middle class white homes (Baumrind 1966; Lareau 2003).

Guo, Brooks-Gunn, and Harris (1996) studied grade retention among urban black children and found that some indicators of parental stress such as unemployment and welfare use were associated with increased grade retention for children; in other words, they found childhood grade retention to be a useful measure of difficulties the students were experiencing at home. Guo, Brooks-Gunn, and Harris (1996:218) identify three potential sources of grade retention: "weak cognitive ability, behavioral problems, and lack of engagement in school." Of these three causes of childhood grade retention, the second two might be partly associated with the quality of the home environment. Students with learning disabilities or physical disabilities which affect learning are also at risk of grade retention, and this type of grade retention would not be indicative of parenting deficits.

Grade retention is closely associated with more serious problems later in life. Students who are held back at least once are at much higher risk for eventually dropping out of high school (Alexander, Entwisle, and Horsey 1997; Guo et al. 1996; Moller et al. 2006; Roderick 1994; Rumberger 1987; Tillman, Guo, and Harris 2006). Failure to graduate from high school is associated with low earnings, high unemployment, low self-esteem, and high mortality rates (Guo et al. 1996; McLanahan 1985; Tillman et al. 2006). Even when grade retention takes place in the early grades, the "crystallization" of behaviors and academic abilities implies that difficulties a child experiences when he or she is 7 or 8 carry forward (more so for girls than for boys) into adolescence and young adulthood (Kowalesi-Jones and Duncan 1999).

There are several theoretical reasons for supposing that children of same-sex couples might have lower school readiness (and therefore higher rates of grade retention) than own children of heterosexual married couples, net of race, parental income, and parental education. First, the legal privileges of marriage are numerous and have direct consequences for the well being of children (Eskridge 1996; Pawelski et al. 2006). Second, evolutionary theory suggests

that parents invest more in their own biological children (Wilson 2002; but see also Hamilton, Cheng, and Powell 2007), and same-sex couples (absent a prior sex change) cannot both be the biological parents of any one child. Third, the large majority of children of same-sex couples from the 2000 census were children from prior heterosexual relationships (only 11% were stepchildren, adopted children, or foster children of the head of household), meaning that most of the children being raised by same-sex couples at the time of the 2000 census had previously lived through divorce or parental breakup, which research has shown to be traumatic for some children (Amato and Cheadle 2005; Chase-Lansdale, Cherlin, and Kiernan 1995; McLanahan and Sandefur 1994; Wallerstein and Kelly 1980; Wallerstein, Lewis, and Blakeslee 2000).

The Benefits of Legal Marriage

Legal marriage confers a host of protections and advantages both to the couples who marry and to their children. Married couples generally share joint legal custody of their coresident children. In a system of employer-based health care insurance, either spouse in a married couple can usually provide health insurance for both spouses and all their children. Marriage is a long-term contract which allows and encourages parents to make long-term investments in their children (Waite and Gallagher 2000). Divorce rights, which are a corollary to marriage rights, provide guarantees for child support and visitation that are intended to minimize the damage of a breakup to a couple's children. Given the many practical, legal, economic, and social advantages of marriage as a childrearing family structure, it should come as no surprise that children of long-term married couples have the best outcomes (McLanahan and Sandefur 1994). The various benefits of marriage extend far beyond income, so one would generally expect children in married couples to have advantages even after SES is accounted for in regressions.

The moral claim for same-sex marriage rests in part on the many practical and psychological benefits of marriage, benefits which conservative family scholars have made the most careful and enthusiastic case for (Waite and Gallagher 2000; Wilson 2002). The benefits of marriage, combined with the exclusion of gays and lesbians (and their children) from those benefits, together form one cornerstone of the case for same-sex marriage (Eskridge 1996).

Relevant Comparison Sets for Same-Sex Couples

Along with the standard comparison to heterosexual married couples, heterosexual cohabiting couples are a second logical comparison group for same-sex cohabiting couples. Both heterosexual cohabiters and same-sex cohabiters are two-parent families living without the rights and benefits of marriage. Certainly, there are differences: heterosexual cohabiting couples can marry if they want to, whereas in the United States at the time of the 2000 census, same-sex couples could not marry. The comparison between children of same-sex cohabiting couples and children of heterosexual cohabiting couples allows for a more specific test of the effect of same-sex parenthood on children, while holding constant legal rights and the number of parents.

A third relevant comparison for children of same-sex couples are the children living in group quarters, since these are the children presumably available for adoption, and because same-sex couples are more likely than heterosexual couples to participate in the adoption market. Some of the difference between children in group quarters and children living with parents and guardians must be due to selection effects—the most troubled children available for adoption may not be adopted and may do poorly in school as a result of emotional or physical disabilities. On the other hand, if gay and lesbian adoptive parents are choosing from the middle or the bottom of the adoptive pool (Stacey 2006), rather than from the population of the most desirable potential adoptees, then the selection effect will be less important. In either case, the census, as a cross-sectional survey, is poorly suited to the analysis of selection effects. Nonetheless, census 2000 does provide strong controls for individual student disabilities, and any comparison between children living with families and children living in group quarters will be made after individual disabilities have been controlled for.

First-Order Predictors of Childhood Grade Retention

Because denominator school populations cover four years (grades 1–4, grades 5–8), but the students who can be identified as over age for their grade come only from the last grade of each four-year span (grades 4 and 8)5, the implied grade retention rate is four times higher than the observed grade retention rate. Our research shows both the observed grade retention rate and the implied grade retention rate, for primary school students using weighted data from the 2000 census.

Our research suggests that childhood grade retention is correlated with family type. Children of heterosexual married couples had the lowest implied rate of grade retention, 6.8%. Children of lesbian mothers and gay fathers had grade retention rates of 9.5% and 9.7%, respectively. Children of heterosexual cohabiting parents had a grade retention rate of 11.7%, while children of single parents had grade retention rates between 11.1% and 12.6%.

The differences in childhood grade retention between all types of non-group-quarters households were dwarfed by the high grade retention rates of children living in group quarters. According to our research, children living in group homes, many of them awaiting adoption or foster parents, had an implied grade retention rate of 34.4%. Children who were incarcerated had a grade retention rate of 78.0%. Later in the paper, I show that the enormous difference in grade retention between children raised in families and children living in group quarters remains even after individual level student disabilities are accounted for.

One way to gauge the advantage of living with families is to note that adopted children (10.6% grade retention) who spent the five years prior to the census living with their adoptive parents, and foster children (20.6% grade retention) with five years of residential stability performed considerably better than children who spent the same 5 years living at a single-group-quarters address (34.4% grade retention for non-inmates). The performance hierarchy which favors own children, and then (in declining order of school performance) adopted children, then foster children, then children in group quarters confirms the long standing research finding that children do best when living with parents who make a long term commitment to the children's development (Bartholet 1999). Selection bias (wherein the children with the most severe disabilities or children who have suffered the worst abuse are the least likely to be adopted) must also play a role, which unfortunately cannot be quantified with these data.

The rest of our research shows implied grade retention along several other dimensions. Asian children had the lowest rates of grade retention, while black children had the highest. Girls were less likely to be held back in the primary grades than boys were. Suburban schools had lower rates of grade retention than city schools, which in turn were lower than rural schools. Household socioeconomic status (SES) was a crucial predictor of childhood school performance. In households with income less than $25,000, 12.6% of the primary school students were left back, compared to only 5.3% for children in households with incomes over $100,000. Householder's education had an even stronger effect on children's progress through school: parents who had less than a high school degree had primary school children who were retained 14.3% of the time, whereas householders with college degrees had children who were retained only 4.4% of the time.

Our research shows that the strongest factor in making normal progress through elementary school is living with a family rather than living in group quarters. For children living in a family, whether the family is headed by a heterosexual married couple or by some less traditional parenting arrangement, the second most important factor in childhood progress through school appears to be parental educational attainment.

Socioeconomic Status by Family Type

Our research shows that gays and lesbians had a higher-than-average educational attainment of 13.6 years (i.e., 1.6 years of college) compared to 13.4 years for heterosexual married heads of household. Across family types, gay couples had the highest median household income at $61,000 per household. It should also be noted that men have higher earnings than women, and gay male couples are the only household type that relied on the earnings of two men. The second Nontraditional Families and Childhood

Grade Retention P. 17 four family types are all single-parent (i.e., single-income) families, so their household incomes were roughly half as high as the household incomes of the first four family types.

Despite the fact that the cost of becoming parents may be higher for gays and lesbians than for heterosexual couples, our research shows that gay and lesbian couples who did have children had substantially lower income and educational attainment than gay and lesbian couples in general. While gay and lesbian cohabiters had relatively high household incomes, gay and lesbian parents had lower SES than heterosexual married parents ($50 thousand per household for gay parents compared to $58 thousand for heterosexual married parents). Excluding marital status recodes, the income and educational level of gay and lesbian parents was even lower. Among gay and lesbian couples, those with lower incomes are more likely to be raising children. Not only were heterosexual married parents economically advantaged, the heterosexual married couples were also racially advantaged. Only 22.9% of children of heterosexual married couple were black or Hispanic, whereas 41.6% of children of gay men were black or Hispanic, and this percentage rose to 53.7% when dual marital status recodes were excluded. The children of lesbians were similarly likely (37.1%) to be black or Hispanic. Never-married mothers were the most likely parenting family type to have black or Hispanic children. The racial breakdown of parents was similar to the racial breakdown of children described in our research. Among heterosexual married heads of household, 22.2% were black or Hispanic, while 40.4% of gay fathers were black or Hispanic, and 36.1% of lesbian mothers were black or Hispanic (not shown in our research).

Among all family types, children of lesbian mothers were the most likely (more than 12%) to be adopted children, stepchildren, or foster children. Because economic disadvantage, minority racial status, and experience with the adoption or foster care system are all challenges for children, a careful analysis of the school performance of children of gay and lesbian parents must take these disadvantages into account.

Comparisons with Children of Unmarried Heterosexual Couples

Our research revisits the regressions from our research (with the same models, covariates, and summary statistics), comparing children raised by same-sex couples to children raised by heterosexual cohabiting couples. Our research shows that children raised by same-sex couples are more likely to make normal progress through school compared to children raised by heterosexual cohabiting couples, but the difference is statistically significant only in Model 1, before parental SES has been accounted for. If children living with dual marital status recoded couples are excluded, the signs are reversed (meaning children raised by heterosexual cohabiting couples do better), but

none of the coefficients are statistically significant. These results suggest that (for the outcome of normal progress through school) children raised by same-sex cohabiting couple parents are no different, and perhaps slightly advantaged, compared to children being raised by heterosexual cohabiting couples. The similarity in school performance between children of same-sex couples and children of heterosexual cohabiting couples fails to support the gender essentialist theories of parenting, which argue that child development depends on having parental role models from both gender groups (Alvaré 2005; Popenoe 1996; Wardle 1997).

Comparisons with Children in Group Quarters

Our research represents a different variation on the type of analysis from. In our research, the sample of children includes children in group quarters, and these children are the comparison category for the analysis. Because neither household income nor parental education can be associated with children in group quarters, these variables are dropped from the analysis. The sample of children in our research includes own children, adopted children, stepchildren, group quarters children, and foster children. Since the children in group-quarters have no head of household to have a relationship with, it seemed appropriate to use the broadest definition of "children" for children who were living with families. Furthermore, the adopted and foster children probably include some children who formerly lived in group quarters.

Our research confirms the robustness of a previous finding from our research, that children who live with parents regardless of family type are much more likely to make normal progress through school than children living in group quarters. Even after student disabilities (more common among group-quarters children than among children living with families) are taken into account, the difference remained between children raised by families and children living in group quarters. Children living at least five years with same-sex couples and children living at least five years with unmarried heterosexual cohabiting couples had odds of making good progress through school that were twice as high as non-inmate children who had spent the previous five years in group-quarters. Using coefficients from Model 2 of our research, which controls for children's race and disabilities, children raised by same-sex couples had odds of making good progress through school that were 2.43 times higher than children living in group quarters (e.886 = 2.43). Children raised by heterosexual cohabiting couples were similarly advantaged compared to children in group quarters (e.810 = 2.25, coefficients from Model 2). The advantage of children raised by same-sex couples over children living in group quarters remains positive and statistically significant across all four models even after marital status recoded couples are excluded.

Discussion

Children raised by same-sex couples are one of the most difficult populations in the United States to study systematically because of their small numbers and their geographic dispersion. The census data are far from ideal, and better data would, of course, be welcome. However, until such time as better nationally representative data are available, the U.S. census is the only nationally representative dataset with a large enough sample of children raised by same-sex couples to allow for statistically powerful comparisons with children of other family types.

To the extent that normal progress through primary school is a useful and valid measure of child development, the results confirm that children of same-sex couples appear to have no inherent developmental disadvantage. Heterosexual married couples are the most economically prosperous, the most likely to be white, and the most legally advantaged type of parents; their children have the lowest rates of grade retention. Parental SES accounts for more than half of the relatively small gap in grade retention between children of heterosexual married couples and children of same-sex couples. When one controls for parental SES and characteristics of the students, children of same-sex couples cannot be distinguished with statistical certainty from children of heterosexual married couples.

Children of all non–group quarters family types, including households headed by same-sex couples, are dramatically more likely to make normal progress through school than students living in group quarters. Any policy that would deny gay and lesbian parents the right to adopt or foster children would force some children to remain in group quarters. A longer stay in group quarters would seem to be contrary to the best interest of the children. In recent years, scholars have arrived at a consensus that moving children out of group homes and into adoptive families should be the goal of public policy. Families, even suboptimal families, are better equipped than the state to raise children (Bartholet 1999; Goldstein, Freud, and Solnit 1979).

Historical restrictions against interracial adoption in the United States represent one relevant historical precedent for the current debate over the adoption rights of same-sex couples. Randall Kennedy (2003) argues that even though restrictions against interracial adoption have been proposed as a way of protecting children, such restrictions have victimized children by taking them away from loving homes or by forcing children to remain in group quarters for too long. Policies which limit the kinds of families that can adopt or foster children ignore the enormous advantages of personal attention that families have (even single parents and other nontraditional family types) over the state in raising children well.

The prior literature has found no evidence that children raised by same-sex couples suffer any important disadvantages (Chan et al. 1998b; Patterson 1995; Stacey and Biblarz 2001; Wald 2006). Yet this same literature has been heavily criticized on the methodological grounds that universally small sample sizes prevent the studies from having the statistical power to identify differences that might actually exist (Alvaré 2005; Lerner and Nagai 2001; Nock 2001). The analysis in this paper, using large-sample, nationally representative data for the first time, shows that children raised by same-sex couples have no fundamental deficits in making normal progress through school. The core finding here offers a measure of validation for the prior, and much debated, small-sample studies.

MARK GOOD is a Professor of Counselor Education at West Chester University and the President of Opn-Wyd, a diversity and communication company. Good argues that diversity in traditional and nontraditional is healthy. In fact, he argues that it can be damaging to hold the traditional family as the ideal familial structure.

EXPLORING THE ISSUE

Are Traditional Families Better Than Nontraditional Families?

Critical Thinking and Reflection

1. What are some arguments made by each side with which you agree or disagree?
2. What are the strengths and weaknesses of the two positions made in this issue?
3. Pick the side with which you most agree. What are some additional arguments you would make to strengthen the case for or against the traditional family?
4. Think more broadly about the issue of the traditional family. Are there some changes in family structure that you support but others you oppose? Why or why not?

Is There Common Ground?

While we can debate the value of the traditional versus the nontraditional family, changing family structure is difficult to alter significantly. However, there are other qualities that need to be provided to ensure that children are afforded as many opportunities as possible. Let's identify those opportunities and advantages. What are some of the ways in which both traditional and nontraditional families can provide such opportunities?

Family structure will not remain static. Perhaps nontraditional families will be on the increase. Perhaps they will be on the decrease. What sort of projections would you make about changing family structure in the future? How should a pluralistic democracy approach such changes in family structure?

Create Central

www.mhhe.com/createcentral

Additional Resources

American Family Association:

www.afa.net

Focus on the Family:

www.focusonthefamily.com/

Human Rights Campaign:

www.hrc.org

Lambda Legal:

www.lambdalegal.org/

Internet References . . .

American Family Association

www.afa.net

Camp Mountain Meadow

www.queercamps.org/camps/mountainmeadow

Focus on the Family

www.focusonthefamily.com

Human Rights Campaign

www.hrc.org

Selected, Edited, and with Issue Framing Material by:
David M. Hall, Ph.D., *Delaware Valley College*

ISSUE

Is Hookup Culture on College Campuses Bad for Heterosexual Girls?

YES: Amy Julia Becker, from "Hookup Culture Is Good for Women, and Other Feminist Myths," *Christianity Today* (September 24, 2012)

NO: Timaree Schmidt, from "Hookup Culture Can Help Build Stronger Relationships," originally written for this book (2014)

Learning Outcomes
After reading this issue, you will be able to:
• Summarize competing arguments related to hookup culture.
• Evaluate the gender imbalance of this debate and why there is particular focus on the impact on women.
• Evaluate the long-term implications of sexual decision-making in college.

ISSUE SUMMARY

YES: Amy Julia Becker argues that hookup culture demeans women. From a Christian perspective, she argues that sex leads to greater life fulfillment when removed from the hookup culture.

NO: Timaree Schmidt argues that hookup culture is nothing new and that it can be healthy for people to have different sexual experiences.

Sexual activity occurs on college campuses, and it sometimes occurs with high frequency. Larger schools allow a level of anonymity that students would never have experienced in high school. Sometimes sexual activity is in the context of a long-term, committed relationship. Other times it is in the context of a one-night stand.

Who benefits from a one-night stand? Is it wrong to want one? Is it wrong to enjoy it? Should there be a different answer for males or females, and for heterosexual, gay, lesbian, or bisexual individuals?

Hooking up in college is not something new. However, there are some newer trends in higher education. For example, women are attending in much larger numbers than men. Some colleges have 60 percent or more female students. Add a few other variables to this: (a) most studies show a higher proportion of gay men versus lesbians in the general population; and (b) some men are already in committed relationships at school or at home. On many college campuses, if a woman is looking for a long-term heterosexual relationship, she is finding that the odds are stacked in the men's favor.

What about the women who are not looking for a long-term relationship? What about the pre-med student who does not want a relationship to tie her down when she is ready to leave for medical school? Or the woman who believes that college is the right time to experiment? One college student recently posted many of her sexual experiences online and wrote, "I turn 20 in two weeks. I feel like I should be making a lot more mistakes right now."

Why does this discussion so often focus on the impact on women? There is often an assumption that men prefer hookup culture and women prefer relationships. The theory goes that women are joining hookup culture at their own expense to please men.

How much is hookup culture today different from generations past? Does it diminish a woman's chances of being in a relationship?

Of course the major point of college is the education that is received there. Yet during our time in colleges, relationships are formed, sometimes long-term, and hookups occur. One mother wrote an open letter to the young women attending Princeton University telling them that they would never again be in such a large pool of marriageable, impressive men. They should be using this opportunity to find a husband rather than engage in hookup culture.

Why do women hookup? Is it because they like sex? Or is it because they want to please men? What about when they keep hooking up with the same person, known as friends with benefits? Are they keeping the relationship light to please a man?

We are in an era today in which there is a sex-positive feminism that is captured by *Sex and the City*, *Girls*, Christina Aguilera, and many others. Do these media depic-tions of sex-positive women capture a real demographic in American society? If so, how big is it? How overestimated or underestimated is it?

The truth is that during college we learn a great deal more than what comes from the instruction of our pro-fessors and the words in our books. We learn a great deal about relationships from the people around us. The gen-eral culture influences how the people around us act.

The articles in this essay help us take a better look at the case for or against the impact of hookup culture on heterosexual girls.

YES

Amy Julia Becker

Hookup Culture Is Good for Women, and Other Feminist Myths

According to Atlantic *essayist Hanna Rosin, we should celebrate that young women are now acting as sexually selfish as their male counterparts.*

Pornography. Casual sex. Crude jokes about sex. Hooking up with no strings attached.

Hanna Rosin's most recent *Atlantic* article, "Boys on the Side," describes highly intelligent, career-oriented women engaging in all of these behaviors with a mere shrug of the shoulders. In the minds of many driven young women on college campuses across the country, sexual promiscuity doesn't harm anyone. Hooking up has become the new sexual norm for young adults, and according to this norm, students shy away from committed relationships and instead enjoy one-time sexual encounters with no expectation of further intimacy. And, Rosin argues, the sexual liberation of the 1960s that led to the more recent "hookup culture" on college campuses is good for women—it allows women to enjoy casual sex without being "tied down" by serious commitment.

Rosin initially substantiates this claim through interviews with her subjects. Most women who are engaging in the hookup culture report that they don't want to return to the days of chastity belts or even more traditional dating, and Rosin takes these positive reports as evidence that the hookup culture is not only here to stay but is also good for the women involved. She provides no evidence, however, that women who hookup a lot during their early 20s go on to lead fulfilling lives, and she doesn't offer a counterpoint of women who have opted out of hooking up. Furthermore, Rosin offers a few statistics to demonstrate positive trends nationwide when it comes to sexual mores. The rate of teenage girls having sex has declined from 37 to 27 percent in the past 25 years, for instance. And the rate of rape and sexual assault against females has declined by 70 percent nationally since 1993. Both of these numbers demonstrate significant progress for women. Whether or not the positive statistics correlate to the rise of the hookup culture, however, remains unclear.

Rosin's stance on hookup culture hinges on two assumptions. First, she assumes that economic productivity and personal independence are the twin goals of every modern person. Feminists shouldn't decry the advent of the hookup culture, she argues, because it "is too bound up with everything that's fabulous about being a young woman in 2012—the freedom, the confidence, the knowledge that you can always depend on yourself." Moreover, "[the hookup culture] is not a place where they drown . . . unlike women in earlier ages, they have more-important things on their minds, such as good grades and internships and job interviews and a financial future of their own." Intimacy, family, and community might be desirable, but only after a woman has established herself as an independent financial entity.

Second, though I suspect she would disagree with me here, Rosin's argument assumes that for women to "arrive," they must become *just like men*. She describes sexually aggressive women at a business-school party as ones who "had learned to keep pace with the boys," and later as ones who were "behaving exactly like frat boys." Instead of challenging male behavior that demeans women (and men), Rosin capitulates to it. Instead of arguing for men and women to change culture in such a way that the responsibility for pregnancy and childrearing falls on the shoulders of both parents, she simply heralds women's ability to avoid pregnancy through birth control and abortion. And instead of promoting an understanding of human flourishing that includes relationships with trust, responsibility, and love, she succumbs to a truncated and depleted view of humanity that esteems individual work as the highest goal and self-serving love as the highest love.

From a Christian perspective, it's easy to critique Rosin's argument, one that she explores in her new book, *The End of Men* (a review of which *Christianity Today* will publish online in the coming weeks). Even if they don't always heed it in practice, Christians at least acknowledge the truth and goodness of the biblical view of human sexuality—that both men and women will honor God and find personal fulfillment in engaging in a sexual relationship with one other person within the covenant of marriage. Christians understand relationships as the core of our humanity, beginning with God's relationship within the Trinity, and extending to humans, who are invited into relationship with God but also into interdependent relationships with one another. Marriage, children, and community are viewed not as problems to be delayed until a career is in place, but rather as blessings to be received. And Christians understand love as, at its core, self-sacrificial, modeled after the love of Christ offered to us on the cross.

In Rosin's view, "Feminist progress right now largely depends on the existence of the hookup culture." But women can continue to find their rightful roles in the workplace and within the home without succumbing to the lie that a fulfilling life is one in which financial independence and self-sufficiency are the primary goals. Instead of assuming that women must become just like the traditional norm of sexually active men, the gospel offers a transformative vision of humanity. And it isn't a picture of the 1950s housewife either. It's a picture that challenges notions of traditional masculinity and femi-

ninity, including, but not limited to, the sexual norms for both. Yes, it's a picture that calls for chastity for both men and women outside of marriage. But it's also a picture that holds forth the possibility not of sexual liberation, but of true freedom.

Christians have done plenty of finger-wagging about the state of our nation's sexual culture, for the same reasons that Rosin extols it. But Rosin's posture, and the norm it extols, calls for more than rebuke. Christians have an opportunity to offer a different understanding not only of sex, but of what it means to know abiding joy and peace as a full human being. Let's make sure we can both articulate and live that understanding of sex and humanity in a world starving for true fulfillment.

AMY JULIA BECKER focuses her writing on faith, family, disability, and ethics. She is identified as a Christian theological conservative and also socially liberal.

Timaree Schmit

Hookup Culture Can Help Build Stronger Relationships

Hookup Culture, if such a thing exists, provides opportunities for young people to be more contemplative and communicative about sexuality, fostering a climate that encourages collaborative, consensual sexual behavior over transactional or predatory behavior. It also holds the possibility of freeing women and men from constraints of traditional gender expectations.

Is Hookup Culture Real?

When a young person says that he or she "hooked up with" someone, this should prompt more questions than commentary. After all, there is no strict definition of the term or even a majority opinion on what, specifically, must happen for a "hook up" to have occurred. Among college students, the phrase can indicate anything from prolonged kissing to oral, vaginal and anal sex. While common, the term is often too vague to be useful.

Researcher Amanda Holman uses the term hookups to refer to sexual behavior that takes place without the expectation of commitment. This is often purported to represent a fundamental change in the dating and sexual patterns of young people from previous generations. However, a comparison of responses to the General Social Survey from 1988–1996 and those of 2002–2010 failed to find evidence this is true. Sociologists Martin Monto and Anna Carey's research found "no evidence that there has been a sea change in the sexual behavior of college students or that there has been a liberalization of attitudes towards sexuality." They found a greater percentage of current college students indicate that they have had sex with a friend within the last year (68% versus 56%) and a larger number report having had sexual activity with a casual partner (44% compared to 34.5%). This degree of change indicates that casual sex was already a common experience and that a significant portion of the population does not engage in commitment-less hookups.

Instead, Hookup Culture is largely a matter of change in conversations about sexual behaviors. Students are more likely to talk with peers about experiences, but use non-specific terms like "hookup" to describe what happened. This intentional vagueness serves several functions. It can retain privacy, diminish embarrassment associated with using more technical or degrading

terminology, or deliberately give the impression that a greater or smaller variety of sexual acts occurred.

There is not much research, about whether most young people approve of Hookup Culture or think it is harmless. Qualitative interviews about hooking up find experiences may range from entirely satisfying to devastating. Additionally, there continue to be different social acceptance levels for males and females in terms of frequency of casual sex and number of partners. While traditional sexual gender norms are expanding for both men and women, many of the stigmas and expectations remain. Males are more likely than females to receive social encouragement to seek sexual pleasure, engage in sexual activity without intimacy or commitment and to be sexually involved with multiple partners.

Social Desirability Bias is a major issue when researching sexual behaviors, as respondents often feel pressure to appear 'normal' among their peers or to align their answers with personal ideals about how much and what kind of sex is OK to have. Perhaps young people now, especially young women, are simply more willing to acknowledge sexual activity that occurs outside of a serious relationship than in previous decades. Holman also suggests that young men now may feel pressured to over-report their experiences, thinking that their peers are engaging in more casual sex than they really are. She argues that the vagueness of the term "hookup" cultivates misperceptions about how much sex young people are having, giving the false impression that committed relationships are no longer the most common context for sexual activity.

What is Wrong with Hookup Culture?

Many discussions about hooking up focus on whether or not it's healthy for young people to have more casual sexual encounters. Some emphasize that Hookup Culture is a result of independent, career-oriented women feeling free to express their sexual desires and seek physical satisfaction without commitment in the way that only men were previously able to do. Others express concern that a climate that encourages strings-free sex will make it harder for young adults to build respectful and loving committed relationships or to say "no" to sex without facing social disapproval.

As for the first claim, longitudinal studies are not yet possible about how Hookup Culture affects women later in life, their relationship outcomes, satisfaction and sense of self. As for the latter claims, we have no evidence either. In fact, rates of sexual assault have dropped dramatically since the 1970s, with evidence that enthusiastic sexual consent may be viewed as more important now than in previous generations. Assessing whether intimacy in relationships is harmed by hooking up is made extra complicated by the variety of other variables of modern life, including: the ubiquity of social media, online dating, and a growing body of research that shows social isolation has increased for all demographics of Americans over the last two decades.

What Might be Right about Hookup Culture

Among the few facts we can ascertain about Hookup Culture, there are positive signs. Any deconstruction of traditional sexual mores bodes well for those who have been historically subjugated by them. For young women, the probability of negative consequences for engaging in premarital sexual behavior is reduced, including: harassment, ostracism, and the perception that she is no longer marriageable. As marriage becomes less and less vital for a woman's survival and sense of self, Hookup Culture enables those women who want to remain single to do so without sacrificing sexual pleasure, an optional luxury long granted to men.

Hookup Culture also supports the "queering" of restrictive sexual norms. Queer Theory aims to deconstruct restrictive essentialist ideas about men, women and sexual identities. Traditional sexual norms divide identities and behaviors categorically: man and woman, straight and gay, good and bad. Through a queer lens, sexuality is viewed as fluid and existing on a continuum, rather than in dichotomous boxes. According to both feminist and queer thought, someone's sex or gender shouldn't limit their behavioral choices. Since Hookup Culture subverts traditional sexual norms, it serves as a de facto "queering." As it expands the parameters of what is possible sexually, it holds the possibility of adding to the liberation of gay, lesbian and bisexual individuals. For those who are oppressed by a system that says sex is only appropriate for a husband and wife, any opportunity to reexamine these beliefs may hold promise.

Finally, Hookup Culture prioritizes sexual pleasure. Traditional sexual norms emphasize male sexual prowess and female sexual purity. These ideas put unrealistic expectations on young men and discourage them from expressing doubt or seeking information about what is pleasurable to female partners. Females, in contrast, are discouraged from demonstrating familiarity with their turn-ons, or expressing sexual desires. This results in a cycle of sexual encounters where men feel uncomfortable asking for direction and females are unable to ask for what they want. Even in the context of long-term relationships, partners may fear communicating uncommon desires out of fear of rejection or upending stability. The commitment-free nature of a hookup allows for partners to express their sexual needs without fear of judgment or compromising the relationship. Within Hookup Culture, individuals may experience a greater variety of partners and sexual acts, possibly introducing them to a diverse array of sexual pleasures that they can integrate into any future sexual interactions, including those in committed situations. Some authors have described this experimental process as helpful "practice" for more significant relationships.

A young person may choose to stop having sexual relations with a partner who is selfish, unwilling to learn, or otherwise unsatisfying, and focus their energies on partners who are more giving and open to experience. A selfish lover may find their reputation disqualifies them with other possible partners. This encourages a culture of reciprocal, mutually pleasurable sexual experiences.

Hookup Culture will never be acceptable to those who espouse the belief that sex is only appropriate between committed partners. However, there is little evidence that those people will have to change to accommodate those who do not share this belief. The possibility of Hookup Culture is not a replacement of traditional norms, but the addition of new norms with different values.

TIMAREE SCHMIT runs a sex-positive podcast and blogs under the title *Sex with Timaree*. She possesses a doctorate in human sexuality from Widener University.

EXPLORING THE ISSUE

Is Hookup Culture on College Campuses Bad for Heterosexual Girls?

Critical Thinking and Reflection

1. What are some arguments made in each side with which you agree or disagree?
2. What are the strengths and weaknesses of the two positions made in this essay?
3. Pick the side with which you most agree. What are some additional arguments you would make to strengthen the case for or against hookup culture?
4. Think more broadly about hookup culture. Are there ways to look at this as a bad thing for heterosexual girls from a non-Christian perspective? If so, what case would you make? Is there a way to make the case for hookup culture from a religious perspective? If so, what would you say?

Is There Common Ground?

Both authors have opposite views regarding the impact of hookup culture on college campus. However, both, to a certain degree, have the same goal: they want young women to do what is in their best interest. Of course one argument is secular and one is non-secular. Beyond that, there are other reasons that are not necessarily anchored in religious faith: transmission of sexually transmitted diseases, finding the right partner, and other goals. What sort of sexuality education can occur on campus—or off campus—that can help students make sexual decisions that are consistent with their best interest and long-term goals?

Create Central

www.mhhe.com/createcentral

Additional Resources

Kathleen A. Bogle, *Hooking Up: Sex, Dating, and Relationships on Campus* (2008)

Donna Freitas, *The End of Sex: How Hookup Culture Is Leaving a Generation Unhappy, Unfulfilled, and Confused about Intimacy* (2013)

Laura Stepp, Sessions, *Unhooked: How Young Women Pursue Sex, Delay Love and Lose at Both* (2008)

Internet References . . .

American Psychological Association

www.apa.org/monitor/2013/02/ce-corner.aspx

Bacchus Network

www.bacchusnetwork.org

Selected, Edited, and with Issue Framing Material by:
David M. Hall, Ph.D., *Delaware Valley College*

ISSUE

Are Teenagers Too Young to Become Parents?

YES: The National Campaign to Prevent Teen and Unplanned Pregnancy, from *One in Three: The Case for Wanted and Welcomed Pregnancy* (May 2007)

NO: Simon Duncan, Claire Alexander, and Rosalind Edwards, from "What's the Problem with Teenage Parents?" in *Teenage Parenthood: What's the Problem?* (2010)

Learning Outcomes

After reading this issue, you will be able to:

- Identify critical research about the state of and consequences of teenage parenting.
- Compare and contrast the major research cited and analysis used in examining teenage parenthood.
- Evaluate the impact of teen parenthood on teens themselves as well as on the larger American society.

ISSUE SUMMARY

YES: The National Campaign to Prevent Teen and Unplanned Pregnancy is dedicated to reducing teenage pregnancy. Their research argues that teens face significant consequences if they have unplanned pregnancy.

NO: Simon Duncan, Claire Alexander, and Rosalind Edwards have written a chapter in a book about teen pregnancy and parenting. This chapter, which takes a global perspective by looking at another Western society, England, argues that teenage pregnancy and parenting is not a problem.

Most people agree that it is important to reduce teenage pregnancy and parenthood. Teens involved in a pregnancy often did not plan that pregnancy. Indeed, about half of all pregnancies in the United States are unplanned—about 3 million each year.

Since the Clinton administration, there has been ongoing debate about the federal government's role in funding programs to reduce teen pregnancy: whether the best way to keep teenagers from having children is to teach them about contraception and abstinence, or only teach them about abstinence so that they fear the consequences of having sex. Although there is debate about whether abstinence-only or comprehensive sexuality education is the best approach, the goals tend to be the same: keep teenagers from pregnancy and parenthood.

In the United States, 30 percent of girls will become pregnant at least once by the age of 20. Many will terminate their pregnancies while others will decide to become parents. Sometimes fathers remain involved; often teen mothers are left as single parents, perhaps with support from their parent(s), guardian(s), and/or caretaker(s).

This issue will focus on adult views of teenage parenthood. However, it is important to take some time to read the perspective of teenage parents themselves. On Pregnancystories.net, teens have posted some of the following stories about their young pregnancy and parenthood:

> **15 and pregnant**—well im 15 and two weeks pregnant. I told my boyfriend at the time and he was happy but as soon as his parents found out they said he was too young to be a dad.... Im looking forward to having my baby and iv got all the support i need. To all the girls who am pregnant and dont have a man . . . dont let him get you down cuz they aint worth it.

> Abi

> **my perfect accident**—hey everyone my name is johanna, i am 18 years old and i have a 5 month old baby. when i was about 4 months off my 17th birthday me and one of my close guy friends started doing a friends with benefits sort of thing, at first it was great but then we let our emotions become involved and i fell in love with him. we decided to end it and he got a girlfriend pretty much straight away which hurt me. soon after i found out that i was pregnant and i told him, but he didnt believe me i had to confirm it with the doctor before anything happened. he was far from

happy with it and started saying that it was all my fault i was a whore and a bitch, eventually his girlfriend broke up with him because of it. he still to this day hates me but i dont care i now have a beautiful 5 month old baby boy dominic jason, who is my world! my mum is so over the moon with everything and im happy to be a single mum, i now realize he did me a favor, i couldve never been with him after that or exposed dominic to that!

johanna

single mommy—Hi my name is Alex, I am 19 and i have a 1 year old daughter. it all started when I was 17 i got pregnant to my boyfriend of 2 years johnny, i was shocked and scared at first but eventually told him and everyone, we decided to keep the baby and be young parents, but as my pregnancy went on johnny started to push away, and eventually when I was 26 weeks he got a football scholarship to college, we talked about it and he wasnt ready to become a father, so he left for college a week later, i was devastated but i had my daughter to think of, i have birth to Lilliana Jayde 4 weeks after i turned 18, i am now 19 and lilliana is 13 and a half months old, we are very happy she is my world, i regularly send johnny pictures we keep in touch he still wants to know that lilliana is okay but she has never met him. But im happy i have a wonderful job, and im renting a nice 3 bedroom house, i have great friends and family.

What do you think about these narratives of teens who are currently or will soon be parents? Their perspective seems fairly positive. Do you think that their experience will meet their expectations? Are they providing a realistic view or an overly rosy view? In your view, are their expectations rational? Are they in denial? Can you see a difference in the support network that some teens have versus others? What impact will that have?

Although there are a great deal of publications about keeping teens from having sex, there is a lack of consensus on this issue—as seen from these teen voices. This Yes selection contains an research from the National Campaign to Prevent Teen and Unplanned Pregnancy, a mainstream American publication, stating that teens are too young to have children.

The opposing viewpoint comes from Europe, and it does so for a number of reasons. First, Europe is not having the same debate about *whether* teens should have sex at all, a topic which has proven highly controversial in the United States (e.g., see the U.S. debate about abstinence-only education versus comprehensive sexuality education). Second, England and much of Western Europe have a more extensive social safety net program than is typically found in the United States. Third, in examining family and personal relationships, it is sometimes valuable to take a global perspective. What does that culture have in common with ours? What is different? What is it about their perspective or approach that you find compelling? What is it about their perspective or approach that you find wrong or even damaging?

We also know that teens in the United States have a much higher rate of pregnancy than they do in England and Western Europe. Research tells us that there is not a significant difference in teenage sexual behavior between the countries. So what causes this difference? Is it an institutional issue of privilege and resources? In the United States, we have a higher proportion of poor citizens per capita than in Western Europe. Or is it a question of education? In the United States, children often receive little if any sexuality education, and many only learn about abstinence. In Western Europe, it is not regarded as controversial to teach children about contraception if they are at an age at which they may become sexually active.

Regardless of the difference in pregnancy rates, this issue provides readers with the opportunity to take a closer look at different views on whether this is a problem.

YES

The National Campaign to Prevent
Teen and Unplanned Pregnancy

One in Three: The Case for Wanted and Welcomed Pregnancy

Defining the Problem

The nation has made extraordinary progress in preventing early pregnancy and childbearing. The teen pregnancy rate declined 36 percent between 1991 and 2002 (the most recent data available) and the teen birth rate has declined by one-third. In fact, few social problems have improved as dramatically as has this one.

When the National Campaign to Prevent Teen Pregnancy began in 1996, we challenged the nation to reduce the teen pregnancy rate in the United States by one-third over a 10-year period. Ten years later, demographic projections suggest that the nation may well have achieved this goal. Even so, it is still the case that one-third of teen girls become pregnant before they are 20, and the rate of teen pregnancy in the United States remains far higher than in other comparable countries. Mindful of the continuing problem, in 2006 we challenged the nation to reduce the rate of teen pregnancy by *another* one-third over the next 10 years.

But when the progress among teens is looked at within the context of pregnancy and childbearing in America more generally, it is increasingly apparent that although teens are moving in the right direction, their older brothers and sisters, friends, relatives, and neighbors are not.

A new analysis of existing data by the National Campaign indicates that about one in three pregnancies in America are unwanted. In this analysis, unwanted pregnancies include (1) pregnancies that end in abortion (about 1.3 million), (2) births resulting from pregnancies that women *themselves* say they did not want at the time of conception or *ever* in the future (about 567,000); and (3) a smaller number of miscarriages that were also of unwanted pregnancies (179,000). In other words, just over 2 million of the 6.4 million pregnancies in America in 2001 (the most recent data available) were unwanted.

Moreover, between 1994 and 2001, the *rate* of unwanted pregnancy in the United States increased slightly (4 percent) from 31.9 to 33.2 unwanted pregnancies per 1,000 women aged 15–44. In fact, the rate of unwanted pregnancy increased among women in every age group with the exception of teens.

An unwanted pregnancy is not to be confused with a pregnancy that may have come at an inconvenient or awkward time; in fact, some women will say, for example, that their third child was a pleasant surprise, and sometimes pregnancy comes a bit sooner than a couple might wish. The children born months later from these mistimed pregnancies are often welcomed into stable and nurturing families.

But some pregnancies are more than unexpected or mistimed; they are greeted by women with anguish—sometimes even alarm—especially when they occur at a time in a woman's life when she is not prepared to raise a child—or, in many instances, *another* child. She may not have adequate personal or financial supports in place or have other serious problems or challenges. It is these pregnancies that are of particular concern, as detailed later in this monograph.

Of the 2 million unwanted pregnancies estimated to have occurred in 2001:

- More than half (54 percent) occurred to women in their twenties (1,092,000 pregnancies): about one third (32 percent) were to women aged 20–24 (651,000 pregnancies); more than one in five (22 percent) were to women aged 25–30 (441,000 pregnancies).
- About three in ten (28 percent) were to women aged 30–44 (577,000 pregnancies).
- About two in ten (18 percent) occurred to teens aged 15–19 (366,000 pregnancies).
- In addition, almost three fourths (72 percent) of unwanted pregnancies are to unmarried women (1,475,000 pregnancies), and just over a quarter (28 percent) of unwanted pregnancies occur to married women (565,000 pregnancies).

What the National Campaign Plans to Do

In response to these important statistics, the National Campaign to Prevent Teen Pregnancy is expanding its mission. We will continue to work on preventing teen pregnancy. And we will now *also* focus on reducing the high level of unwanted pregnancy in the United States among young adults in their twenties where the majority of such pregnancies occur. This expansion is made possible by the William and Flora Hewlett Foundation, which has made a ten-year commitment to preventing unwanted pregnancy and reducing the need for abortion in America.

In opening this new front, the National Campaign will use the experience and knowledge we have gained in our work with teens to encourage young adults to bring more intentionality and planning to their pregnancies. We will continue in a common sense, bipartisan, and research-based fashion using many of the same strategies that have contributed to the nation's progress in reducing teen pregnancy over the past 10 years. In this new work with young adults, we will encourage personal responsibility among women and men and responsible public policies as well. We will:

- work with opinion leaders, policymakers, and program leaders at the national and state levels;
- support public information and education about a wide range of topics;
- encourage careful, consistent use of family planning by all who are sexually active and not seeking pregnancy;
- encourage responsible, healthy relationships among young adults (which can include refraining from sexual activity in some circumstances) to help them achieve their future family and career goals;
- engage the entertainment media, faith communities, parents, and others;
- emphasize the role of men in pregnancy prevention and planning; and
- support practical, evidence-based polices that advance our mission.

Helping Americans reduce their high levels of unwanted pregnancy is a complex challenge, of course, and it will require intense attention and ongoing action from many sectors. Although the National Campaign has many ideas about what to do, there is much we need to learn about underlying causes and possible remedies. Accordingly, over the next several months, the National Campaign will be continuing to learn from a wide variety of experts, policymakers, those on the front lines, and young adults themselves about unwanted pregnancy and what might be done to improve the situation. This outreach has already begun and will be intensifying in the upcoming months.

Taking strong steps to increase the proportion of pregnancies that are fully wanted and welcomed is long overdue. It is worth repeating: one in three pregnancies—over *2 million* each year—are unwanted. We think the country can do far better.

Why Preventing Unwanted Pregnancy Matters

Reducing unwanted pregnancy will bring significant benefits to women, men, children, families, and society in general.

> *Increasing the proportion of pregnancies that are wanted and welcomed will help ensure healthier pregnancies, healthier babies, and enhanced child development.*

New guidelines about preconception care from the Centers for Disease Control and Prevention underscore how planning for pregnancy and being at optimal health before pregnancy can help to dramatically improve a woman's chance of having a healthy pregnancy and baby. Unfortunately, women who experience an unwanted pregnancy often do not have the opportunity to engage in such preconception care.

Even when taking into account the existing social and economic factors, women experiencing an unwanted pregnancy are less likely to obtain prenatal care and their babies are at increased risk of both low birthweight and of being born prematurely, both of which increase the risk of many serious problems including infant mortality. These mothers are also less likely to breastfeed their infants.

Children born from unwanted pregnancies also face a range of developmental risks as well. For example, these children report poorer physical and mental health compared to those children born as the result of an intended pregnancy. They also have relationships with their mothers that are less close during childhood (and possibly into adulthood) when compared to peers who were born as the result of an intended pregnancy.

A new analysis from Child Trends indicates that, after controlling for numerous background factors, children two years old who were born as the result of an unwanted pregnancy have significantly lower cognitive test scores when compared to children born as the result of an intended pregnancy. These cognitive test scores include direct assessment of such skills as listening, vocabulary, exploring, problem solving, memory, and communication, as well as a child's overall mental ability relative to other children in his or her age group.

> *Increasing the proportion of pregnancies that are wanted and welcomed will help reduce both out-of-wedlock births and child poverty.*

Over two decades of social science research makes clear that children fare better when their parents are older, have completed at least high school, are in stable and committed relationships—marriage, in particular—and are ready to take on the complex challenges of being parents. But many children born as the result of unwanted pregnancies are not welcomed into such families.

The majority of children from an unwanted pregnancy are born to women who are either single or cohabiting. This is important because children who are raised in single-parent families face a number of challenges. For example, when compared to similar children who grow up with two parents, children in one-parent families are twice as likely to drop out of high school, 2.5 times as likely to become teen mothers, 1.4 times as likely to be both out of school and out of work, and five times more likely to be poor. Even after adjusting for a variety of relevant social and economic differences, children in single-parent homes have lower grade-point averages, lower college aspirations, and poorer school attendance records. As adults, they also have higher rates of divorce.

Moreover, an analysis of data from 1970 to 1996 by National Campaign President Isabel Sawhill shows that virtually all of the increase in child poverty over that period was related to the growth of single-parent families. In the 1970s, some of this increase was the result of rising divorce rates, but since the early 1980s, virtually all of the increase has been driven by the increased numbers of never-married mothers.

All such data suggest that reducing unwanted pregnancy will increase the proportion of children born into circumstances that better support their growth and development. For example, the National Campaign estimates that preventing unwanted pregnancy has the potential to reduce non-marital childbearing by 26 percent.

Increasing the proportion of pregnancies that are wanted and welcomed will reduce the need for abortion.

Although there are many deeply felt and strongly held beliefs nationwide about the proper place of abortion in American life, virtually all of us see value in lessening the need for abortion and would prefer that fewer women have to confront an unwanted pregnancy in the first place. Through primary prevention—that is helping couples avoid unwanted pregnancy—the 1.3 million abortions in America each year can be dramatically decreased.

Increasing the proportion of pregnancies that are wanted and welcomed will help reduce disparities.

Disparities in unwanted pregnancy are on the rise. A woman below the poverty line is now nearly four times as likely as a woman at or above 200 percent of poverty to have an unintended pregnancy—a complex measure that includes *both* unwanted and mistimed pregnancy. Reflecting this trend, the abortion rate for low-income women increased 22 percent between 1994 and 2000. Still, 40 percent of all unintended pregnancies are to women at or above 200 percent of poverty.

Increasing the proportion of pregnancies that are wanted and welcomed will help women and men better plan their future.

That an unwanted pregnancy can derail the future plans of individuals is self-evident. For example, an unexpected, unwanted pregnancy can interrupt a young person's education and diminish future job prospects—a scenario that is becoming ever more serious with the increasing demand for a well-educated workforce. Reducing the high level of unwanted pregnancy in this country will unquestionably help many teens and adults achieve economic security and more stable relationships, which benefits not only them but also their children and society.

What the American Public Knows and Believes

Public opinion surveys conducted on behalf of the National Campaign by two widely respected communications firms, the Glover Park Group and Public Strategies Inc., make clear that there is broad and deep public support for the goal of reducing the number of unwanted pregnancies. In fact, over two-thirds (69 percent) of the American public believes it is important to reduce the number of unwanted pregnancies in the United States.

The public also supports several ways to encourage more young adults to increase the proportion of pregnancies that are fully wanted and welcomed by both partners:

- 87 percent support strengthening a culture of *personal responsibility* regarding sex, getting pregnant, and bringing children into the world, as well as strengthening the norm of always practicing family planning when a couple is not ready to have a child.
- 82 percent support *responsible policies* that will increase the use of contraception, particularly by those who cannot afford it and by those at greatest risk for having an unwanted pregnancy.
- 90 percent of the public support the idea of providing *more education* to teens, parents, and young adults in their 20s and 30s that encourages them to take sex, pregnancy, and family formation seriously; stresses personal responsibility and respectful relationships; and includes extensive information about contraception.

In this same survey, the most commonly cited reason for reducing unwanted pregnancy was to improve the quality of life for children:

- 24 percent of adults say that the single most important reason for reducing teen and unwanted pregnancy is because children who grow up wanted have a better future.
- 20 percent say it is because more children are likely to grow up living with both a father and a mother.

More generally, the vast majority of Americans believe that young people should complete their education, have the means to raise a child, and be married before becoming pregnant:

- 88 percent of the American public believes that children generally do better when they are raised in two-parent, married families.
- 97 percent believe it is important to have the means to take care of a child without outside assistance before becoming a parent.
- 96 percent believe that finishing one's education before becoming a parent is important.
- 90 percent believe that being married before becoming pregnant is important.

Despite these widely shared sentiments, the *magnitude* of the unwanted pregnancy problem in the United States—and which groups are most at risk—are not well understood. In particular, very few Americans realize that teens are only a small part of the problem. For example:

- Even though less than 20 percent of all abortions are to teens, 4 out of 5 Americans think that the percentage is higher (often much higher).
- 77 percent of Americans assume that teens have the highest number of unplanned pregnancies; in fact, young adults do.
- Only 15 percent of the public knows that unmarried teens are *more likely* than unmarried women in their 20s to have used an effective method of contraception the last time they had sex.

Teens Still Matter a Lot

This monograph makes the case that adults, not just teenagers, are having difficulty in overall pregnancy planning. Even so, there are two primary reasons why the nation should continue to focus on teen pregnancy given all its serious consequences.

Despite a one-third decline in teen pregnancy and birth rates since the early 1990s, the teen pregnancy rate in the United States is *still* the highest among comparable countries. One in three teens becomes pregnant at least once by age 20. For some subgroups, the news is even more sobering. For example, 51 percent of Latina teens become pregnant by the time they leave their teen years. There is also some evidence to suggest that the progress the nation has made in preventing teen pregnancy

and childbearing has begun to slow or, in some cases, to reverse—all of which suggests that the nation's efforts going forward will need to be more intense and creative.

A crisp focus on preventing teen pregnancy and childbearing is also important because the knowledge, attitudes, and behavioral patterns that develop in adolescence strongly affect behavior in the years that follow. In other words, the teen years are a critical place to start to prevent unwanted pregnancy among women of all ages. In our work with teenagers, the National Campaign will continue to encourage teens to delay sexual activity—their best choice—and to practice family planning if they are sexually active.

A Final Note

Unwanted pregnancy among young adults is a complex problem, and getting people to change their behavior is a difficult proposition at best. Even so, we believe this nation can do far better and are optimistic about the chances for success. When the National Campaign began a decade ago, there was a sense that teen pregnancy was an intractable problem and the organization's goal of reducing the teen pregnancy rate by one-third was greeted with great skepticism. Ten years later, the situation has improved dramatically. This progress suggests that *adults* can do a better job, too, and that a higher proportion of all pregnancies can be wanted and welcomed.

If the National Campaign's efforts and those of others lead to less unwanted pregnancy, more young adults will be deliberate, serious, and intentional about pregnancy, childbearing, and family formation. In so doing, more children will be welcomed into the world by parents who are ready to provide them with the love, care, and nurture we want for every child in this country. More children will grow up in two-parent, married families or other fully supportive and stable circumstances; there will be less poverty, a lighter tax burden, less stress on families, and stronger communities. And there will be far less need for abortion.

THE NATIONAL CAMPAIGN TO PREVENT TEEN AND UNPLANNED PREGNANCY is dedicated to reducing teenage pregnancy. Their research argues that teens face significant consequences if they have unplanned pregnancy.

Simon Duncan, Claire Alexander,
and Rosalind Edwards

 **NO**

What's the Problem with Teenage Parents?

[**W**]hy is there such an invested need in presenting an unremittingly negative image of young parents, and what does this say about the values placed on family and the role of paid work in twenty-first-century Britain? How—and why—have policy makers and news makers got the story about teenage parents so wrong?

New Labour and Teenage Parenting: An Economic or Moral Agenda?

2010 marks the year by which New Labour pledged to halve the number of pregnancies for under-eighteen-year-olds in the UK. The government's ten year Teenage Pregnancy Strategy was launched in 1999 in a report from the Social Exclusion Unit (SEU), then at the heart of government in Cabinet Office and itself resulting from a putative 'underclass unit' set up by Peter Mandelson, then Minister without Portfolio, in 1997. The report, which has set the framework for government policy since then, saw teenage pregnancy as a major social and economic problem, where Britain did much worse than other west European countries. Or as Tony Blair, then Prime Minister, put it, in his forward to the Social Exclusion Unit report:

> Some of these teenagers, and some of their children, live happy and fulfilled lives. But far too many do not. Teenage mothers are less likely to finish their education, less likely to find a good job, and more likely to end up both as single parents and bringing up their children in poverty. The children themselves run a much greater risk of poor health, and have a much higher chance of becoming teenage mothers themselves. Our failure to tackle this problem has cost the teenagers, their children and the country dear.

The SEU report identified the causes of this problem as low expectations and ignorance among teenagers, and mixed messages from the media. While the SEU report made clear a strong relationship between teenage pregnancy and social disadvantage, this association was downplayed either as cause or remedy, rather young parenting was seen to strongly reinforce disadvantage. And the way

out was through a dual goal of prevention and direction—to reduce the number of under-eighteen pregnancies by half, and increase the number of teenage parents entering education, training, or employment to sixty per cent.

The heady political symbolism and mobilisation created by the media's moral panic reinforced the need for government to be seen to tackle what was already identified as a problem for 'teenagers, their children and the country.' All this was underlined by contrasting national teenage birth rates or, as Tony Blair put it in his forward to the SEU's 1999 document, Britain's 'shameful record.' British rates remained among the highest in the 28 OECD developed countries (30 per 1000 in 1998, compared to 10 or less in Germany, France, Scandinavia and the Netherlands). Only the USA at 52.1, and more marginally Canada and New Zealand, had higher rates. This comparative failure has an important policy impact, as suggested by the highlighting of international comparisons in most government and policy reports. For while the UK seemed to be 'stuck,' as the SEU put it, the experience of western Europe implied that teenage pregnancy and parenting, perceived as a difficult social problem, was nonetheless amenable to policy solution. Underlying this comparison is an issue around economic, as well as social, competition—how can Britain compete with an inadequate workforce, where teenage pregnancy supposedly restricts educational achievement and employment participation.

This international comparative lesson was emphasised by the appreciation that local rates also vary widely across Britain; it is not just young women who are poorer that are more likely to become pregnant, and least likely to use abortion to resolve pregnancy—they also live in poorer areas. In contrast, some richer areas in Britain have teenage abortion and pregnancy rates more like supposed European exemplars such as The Netherlands. The 'problem' of teenage pregnancy was ripe for intervention by a reforming new government.

Hence the New Labour government rolled out its teenage pregnancy strategy from 1999 onwards, originally under the direction of a Ministerial Task Force, and coordinated by the Teenage Pregnancy Unit (TPU). Starting in 2001, each top tier local authority had an agreed teenage pregnancy strategy to reach local 2010 targets around the desired national average. Each local strategy was led by a Teenage Pregnancy Coordinator, working with a Teenage Pregnancy Partnership Board, and supported by a Local Implementation Grant. These local Strategies were supported and performance managed by a Regional Teenage Pregnancy Coordinator, based in the regional government office. Local indicators, such as levels of conceptions in targeted age groups, availability and use of services, and health outcomes, were devised to help monitor progress towards achieving these targets. In line with government objectives for 'joined-up' approaches to service and policy development, work locally was intended to proceed in conjunction with other national government initiatives such as Sure Start, Sure Start Plus and the Children's Fund, and other national government departments were expected actively to support the strategy. In this way the TPU would hopefully reach the two main targets, as set by the Social Exclusion Unit—to halve the under—eighteen teenage conception rate by 2010 and to substantially increase the participation of teenage parents in education, training or employment.

This is an impressive machinery. But the 'low expectations' explanation—which points towards tackling social disadvantage—seems to have been neglected. Rather, policy in practice focused on the 'ignorance' explanation—British youth were seen as deficient in their sexual health knowledge, poor users of contraception, shy about sex, and wary about accessing services. Perhaps this focus was the more appealing when current policy thinking tends to stress individual behaviour and motivations, rather than structural influences on behaviour, like social disadvantage. Certainly, on a relatively low budget (the initial TPU budget was only £60 million) it might have been here that the policy implementers hoped for 'quick wins,' when taking on social disadvantage would cost a lot more and take a lot longer. Policy then ended up pathologising teenage pregnancy and childrearing, when it was seen to arise from 'inappropriate motivations, ignorance and sexual embarrassment,' rather than supporting the positive features of parenting.

How has this approach endured the experience of implementation? The Department for Communities, Schools, and Families report *Teenage Parents: the next steps* was to give new guidance to local authorities and primary care trusts given the previous eight years experience. The report recognises failures in reaching the desired targets—the reduction rate in teenage births was only 11.8% over the period, rather than approaching the desired 50% by 2010; similarly only about 30% of teenage mothers were in employment, education and training (EET), rather than 60%. Hence the need for a 'refreshed strategy' as the report's introduction puts it. There was also a whole battery of research produced since the SEU's original 1999 report, which as a whole pointed to a substantial gap between policy and experience, indicating both that the outcomes for teenage parents were not as dire as assumed and that young parenting encapsulated many positive fea-tures as well as problems. This includes research reviewed, or directly commissioned, by the TPU itself. But despite recognition of 'What teenage mothers and young fathers say' in the new 2007 report (in its chapter four), the existing two-track approach remained. Teenage parenting was as a problem in and of itself and should be cut, and the further need was to integrate remaining young parents into a productive workforce. 'Refreshed' was more about changing the implementation channels from specialised services into mainstream midwifery and health visiting services, Children's Centres, and Youth Support Services.

The report bases the essential continuation of the two-track approach on its enumeration of the disadvantaged characteristics of teenage mothers, and the poor outcomes they—and their children—experience, using a whole range of social and economic indicators. There are a number of key features that can be identified in this policy portrait of teenage parenthood, and that echo the media and political representations discussed above. First there is the clear gendering of this discourse, with the focus being primarily on young mothers, while young fathers play a very secondary role. This links into an assumed conflation between young motherhood (where many will live with partners or grandparents, and others will have 'live apart together' relationships') and single motherhood. Second, there is the insistence on the negative consequences of teenage pregnancy on both the mother and child, in which health, emotional and economic 'wellbeing' are taken as the key problem areas (and largely seen as interchangeable). Third, there is the emphasis on prevention of pregnancy rather than support for teenage parents—and in the 2007 report, rather chilling, concern to prevent further pregnancies for young mothers (for some young mothers, especially those with partners, would like to reach a desired family size). Fourth, is the conflation of socio-economic deprivation with teenage pregnancy, the implication being that teenage pregnancy is a cause of poverty. The report asserts that these poor outcomes are partially independent of wider factors of social deprivation and rather points to 'the lifestyles and behaviour of teenage mothers' as contributory factors. Fifth, there is the 'classing' of the issue, with teenage pregnancy linked to specific socio-economic groupings, and their associated problems, in particular the low levels of labour market participation. Sixth, there is the insistence on education, training and paid employment as the sole legitimate pathway to social inclusion and to ameliorating the negative effects of young parenthood.

Hence Beverley Hughes, then Minister for Children, Young People, and Families, wrote in her forward to the 2007 report that:

> Children born to teenage mothers are more likely to live in deprived areas, do less well at school, and disengage from learning early—all of which are risk factors for teenage pregnancy and other poor outcomes.

Equally, one could write that teenage mothers commonly show resilience and motivation, and become more socially connected and purposeful, where pregnancy usually marks a turning point for the better, become more likely to take up education and employment, and do no worse—and often better—than their social peers once pre-existing disadvantage is allowed for. This contrast is the terrain of this book.

The Myth of the Teenage Pregnancy Epidemic

The perceived social threat from teenage parenting is buttressed by a negative public consensus around teenage conception and pregnancy itself. This consensus assumes that teenage pregnancy is increasing rapidly, that this increase is particularly marked among younger teenagers, that all teenage pregnancies are unplanned, that all these unplanned conceptions are unwanted, and that new teenage mothers are inevitably also single mothers without stable relationships with partners. All these assumptions are unfounded, but all serve to bolster the negative evaluation of subsequent teenage parenting, and hence the nature of the policy response.

Newspaper headlines frequently announce 'soaring' teenage birth rates, creating an 'epidemic' of births to teenagers. Indeed as many as 81% of respondents to a 2008 Ipsos MORI poll thought that teenage pregnancy was increasing, while about a quarter of the 16–24 age group thought that 40% of 15–17 year-old girls became parents each year. In fact there have been substantial declines in both birth rates and absolute numbers of births to teenagers since the 1960s and early 1970s (see Table 1). By 2007 only 11.4% of conceptions were to women aged under 20, with an even smaller share of births—6.4%. In addition few teenage mothers are under 16, only around 6% in 2006, accounting for just 0.9% of all births in Britain by 2007, while around 80% of teenage mothers were 18 or 19 years-old. Overall, teenage birth rates are now at around the same level as in the 1950s, that supposed 'golden age' of family.

What *is* different is that in the 1950s and 1960s, the majority of teenage parents married—although many seem to have been hastily enforced 'shotgun marriages,' notorious for high rates of dysfunctionality and breakdown. In addition, probably around 20% of the children were adopted shortly after birth. In contrast, by the 2001 census only 9% of teenage parents were married; although around 30% cohabited; in addition, around another quarter jointly registered the birth with the father at another address—which suggests some continuing parental relationship on the 'living apart together' (or LAT) model. There are now very few adoptions of teenage mothers' children. These trends away from marriage, and towards unmarried cohabitation and 'living apart together' reflect those for the population as a whole, especially among younger age groups. Thus in 2006, around 0.5% of all 18–24 year-olds in Britain

Table 1

Live Births and Birth Rates for Women Under 20, 1951–2008

	Numbers of live births	Birth rate per 1000 women aged 15–19
1951	29,111	21.3
1956	37,938	27.3
1961	59,786	37.3
1966	66,746	47.9
1971	82,641	50.6
1976	54,500	29.8
1981	60,800	30.9
1986	57,406	30.1
1991	52,396	33.1
1996	44,667	30.0
2001	44,189	28.0
2004	45,028	26.9
2005	44,830	26.3
2006	45,509	26.6
2007	44,805	26.0
2008	44,683	see note

Sources: ONS Birth Statistics, Health Statistics Quarterly.

Note: 2008 birth rate not available at time of press.

were married, with 12% cohabiting, while as many as 35% were in 'living apart together' partner relationships.

Whatever the level of teenage pregnancy, it is assumed in the public and media discourse that all teenage pregnancies are unplanned, that all unplanned conceptions are unwanted, and that most result from ignorance if not wilful immorality. Certainly the Social Exclusion Unit's framework 1999 report identified 'ignorance'—the 'lack of accurate knowledge about contraception, STIs (sexually transmitted infections), what to expect in relationships and what it means to be a parent' as major cause of teenage pregnancy. This is repeated in succeeding policy and guidance documents. But there is little support for the assumption that teenage parents are particularly ignorant about sex, contraception, and parenting, that low levels of knowledge 'cause' teenage pregnancy, or that increased knowledge reduces pregnancy. It is hard to find young mothers who become pregnant due to ignorance about sex and contraception. Similarly, a meta-analysis of preventative strategies focusing on sex education, and improved access to advice and contraceptive services, concluded that this did not reduce unintended pregnancies among young women aged between 11–18.

Indeed, a significant minority of teenage mothers, and fathers, positively plan for pregnancy. Some are hoping for birthing success after an earlier miscarriage, others in this group, especially those with partners, plan for subsequent children so as to complete their desired family size and hence 'build' a family. Many other teenage parents are 'positively ambivalent' towards childbirth—that is, they do not actually plan it but would quite like a baby and do not use contraception for that reason. For most teenage parents, pregnancy may well be 'unplanned,' but then so are many, if not most, pregnancies for all women—the very idea of 'planning pregnancy' is something of a grey area to say the least. Few teenage mothers, it seems, regret early childbirth, as many of the succeeding chapters show. As with other women 'unplanned' pregnancy does not necessarily mean 'unwanted' pregnancy for teenage parents. Or, as Germaine Greer put it: 'We have 39,000 unwanted pregnancies a year unwanted by the Government that is. No one is speaking for the mums.'

This set of policy and public assumptions is the starting point for Pam Alldred and Miriam David in their examination on the role and importance of education in young mothers' lives, and on their gendered expectations regarding parenthood. For their research shows how the values and priorities expressed by young mothers do not fit comfortably within the model presented in the Teenage Pregnancy Strategy (TPS), nor with many of the values assumed in, or explicitly asserted by, the TPS. In particular, the chapter questions the assumptions that early mothering is undesirable or aberrant; that education or training in the child's early years is desirable or even accessible to young mothers; and that either 'parenting' or 'studying' can be assumed to be gender-neutral activities. The logic the authors find at work in the young women's lives in their study seems to reflect the dominant values in their community and this logic questions the link between teenage pregnancy and social exclusion asserted in government policy. Similarly; in chapter three, Jan Macvarish and Jenny Billings discuss how the teenage mothers in their study, living in Kent, made moral and thoughtful decisions about contraception, proceeding with their pregnancy, and engagement with health and welfare services. Rather than suffering 'broken' family circumstances, teenage parents were often embedded in networks of support, and were optimistic that parenthood would shift them onto a positive life trajectory.

Statistical Outcomes—Social Disadvantage Versus Teenage Mothering

The influential UNICEF report *Teenage Births in Rich Nations* claims that:

> giving birth as a teenager is believed to be bad for the young mother because the statistics suggest that she is much more likely to drop out of school, to have low or no qualifications, to be unemployed or low paid, to grow up without a father, to become a victim of neglect and abuse, to do less well at school, to become involved in crime, use drugs and alcohol.

But in fact the statistics show nothing of the sort—if we deal with the errors committed by statements like these. For the statement does not compare like with like in reaching its 'much more likely' attribution of statistical causation; ascribing causal effects to teenage motherhood is pretty meaningless if we compare teenage mothers with all mothers, rather than those of a similar background. Rather, if we wish to measure the statistical effect of teenage motherhood (and then go on to ascribe a social effect, which is not necessarily the same thing), we need to control for variation in other variables, so that we do compare like with like. In more formal terms, statistical analysis needs to control for 'selection effects:' This is a variant of the correlation problem so beloved in statistical textbooks. Variable X may be highly correlated with 'dependent' variable Y, but this does not mean that X causes Y; rather both may be caused by an unacknowledged variable A. In this case, becoming a young mother may not cause the poor outcomes—in terms of education, employment, and income—experienced by many teenage mothers; rather, both young motherhood, and poor outcomes, may be caused by pre-pregnancy social disadvantage. In this sense, social disadvantage may 'select' particular young women, and men, to become teenage parents, and this disadvantage will continue post pregnancy. Teenage parenting may therefore be a part of social disadvantage, rather than its cause. But if statistical studies do not control for these selection effects, then they will not be able to recognise this.

In fact, there has been a tradition of statistical studies which do try to take account of these selection effects. Some researchers devised 'natural experiments' where selection effects would be better controlled, such as comparisons between cousins whose mothers were sisters, between sisters, or between twin sisters (only one of whom was a teenage mother), and between teenage mothers and other women who had conceived as a teenager but miscarried (who presumably would have gone on to become mothers). This type of research began in the USA, and found that the social outcome effects of mother's age at birth were very small, or as Saul Hoffman put it in his systematic review of the US research 'often essentially zero.' Indeed, by their mid/late twenties, teenage mothers in the USA did better than miscarrying teenagers with regard to employment and income and this meant, ironically, that government spending would have increased if they had not become young mothers.

The UK-based studies available at the time the 1999 SEU report was produced did not take this 'natural experiment' approach to controlling selection effects, and instead relied on more general statistical controls of social background, like educational level, socio-economic status, housing type, and so on. Although they also concluded that much of the adverse social conditions linked with teenage parenting were associated with pre-pregnancy social disadvantage, this is perhaps why they nevertheless came to more ambivalent conclusions about the social effect of teenage pregnancy in itself. Since the publication of the SEU report, however, a number of British studies have taken up the 'natural experiment' approach, with the same results as in the USA. John Ermisch and David Pevalin, using the British Cohort Study to assess differences between miscarrying and successful teenage pregnancies, found that teen birth has little impact upon qualifications, employment or earnings by thirty years of age. While teenage mothers' partners were more likely to be poorly qualified or unemployed, and this then impacted on the mothers,' and their children's, standard of living, this is also akin to a selection effect. In itself, age of birth has little effect. A complementary study using British Household Panel data to follow teenage mothers over time came to similar conclusions, as does a study by Denise Hawkes on twins, where only one became a teenage mother. Finally, Karen Robson and Richard Berthoud used the Labour Force Survey to assess the link between high rates of poverty and high rates of teenage fertility among minority ethnic groups, particularly for the extreme case of Pakistanis and Bangladeshis where both variables are particularly high. They concluded that teen birth has little effect on future poverty, and does not lead to any further disadvantage beyond that experienced by the ethnic group as a whole.

In chapter four, Denise Hawkes follows this work in providing a wide-ranging statistical review of the life experiences and circumstances of teenage mothers and their children in Britain, compared with other mothers, based on the Millennium Cohort Study. She uses three indicative sets of statistical analyses to examine: (1) life course experience for mothers prior to the birth of the first child, (2) the early life circumstances of children at nine-months, and (3) health, cognitive, and behavioural outcomes for children at ages three and five. The first set of analyses, confirming earlier statistical studies, shows that teenage motherhood is really a symptom of a disadvantaged life course rather than the cause of it. The second set shows that those children with teenage mothers are indeed born into families experiencing multiple disadvantages. However, it is not the mother's age at first birth which is the main driver of these disadvantages—rather, it is the prior disadvantages experienced by the young mothers during their own childhoods. Again, this finding substantiates earlier research. The final set of statistical analyses takes comparison into a new area, and show that having a teenage mother does not significantly affect the chances of a pre-school child experiencing poor health, and makes little difference to how children score on cognitive tests. There is some difference for a few behavioural indices, but this largely disappears once prior life disadvantage is accounted for.

Hawkes notes that the starting point for most policy interventions around teenage parenthood is that the root of the problem is that the mother is a teenager—but her statistical analyses find that being a teenage mother does not in itself lead to poorer outcomes either for the mothers themselves or their children. Rather teenage mother-

hood often signals a life of exposure, for both mothers and children, to a range of social and economic disadvantages. She concludes that these results suggest a shift in government policy away from incidence of teenage motherhood itself, and a refocusing on the social and economic causes of teenage motherhood. What is more this sort of policy would be sensible because the factors associated with becoming a teenage mother appear to be the same factors as those influencing the life chances of their children.

Perhaps there can never be an accurate statistical measurement of the 'effect' of teenage motherhood, in the sense of finding some ultimate truth. Nonetheless, this statistical research tradition shows that—in these outcome terms—teenage childbearing in itself can be seen as only a minor social problem. It is not the teenage bit which is particularly important in these terms, but rather it is social and economic disadvantage which produce poor outcomes. In so far as teenage mothers are over-represented among the disadvantaged, this is because of their 'selection' through pre-existing disadvantage. A policy focus on being a teenage mother can only approach this wider problem of social disadvantage obliquely. Or as Hoffmann concluded for the USA, this sort of statistical study 'no longer supports the notion that teenage childbearing is a devastating event' and 'casts considerable doubt on the received wisdom about the consequences of teenage childbearing.'

Qualitative Accounts of Agency— Young Parents' Values and Experiences

What about the mothers and fathers themselves? A tradition of small-scale qualitative research focuses on their actual understandings and experiences of becoming a parent. In this way, qualitative research can help explain just why the statistical studies find that age of pregnancy has little effect on social outcomes, and may actually make things better. While Hilary Graham and Elizabeth McDermott see quantitative and qualitative research as contradictory (the former seeing teenage motherhood as a route to social exclusion, the latter as an act of social inclusion), this contradiction perhaps relates more to the way these results have been framed, interpreted and used within opposing discourses, rather than to the findings themselves. Instead, we can profitably see quantitative and qualitative studies as complementary in providing, on the one hand, extensive evidence about overall social patterns and, on the other, intensive evidence on the social processes that create these patterns.

What these qualitative studies find is that many mothers express positive attitudes to motherhood, and describe how motherhood has made them feel stronger, more competent, more connected to family and society, and more responsible. Resilience in the face of constraints and stigma, based on a belief in the moral worth of being a mother, is one overriding theme. For some, this has given the impetus to change direction, or build on existing resources, so as to take up education, training, and employment. There has been less research on young fathers, but what there has been tends to contradict the 'feckless' assumption. Like teenage mothers, most of the fathers are already socially disadvantaged, and it does not appear that fathering will in itself make this any worse. But, also like teen mothers, most express positive feelings about the child and want to be good fathers. Most contributed maintenance in some way, and many were actively involved in childcare (this varies by age, with the youngest least likely to be involved). And, like teenage mothers, there is some evidence that successful fathering could be a positive turning point in young men's lives. In fact, it was an invisibility to professionals, as well as housing problems, which often excluded them from the parenting they desired. Again, like teen mothers, young fathers may be less of a social threat, more of a social possibility.

That teenage motherhood has a positive side is an enduring finding over time in this research tradition. Nearly two decades ago, the study by Ann Phoenix of teenage mothers in London, in the mid-1980s, found that most of the mothers and their children were faring well. Most (and their male partners) had already done badly in the educational and employment systems, and it did not seem that early motherhood had caused this or that deferring motherhood would have made much difference. Rather, if anything, motherhood was something of a turning point which 'spurred some women on' into education and employment. Contributions to this edited collection testify that, two decades later, this more positive picture remains pertinent.

While Phoenix's research prefigures the statistical 'natural experiments,' it remains unacknowledged in that tradition, and does not feature in the SEU 1999 framework report. The positive side to research findings about teenage mothering seems to be regularly disregarded in the more official literature, even when government commissions the research. Recent examples include TPU commissioned research on teenage mothers in rural and seaside 'hotspots', and on teenage mothers and education. The former noted how for some young women, motherhood: 'increased their self-esteem and enhanced their lives, providing a sense of security and stability in lives characterised by transience, detachment and low economic aspirations', while the TPU's own evidence showed that having a child provides motivation for young mothers to aspire to new educational and employment goals.

That teenage parenting can have many positive sides is a theme that reappears in most of the chapters in this book. In chapter five, Eleanor Formby, Julia Hirst, and Jenny Owen provide a compelling illustration across three generational cohorts of teenage parents from Sheffield and Doncaster. Having a baby as a teenager did not necessarily predict adversity, and the problems experienced arose more from the particular social and economic circumstances the

mothers and fathers found themselves in, rather than the age at which pregnancy occurred. For mothers, difficulties in accessing appropriate housing was a major problem, while fathers recounted their sense of exclusion or marginalisation from the processes of antenatal care, childbirth, and postnatal care. While the mothers and fathers in the sample had not planned pregnancy, all recounted their pleasure at having a baby and never regretted the decision to continue with the pregnancy. Parents across all generations and social classes spoke of their parenting in positive terms, even if early parenthood for the mothers (but not the fathers) was accompanied by a sense of 'loss' of teenage life. All made explicit references to the positive 'turning-point' offered by pregnancy: the opportunity to make new plans, including the beginnings of a strong family unit or renewed efforts to gain qualifications and secure more certain futures. Despite the pleasure and pride that all participants described, stigma was also a feature of parenting that each generation, but mostly mothers, highlighted. Hence, living in a community where young parents were not unusual was cited as hugely influential, contrasting to the isolation experienced by some older and middle generation mothers who lived in middle-class communities where young parenthood was less visible. This theme is continued in chapter six by Ann McNulty. Exploring three generations of related young mothers down the generations in particular families, in the northeast of England, she challenges ideas about intergenerational transmission of low aspirations, and shows how each generation of young mothers in a family wanted to achieve, and wanted their daughters to achieve, in education and employment. Unmet expectations in relation to career options were more a matter of the (often declining) economic circumstances in their localities, rather than any culture of low aspiration. The chapter also notes the marked shift, over recent decades, towards a negative conceptualisation of young motherhood.

This positive theme is replicated in other national contexts. Lee Smith-Battle's research in the USA is paradigmatic. She followed a small, diverse group of teenage mothers over 8 years, finding that many described mothering as a powerful catalyst for becoming more mature, and for redirecting their lives in positive ways. Mothering often 'anchors the self, fosters a sense of purpose and meaning, reweaves connections, and provides a new sense of future.' Indeed, two of the themes identified in a metasynthesis of US qualitative studies of teenage mothers undertaken during the 1990s are 'Motherhood as positively transforming' and 'Baby as stabilising influence.'

In this way, qualitative research can explain the patterns found by extensive statistical studies; they suggest just why teenage parenting does not produce particularly poor outcomes, and can sometimes make things better for young people. In addition, the qualitative research can go further in explaining the processes involved in teenage parenting just because it allows more attention to context and diversity—usually stripped out by extensive studies in their concentration on average measurement. This is not just a qualification to the statistical results, whereby teenage parents' experiences can be shown to vary significantly in different social groups and geographical places. For this also takes us to a vital 'missing link, and a key to understanding the agency of teenage parents—the life worlds in which they live. Becoming a teenage mother, and it seems a father, can make reasonable sense in the particular life worlds inhabited by some groups of young women and men. Recently, Rachel Thomson has conceptualised this as the 'economy of values' particular to different communities, and earlier Ann Phoenix found that early motherhood was common, and normally uncensured, in the social networks inhabited by the working-class teenage mothers in her 1980's London sample. Smith-Battle shows much the same for the USA; early motherhood often made sense in terms of local constitutions of opportunity, constraint, and social practice.

In chapter seven, we discuss our own research findings, from a small sample in Bradford, that teenage parents saw themselves unexceptionally as 'just a mother or a father' like any other. They were motivated to achieve well in education and employment so as to provide a stable future for their children, while at the same time they lived in communities where family and parenting was placed centrally as a form of local inclusion and social participation. The case of the two Asian mothers, who were married, is an indicative example. In this way, ethnicity, as well as class, shaped expectations around motherhood. The young mothers and fathers in the sample spoke of their positive experience and the ways in which having children had given them a sense of responsibility and adult status. The teenage mothers in the study were little different from many other mothers who morally and socially prioritise motherhood, not employment. It is not that the young mothers rejected education and employment; rather, self-esteem and identity are centred round motherhood; paid work was important more as a secondary and supportive part of life. While they faced many struggles, these were often linked to problems of wider social disadvantage, and they themselves strongly challenged the idea that these were related to their position as *young* parents. They resisted being characterised solely as a teenage mother or father and saw themselves as having multiple roles and identities, as individuals, partners, workers, students.

In chapter eight, Jenny Owen and colleagues develop this theme with respect to ethnicity. Drawing on a study of teenage mothers in Bradford, Sheffield, and three London boroughs, they examine in depth the transition to motherhood by young minority ethnic mothers. This reveals the strengths that these mothers draw on to deal with double-faceted prejudice—based on age and race/ethnicity—and their determination to make something of their own and their children's lives. However, at the same time many of the experiences of these young moth-

ers are 'strikingly unremarkable': like older mothers, they are proud of their children; they aim to put them first; and they encounter familiar dilemmas in reconciling 'care' commitments with making a living and reaching accommodations with partners and other family members. This adds further weight to the general argument that 'teenage parents' should not be described as a homogenous group somehow separate from other mothers.

Conclusions: Experience v Policy?

The evidence substantiated in the chapters which follow shows that teenage childbirth does not often result from ignorance or low expectations, it is rarely a catastrophe for young women, and that teenage parenting does not particularly cause poor outcomes for mothers and their children. Expectations of motherhood can be high and parenting can be a positive experience for many young men and women. Furthermore, becoming a teenage parent can make good sense in the particular life worlds inhabited by some groups of young women and men. Policies about teenage parenting, however, assume the opposite. Unfortunately, this also means that policy will be misdirected in its aims, use inappropriate instruments, and may be unhelpful to many teenage parents.

This brings us to the last question posed by the 'problem' of teenage parenting. Why then, is there such a yawning gulf between policy assumptions and the experiences of its subjects? And why does policy seem so resistant to evidence? This is the subject of our concluding chapter nine; the way forward, we claim, necessitates a 'smashing' of the policy making mould maintained by the 'epistemic community' existing around teenage parenting. We refer here to a network of professionals and policymakers with a shared set of normative, analytical and causal beliefs, with an agreed, shared and self-reinforcing knowledge base, and a common set of interests. Parameters of preferred policy models and narratives of cause and effect are set, to the exclusion of other ideas and information, even if those other data are more representative of everyday reality. The impetus is to retain these dominant and agreed conceptions in developing (further) policies, protecting them not only from critical scrutiny but even from recognising the existence of challenging alternative scenarios. Researchers working outside of these favoured models, with messages at odds with current policy directions, are unlikely to be heard or, if heard, considered relevant.

In this way, a monochrome, negative, stereotype of teenage parents and parenting has become embedded in policy, bolstered by shared assumptions about social participation and the nature of social mobility, and by neo-liberal ideas about individual choice and rationality. Ideas about what is 'rational' are integrally linked to what is held to be socially acceptable, which in turn is regarded as a universal 'common sense' applicable in all contexts, rather than being rooted in the specific perspectives of a particular classed and gendered group of people who have the ability to judge others and place them as outside of rationality. In the case of teenage mothers and fathers, they are envisaged as ignorant, immoral or both because they have deviated from the cost-benefit calculative, future-oriented planned pathway of life. As other chapters show, this thinking is at odds with the complex reality of young mothers' and fathers' understandings and motivations, and yet is unequivocally accepted as an accurate portrayal. And all this, we suggest, is underlain by idealisations of children and childhood, where teenage parents, and mothers especially, are regarded as taking on the 'adult' responsibilities of parenthood before they have undergone the necessary sloughing off of the immaturity of childhood. They are (almost) children who have disrupted the regulation represented by the boundaries of adulthood and childhood, embodying the breakdown of social order and the nation's moral turpitude.

The question remains of how to move on. On the basis of the evidence presented in this book, we suggest there needs to be a refocus on the value of parenthood in itself, both socially and for individuals. For teenage parents, this might focus on the positive experience of becoming a mother and father, and on young parents' own resilience and strengths. Education and employment for young parents should be recognised as a components of parenting (which would also include 'full-time' mothering at home), rather than as a return to individualised rational economic planning where children are seen as an obstacle. Policy may also be better directed at improving employment for young people as a whole in declining labour markets, and regenerating disadvantaged neighbourhoods, rather than targeting teenage parenting in itself. Teenage parenting might then be approached as a way through and out of disadvantage, given its positive potential, rather than a confirmation of it. It could be seen as more opportunity than catastrophe. Certainly stigmatising policies directed at the assumed ignorance and inadequacy of teenagers will be inappropriate.

SIMON DUNCAN, CLAIRE ALEXANDER, AND ROSALIND EDWARDS have their chapter on teen pregnancy and parenting. This chapter, which takes a global perspective by looking at another Western society, England, argues that teenage pregnancy and parenting is not a problem.

EXPLORING THE ISSUE

Are Teenagers Too Young to Become Parents?

Critical Thinking and Reflection

1. What are some arguments made by each side with which you agree or disagree?
2. What are the strengths and weaknesses of the two positions made in this issue?
3. Compare and contrast the competing arguments made about teenage parenthood. What conclusions do you reach about the different research cited?
4. Think more broadly about the amount of teen parenthood. If it is a problem, what is the cause of this problem? If it is not a problem, should society be concerned in any way with the ways in which we educate and prepare teens for sexual activity as well as the potential for parenthood?

Is There Common Ground?

Virtually everyone will agree that the outcome that they want is for (a) teens to make decisions about their sexual behavior that are consistent with their long-term goals and (b) children of teen parents to be raised with opportunities to achieve their American dream. What needs to be done to ensure that? Do we need to take a look at how we prepare teens with sexuality education? Should the approach we take be abstinence-only education? Should it be comprehensive sexuality education? What role does it play to help teens identify their long-term goals? When teens have children, what sort of role does family and society play in providing that young child with a social safety net? Is that solely the responsibility of the teen parent(s)? Or is there a larger societal responsibility at play?

Create Central

www.mhhe.com/createcentral

Additional Resources

Bilingual site for teenage parents:

> **www.teenageparent.org/**

American Academy of Pediatrics:

> **www.healthychildren.org/English/ages-stages/ teen/dating-sex/pages/Teen-Parents.aspx? nfstatus=401&nftoken=00000000-0000-0000-0000- 000000000000&nfstatusdescription=ERROR%3a+ No+local+token**

TeenPregnancy.com provides advice:

> **www.teenpregnancy.com/**

About.com on teen pregnancy:

> **pregnancy.about.com/od/teenpregnancy/a/ Teen-Pregnancy.htm**

Internet References . . .

American Family Association

> www.afa.net

Focus on the Family

> www.focusonthefamily.com

Planned Parenthood

> www.plannedparenthood.org/

The National Campaign to Prevent Teen Pregnancy

> www.thenationalcampaign.org/

Unit 4

UNIT

Twenty-First Century Family and Relationship Issues

*W*ith technology today, relationships develop through the Internet and sexting. With reality television, anyone can become a star if the reality television camera shines on them. When shifting gears to law and relationships, statutory rape laws have become gender-neutral. In the midst of all of this, a small but increasingly visible minority are rejecting monogamy. These issues account for changing concepts of what constitutes agreed upon rules for families and relationships. This section examines important questions about twenty-first century families and relationships.

Selected, Edited, and with Issue Framing Material by:
David M. Hall, Ph.D., *Delaware Valley College*

ISSUE

Is Cybersex "Cheating"?

YES: Susan A. Milstein, from "Virtual Liaisons: Cybersex Is Cheating," written for *Taking Sides: Family and Personal Relationships* (2009)

NO: Crystal Bedley, from "Virtual Reality: Cybersex Is Not Cheating," written for *Taking Sides: Family and Personal Relationships* (2009)

Learning Outcomes

After reading this issue, you will be able to:

- Identify the major arguments made for and against whether cybersex is cheating.
- Compare and contrast the competing arguments made for and against cybsersex as cheating in this issue.
- Evaluate the implications of cybersex on the impact this has on dating, marriage, and other intimate relationships.

ISSUE SUMMARY

YES: Susan Milstein is a Certified Health Education Specialist and a Certified Sexuality Educator. She is an Associate Professor in the Department of Health Enhancement at Montgomery College in Maryland, as well as the Lead Consultant for Milstein Health Consulting. Milstein contends that while it is diffcult to create a universal definition of cheating, the majority of people feel that cybersex outside of a primary relationship is cheating.

NO: Crystal Bedley argues that the anonymous nature of cybersex means that it is not cheating.

What is your definition of infidelity? Does it include flirting? Phone sex? Sexting? If you are in a committed relationship, does your significant other have the same definition? Too often, couples fail to have this conversation. In the event that this conversation occurs, they may find that they have significantly different definitions of what is monogamy as well as what is infidelity. This divergence in definitions can lead to significant conflict within a relationship. The differences may very well be vast without even raising the topic of cybersex.

Infidelity is a common occurrence in American society. Most people know more than one person who has been unfaithful. National headlines are full of famous Americans who had been unfaithful to their spouses: Eliot Spitzer, John Edwards, A-Rod, Tiger Woods, and Peter Cook, Christie Brinkley's former husband. All of these cases involved real life, in-person affairs.

However, cybersex is creating new types of headlines among the powerful. A conservative Congressman from Florida was caught sending sexually explicit text messages to teenage pages working in Washington, DC. A couple of years later, a liberal Congressman from New York was caught

sending similar photos, but these were to young women on Twitter. For both men, the scandal destroyed their political careers. While this case did not involve the question of whether this was cheating, it raised a national dialogue regarding the expected norms related to virtual sex.

Infidelity dates as far back in human history as marriage. Sometimes infidelity is sanctioned by society or the spouse, but it is typically forbidden. Infidelity can lead to marital breakups, creating great stress and instability in people's lives. It is highly unlikely for in-person infidelity to guarantee anonymity.

Cyberspace has fundamentally altered the landscape for meeting others, particularly for anonymous sexual encounters. Now without leaving one's home, with minimal risk of meeting someone one knows, a person can have written, spoken, or streaming video cybersex with different people at any time. Indeed, one can log on at any time and find a significant number of people looking to meet someone.

In fact, there is not even a need to be yourself. Online, people change their hair color, height, weight, eye color, sexual history, age, race, and gender. It is possible to have cybersex with a level of anonymity that cannot be realized in person. One can live out their sexual fantasies without fear of rejection from someone they care about, or even know who they are. With the opportunity for sexually explicit virtual meetings, the personal risk of being identified recedes.

Cybersex has created a new dimension, a potential form of twenty-first-century infidelity, depending on one's definition of infidelity. This is new terrain that presents a unique set of challenges. The lines of what is cheating may be difficult to draw with new technology. Even if you determine that certain scenarios are off limits, temptation to stray is virtually omnipresent when in the privacy of your own residence.

Before reading this issue, write down your definition of infidelity. Include a definition of what types of cybersex, if any, you regard as being unfaithful. Does anything on your list surprise you? While reading, examine the ways in which the authors' assessment compares and contrasts with your values. What are some ways in which your beliefs were supported? What are some of the ways in which they were challenged? In addition, what are the generational differences, if any, of views of cybersex and infidelity?

Have you ever hid something from your significant other that you feared would make him or her jealous? Maybe texting an ex? Visiting a strip club? Going out to a platonic dinner with someone you find attractive? While none of these incidents are physical sexual encounters with another person, many people will conceal these encounters out of fear that their significant other will regard them as being unfaithful in their relationship. Each incident described has some degree of emotional or physical interaction. In contrast, cybersex can be nonphysical and anonymous. Facing reduced risks for exposure and regular access to virtual sexual encounters, cybersex creates a new set of boundaries to be negotiated in a relationship.

Cybersex potentially changes the ways in which trust is extended within a relationship. While access to anonymous sexual encounters may be a threatening prospect to many, there is a fundamental question which needs to be asked and evaluated that has not changed despite the virtual world of sexual relations: What is a healthy relationship?

Write down what you consider to be the most important qualities of a healthy relationship. Then rank how important the different qualities are. This should provide a larger perspective related to cybersex and infidelity.

Whether the Internet exists or not, the qualities of healthy relationships should remain constant.

Once you have identified your views about sexual infidelity and cybersex, are you ready to talk about your criteria with a significant other? How might you respond to answers that may differ from yours? Specifically, weigh whether or not you can negotiate if you have decidedly different values related to cybersex and infidelity. How much are you willing to compromise your beliefs? What are your expectations related to how your significant other will compromise his or her beliefs?

If you are in a relationship that lacks equality or fails to communicate respectfully, you may find that this conversation is difficult to have. If you are in a relationship of equality and mutual respect, this conversation is far easier, provided that you and your partner feel comfortable having frank conversations about sexuality. Keep in mind that it is normal to struggle when having frank conversations about sexuality. It might be a good idea to acknowledge that at the start of such a conversation and not to be too hard on yourself if the conversation is challenging.

Melanie Davis, an expert on communicating about sexuality within families and relationships, advises that a person do the following in starting this conversation: "The first thing is for the person who wants to bring up the conversation to define the purpose of the conversation. It is just curiosity, or is there some sort of fear? Or is there a need to disclose something? That can help you get into the right frame of mind. If you think your partner is cheating on you, it might come across as accusing the person, and that is never an effective way to start a conversation. The other thing to consider is where you're going to have the conversation. It is probably not a conversation you want to have in the middle of a crowded restaurant. If you fear what will be disclosed, you might want to have the conversation in the presence of a counselor or a therapist who can help guide the conversation."

Davis adds, "Sometimes you just want to test the waters conversationally. A good way to do that is to remark about a TV show or an article that you read, something that can get you to that topic of conversation in a neutral way."

Once these conversations begin, you may find that they are likely to get easier, provided you have a cooperative and supportive partner. If these conversations cannot occur, it may not be surprising if people get hurt when they lack a full understanding of each other's boundaries and their rationale behind them.

YES ↵   **Susan A. Milstein**

Virtual Liaisons: Cybersex Is Cheating

Consider the following behaviors: flirting with a coworker, engaging in intimate phone calls or sending love letters to someone other than your partner, looking at sexually explicit images while masturbating, having a one-night stand. Would any of these behaviors be cheating?

You may have answered "yes" to none, some, or all of these behaviors, whereas your partner's answers may have been very different. For this reason, defining cheating can be difficult. Many couples may never take the time to sit down and discuss what behaviors they consider to be cheating but feel betrayed nonetheless when certain lines are crossed. The lines of what is considered cheating may become even more blurred when the actions in question take place online.

Enter the world of cybersex.

What Is Cybersex?

There is no single definition of cybersex. It is a broad term that may be used to encompass a variety of behaviors, including different methods of communication that happen online like love letter e-mails or instant messages. Sex, Etc. (http://www.sexetc.org/) defines cybersex as "Sexual encounters that take place entirely via the Internet." This would include going on a virtual "date" in a chat room that may involve one or both people masturbating in real life. These dates may happen simply by typing on a keyboard, or they may include the use of webcams and microphones.

Meeting for cybersex can take place in a multitude of places, including chat rooms, inside online games like World of Warcraft, or inside the virtual world of Second Life. Thanks to webcams, Skype, and Googlechat, you don't necessarily need a specific site like a chat room to meet—you just need the time, the technology, and another person. The definition of cybersex will continue to evolve as technology changes, and for some, the new definition will include the use of teledildonics.

For some people, the use of teledildonics with a person other than a significant other crosses yet another boundary in the world of cybersex and infidelity.

So, What Is Cheating?

Many of us associate sexual infidelity with the word "cheating." It involves having sexual contact with someone other than your partner. How much sexual contact is required for it to be cheating will vary from one person's definition to another. It may extend beyond sexual intercourse to include oral sex or kissing, but regardless of how much contact is involved, most of us usually think of something physical when we think of cheating. But, there's more to it than that. Online or offline, cheating on a significant other may involve physical acts, which is called sexual infidelity, or it may involve emotional infidelity (Whisman & Wagers, 2005).

Emotional infidelity occurs when someone is spending time with, giving attention to, or falling in love with someone other than their partner (Shackelford, LeBlanc, and Drass, 2000; Whitty and Quigley, 2008). Regardless of whether it is emotional or sexual infidelity, violating the bounds of one's relationship can lead to anger, jealousy, hurt, resentment, and potentially the ending of the relationship.

Subotnik and Harris (2005) describe four different types of affairs one might see in offline relationships. The first type is the serial affair, where there are a string of one-night stands or affairs that lack both an emotional connection and commitment. The second type of affair is the fling, which can be seen in one-night stands. The other two types of affairs are the romantic love affair and the long-term affair. These two affairs are similar in that there is a deep emotional component to each. One thing that differentiates these two affairs is the amount of time that is invested in each. All of these types of affairs can be carried out online through cybersex, and like offline affairs, they can have a tremendous negative impact on relationships.

Then there's the emotional affair, or what Glass and Staeheli (2003) describe as the "extramarital emotional involvement" (p. 35). This emotional involvement consists of three components: emotional intimacy, secrecy, and sexual chemistry. All three of these components may happen during cybersex, whether it's a one-time "date" in a chat room or an affair which is taking place solely online.

As with offline affairs, relationships where cybersex has occurred face many challenges. The affair may lead to conflict and a decision to separate or divorce as a result of the online cheating (Docan-Morgan and Docan, 2007; Schneider, 2000; Young, Griffin-Shelley, Cooper, O'Mara, and Buchanan, 2000). The partner who was cheated on may feel a host of emotions, including betrayal, abandonment, and shame (Schneider, 2000). Part of the healing process for the partner who was cheated on through cybersex involves learning to cope with what happened and trying to find closure (Maheu and Subotnik, 2001).

Cybersex and Cheating

Research is showing that people do believe that cybersex is cheating and that it can have a negative impact on relationships. One study found that 33 percent of respondents felt that cybersex of any kind was cheating. If certain circumstances occurred, for instance, the use of webcams, or having cybersex repeatedly with the same person, then the number increased to 58 percent (McKenna, Green, and Smith, 2001).

One researcher, Monica Whitty, has completed a number of studies looking at which specific cybersex behaviors people believe constitute infidelity. What she has not been able to do is come up with one list of cybersex behaviors that everyone agrees is cheating. But this is to be expected. If you look back at the behaviors at the beginning of this article, you'll see why one list of "cheating behaviors" will probably never exist for cybersex or for offline behaviors. What her research has shown is that there are many who believe that cybersex is infidelity and that it can have just as much of a negative impact on a relationship as cheating that is done offline (Whitty, 2003, 2005).

The research previously mentioned was done using respondents' opinions based on hypothetical situations. It would be easy to say that what someone says in a hypothetical situation may be different from what that person would say if faced with the same situation in real life. This may be true in that people who have found out that their partners had been engaging in cybersex might be more likely to say that they feel like they were cheated on.

When looking at studies that involved people who had direct experience with cybersex, you can see the negative impact that it has on people and their relationships. One study found that the offline partners of those engaging in cybersex reported feeling hurt, abandoned, and betrayed (Schneider, 2000). In another study, one-quarter of the people surveyed who were engaging in cybersex admitted that it had affected their primary relationship (Underwood and Findlay, 2004).

Given the findings of these studies, it should come as no surprise that therapists are seeing the impact of cybersex among their clients. In one study, a majority of marriage and family therapists reported having clients where cybersex was a problem, and 16 percent of the therapists reported that cybersex was the primary reason why the couple was in therapy (Goldberg, Peterson, Rosen, and Sara, 2008). And this is just the beginning, as the number of people affected seems to be increasing. In the two years prior to the survey, more than half of the therapists said their cybersex caseload had increased (Goldberg, Peterson, Rosen, and Sara, 2008).

Cybersex Is Cheating

We know that people who are involved in committed relationships are having cybersex. In a survey done in 1998, almost 85 percent of people who reported that they were engaging in online sexual activity were either married or in a committed relationship (Maheu and Subotnik, 2001).

We also know that cybersex is viewed by many as cheating and that it can have the same long-term negative impact on relationships that offline infidelity has.

So what's the bottom line? If what one person is doing is going outside the bounds of his or her relationship, then it's cheating, and it doesn't matter if it's in a hotel room or a chat room.

References

T. Docan-Morgan and C. A. Docan, "Internet Infidelity: Double Standards and the Differing Views of Women and Men," *Communication Quarterly* (vol. 55, no. 3, 2007).

S. P. Glass and J. C. Staeheli, *"Not 'Just Friends.' Rebuilding Trust and Recovering Your Sanity after Infidelity* (New York: Free Press, 2003).

P. D. Goldberg, B. D. Peterson, K. H. Rosen, and M. L. Sara, "Cybersex: The Impact of a Contemporary Problem on the Practices of Marriage and Family Therapists," *Journal of Marital and Family Therapy* (vol. 34, no. 4, 2008).

M. M. Maheu, and R. B. Subotnik, *Infidelity in the Internet. Virtual Relationships and Real Betrayal* (Naperville, IL: Sourcebooks, Inc., 2001).

K. Y. A. McKenna, A. S. Green, and P. K. Smith, "Demarginalizing the Sexual Self," *The Journal of Sex Research* (vol. 38, no. 4, 2001).

J. P. Schneider, "Effects of Cybersex Addiction on the Family: Results of a Survey," *Sexual Addiction & Compulsivity* (vol. 7, 2000).

Sex, Etc., "Cyber Sex" (n.d.). Retrieved March 15, 2009, from http://www.sexetc.org/glossary/1148.

T. K. Shackelford, G. J. LeBlanc, and E. Drass, "Emotional Reactions to Infidelity," *Cognition & Emotion* (vol. 14, no. 5, 2000).

R. B. Subotnik and G. G. Harris, *"Surviving Infidelity. Making Decisions, Recovering from the Pain* (Avon, MA: Adams Media, 2005).

H. Underwood and B. Findlay, "Internet Relationships and Their Impact on Primary Relationships," *Behaviour Change* (vol. 21, no. 2, 2004).

M. A. Whisman and T. P. Wagers, "Assessing Relationship Betrayals," *Journal of Clinical Psychology* (vol. 61, no. 11, 2005).

M. T. Whitty, "Pushing the Wrong Buttons: Men's and Women's Attitudes toward Online and Offline Infidelity," *CyberPsychology and Behavior* (vol. 6, no. 6, 2003).

———— "The Realness of Cybercheating. Men's and Women's Representations of Unfaithful Internet

Relationships," *Social Science Computer Review* (vol. 23, no. 1, 2005).

M. T. Whitty and L-L. Quigley, "Emotional and Sexual Infidelity Offline and in Cyberspace," *Journal of Marriage and Family Therapy* (vol. 34, no. 4, 2008).

K. S. Young, E. Griffin-Shelley, A. Cooper, J. O'Mara, and J. Buchanan, "Online Infidelity: A New Dimension in Couple Relationships with Implications for Evaluation and Treatment," *Sexual Addiction & Compulsivity* (vol. 7, 2000).

SUSAN A. MILSTEIN, PhD, is a Master Certified Health Education Specialist and a Certified Sexuality Educator. She is a Professor in the Department of Health Enhancement, Exercise Science and Physical Education at the Rockville Campus of Montgomery College in Maryland. Milstein contends that while it is difficult to create a universal definition of cheating, the majority of people feel that cybersex outside of a primary relationship is cheating.

Crystal Bedley

Virtual Reality: Cybersex Is Not Cheating

As the Internet continues to expand and evolve, so do the possibilities for engaging in sexual encounters online. From chat rooms, to social networking sites, to virtual boy/girlfriends, new technologies are shaping the ways in which desires can be explored and indulged. Couples must navigate these new technologies to determine the role(s) that virtual encounters may or may not play in their relationships. Some people might enjoy engaging in cybersex, whereas their partners may not; some couples may enjoy engaging in cybersex together, whereas others may not. To understand whether a particular cybersex act is a form of cheating, therefore, one must take into account the nature of the relationship. Ultimately, whether cybersex is a form of cheating depends largely on both the interpersonal dynamics of the couple *and* the intentions and perceptions of the cybersex participant.

The term "interpersonal dynamics" refers to the nature of the relationship between the two romantic partners. More specifically, interpersonal dynamics shape how partners come to agree or disagree about the meanings of particular acts (e.g., whether cybersex is a form of cheating). Importantly, the ways in which couples negotiate their relationships, especially when each partner has different expectations, shape how both partners will interpret particular behaviors. For example, few people would argue that, if both partners agree to participate in cybersex together, that their shared action is a form of cheating. Moreover, if one partner communicates to the other partner that she or he would like to engage in cybersex and the other partner consents, then most would agree that the partners are being faithful to one another. Each of these examples demonstrates how the interpersonal dynamics of the couple determine whether cybersex is cheating. The ways partners choose to communicate with one another and the decisions they reach are critical for understanding whether cybersex is cheating or an expression of sexual desires. If both partners share an understanding of cybersex as an expression of sexual desire that does not constitute cheating, then it is clear that cybersex is not cheating. By the same token, if both partners believe the act of cybersex is cheating, then there is no reason to draw a different conclusion.

In contrast, if a partner deceives the other partner in order to engage in cybersex, one could argue that in this context, cybersex is an act of infidelity. Because relationships are built on mutual trust (among other factors), deception not only serves to destabilize the relationship but also becomes the framework for interpreting the cybersex act as an act of cheating. Importantly, recent research suggests that deception and emotional unavailability are primary reasons why partners view cybersex as equivalent to adultery (Schneider, 2003). In these cases, it is clearer that cybersex is an act of infidelity.

Although there are a variety of ways to engage in cybersex, when it comes to interpreting cybersex as cheating, traditionally the virtual form of the sex act is often inconsequential, trumped by the emotional toll paid by the partners involved in the relationship. Consider the following example:

> Shannon and Kendall are in a long-term committed relationship. Neither partner has been physically or emotionally intimate with anyone outside of the relationship. One day, Kendall decides to participate in a mutual masturbation session with an anonymous person he meets in a chat room. Minutes later, Shannon walks into Kendall's office and witnesses the masturbation session. Devastated by what she sees, Shannon feels that Kendall has cheated. From Shannon's perspective, Kendall's online session is a form of cheating because of the sexual intimacy Kendall shared with the other person. From Kendall's perspective, Shannon is overreacting. Kendall believes that because cybersex does not involve physical contact, it is not cheating. So, Kendall views the cybersex act as a way of exploring one's fantasies in a safe environment.

This scenario illustrates the notion that the same act (in this case, the act of participating in a mutual masturbation session) can be interpreted in different and sometimes conflicting ways. For this reason, I argue that the individual perceptions of each partner are important to understanding whether cybersex should be considered cheating. The expression "individual perceptions" refers to the beliefs and/or attitudes of a person, which shape how the individual will interpret a particular behavior. Unlike interpersonal dynamics, which involve a negotiated agreement (or disagreement) about the meanings attributed to particular acts, individual perceptions are those beliefs held by each individual about the meanings attributed to particular acts, *regardless* of the beliefs of one's partner. To clarify the distinction between individual perceptions and interpersonal dynamics using the current example, it is clear that Kendall's individual perception is that the cybersex act is not a form of cheating, whereas Shannon's perception is that it is cheating. The interpersonal dynamics of the couple can be described as a disagreement over the cybersex act because each partner's perceptions are at odds with the other's.

Because partners can have differing perceptions of the same act, it is critical to also consider each partner's perception of cybersex to understand whether the cybersex is a form of infidelity. On the one hand, let's assume that Shannon is not emotionally hurt by the act of masturbation alone, but rather is hurt that Kendall transgressed upon an important moral boundary in their relationship; namely, that partners are to remain sexually faithful to one another. On the other hand, Kendall does not see cybersex as cheating because the cybersex was used only to facilitate masturbation. Because masturbation has never been considered an act of cheating throughout the course of their relationship, Kendall believes that cybersex is merely another form of masturbation. Therefore, Kendall's perception of cybersex as masturbation reinforces the belief that Kendall is remaining sexually faithful to Shannon. Undoubtedly, Shannon and Kendall have differing views about the same act. If Shannon and Kendall cannot come to an agreement about whether or not the online mutual masturbation session was indeed an act of cheating, then whose perception helps us to best understand whether this act of cybersex is a form of cheating?

Traditionally, the perceptions of the partner not involved in the act of cybersex determine whether the act is considered cheating. In other words, if the partner not involved in the act of cybersex believes cybersex is cheating, then it is cheating.

But why should the perceptions of the partner prevail over the perceptions of the cybersex participant? The short answer is that they should not. Instead, whether an act of cybersex is cheating depends primarily not only on the intentions of the person who engages in cybersex but also on how this person perceives the cybersex act. I am arguing that rather than privilege the perceptions of the person not directly involved in the cybersex act, one must focus instead on the cybersex participant. Specifically, it is important to take into account both the intentions *and* perceptions of the cybersex participant in order to determine whether an act of cybersex is a form of infidelity.

To demonstrate the significance of one's intention in relation to the cybersex act, it is helpful to think about the following contrasting examples. In the first example, the cybersex participant intends to seek sexual and/or emotional pleasure from a person who is outside the participant's relationship. The person may feel guilty for engaging in cybersex because she believes that she is being unfaithful given the nature of the cybersex encounter (e.g., cybersex acts that foster emotional and/or sexual intimacy). In this case, because the cybersex participant's intentions and perceptions of her behavior are adulterous, then this act should be interpreted as cheating. Even

if a cybersex encounter does not begin with adulterous intentions, if the cybersex participant's intentions and/or perceptions of the act change during the course of the encounter, then the act could still be considered cheating. For many cybersex participants, however, this is not the reality of their experience. To state this point differently, many people who engage in cybersex do not engage in cybersex in order to cheat on their partners. Because people often do not engage in cybersex to harm their relationship, it is important to consider other intention/perception understandings of the cybersex act.

Now consider the case of a person who engages in cybersex with the sole intention of having an orgasm. It is important to point out that this person is not engaging in deceptive behavior in order to take part in the cybersex act. In this case, the cybersex participant is not looking to create an emotional connection with another person but instead is seeking out a stimulating aid for the purpose of masturbating. This person could choose to watch a pornographic movie, for instance, but instead chooses a chat room for arousal. In fact, an in-depth interview study of cybersex participants found that these participants often "equated participation in chat rooms with watching a movie or reading a novel" (Mileham, 2007, p. 16). Therefore, not only does the person involved in the cybersex act intend to engage in masturbation (a sexual act that is not generally considered to be a form of cheating), his perception of the experience is the same. Specifically, the cybersex participant perceives the cybersex act as an act of masturbation, not infidelity. From this perspective, I argue that the cybersex participant did not cheat on his partner because he did not intend to cheat, nor did he perceive the act as cheating.

For those who still remain skeptical as to whether cybersex is cheating, it is critical to understand the implications of this position. If someone believes that, although the cybersex participant thinks he is simply masturbating, he is actually cheating on his partner, then where can we draw the distinction between other forms of masturbation and cheating? Is the person who masturbates to a racy magazine cheating on her partner? Moreover, how do we make sense of situations where a person's mind wanders during sex? Is one cheating if he thinks of someone other than his partner during sex? Clearly, neither of these cases seems to constitute cheating. Skeptics must be aware that if the intentions and the perceptions of the cybersex participant are overlooked, then a variety of sex acts should also be considered alternative forms of cheating. Yet, if these masturbatory acts were all considered cheating, many of us would have to acknowledge that we've cheated on our partners!

By privileging the perceived "victim's" individual perceptions of the cybersex act above the intentions and perceptions of the cybersex participant, one is more likely to conclude that cybersex is cheating. It has been my aim to question this traditional bias to suggest that many of the acts typically considered cheating are vastly more complicated. By highlighting the intentions and perceptions of the cybersex participant, it becomes clear that many cybersex acts are not necessarily acts of infidelity. Often, cybersex is used to sexually enrich the lives of those who take part, which can ultimately benefit a relationship rather than destroy it.

References

B. L. A. Mileham, "Online Infidelity in Internet Chat Rooms: An Ethnographic Exploration," *Computers in Human Behavior* (vol. 23, 2007), 11–13.

J. Schneider, "The Impact of Compulsive Cybersex Behaviours on the Family," *Sexual and Relationship Therapy* (vol. 18, no. 3, 2003), 329–354.

CRYSTAL BEDLEY holds an MA in Sociology and is currently a Doctoral Student in Sociology at Rutgers University. Bedley has developed and taught interdisciplinary courses on the topics of the research process, methodology and graduate education preparation. Bedley argues that the anonymous nature of cybersex means that it is not cheating.

EXPLORING THE ISSUE

Is Cybersex "Cheating"?

Critical Thinking and Reflection

1. What are some arguments made by each side with which you agree or disagree?
2. What are the strengths and weaknesses of the two positions made in this chapter? Pick the side with which you most agree.
3. What are some additional arguments you would make to strengthen the case for or against cybersex constituting cheating?
4. Think more broadly of the issue of cybersex. What are some of the ways in which it is or can be unhealthy? What are some of the ways in which it is or can be healthy?

Is There Common Ground?

The truth is that couples may often disagree in many ways over what constitutes cheating. There is a long list of questions that will elicit different answers from individuals. Is kissing someone else cheating? Does talking with your ex constitute cheating? How about dinner with your ex? Getting a lap dance from at a strip club? Getting a lap dance at a party? Looking at pornography? A lack of understanding of your partner's definition of monogamy can lead to serious problems in a relationship. Refer to the advice of Melanie Davis in the Introduction to this section and work on communicating openly and honestly within relationships.

Create Central

www.mhhe.com/createcentral

Additional Resources

The following Web sites examine the question as to whether cybersex is cheating:

http://marriage.families.com/blog/is-cybersex-cheating#

www.lovematters.info/cybersex-cheating-does-it-count

www.ivillage.com/cybersex-really-cheating-0/4-n-282345

Internet References . . .

Organizations exist online solely to classify cybersex as an addiction—or to encourage cybersex. Those results are either one-sided or not the right fit for this section.

To learn more, please Google, "Is Cybersex Cheating?" and a wide array of articles will be available for further study.

Selected, Edited, and with Issue Framing Material by:
David M. Hall, Ph.D., *Delaware Valley College*

ISSUE

Is Internet Pornography Harmful to Teenagers?

YES: Wayne Grinwis, from "Is Pornography Harmful to Teenagers? Yes!" revised from *Taking Sides: Family and Personal Relationships* (2009)

NO: Justin A. Sitron, from "Why Porn Is Not Harmful to Teens," revised from *Taking Sides: Family and Personal Relationships* (2009)

Learning Outcomes

After reading this issue, you will be able to:

- Identify critical research about the impact of pornography on teens.
- Compare and contrast interpretations of research in determining how to help teens develop in a way that is consistent with being sexually healthy.
- Evaluate the unique role of the Internet and pornography on teens.

ISSUE SUMMARY

YES: Wayne Grinwis has been a Sexual Health Educator for Planned Parenthood for 15 years. He is also Adjunct Professor in the Department of Health at West Chester University. Grinwis credits Andrea Daniels for help with this article. Grinwis argues that pornography is all right for adults, but for teenagers, it can create unrealistic expectations about sex, provide a negative and inaccurate sexuality education, and increase sexual violence against women.

NO: Justin Sitron is an Assistant Professor of Education at Widener University. Sitron argues that pornography has no negative impact on teenagers and, in fact, has potential benefits. Sitron contends that Internet pornography can be helpful in providing teens an opportunity to see real bodies, a chance to learn about sex from seeing rather than doing, and an open door for communication with parents.

The First Amendment to the U.S. Constitution states, "Congress shall make no laws . . . abridging the freedom of speech." While this amendment is written as an absolute, there are limitations to speech that are known as unprotected speech, including libel, slander, seditious speech, and obscenity. It is the latter form of unprotected speech that is the focus of this issue, as obscenity is often used as synonymous with pornography. For many children, the Internet has allowed greater access to pornography than ever before.

In the United States, federal censorship of obscene materials began with the Tariff Act of 1842. While prosecutions were initially limited, the American middle class grew following the Civil War. Many social reformers believed that America too often failed to apply proper moral values, thus leading to social problems. Anti-vice societies were formed and worked to create laws regarding labor, prison reform, temperance, welfare, and obscenity. By 1873, America had a federal anti-obscenity law, often referred to as the Comstock Law.

During this time, anti-obscenity laws were designed to protect three groups who were considered to be particularly vulnerable, which included women, the lower classes, and children. Today, women and the so-called lower classes are not considered groups that deserve legal protections, though the primary audience for pornographic pictures and films today is men.

A challenge that has existed regarding censorship has been to determine specifically what is obscenity. In 1973, The Supreme Court of the United States provided the following standard for evaluating whether materials are pornographic in the case of *Miller v. California*:

1. That the average person, applying contemporary standards, would find a work, taken as a whole, appeals to the prurient interest;
2. Whether the work depicts or describes, in a patently offensive way, sexual conduct specifically defined to be offensive and "hard core" by the applicable state law;

3. That the work, taken as a whole, lacks serious literary, artistic, political, or scientific value.

Therefore, there exists a legal standard of how to define pornography and legal precedent that pornography is regarded as unprotected speech. In addition, there is legal precedent that children do not have the right to have access to pornography. As a result, the federal government sought to create new censorship policies in the face of children's access to pornography online.

Congress passed and President Clinton signed into law both the Communications Decency Act of 1996 and the Child Online Protection Act of 1998. Each of these laws was struck down by the Supreme Court. The Supreme Court did not challenge the fact that pornography can be censored for children. However, there was no mechanism to limit children's access to online pornography without also limiting adult access to pornography. When censoring unprotected speech, in this case children's access to pornography, laws cannot be so broad that they also censor protected speech, in this case adults' access to pornography.

With limited means for government censorship, controlling access to pornography becomes almost entirely the domain of parents and children. The access to sexually explicit materials that exists is unprecedented in human history. Children today have more access to sexually produced materials than ever before. Previously, parents were urged to leave their computer in a common, public space in their house. Today, however, few families buy desktop computers, opting instead for a portable laptop which can be privately used more easily. In fact, many children access the Internet whenever they want, wherever they want, via their iPhone or another portable device.

This issue examines the debate over the impact of pornography on teenagers. The conclusions that one reaches should have significant implications in what teenagers should be taught by their parents about pornography.

Pornography is one of the most controversial issues addressed in this volume. What are some of the ways in which these articles reinforced your value system? What are some of the ways in which these articles challenged your value system? How did it feel when your value system was challenged?

In some sections of this issue, Grinwis and Sitron addressed the same issue but cited different research, therefore reaching different conclusions. For example, Grinwis stated that pornography can lead to sexual violence, in part by citing research published by the National Online Resource Center on Violence Against Women. In contrast, Sitron argued that the research is divided but that a meta-analysis published in the *Annual Review of Sex Research* found no association between pornography and "high levels of sexual aggression." What are some ways that you can examine these resources to determine which research you think is accurate?

Students may find important research topics raised in this issue. That can include topics that were specifically examined in this issue as well as other issues not specifically examined. What are some related topics that are important to address?

For example, Sitron's article cites the significant amount of amateur pornography uploaded onto the Internet when he addresses the diversity of body images available online. A separate issue to consider, particularly for young people, are issues of consent for uploading photographs and video online. One significant technological difference for teenagers today as compared to generations past involves the degree of access to photo and video cameras. Some questions that can be considered are the following:

- What are some of the ways, if any, that teenagers today feel pressure to photograph and record themselves hooking up?
- How does seeing amateur pornography online influence discussions or actual behavior with teenagers about recording themselves when hooking up?
- How can teenagers ensure that their pictures or video will never be posted online without their consent?
- Have teenagers had experiences being recorded without first giving consent?
- Does consent to be recorded mean that there is consent to show the footage to others?
- Sometimes amateur footage is seen by millions of people. How might seeing amateur pornography featuring people one meets in their everyday lives possibly affect their college admissions? College scholarships? Job prospects? Familial relationships?
- In short, what are the rights of people featured in amateur pornography available online?

Beyond these questions, middle school and high school students need to know that some teenagers are being prosecuted for creating child pornography when recording themselves engaged in sexual activities before they have reached the age of 18. Crimes that teenagers are charged with can range from public indecency to the creation of child pornography, possession of child pornography, and distribution of child pornography. Some of these young people have been convicted of felonies, sentenced to long prison terms, and will be required to register as sex offenders after their release.

Today, teenagers have not just access to pornography but also the ability to create pornography with greater ease than ever before. While it is important to research the impact of viewing pornography on teenagers, it is also necessary to conduct more research to better understand the ways in which the creation of amateur pornography may be affecting the young people involved.

YES ↵

Wayne Grinwis

Is Pornography Harmful to Teenagers?

There are some who would argue that pornography has no acceptable audience or any valid place, even for entertainment purposes, in a healthy relationship. In this mindset, pornography might even be considered harmful and its effects wide-reaching enough to encapsulate every age group who may be attracted to the lure of a little adult fantasy. High school students, grandparents, Baby Boomers, Gen Xers—all would fall victim to its inappropriate ideals if we were to place a general label of "harmful"—a sort of "Mr. Yuck" sticker for grown-ups, if you will—onto pornography. I am unable to do such a thing. In the right setting and with the right frame of mind, pornography can be a pleasurable addition to an adult individual's or couple's sexual life.

When speaking of teenagers, however, the term *harmful* may well apply. Without the proper maturity and level of experience, navigating through the very adult world of relationships and sex, most teens simply do not possess the necessary tools needed for their first foray into fantasy, and many of the themes found in a good deal of easily accessible pornography may actually be harmful to their adolescent development.

Access to Pornography

Before we can examine pornography's harmful effects on teenagers, we must first discuss the specifics of what pornography actually is. Former Supreme Court Justice Potter Stewart said, in discussing a potential definition of pornography, "I know it when I see it" (*Jacobellis v. Ohio*, 1964). That statement, albeit somewhat glib, brings to mind a serious thought: In the high-tech, ever-evolving cyber-realm that young people today inhabit, they are inundated with more varied forms of pornography than ever before, stumbling upon sites that they probably shouldn't and gaining access to those deemed "adult-only" by easily tiptoeing around safeguards as flimsy as a few keystrokes and the honor system.

In the past, teens had to seek out pornography by obtaining and viewing magazines (*Playboy* and *Hustler* are among the more tame periodicals), locating old VHS films or DVDs not hidden quite carefully enough in their own homes, or watching soft-core versions of these films on cable (good 'ol' "Skinemax"—an informal reference to occasional late-night viewing opportunities on Cinemax—has long been a favorite). However, tech-savvy young people have more opportunities than ever before to satisfy their sensual cravings. In recent years, pornographic-like activity has been added to some video games (*Grand Theft Auto*, one of the most popular video games among this demographic, is rife with sexual content), and then, of course, there is the ever-pervasive Internet, which, to many teens, is just as tangible a home as the concrete structures they inhabit with their family members. Although the one-time estimate that over 80 percent of Internet sites are pornographic was proven false (Godwin, 2003), recent estimates are that 12 percent of all Web sites are porn and that a quarter of all search engine requests are for porn (Ropelato, 2003). Even if someone were trying to avoid this type of explicit sexual material, it would only be the über-diligent who would succeed in avoiding pornography on the Internet, and it is important to note that not all teenage exposure to pornography is intentional; contact may be unintended—stumbled upon when receiving emails advertising porn sites or even through the simple act of employing an Internet search (Bryan, 2009). For those who do take the time to seek out pornography, their fingers don't have far to travel on their computer keyboards. From things as basic as still pictures to home videos of sexual encounters, from monthly subscription services to "fetish" sites, thousands upon thousands of hours of porn can easily be found online.

It is true that most adult sites stipulate that a viewer must be "18 to enter;" however, age is often established by a simple mouse click stating that the visitor is, indeed, the required age or by asking the visitor to enter in his or her birthdate. Young people can handle the simple math of subtracting a few years from the date on which they were born in order to appear age-appropriate for viewing.

Now that we have determined the ease with which pornography can be viewed and before we begin to examine the harmful effects of pornography on teenagers, we must first establish the gender of which we speak. Do we mean male teens or female? The simple answer is both. Although teens actively seeking out and viewing pornography are predominantly male, girls are also affected by the messages boys receive.

But all of this—the pervasive and easily accessible nature of pornography—is not in and of itself proof positive of its harmful nature when speaking in terms of teens. We must now begin to dig deeper to unearth the negative effects that exposure to an adult-oriented fantasy world has upon adolescent development by examining pornography's fostering of unrealistic expectations when it comes to sexual encounters and body image, its role as an unqualified sexuality educator, and its bent toward violence.

Unrealistic Expectations

How many times has this happened to you? You're in your office making copies, perhaps scantily clad and probably glistening a little from the heat of the copier, and in walks a very attractive member of the opposite sex, who immediately begins complimenting your body and undressing you. Moments later, you are in the throes of passion, with the copier working overtime capturing fantasy, flipbook-worthy images of all that is happening on it.

This has never happened to you? Then clearly you are not living in the world of pornography.

Most teenagers lack the abstract processing skills that advise them that the incidents and images displayed in pornography are not representative of most adults' sex lives. Teens exposed to what the pornography industry and, indeed, its consumers ordain as "sexy" or "passionate" or "hot," and who lack the aforementioned skills, eventually begin to think that the sexual acts displayed are necessary to have the desired adjectives listed above become attributes of their own lives.

This is especially true when it comes to body image. Average people, who are endowed in a very average way, are not typically stars of the pornographic industry, or at least not pre–surgical alteration. As teenagers watch pornography, they cannot help but make comparisons to the unrealistic images they see and, consequently, may begin to find themselves and perhaps their own partners less attractive. As if being a teenager and dealing with hormonal changes and body image insecurities weren't difficult enough, now teenagers are comparing pornographic superstars to their own developing young bodies and those of their partners.

However, it is not body image alone that suffers through the consumption of pornography. Often a teen's view of the sex act itself becomes skewed in an unrealistic and unhealthy way, especially when pornography becomes the educator through which he or she learns about sex.

Pornography as Education

Where do young people actually learn to have sex? Comprehensive sexuality education, although widely favored in this country (despite the current trend of abstinence-only education), doesn't include demonstrations or lessons on how to engage in the act of having sex. Likewise, most parents surely don't advise their children on the virtues and techniques of making love. When people lose their virginity, one hopes the experience will happen with a partner whom they are able to feel comfortable with and who will accept their genuine selves. In an ideal situation, one inexperienced partner should be able to say to the

other: "I don't really know what I'm doing!" However, sad truth though it may be, that is not usually the case. Many times, people lose their virginity with someone they've just met, or when they've been drinking or using drugs, or with someone they care about but with whom they aren't completely intimate—in other words, not someone with whom they can allow themselves to be completely vulnerable. That leaves pornography as the most viable sexual education tool.

We've already established that pornography sets up unrealistic expectations, and that most certainly poses a problem when people are modeling their sex life after knowledge—albeit knowledge that has no basis in reality—gleaned from pornography and when they lack any other alternative. But consider the advantages film has over real life. What appears to the viewer as a 15-minute sexual encounter may have taken eight hours to film, incorporated multiple camera angles to find the best view of the bodies, and required extensive editing in order to make it work—all advantages that the fantasy world of pornography has over typical sexual experiences.

This leads us to our last concern: Besides the unrealistic expectations created by viewing and utilizing pornography, even inadvertently, as an educational tool, the simple, yet serious fact is that pornography can contribute to greater acceptance of sexual violence. This is because much of pornography is based around images and incidents that are degrading toward women, exhibit misogynistic attitudes, and largely focus on the pleasure of the male as its utmost goal.

Sexual Violence

Pornography is rarely about love, intimacy, tenderness, and affection. It is about sex. People don't view pornography to feel closer to themselves or their partner emotionally. They view it for the purpose of arousal and, often, use it as an impetus for masturbation or intercourse. As previously stated, viewers of pornography are predominantly male, and because of this and of its aforementioned purpose, pornography often objectifies women—props who become a means to an end, with an end most likely translating into male orgasm.

In much of the pornographic world, women are there to serve men and to be dominated by them, the ideas of sexual arousal and power becoming intertwined in a way that can be processed cognitively by an adult, but not by a teenager whose emotions and hormones so often overrule any rational thought (Peter and Valkenburg, 2007). Think of the underlying meaning of a porn staple, "the money shot," where the male subject in a pornographic film ejaculates onto his partner, expressing his regard for her with an action devoid of any feeling or affection. If this doesn't model the idea that women are objects, then what does?

The fact is, young men who view pornography are more likely to have negative perceptions of women and be more accepting of violence toward them (Jensen and Okrina, 2004). This is not to say that all men who view pornography will engage in an act of sexual assault, but viewing pornography certainly contributes to a misogynistic culture, a culture where men feel entitled to view and treat women as sexual objects, and in that type of culture, men are more inclined to take advantage of women and, indeed, have an easier time justifying sexual violence.

Although adult men may have the internal processing skills to understand that what they see in porn is not an accurate portrayal of how men should treat women, teenage boys often have not developed that capacity. When they continually see a man belittle a woman in pornography—either emotionally or physically—they view that attitude as acceptable. This is especially true if young men view porn with their friends, as the pack mentality increases the support for this notion—further proof that no good can come of inappropriate sexual content coupled with immaturity.

Conclusion

A healthy sexual appetite is normal and can be expressed in myriad ways. For adults, viewing pornography with a partner can be a fun and "inspiring" experience, but it requires maturity to keep it in the proper context.

Though youth has its advantages, it also has its limitations. Young men and women who are just beginning to develop as sexual beings should take care to learn from examples of loving, mature, and healthy relationships. Pornography does not provide the proper model for any of these and is more likely to prove harmful to teens than advantageous in any way. A healthy sex life is not teeming with unrealistic expectations or fraught with an underlying sense of violence or disrespect. Teenagers whose sexual education is informed through the dark, sensual world of pornography are sure to come to the opposite conclusion, and their relationships will only suffer because of it.

References

C. Bryan, "Adolescence, Pornography, and Harm," *Trends and Issues in Crime and Criminal Justice* (vol. 368, 2009).

M. Godwin, *Cyber Rights: Defending Free Speech in the Digital Age* (Cambridge, MA: MIT Press, 2003).

Jacobellis v. Ohio, 378 U.S. 184, 197 (1964).

R. Jensen and D. Okrina, *Pornography and Sexual Violence* (2004). Retrieved March 14, 2009, from National Online Resource Center on Violence Against Women, http://new.vawnet.org/Assoc_Files_VAWnet/AR_PornAndSV.pdf.

J. Peter and P. M. Valkenburg, "Adolescents' Exposure to a Sexualized Media Environment and Their Notions of Women as Sex Objects," *Sex Roles* (vol. 56, 2007).

J. Ropelato, *Internet Pornography Statistics* (2003). Retrieved March 22, 2009, from Top Ten Reviews, http://www.internet-filter-review.toptenreviews.com/internet-pornography-statistics.html.

WAYNE GRINWIS has been a Sexual Health Educator for Planned Parenthood for almost 20 years. He is also Adjunct Professor in the Department of Health at West Chester University. Grinwis credits Andrea Daniels for help with this article. Grinwis argues that pornography is all right for adults, but for teenagers it can create unrealistic expectations about sex, provide a negative and inaccurate sexuality education, and increase sexual violence against women.

Justin A. Sitron

Why Porn Is Not Harmful to Teens

The question about whether pornography is harmful is something that has been on the minds of researchers, parents, and others for decades (Malamuth, Addison, and Koss, 2000). Since the invention of the Internet, the question has become more and more popular, as access to pornography has become as easy as pressing the keys on a keyboard and clicking a mouse. While years ago most people had to go to a bookstore, video store, or adult sex shop to access pornography, now one does not even need to leave one's home or even pay for it. With much more explicit cable television programming and the advent of the Internet, accessing pornography for teens is as easy as finding out the answers to a question on their geography homework (and, the teens might say, infinitely more interesting!). Some researchers even have shown that some youth who access porn do so unintentionally (Sabina, Wolak, and Finkelhor, 2008; Ybarra and Mitchell, 2005).

The question about whether pornography is harmful, dangerous, or leads to aggressive sexual behavior has been studied in adults with varying results (e.g., Fukui and Westmore, 1994; Kutchinsky, 1991). Quite simply, some researchers have found that it makes men more aggressive, whereas others find that it does not. Malamuth, Addison, and Koss (2000) conclude in their meta-analysis of such studies that ". . . for the majority of American men, pornography exposure (even at the highest levels assessed here) is not associated with high levels of sexual aggression" (p. 85). So why the big concern about teens having access to porn?

While in recent years there is growing interest in the effects of online pornography on youth, there has been little research done to date (Sabina, Wolak, and Finkelhor, 2008). In maintaining my position that porn is not harmful to people—teen and adult alike—I need to describe the context in which pornography exists. By and large, the opposing viewpoint—that pornography is harmful to teens—comes from a place of fear; fear of sex and sexual pleasure that has been a part of American society since before the word "American" even existed (Klein, 2006).

The sexual value system that prevails in the United States sees sex as St. Augustine of Hippo saw it after his conversion from a period of lust and sexual promiscuity to a Christian man of high morals—sexual behaviors are only appropriate between a man and a woman, within the confines of marriage, and for procreative purposes. This same value system is one that leaves out something that has become a part of American mainstream media

in recent years with sex therapists and relationship counselors on America's talk shows, like *Oprah*, *Tyra Banks*, and *Dr. Phil*, among others, as well as the nightly news: sexual pleasure. Sexual pleasure is a part of pornography, whether it is something that filmmakers aim to represent on the screen or it is being experienced by pornography's viewers. It is a part of sexual expression and sexual behaviors. If it were not, our culture would not be spending as much time discussing it—and certainly nowhere nearly as much money on it—as it does.

In a society that values sex for reproduction rather than for sexual pleasure and an individual's right to ecstasy and self-fulfillment, the very idea that our teenagers might be experiencing pleasure or witnessing others doing so incites an even more pronounced fear. Certainly, these fearful individuals speculate, indulgent pleasure can only have one outcome—danger or harm. Therefore, the idea of consuming pornography is reserved for the lowest members of society—criminals, perverts, sex maniacs, and so on. Those who aim for achieving the greater good by being successful in our careers, raising families, and experiencing a sense of spiritual satisfaction wouldn't allow ourselves to stoop to self-satisfying physical pleasure. It is far too much of a distraction, and therefore not valued.

Varying media, when relating stories about the Internet, frequently discuss either the wealth of information that it offers or the dangers of its use. Sutter (2000) connects the statements I make above with a recurring fear of humanity since its very first scholars: "The furor over Internet pornography follows the classic pattern of moral panic throughout the ages. From Plato's concerns regarding the 'dramatic poets' effects on the young to the 1980s 'video nasties' scare, to screen violence and internet pornography in the 1990s and beyond: the contexts change but the arguments are consistent" (p. 338). So, I ask that we reconsider the question and begin to explore the panic from a new angle: an angle that begs us to ask what the harmful effects of the panic itself may be.

The panic in which our society engages around the harmfulness of pornography, as I mentioned before, is about the assumption that sexual pleasure is harmful and therefore something from which teens must be protected. Consider this short scenario:

> A parent and 10-year-old child are sitting around
> the living room, and perhaps the child is sitting
> on the floor playing with a toy while the parent is

flipping through prime-time television. After flipping through the channels, the parent decides on a favorite love story. Although the story itself is over the child's head, the child is otherwise occupied. As the story progresses, the child begins to watch and ends up captivated until the parent switches the channel, which sparks protest in the child because the story was so engaging. The parent's response is, "Go back to playing with your toys, I want to watch something else." What sparked the change of channel? The two main characters engaged in a kiss that transformed into the removal of clothing and rolling in the sheets. No nudity. No words between the characters of any kind, just a romantic ballad in the background and two people beginning to kiss passionately and remove clothing.

Although the child in the story objects to the channel being changed, the parent does nothing to engage the child in a discussion about why the channel was changed or what was going on in the story before the flick of the remote. The message that is entirely implicit in this situation is that kissing and the touching of naked bodies between two adults is not something a child should see. If something suitable for prime-time television is too harmful for children, the mainstream thinking would certainly hold that pornography is harmful as well, if not more so.

I disagree. I posit here that there are benefits to teens watching pornography: (1) Internet pornography offers teens an opportunity to see real bodies; (2) pornography offers an opportunity for teens to learn by watching rather than by doing; and (3) pornography opens doors for communication.

Internet Pornography Offers Teens an Opportunity to See Real Bodies

The days of pornography being only accessible in commercially produced formats (DVD, VHS, film, etc.) are gone. Such content has been described by researchers as being responsible for promoting artificial and unrealistic body types in women and men alike. Certainly, this is not a phenomenon left to the pornography industry alone; producers of mainstream film, television, and video all contribute to the perpetuation of unrealistic body types as more beautiful than that of the average viewer. Why, then, should pornography be held to a higher standard than any other type of media?

On the Internet, there is a multitude of sites where Internet users can generate their own original video content and post it on Web sites for others to see. A visitor to sites like XTube.com and Bigbeautifulwomen.com can see a variety of different film clips that include a diversity of body types, sexual orientations, gender, body hair levels, and sexual behaviors ranging from the most mainstream to fetishes. Such a site can build a sense of self-esteem for individuals who might never have seen other people whose nude bodies are like their own.

Pornography Offers an Opportunity for Teens to Learn by Watching Rather Than by Doing

Howard Gardner's (1983) theory of multiple intelligences, which articulates the varying ways in which people express their learning styles, has had a great impact on the ways in which educators approach teaching students. Two of the intelligence styles are kinesthetic, which learns best by physically doing and/or handling something, and visual, which prefers seeing. Teens who match either of these two learning styles may be able to use pornography as a substitute for actual sexual behaviors. Although the kinesthetic learners might be motivated naturally to engage in sex, they may find watching it or masturbating while watching it to be a learning experience. They can understand what they do and don't find arousing; they can learn about their own bodies and what feels and does not feel good. Pornography, and any sexually explicit material for that matter, can actually serve as an excellent teaching tool. Considering that no one has ever gotten pregnant or acquired a sexually transmitted infection from masturbation, one might go so far as to argue that teens who view porn might be able to maintain a decision to remain abstinent longer than teens who do not.

In addition to pornography serving as a tool for varied learning styles, it also serves as a medium through which to portray sexual behaviors. There are few educational venues for teens to see sex in this way. Sexuality, as it is taught in schools, is taught very much separate from the rest of the human body, often even in a different set of classes from other body parts and their functions. Sexual health and reproduction are usually a stand-alone unit in a health class or biology class. The focus of such education is on how the parts work, what their purpose is (procreation), and how to avoid disease. So, although the body parts (uterus, vagina, ovaries, penis, testicles, prostate, etc.) are explained, and often their functions described, all of it is done as if they are detached organs from the rest of the body and without discussion of pleasure.

From a learning standpoint, adolescents and teens are concrete learners—they must have very specific, straightforward examples to support teaching in order for that teaching to resonate. Talking hypothetically about sexual behaviors is often much more challenging for a teenager to understand than seeing an actual representation of it. Pornography provides teens with that representation.

Pornography Opens Doors for Communication

Finally, pornography offers us, as adults, an opportunity to engage young people in conversations about sexuality. If we engage in conversations with young people about sexuality, sexual bodies, and sexual pleasure, we provide teens with valuable lessons. Pornography as a medium, therefore, becomes neutral, neither good nor bad. It is merely another teachable moment for educators and parents alike.

Realistically speaking, the context in which pornography is viewed is the complicated and potentially troubling component. Sure, some pornography depicts stereotypical sexual behaviors, unrealistic body types, and even behaviors that some perceive to be violent or degrading, but this all presents just as many challenges for teens as it does for adults. Viewing pornography, if not done critically and with discussion, may leave the viewer with misconceived notions of sexual behavior and pleasure. The problems with pornography are cultural and social and can be further understood and framed appropriately with teens only if adults are willing to engage teens in a discussion—a discussion that may even include watching pornography together. Adults sometimes expect that they can control their children's lives, their exposure to the world, and their behaviors. The reality is that while many parents take action to censor their children's Internet access, friends, and media viewing, children who aim to find pornography will always be able to do so. In addition, as mentioned earlier, even children who do not aim to find or view pornography sometimes come upon it unwittingly. The irony of the situation is that enough studies have been done to demonstrate that adolescents and children are sexual, whether alone or with someone else, and even without engaging in sexual behavior, they have fantasies and think about it. As most adults who work with children and teens will tell you, when adults are not present, sex is something teens talk about.

If adults and children don't discuss sex and sexuality, then where are the models for adults to discuss it as well? Pornography, whether viewed in secret, in groups, or with adults present, opens the door for young people to talk about sex and their feelings about it and to find out what important adults in their lives think about it. Pornography presents an opportunity to raise many questions, if the questions are allowed to be asked. Openly discussing sexuality can bring a lot of potential benefits to teens as they age. To consider the ramifications of a culture where sex is taboo, one only needs to read through a chapter in a text on the treatment of sexual dysfunctions. So many of the problems that adults face with the expression of their sexuality have their roots in their lives as children, teenagers, and young adults—times in their lives when sex was not discussed openly, positively, or in constructive ways. Rather than predispose our teens to a future with sexual dysfunction and a fear of finding support around their sexuality, why not begin conversations about sex when young people naturally want to have them?

If our answer to the question posed as the title of this section—Is viewing pornography harmful to teens?—is "yes," we begin on a misguided, thorny path of protecting children and teens from pornography, sexual pleasure, and sex in general by shutting and locking the doors to learning and communication. On the other hand, if the answer is "no," doors open to begin a dialogue about pornography, its use, misuse, benefits, and detriments, and an invaluable conversation can begin between adults and children about healthy sexual expression.

References

A. Fukui and B. Westmore, "To See or Not to See: The Debate over Pornography and Its Relationship to Sexual Aggression," *Australian and New Zealand Journal of Psychiatry* (vol. 28, 1994).

M. Klein, *America's War on Sex* (New York: Praeger Publishers: 2006).

B. Kutchinsky, "Pornography and Rape: Theory and Practice? Evidence from Crime Data in Four Countries Where Pornography Is Easily Accessible," *International Journal of Law and Psychiatry* (vol. 14, 1991).

N. M. Malamuth, T. Addison, and M. Koss, "Pornography and Sexual Aggression: Are There Reliable Effects and Can We Understand Them?" *Annual Review of Sex Research* (vol. 11, 2000).

C. Sabina, J. Wolak, and D. Finkelhor, "The Nature and Dynamics of Internet Pornography Exposure for Youth," *CyberPsychology & Behavior* (vol. 11, 2008).

G. Sutter, "'Nothing New Under the Sun': Old Fears and New Media," *International Journal of Law and Information Technology* (vol. 8, 2000).

M. L. Ybarra and K. J. Mitchell, "Exposure to Internet Pornography Among Children and Adolescents: A National Survey," *CyberPsychology & Behavior* (vol. 8, 2005).

JUSTIN A. SITRON is an Assistant Professor and Director of PhD Programs at Widener University. Sitron argues that pornography has no negative impact on teenagers and, in fact, has potential benefits. Sitron contends that Internet pornography can be helpful in providing teens an opportunity to see real bodies, a chance to learn about sex from seeing rather than doing, and an open door for communication with parents.

EXPLORING THE ISSUE

Is Internet Pornography Harmful to Teenagers?

Critical Thinking and Reflection

1. What are some arguments made by each side with which you agree or disagree?
2. What are the strengths and weaknesses of the two positions made in this issue? Compare and contrast the competing arguments made about the impact of Internet pornography on teens. What conclusions do you reach about the different research cited?
3. Think more broadly about the amount of privacy that teens have to view pornography. Also, consider the wide access that they have to cell phones that record video. How might this combination affect their own sexual behaviors, the recording of the own sexual behaviors, and sending/posting video recordings of their sexual behaviors?

Is There Common Ground?

While the authors may disagree over the impact of pornography, they both would probably agree about the potential dangers of recording and posting teens' own sexual behaviors. We have seen some cases of teens committing suicide after sexually explicit video of them has been posted online. What are some things that can occur to create a generation of more sexually literate teenagers who make decisions that are consistent with their long-term goals? What responsibilities do families have to teach their children about creating sexually explicit videos? What responsibilities do schools have to teach children about creating sexually explicit videos?

Create Central

www.mhhe.com/createcentral

Additional Resources

C. Bryan, "Adolescence, Pornography, and Harm," *Trends and Issues in Crime and Criminal Justice* (vol. 368, 2009)

M. Godwin, *Cyber Rights: Defending Free Speech in the Digital Age* (MIT Press, 2003). *Jacobellis v. Ohio*, 378 U.S. 184, 197 (1964)

R. Jensen and D. Okrina, *Pornography and Sexual Violence* (2004). Retrieved March 14, 2009. Accessible online at National Online Resource Center on Violence Against Women, http://new.vawnet.org/Assoc_Files_VAWnet/AR_PornAndSV.pdf

L. Margolies, *Teens and Internet Pornography* (2010). Psych Central. Retrieved September 4, 2011. Accessible online at http://psychcentral.com/lib/2010/teens-and-internet-pornography.

Optenet. More than one third of Web pages are pornographic [Press release]. (2010). Retrieved September 10, 2010. Accessible online at www.optenet.com/en-us/new.asp?id=270

J. Peter and P. M. Valkenburg, "Adolescents' Exposure to a Sexualized Media Environment and Their Notions of Women as Sex Objects," *Sex Roles* (vol. 56, 2007).

Internet References . . .

Googling this tends to result in sites supporting Internet pornography. To read more, search this under the "news" section of your favorite search engine.

Selected, Edited, and with Issue Framing Material by:
David M. Hall, Ph.D., *Delaware Valley College*

ISSUE

Are Statutory Rape Laws Effective at Protecting Minors?

YES: Sherry F. Colb, from "The Pros and Cons of Statutory Rape Laws," CNN.com (February 11, 2004)

NO: Carolyn E. Cocca, from "Prosecuting Mrs. Robinson? Gender, Sexuality, and Statutory Rape Laws," *Deviance* (2002)

Learning Outcomes
After reading this issue, you will be able to: • Compare and contrast the competing arguments made for and against statutory rape laws.   • Evaluate the implications of statutory rape laws on the impact this has on issues such as adolescent sexual behavior, spreading of sexually transmitted infections, and teenage pregnancy.

ISSUE SUMMARY

YES: Sherry F. Colb, Columnist and Law Professor, uses a case study involving a statutory rape case to raise concerns about whether rape and assault cases would be prosecuted sufficiently without statutory rape laws. Although not perfect, statutory rape laws can be assets in such rape cases when the older partner denies the rape occurred or denies responsibility for a resulting pregnancy or infection.

NO: Carolyn E. Cocca argues that while the laws are written in a gender-neutral way, the enforcement of these laws is heavily influenced by societal attitudes toward males and females. She argues that in effect these laws punish consensual sex and disproportionately punish same-sex relationships.

The term "rape" refers to forced sexual contact between two people that usually involves the insertion of a penis or inanimate object into another person's vagina, anus, or mouth. Rape is against the law in every state in the United States and usually results in heavy penalties on the rapist.

Statutory rape laws say that sexual behavior between two people where one individual is below a certain age is against the law, even if there was no force involved. These laws, which were originally created to protect adolescent girls from predatory adult males, are different in every state. The age at which a person is considered legally able to engage in sexual behavior, called the "age of consent," is different in every state, too. Most state laws are no longer restricted to a female victim and male perpetrator; they now apply to couples of any gender combination, including same-sex relationships. Yet some cases receive far more attention than others. For example, the media has carried news of former schoolteacher Mary Kay Letourneau, an adult who was convicted of statutory rape for having a sexual relationship with an adolescent student. Even though the two claimed then (and maintain

now) that they were in love, the law said that this relationship was illegal, and Ms. Letourneau went to prison.

People who support statutory rape laws argue that in any relationship where there is a significant age difference, the older of the two people has an inherent power advantage over the younger. Even if the younger partner agrees to have sex, statutory rape law supporters argue, that person was not old enough to make a well-thought-out decision—and may have been coerced emotionally, even if not physically. What an older partner has can be very seductive—power, money, a job, a car, and more. These tangible things, they argue, play a powerful role in a younger person's decision-making process. In addition, it is quite flattering for a 14-year-old to have a 24-year-old person interested in her or him. One wonders, however, what a 24-year-old could possibly have in common, developmentally and experientially, with a 14-year-old. Statutory rape laws are designed, in part, to keep these types of unequal relationships from becoming sexual in nature.

Others disagree, saying that statutory rape laws are ineffective, judgmental, patronizing, and sexist. Opponents to statutory rape laws argue that adolescents and teenagers are able to make their own decisions about their sexual behavior, even if their partner is older. Opponents maintain that relationships are about much more than sexual behavior, and that if a relationship is otherwise healthy and loving, penalizing the couple for their age difference does more to ruin lives than save them. There are young men, they argue, who have gone to jail because the parents of their younger partners learned that they were having sex and wanted to punish them. As a result, these young men have a jail sentence on their records forever, solely because of an age difference.

What do you think about statutory rape laws? Do they protect, or do they discriminate? Do you think that an adult has more power than a teenager just because she or he is older? If so, is this power strong enough that the adolescent or teen could not say whether she or he wanted to have sex with that adult? What are some of the inherent problems with a significant age difference in a relationship? What are some of the positive things that can happen from two people of different ages having a relationship?

The combination of age and sexuality is a sensitive subject in many cultures and societies. In the United States, we have many double standards about the age difference between sexual and romantic partners and the gender of the people involved in the relationship. An older man with a much younger woman is much more commonplace than an older woman with a much younger man. An adult male pursuing a teenage girl is seen as a predator, while an adult female doing the same is seen as much less threatening. Even in some court cases, judges have dismissed charges in cases where the older partner was female and the younger

one male. It is as if the law does not see an adolescent girl as being able to consent, but a younger male is simply "coming of age" by being sexual with an older partner. In our mainstream society's eyes, an adolescent girl has lost something by being sexual so young; she has shown poor judgment and has been taken advantage of by this terrible older male. An adolescent male in the same situation with an adult woman, however, is often seen as having gained from the relationship—respect and experience. Are these assumptions prejudicial to boys? To girls?

There is an episode of *South Park* in which one of the characters finds his younger brother, who is in Kindergarten, in bed with his female teacher. The character goes to the police to report that there is a teacher at school having sex with a child at school. The police are concerned, then they learn that the child is male and the teacher is female. At that point, they respond with, "Nice" and "She's hot."

While this exchange is meant to be funny, what does it reveal about our society's larger views about whether or not someone is a victim of statutory rape?

There are far too many unhealthy and abusive relationships. People bring different things to their relationships, including different levels of power. In some cases, age brings power with it; in others, money and experience; race or ethnicity; physical ability—the examples can continue almost endlessly. The questions that remain are these: In what way can people have healthy, respectful, equal relationships given the inherent power differences that are there? To what extent can and should personal relationships be governed by law?

Sherry F. Colb

The Pros and Cons of Statutory Rape Laws

A 10-Year Sentence for Marcus Dwayne Dixon

Recently, the Georgia Supreme Court heard arguments in *Dixon v. State*. The case involves the conviction of Marcus Dwayne Dixon for statutory rape and aggravated child molestation. (Dixon was acquitted of rape and several other charges.)

Statutory rape is sex between an adult and a minor, while aggravated child molestation also involves an injury. At the time of his offense, Dixon was an 18-year-old high school football player who had sex with a 15-year-old female classmate. The aggravated child molestation statute mandates a ten-year minimum sentence, and Dixon challenges the harshness of the resulting penalty.

The case has attracted claims of racism, because the victim was a white girl and the convict an outstanding African-American student with a football scholarship to Vanderbilt.

One provocative underlying (though unstated) question that has contributed to the notoriety of this case is whether the law can legitimately send teenagers to prison for having sex with other teenagers, in the absence of force. Because every state has a statutory rape law in some form, this case presents a challenge to a long and continuing tradition of criminal laws that confine men for what could be consensual sex with minors who are close to the age of majority.

Such liability is controversial in a number of ways, but it also has some benefits that are often overlooked by critics, thus leaving us with a difficult dilemma that admits of no easy answers.

Statutory rape laws have a checkered past. A primary purpose was to guard the virginity of young maidens against seduction by unscrupulous cads. To give up one's "virtue" to a man who was unwilling to pay with his hand in marriage was foolish and presumptively a product of youthful, poor judgment.

Such laws had more to do with preserving female virginity than with the force and violence that define rape. One sign of this is the fact that a man could (and in some states still can) defend himself against statutory rape charges by proving that his victim was already sexually experienced prior to their encounter (and thus not subject to being corrupted by the defendant).

Justifications for Statutory Rape Laws

Despite their unsavory beginnings, however, some feminists have favored these laws as well. Progressive women supported such statutes mainly as measures to help combat the sexual abuse of young girls.

Though a statutory rape charge would not require proof of force or coercion, feminists observed, young girls were (and may continue to be) especially vulnerable to being raped by the adults in their lives. In one study, for example, 74 percent of women who had intercourse before age 14 and 60 percent of those who had sex before age 15 report having had a forced sexual experience.

In addition, prosecutors attempting to prove rape in court have historically faced significant burdens, such as corroboration requirements premised on the complaining witness's presumptive lack of credibility.

For many years, legal thinkers like 18th-century British jurist Sir Matthew Hale were convinced that rape "is an accusation easily to be made and hard to be proved, and harder to be defended by the party accused, though never so innocent." Thus, rape law did not provide a reliable or efficacious vehicle for addressing most sexual violence, and it continues to be of limited utility for acquaintance rapes. . . .

For this reason too, feminists may have viewed statutory rape laws as a godsend. As long as there was sexual intercourse and an under-age victim, the jury could convict. And more importantly, that possibility itself might deter real sexual abuse.

Is Statutory Rape Just Rape Without Proof of One Element?

Viewing statutory rape laws as salutary in this way does raise a serious problem, however. In *In Re Winship*, the U.S. Supreme Court required that prosecutors prove every element of a crime beyond a reasonable doubt before a conviction can be constitutionally valid. Removing the "force" element of rape and leaving only intercourse and age might seem to amount, from some perspectives, to a presumption that the force element of rape is established, without the prosecutor's having to prove it and without the defense even having the option of affirmatively disproving it.

Such a presumption allows for the possibility that a fully consensual sexual encounter will be prosecuted and punished as rape. Some might understandably believe that this unfairly subjects essentially innocent men to unduly harsh treatment, simply in the name of deterring other, unrelated men from engaging in very different and far more culpable sorts of conduct.

Responses to Concerns About Prosecuting Consensual Sex

There are two potential responses to this concern. First, at some level, we might have doubts about the competence of a minor to "consent," in a meaningful way, to sexual activity. Because of her youth, the minor might not fully appreciate the full physical and emotional implications of her decision (including the possibility of offspring for which she will likely have little means of support).

Of course, many adults might also fall into this category, and the decision to treat intercourse as distinctive in this way may simply represent a revival of the old view that maidens should be protected from the corruption of their virtue. Why, otherwise, should girls who are sexually attracted to men be considered the men's victims rather than participants in arguably unwise and socially costly, but mutually gratifying, activity?

Another response to the concern about innocent men is more in keeping with feminist concerns. It is that when sexual activity with a minor is truly consensual, the activity is unlikely, at least in modern times, to be prosecuted. In other words, to the extent that statutory rape is truly a consensual and therefore victimless crime in a particular case, it is highly unlikely to generate a criminal action.

In the Dixon case, for example, the 15-year-old victim claimed that the defendant "tracked her down in a classroom trailer that she was cleaning as part of her duties in an after-school job, asked if she was a virgin, grabbed her arms, unbuttoned her pants, and raped her on a table." This description renders the statutory rape and aggravated child molestation prosecution something other than the state targeting consensual activity for unduly harsh punishment.

Though Dixon was acquitted on the rape charge, that fact does not rule out the possibility of sexual assault. It means only that the jury was not convinced beyond a reasonable doubt that Dixon forced the 15-year-old girl to have sex against her will.

The normative question, then, becomes this: Is the likelihood that consensual sex will be punished by imprisonment sufficient to override the benefits of statutory rape legislation in facilitating the fight against actual sexual abuse of young adults?

Is Convicting in the Absence of Force Unacceptable?

One reaction to this question is that even the theoretical possibility of convicting in a case of consensual sex is unacceptable and unconstitutional. Prosecutors and juries, on this reasoning, should not have the option of finding a person guilty in the absence of force, regardless of how unlikely they are to exercise that option. Consensual sex is not criminal, period.

The assumptions underlying this reaction, however, though understandable, are at odds with other areas of the criminal law. Consider drug laws. Possession of a large quantity of narcotics is regularly treated as a far more serious offense than possession of a smaller quantity. One reason is that the first is viewed as possession with the intent to distribute (that is, drug dealing), while the second is thought to be consistent with personal use. Since legislators and others view dealing as much more harmful than mere possession, the penalties are accordingly more severe.

Yet possession of a large quantity of drugs, though highly suggestive, is not necessarily accompanied by an intent to distribute. A person might, for example, possess large amounts of drugs to avoid having to risk apprehension, or sources drying out, through repeated purchases.

Suppose the drug statute did require proof of intent to distribute. If so, then the judge would, on request, have to instruct the jury that the bare fact of quantity alone is enough for a conviction only if the jury draws the inference, beyond a reasonable doubt, that the defendant intended distribution. Without such a finding of intent, the jury would have to acquit.

With the statute providing instead that quantity is the sole element, however, intent becomes legally irrelevant. As a result, even a prosecutor and jury who know that the defendant is simply saving up for an anticipated heroin shortage rather than planning to deal drugs can convict the defendant of the more serious felony without giving rise to any grounds for appeal.

By crafting a statute without an "intent to distribute" element, in other words, legislators target distribution without requiring its proof (or even allowing for its disproof). One might characterize this as an end run around the constitutional requisite of proving every element of guilt beyond a reasonable doubt.

The same "end run" accusation can be leveled against statutory rape laws. Young girls may represent a substantial portion of rape victims, perhaps because they are vulnerable and have not yet become sufficiently suspicious of the people around them. In most cases, moreover, a truly consensual encounter with a minor will probably not be brought to a prosecutor's attention or trigger the prosecutorial will to punish.

As with drug possession laws, then, the omission of a requirement that would pose proof problems might generally serve the interests of justice, despite appearances to the contrary.

Consensual Sex with Minors Is Not a Fundamental Right

What permits legislatures the discretion to enact such laws, ultimately, is the fact that (like drug possession), consensual sex with minors is not a constitutionally protected activity. Even if it is victimless, sex with a minor may be criminalized and punished severely without resort to a force requirement. Indeed, it once was punished routinely in this way because of misogynist concerns about preserving female purity.

In modern times, though, when consensual sex among teenagers is generally understood to be both common and profoundly different from the crime of rape, there might still be a role for statutory rape laws in protecting young girls from actual rapists, through deterrence and through the real possibility of retribution.

Racism Raised in the Dixon Case

A remaining concern is the worry about racism specifically, and discrimination more generally, that arises whenever officials are vested with a large amount of discretion. In Dixon's case, one witness testified that the victim said that the sexual intercourse in question was consensual but that she claimed it was rape to avoid the wrath of her violent, racist father. This testimony may have given rise to reasonable doubt in the jury on the rape charges.

In easing the burden of proof at trial by eliminating the requirement of proving force, then, the law does permit unscrupulous prosecutors and complainants to bring charges on the basis of what is truly victimless behavior.

One does wonder, though, why a girl would tell a violent and racist father about a sexual encounter with a black man in the first place, rather than simply keeping the information from him, if the encounter were actually consensual.

Are Statutory Rape Laws Worth Their Cost?

In short, the crime of statutory rape may have originated from repressive and misogynist conceptions of sexuality. Nonetheless, it has (and may always have had) redeeming characteristics, even from an enlightened perspective that takes into account the realities of prosecuting rape and of women's equality. It makes it easier, for example, to prosecute and thus to deter real rapists who count on jury skepticism about acquaintance rape allegations.

Still, reducing burdens of proof relies a great deal on trust—in victims and in prosecutors—that the omitted element will truly be present when cases come to trial. If and when that trust is misplaced, . . . a grave injustice can result.

SHERRY F. COLB, ESQ. is a Professor at Rutgers Law School and a columnist for CNN.

Carolyn E. Cocca

 **NO**

Prosecuting Mrs. Robinson? Gender, Sexuality, and Statutory Rape Laws

Introduction: Statutory Rape Laws

State statutory rape laws prohibit sexual intercourse with an unmarried person under a certain age, ranging from 14 to 18 (generally, 16). Those under this age, who are not married to their sex partner, are deemed incapable of consenting to such activity; therefore, consensuality is not permitted as a defense to the crime. Proscribing the sexuality of young people is thus said to be a protective measure. In many states, the perpetrator may be the same age as the victim and still be charged with a felony; in most of the states that mandate that the perpetrator be a certain number of years older then the victim, a same-age perpetrator can still be charged with a misdemeanor. When the activity is heterosexual, it is usually the male who is charged.

The laws originally were gender-specific: they punished a male who had sexual intercourse with a female not his wife under the age of consent. As of August 2000, all fifty states have gender-neutral statutory rape laws, in which either a male or female may be prosecuted for engaging in sexual activity with a male or female (who is not the perpetrator's spouse) under the age of consent. While a solely heterosexual framework would assume that this was meant to prohibit sex between an older female and younger male, prosecutions under the laws have targeted homosexual relationships as well.

Considering the marital exemption, the prosecutions of same-age perpetrators (usually males), and the use of the laws against homosexual activity even as most states have decriminalized sodomy, one wonders if "age" is really the operative category in statutory rape laws. I would argue, rather, that such laws are based on—and serve to reinforce—cultural stereotypes of gender. That is, heterosexual males are perceived to be the active, aggressive, party in sexual intercourse (defined in the laws as penetration); heterosexual females as the passive, victimized, party.

This article explores the ways in which cultural narratives of sexuality work to undermine the gender-neutral language of statutory rape laws. It examines the discourses surrounding statutory rape cases involving both male and female perpetrators with both male and female victims, in order to discern whether or not gender is treated "neutrally" both in the courtroom and in media coverage

of cases. I find that while much of the discourse still categorizes statutory rape with a male victim as abuse, the "older woman" perpetrator is more often described as a manipulative or mentally ill seductress while the "older man" perpetrator is usually likened to an abusive predator, doubly outside the bounds of society by being homosexual as well. Such language maintains the boundaries of traditional gender roles: the older woman is constructed as an almost sympathetic aberration of her gender who tries to obtain love by seducing a young male, while the older man is seen simply as a sexual aggressor and is therefore more universally excoriated for his behavior. The presumption of innocence, or of consensuality, begins to fade when the perpetrator is male, and in particular, when the perpetrator is a homosexual male. At the same time, victims of statutory rape, particularly by older males, are virtually always constructed as unwilling, or at best, passive and manipulated participants in sexual conduct. Yet children are also perceived to be "invested with sexual capacity." Cases involving young males with older females are most readily perceived as falling into this category, as if one's male gender surpasses one's age as enabling or encouraging sexual behavior.

The paper begins with a brief overview of statutory rape laws, and then details the feminist debate over the laws and over gender-neutral language. It then moves to case studies of three statutory rape cases of national notoriety, those involving Mary Kay LeTourneau, Stephen Simmons, and Sean O'Neill. Finally, it concludes with a discussion of the implications of gender-neutral statutory rape laws and the prosecutions brought under them.

Statutory Rape Reform

Following English common law, the age of consent in the American colonies was generally set at 10 or 12. The laws in some sense served to preserve female virginity, which was a valuable commodity, until marriage. The "theft" of that chastity was considered a property crime against the girl's father and future husband. This in practice applied only to white females; many young black females, for instance, were enslaved or otherwise treated discriminatorily by the legal system.

In the late nineteenth century, an alliance of organizations such as the Women's Christian Temperance

Union, suffragist groups, and some conservative religious groups and white workingmen's organizations lobbied to have the age "at which a girl could legally consent to her own ruin" raised to 16 or 18. This occurred most rapidly in the states in which women could vote. In response, male legislators made prosecutions more difficult. A number of states passed provisions that required the female victim to be "of previous chaste character," i.e., a virgin, and be able to prove that fact. Others allowed perpetrators to claim that they had made a "mistake of age" and thought the female older than she was. Such provisions call into question if the concern was with protecting a young woman per se, or with policing gender boundaries; if a female had previously been sexually active, or could have been perceived as older and experienced, it was as if no crime had been committed.

The laws were not amended again until the 1970s. This was due in large part to activism by second wave feminists, represented in particular by such groups as the National Organization for Women. They sought to do away with gendered inequities in a variety of laws, including both forcible rape and statutory rape laws. In general, most of these feminists felt that the laws as written (prohibiting sexual intercourse with a female under a certain age) reinforced stereotypes of gender and inscribed patriarchal notions of female sexuality and mental capacity into law. They therefore sought to restore some formal agency and formal equality to young women while also retaining the ability to safeguard them from sexual coercion. Specifically, they lobbied for 1) gender-neutral language, which would include young males as part of the protected class and enable the charging of females as perpetrators, and 2) age span provisions which mandate that the perpetrator be a certain number of years older than the victim, thus catching potentially more coercive relationships while exempting those more likely to be consensual.

These two proposals began a multifaceted debate among feminists, reflective of the virtually simultaneous debates over sexuality, sexual consent, and pornography. Radical feminists in particular critiqued the legal construct that sex fell into two categories: consensual sex or rape. They argued that for socially constructed reasons men and women were simply not similarly situated in modern society; some extended that argument to suggest that the idea of a woman being able to give true consent was untenable. As such, pornography reflected the degraded status of women and should be regulated as a means of pursuing equal protection for women. In this environment, radical feminists were concerned that gender-neutral statutory rape laws could not acknowledge that adolescent males and females in particular were not similarly situated in regard to psychological needs and sexual power. The problem was one of "social inequality, of sex aggravated by age."

In other words, gender-neutral laws would not serve to advance the substantive equality of females in the law and in real life, but instead would grant females only formal equality which would do them a disservice. "Boys and girls may both be harmed by early sexual activity, but they are harmed differently and we gain nothing by pretending the harm is the same." A number of studies recount that adolescent females have low self-esteem, are uncomfortable with speaking their minds for fear of appearing unfeminine or intellectually threatening to their male counterparts, and are insecure and willing to please. Beyond the potential for pregnancy, disease, pain, and shame, a young female might regret having decided to engage in sex—but socialized as she is to believe that sex and love go together, still see such an encounter as consensual because she was not physically forced to do so. Therefore, these feminists would worry, gender-neutral language might actually worsen the situation by allowing public officials, and feminists, to claim credit for advancements in the cause of gender equality, causing any fervor for change to be undercut with no progress made on the underlying structures of gender inequality that pervade (adolescent) heterosexual relationships.

Feminist sex radicals were on the opposite side of the sexuality and pornography debate from the radical feminists. They felt that the latter essentialized all females as victims and all pornography as problematic, rather than acknowledge that many women were actively confronting inequalities and that pornography in and of itself could be received differently by different audiences—perhaps even re-constructed in a feminist fashion. Worse, they worried, the radical feminist position that women are different (for socially constructed reasons) could play right into the hands of conservative censorial forces, who were all too willing to agree with that notion (for biological reasons); indeed, radical feminists and social conservatives joined forces to pass anti-pornography ordinances in the Midwest.

While they acknowledged that statutory rape laws had a protective function, the sex radicals were concerned that their patriarchal and proscriptive roots punished potentially consensual unmarried sex, painted young people and particularly young females as a monolithic group unable to make decisions about their own bodies, and sent a message that nonmarital sex and female sexual agency in and of themselves were wrong and harmful. Therefore, they saw the laws as violating rights of privacy and personal autonomy in sexual matters.

Sex radicals also argued that the laws' marital exemption which allowed those under the age of consent and married to be free from prosecution showed that the laws had little to do with one's age and everything to do with one's marital status. Along the same lines, the gender-neutral language would enable the prosecution of homosexual couples already suffering from other forms of legalized discrimination based on their sexuality. Indeed, in the battle over pornography, many sex radicals were appalled but not surprised that one of the arguments used to win over male judges was to tell them that in gay porn, males were just as degraded as females. The intertwining of sex and violence in statutory rape laws might only serve to further marginalize, rather than protect, homosexuals.

The liberal feminists who themselves often drafted gender-neutral statutory rape laws were somewhere in the middle of these two poles. They felt that young males should not be neglected as victims, and that the gender-specific laws formally inscribed the stereotypes of male-as-aggressor and female-as-victim in the realm of sexuality and therefore had to go. "If sex is viewed as a privilege, for a state to say that a girl of a certain age is neither legally nor factually capable of consenting to that act while boys are able to consent to sex at any age with any women, that girl has been deprived of a right that her male counterpart has been allowed to engage in." The change in language would treat males and females as if they were similarly situated, thereby perhaps accelerating the process of equal treatment in nonlegal realms as well.

Liberal feminists lobbied so successfully for statutory rape reform that by 1981 all but ten states had made their statutory rape laws gender-neutral. But in that year, the Supreme Court upheld the gender-specificity of California's statutory rape law. The majority opinion argued that because only the female party could get pregnant from a (heterosexual) sexual encounter, a law punishing only the male would equalize the burden placed on the two parties when they decided to engage in sexual activity. The court's rationale was much-criticized in legal circles and feminist circles; in short, neither the plurality opinion, nor the concurrences, nor the dissents addressed feminist concerns about statutory rape laws as described above, but rather reflected that the justices' assumptions about teenage sexuality were strongly based on stereotypes of gender. By 2000, regardless of the Supreme Court's decision, all fifty states had gender-neutral statutory rape laws; they now read that "any person" who has sex with "any person" under the age of consent has committed a criminal act.

But has the change in the language of the law resulted in a change in prosecutions under the laws, or a change in cultural discourses about statutory rape? The next section addresses statutory rape prosecutions in general; the section following details three prominent statutory rape cases in order to examine the discourses surrounding the crime.

Prosecutions under Gender-Neutral Statutory Rape Laws

It is somewhat difficult to generalize about statutory rape prosecutions because of the methods by which arrest and conviction records on the crime are collected. The Federal Bureau of Investigation's Uniform Crime Reporting Program (UCRP) requires that statutory rape be bundled with other crimes and reported as "Sex offenses: (Except forcible rape, prostitution and commercialized vice)—statutory rape and offenses against chastity, common decency, morals, and the like. Attempts are included." The Bureau of Justice Statistics (BJS) sometimes bundles several datasets

and then lumps statutory rape in with "Other Sexual Assault: Includes statutory rape, lewd acts with children, forcible sodomy, fondling, molestation, indecent practices, and other related offenses." The National Judicial Reporting Program (NJRP) includes statutory rape in the figure for "Sexual assault: Forcible or violent sexual acts not involving intercourse with an adult or minor, nonforcible sexual intercourse with a minor, and nonforcible sex acts with someone unable to give legal or factual consent because of mental or physical defect or intoxication." Sometimes, however, NJRP tables bundle "sexual assault" with "[forcible] rape." Lastly, the Office of Juvenile Justice and Delinquency Prevention tracks the crime a fourth way in the juvenile court system, "Public Order: Liquor law violations, weapons offenses, disorderly conduct, obstruction of justice, nonviolent sex offenses, and other public order offenses." Local law enforcement collect data on their arrests and convictions within these categories, rarely breaking out the numbers for the crime of statutory rape alone; when they do tally statutory rape rates separately, it is rare to find them broken down by the sex of the offender. This is perhaps because of the assumption that the perpetrator will be male.

Having said this, the NJRP survey for 1998 that breaks down crimes by the sex of the offender found that of persons convicted for "Sexual Assault" (including forcible rape) felonies, 97% were male and 3% were female. A BJS survey that combines datasets reports that of all offenders in state prison for "Other sexual assault," 98.8% were male and 1.2% were female. In terms of probated sentences, a Georgia Department of Corrections spokesman said recently that of the approximately 800 people on probation in that state for statutory rape, eighteen are women—about 2%. In short, the number of women prosecuted for statutory rape does not appear to have skyrocketed since the adoption of gender-neutral language. However, according to a recent UCRP study, the number of male victims has risen to include about 14% of all types of sexual assaults reported to law enforcement. This indicates that while those prosecuted are still overwhelmingly male, a not insignificant number of them were prosecuted for same-sex activity.

Two types of prosecutions in the 1990s have further buttressed the gendered undercurrents of statutory rape laws. Spurred on by bonus monies offered through the welfare reform act (the Personal Responsibility and Work Opportunity Reconciliation Act of 1996) for decreasing their number of teenage pregnancies, several states have begun using stepped-up statutory rape prosecutions as a means of accomplishing that goal. That such an approach could actually stem the number of teenage pregnancies is extremely unlikely; indeed, young pregnant females may be deterred from seeing their doctors if they fear their partner will be punished. Focusing on this one particular type of relationship not only excludes cases in which abuse but no pregnancy has occurred, but also subverts the gender neutrality of the law by purposely prosecuting only males who have impregnated young females.

A second type of case making its way through the court system in various states encompasses females convicted of statutory rape for relationships with young males, but who have then become pregnant, chosen to give birth, and have sued the male for child support. Thus far, in a number of different states, those young males have been forced to pay—even though they are minors as well as victims of sex crimes and their partners are in some cases felony-level sex offenders. "The State's interest in requiring minor parents to support their children overrides the State's competing interest in protecting juveniles from improvident acts, even when such acts may include criminal activity on the part of the other parent." That the young male may have been emotionally or physically harmed is virtually dismissed, outweighed by the cultural assumption that he should be a provider.

Looking at the general patterns of convictions demonstrate that while the number of male victims has risen, the numbers of women prosecuted has changed little, and the number of men prosecuted has risen. Cases involving pregnancy, in general, tend to reflect gendered assumptions: females are the victims, and males are the perpetrators, regardless of their respective ages. But these facts in and of themselves do not serve to illuminate whether or not stereotypes of gender are implicated in statutory rape prosecutions themselves and the discourses surrounding them. I turn at this point to three statutory rape cases of national prominence.

Case Studies: Implementation of Gender-Neutral Statutory Rape Laws

This section examines a heterosexual statutory rape, Mary Kay LeTourneau and her victim Vili Fualaau; a homosexual statutory rape, Stephen Simmons and his victim Samuel Manzie; and another case labeled "homosexual" but which was complicated by the perpetrator's flexible construction of gender, that of Sharon Clark/Sean O'Neill. The differences between the types of cases lies in the way in which the female perpetrator, LeTourneau, was treated not so much as a sexual predator but more as an oddity with mental problems—she fell outside a cultural narrative of females as sexually passive rather than sexually active. As such, the discourses describing LeTourneau and Simmons, who by law had committed the same crime, were quite different because of the assumptions made about Simmons; namely, that he was predatory based on both his gender and his sexuality. O'Neill, a transgendered person with vaginal sex organs who identifies as male, was treated less like LeTourneau and more like Simmons. While he stood outside the boundaries of gender as a sexual agent like LeTourneau, his sexual activities themselves as well as and what was labeled his "homosexuality" masculinized him. The implications of this are discussed in the conclusion.

Case 1: State of Washington v. Mary Kay LeTourneau

The arrest and re-arrest of Washington teacher Mary Kay LeTourneau in 1997, and the extensive coverage surrounding it, provide an opportunity to look at the language used to describe a relationship between an older female and younger male. Her first arrest on statutory rape charges ended in a suspended 89-month prison term, completion of a three-year sex offender treatment program, and avoiding all contact with minors (including Vili Fualaau, the victim). For a repeat statutory rape offender, to serve no jail time is extremely unusual. Her second arrest, after she violated these terms by seeing Fualaau and indeed becoming pregnant with their second child, resulted in the 89-month sentence being imposed.

In television interviews, Fualaau objected to being called a victim although he was thirteen at the time of the initial offense. He told of his pursuit of LeTourneau which she at first resisted, and professed his love for her and his willingness to wait to be able to be with her. He wrote a book in 1998, "Only One Crime, Love," that was published in France. His own mother pleaded with the judge not to sentence LeTourneau to prison. In the spring of 2001, Fualaau noted that he was about to turn 18, and was hopeful that prison officials would allow him to marry LeTourneau.

In reviewing newspaper articles (including some from foreign presses), magazine articles, transcripts of several television news items from CNN, NBC, and ABC, as well as an hour-long installment of "Oprah," it appears that, somewhat like the discourse on infanticide, women "offenders" are more subject to solely medicalized language than their male counterparts, who tend to be described with a mixture of medical and criminal terms. Her lawyer's main argument, repeated frequently, was that, "Mary still does need treatment . . . locking her up is not going to cure her and, in fact, could cause her delusional beliefs and the boy's to continue to grow. . . A developmentally disabled person cannot be held responsible for some of their actions . . . she needs some help, she needs some extra supervision." A number of therapists echoed this view: Roger Wolf, a Washington State Sex Offender Treatment Specialist, said "What we're dealing with here is obviously not 'love' as most people define it. . . . We treat this as just another cognitive disorder." Robert Kolodny, a Sexologist at Behavioral Medicine Institute, commented, "To behave in such a dangerous way, one would think this woman is indeed psychologically unstable. We are talking about someone who needs professional care."

When LeTourneau pled guilty the first time she was arrested, she used this same language—apparently in order to receive a more lenient sentence. After her second arrest and during her interview on "Oprah," she said that she preferred being in jail and being "true" to herself, rather than pretending in the sex offender program that she felt remorseful and wanted treatment. LeTourneau wrote in

January 2000 on a website dedicated to her point of view, "If the most merited psychologists are saying that I have no psychiatric or psychological disorder or illness . . . then why is it so uncomfortable for some people to accept that there was and is nothing 'wrong' with me?" The answer appears to be that to accept that she is not unusual would be to interrogate a traditional cultural stereotype of what female sexuality is or should be like.

The word "abuse" occurs less frequently in these sources than in the example below in which the older party was male. She is portrayed more as influential and exploitative seducer than coercive or violent abuser. This appears to reach back to a construction of a woman as a temptress, who while invested with sexuality still required a male to act. Such a narrative withstands the language used for men who commit the same crime—that of pedophilia.

Case 2: State of New Jersey v. Stephen Simmons

In September 1997, 11-year-old Edward Werner was killed by 15-year-old Samuel Manzie in New Jersey. It was soon revealed that over a period of several months, the latter had frequent phone and email contact with and was "sexually abused . . . by [Stephen Simmons, 43] who lured him from an on-line chat room [for gay men]." Manzie's parents found out, forced him to end the relationship, and sent him to counseling. The police enlisted the teen's help to entrap Simmons; and Manzie went along briefly with the plan, but eventually smashed the recording equipment, refusing to cooperate further. His parents first forced him to stay in a shelter for teen runaways and then tried to have him committed to long-term psychiatric care—the hospital refused; and a few days later he sexually assaulted and killed Werner. In a 20/20 interview with Barbara Walters, Manzie's parents admitted that their son knew that they found homosexuality to be contrary to the teachings of their church, but could not understand why he had suddenly become withdrawn after they forced him to end the relationship. They were similarly puzzled by his violent behavior after he had appeared to cooperate with the police to arrest Simmons. They sought to place the blame for their son's disrespectful behavior, disturbed mental state, and murder of the boy on two sources: the psychiatric unit that refused to accept Manzie into their program, and Simmons. Walters commented to Hugh Downs that the puzzle remained, "Here are two parents who seemed to do everything for their son. What happened?"

Simmons was charged under New Jersey's gender-neutral statutory rape law, among others. The potential penalty for his nine offenses totaled 46 years. Manzie, on the other hand, had committed murder which had a potential sentence of 30 years. One typical front-page article noted that the teen was not forced to have sex, yet referred to Simmons as "the pedophile" four times, roughly the same number of times he was referred to by his last name. While using the subject's last name is journalistic convention, using the term "pedophile" reinforces the repeatedly constructed link between homosexuality and pedophilia that is unshaken by evidence to the contrary. At Simmons' sentencing hearing, Manzie told the judge as he refused to testify against Simmons, "I would like to shed some light on my relationship with Simmons. It was a good one. . . . Please keep in mind that he never forced me to do more than I wanted to, and please keep in mind that I never regretted the relationship." While the prosecutor did note how "clever" Manzie was in setting up meetings with Simmons, the assistant prosecutor dismissed this agency, saying "Mr. Simmons committed a criminal act which we believe not only victimized Sam Manzie but was also an assault on our society."

In both the Simmons and LeTourneau cases, the victims asserted that they were active and willing participants in the sexual activity. But in striking difference from the LeTourneau case is the use of the terms "sexual assault" and "sexual abuse" in every article on the Simmons case. A typical article on LeTourneau is titled "Lovesick" or "Statutory Rape: A Love Story;" a typical article on Simmons is titled "Pedophile Admits He Abused Young Killer." Simmons was not portrayed as having some sort of medical disorder; he was merely a violent offender, assumed to have indirectly caused a murder, facing jail time. He was not given the possibility of outpatient treatment as was LeTourneau. No feature articles were written about whether or not he was a sympathetic figure in love with Manzie (or vice versa). By the same token, LeTourneau was never referred to as a pedophile although Fualaau was actually younger than Manzie. It appears as if the homosexual nature of the sexual encounters feminized Manzie; during Simmons' prosecution while it was assumed that LeTourneau's victim was a sexual agent, it was assumed that Simmons' was not.

But the above cases do not appear readily able to tell us much about statutory rape cases involving a female perpetrator with a female victim. Given that the laws prohibit sexual intercourse, are there such cases? If so, would a "lesbian" perpetrator be treated in media coverage as more like LeTourneau or more like Simmons?

Case 3: State of Colorado v. Sharon Clark [Sean O'Neill]

While it is not difficult to find statutory rape cases in which males have been charged for statutory rape of young females, and there are a small but increasing number of cases involving females charged for statutory rape of young males, there is but one accessible case over the last decade that involves two females—and the perpetrator, Sean O'Neill, would undoubtedly say that this characterization of him would not be accurate. Because the laws as written criminalize sexual intercourse; i.e., penetration of a vagina by a penis, a female perpetrator would not technically fit into this legal definition of the crime. She could be charged with statutory sodomy (or oral copulation depending on the phrasing used by that state), or perhaps under a sexual contact law that includes digital or object penetration. The lack of such cases in itself serves to remind us of the limits of legal language, of the heterosexual assumptions of the laws, and of the strict gender stereotypes enshrined by rape and statutory rape laws in particular.

In Colorado in 1994, 19-year old Sean O'Neill was prosecuted for having sexual relationships with four young females, two of whom were underage. "The parents [of the females] made no objection to the relationship, until it emerged that Sean had a vagina and the relationship was 'lesbian.'" Apparently, he had "posed as a 17-year-old boy to woo young girls into sexual encounters." Born Sharon Clark, O'Neill was in the end charged with twelve counts of sexual assault, sexual assault on a child, and criminal impersonation (having represented himself as a male rather than a female), crimes that together could have brought him almost 50 years in prison. Recall that Simmons' potential penalty for nine counts could have brought him 46 years in jail; LeTourneau's potential penalty was at first a probated seven and one-half years, imposed only when she violated the terms of the probation.

Each of the females, who apparently did not want to prosecute, stated that they never suspected that Sean "was a woman." One recalled at trial, "She had her shirt off, had her jeans on, and had a condom and was putting it on herself." Another testified that "during the fifty or so sexual encounters, the defendant never removed his shirt completely and that she never saw a penis, but felt it;" she later said that she had performed oral sex on him. Most of the news coverage identified O'Neill as "Clark" or "Ms. Clark," and when using pronouns such as "he," tended to put them in quotation marks. A typical headline read "Woman Accused of Playing Boyfriend to Girls."

"I don't call myself gay or straight. I consider myself in the masculine form," said O'Neill. Because he identified as male, but did not identify as lesbian or transgendered, it is difficult to make generalizations from this case about how a perpetrator who claimed such an identity might be treated. It seems though that the use of an object for penetration, coupled with a fluid sense of gender identity, both masculinized and queered O'Neill for the purposes of statutory rape prosecution, "During cross examination and closing arguments the DA repeatedly cast Sean as a dangerous predator, a pedophile of the worst sort, driven to sexual relations with 'children.'" Noted only once as he was characterized this way was O'Neill's physical appearance: he was less than five feet tall, and weighed less than one hundred pounds.

His lawyer remarked, "The disparate treatment between transsexuals and 'normal' sex offenders makes it that much easier for the prosecution to stack and maximize the charges. . . . The simple fact of a defendant's being transgendered dramatically shrinks the 'presumption of innocence,' impossibly complicating any chance of mounting a fair and effective defense." As in the Simmons and LeTourneau cases, the victims did not want to prosecute, but the language surrounding this case is much more similar to that of Simmons' crime than that of LeTourneau's. O'Neill was not assumed to be a "sick" heterosexual female like LeTourneau, with her mental illness explaining how she could stand outside gendered boundaries as a female sexual agent. Rather, he was assumed to be a lesbian, with his sexuality itself placing him outside the boundaries of femaleness and enabling his sexual agency.

O'Neill's sexuality and his gender were collapsed so that he was constructed not as a transperson, but rather as homosexual and as male, both suspect categories in statutory rape prosecutions. Indeed, the legal director of the Lambda Legal Defense and Education Fund commented that statutory rape cases in which the parties are close in age are more likely to be prosecuted when the parties are of the same sex. In statutory rape prosecutions, one who is deemed outside of constructed boundaries of gender and sexuality is considered deviant.

Conclusions: Gender-Neutral Statutory Rape Laws

These case studies have served to point out the small yet telling differences between depictions of Mary Kay LeTourneau and Stephen Simmons, who had committed the same crime—statutory rape of a teenage male. The language used to describe Sean O'Neill was closer to that used to describe Simmons. LeTourneau, female and heterosexual, was constructed as "sick," "fixated," and needing treatment; Simmons and O'Neill as homosexual and "predatory pedophiles" who deserved long jail sentences for "assault." "The reason anyone even questions whether LeTourneau is a pedophile is clear: she is a woman. Had a thirty-five year old male teacher impregnated a thirteen year old student, would late night talk show hosts really be making wink wink jokes about high-fiving the victim in the halls? It is the typical double standard: when a man commits adultery, it is assumed he did it for the sex. When a woman does, we assume she did it for love."

As Kincaid notes, "Our culture has produced a story of molestation that is not only widely believed, but, more important, widely sanctioned, and, more important still, widely circulated. According to this story. . . . They are all male, maladjusted or sick (but criminal certainly), violent and dangerous. . . ." Simmons, as a male, and O'Neill, as a transperson, were fit into this narrative while LeTourneau was not. A few sources noted the apparent consensuality of these sets of sexual relationships, and used feature stories as a means by which to probe sexual abuse. The gender-neutrality of the laws does not appear to erase the idea of young women as victims of predatory older men; indeed, O'Neill's case was forced into that box. It adds young males to the protected class but gives more credence to their claim if their sex partner is male. Gender stereotypes remain, regardless of the changes in legal language, to describe both the victims and the perpetrators.

Liberal feminists' goals for gender-neutral statutory rape laws—that they would enshrine gender equality into law and thus dismantle stereotypes of female sexuality as passive and male sexuality as aggressive—may have been unfortunately too ambitious, particularly in a climate in which homosexuality is still often constructed as suspect. Rather, the criticism by feminist sex radicals that such laws might essentialize young people as victims, punish

consensual sex, and single out homosexual relationships may prove to be more accurate. It appears that the reconstruction of the category of gender and its meaning vis-à-vis sexuality is a longer and more complex process than can be accomplished through amendments to laws on the books. The question remains as to how to move that process forward as quickly and comprehensively as possible.

Carolyn E. Cocca is the author of *Jailbait: The Politics of Statutory Rape in the United States.*

EXPLORING THE ISSUE

Are Statutory Rape Laws Effective at Protecting Minors?

Critical Thinking and Reflection

1. What are some arguments made in each side with which you agree or disagree?
2. What are the strengths and weaknesses of the two positions made in this chapter?
3. Pick the side with which you most agree. What are some additional arguments you would make to strengthen the case for or against statutory rape laws?
4. Think more broadly of the issue of statutory rape laws. What is required to give consent to sexual behavior and what age or ages are clearly fair criteria in making sex illegal?

Is There Common Ground?

Both authors in this chapter would not want someone to engage in sex with someone with which they have not consented. However, drawing this line is difficult. While age is one criteria for consent, what are some others? How mature should a person be (which is not always tied directly to age)? How much should a person know about sexually transmitted infections and their prevention? How much should a person know about pregnancy prevention? How should a person evaluate whether they are ready to have sex?

Additional Resources

Carolyn Cocca, *Jailbait: The Politics of Statutory Rape Laws in the United States* (2004)

Asaph Glosser, et. al., *Statutory Rape: A Guide to State Laws and Reporting Requirements (Department of Health and Human Services)*, 2004

Judith Levine, *Harmful to Minors: The Perils of Protecting Our Children from Sex* (2003)

Create Central

www.mhhe.com/createcentral

Internet References . . .

Find Law: Statutory Rape

http://criminal.findlaw.com/criminal-charges/
statutory-rape.html

National Sexual Violence Resource Center

www.nsvrc.org/publications/taxonomy/term/41

State Legislators' Handbook for Statutory Rape Issues

www.ojp.gov/ovc/publications/infores/statutoryrape/
handbook/

Selected, Edited, and with Issue Framing Material by:
David M. Hall, PhD, *Delaware Valley College*

ISSUE

Do Reality Television Shows Have a Negative Influence on Teenage Pregnancy and Parenting?

YES: Jessica Isner, Annie Koval, and Lisa Paul, from "True-Life Teen Moms, Experts Say MTV's 'Reality' Off the Mark," *NWI Parent* (March 9, 2011)

NO: The National Campaign to Prevent Teen and Unplanned Pregnancy, from "Evaluating the Impact of MTV's *16 and Pregnant* on Teen Viewers' Attitudes About Teen Pregnancy," *Science Says* (October 2010)

Learning Outcomes

After reading this issue, you will be able to:

- Identify critical research about the impact of reality television on teenage parenting.
- Compare and contrast the major research cited and analysis used in examining the impact of reality television on teenage pregnancy and parenting.
- Evaluate the impact of reality television on the larger spirit of teen behavior and decision making.

ISSUE SUMMARY

YES: Jessica Isner, Annie Koval, and Lisa Paul wrote this article for *NWI Parent*, which advertises that their publication provides "Real Solutions for Real Families." The authors are concerned that MTV's episodes related to teenage parenthood fail to capture accurately the true challenges of teenage parenthood.

NO: The National Campaign to Prevent Teen and Unplanned Pregnancy is dedicated to reducing teenage pregnancy. Their research reveals that teenagers who watch *16 and Pregnant* are more likely to express a negative view about the ways in which parenthood affects a teen's life.

$\mathbf{S}$ome people claim that the first reality show was *Candid Camera*, a show that dates back to the late 1940s, and was intended to catch people in mildly embarrassing situations. Allen Funt said that *Candid Camera* "caught people in the act of being themselves." A modern-day version of that would be *America's Funniest Home Videos*. On both shows, participants might be mildly embarrassed at having been caught getting frustrated in an encounter, but it did not result in the kind of shame that would be experienced by the participants in some of today's reality television shows.

A show from the 1950s, *Queen for a Day,* had housewives talk about how difficult their lives were with all of their children. Whoever had the worst life won a wide variety of cleaning products and appliances intended to save her time and make her life easier. Other shows exist today that intend to make viewers feel better for helping someone whose life is in a difficult position. *Extreme Makeover Home Edition* captures this very concept.

However, reality television began to change. Robert Thompson, director of the Center for the Study of Popular Television at Syracuse University, explains that reality television is "a new way of telling a story which [is] half fiction—the producers and creators set up a universe, they give it rules, they make a setting, they cast it according to specific guidelines as to who they think are going to provide good pyrotechnics. But then they bring in non-actors with no scripts and allow this kind of improvisation like a jazz piece to occur."

Reality television took on increasing popularity when MTV debuted *The Real World* during the 1990s. Less than a decade later, competitive reality television would emerge in a genre significantly different from *Star Search*. Huge ratings were realized by a reality television show, *Survivor*. *Survivor* had viewers transfixed over contestants catching and eating rats, treachery toward best friends, illicit romance, and attempts to capture the $1,000,000 prize.

The success of *Survivor* would have major implications for television programming. All of a sudden, all you needed was a film crew and production costs. There was no negotiating with stars about what they should get paid. There were people who just wanted to be on television, who just wanted a chance to win the big monetary prize, or who thought that they could turn their reality-show appearance into wider fame.

Indeed, some have done just that. From *Jersey Shore*, Snooki and the Situation are reported to earn $10,000–$30,000 per episode. Snooki is reported to earn an additional $20,000 per appearance to attend events or speak in public. The Situation is reported to earn millions of dollars per year.

Reality television, by some estimates, makes up 17 percent of the programming on television. Research about the most successful reality television series shows that they have three elements: curiosity, family, and social contact. Additional popular themes for viewers of reality television include romance, idealism, and honor. Think of the reality shows that you have watched. Are these characteristics present in the shows that you have watched most?

If you were to write a reality show to be popular based on these criteria what topic might it be about? Would that topic be merely entertaining, or would it have a positive impact on society? In what ways might there be a conflict with giving viewers what they want and creating a show that reinforces good and positive messages?

There was a time when people had to achieve something in order to become famous. They had to exceed at athletics, acting, singing, or playing an instrument. Or at least they had a lucky break, with the right person seeing them perform, leading to stardom.

Today, that is no longer required. A few people achieve stardom merely by the reality television camera turning its lens their way. In some cases, fame is achieved for what is commonly regarded as wrong, or even outrageous, behavior.

If we live in a society that tends to have a negative view of teenage pregnancy and parenthood, what level of interest would there be in television shows that highlight teenage pregnancy? Let's revisit the characteristics that researchers say viewers most want in reality television. Would a television show about teenage mothers have the most desired characteristics of reality television? Curiosity? Yes, for those who do not personally know teen parents. Family? Absolutely. Social contact? Clearly. Romance? There is room for that—or the absence of it—in these episodes. Idealism? Without question. Honor? Certainly.

Many people believe that reality television tends to be morally wrong. Indeed, just think about what was considered objectionable when *Survivor* first aired. Today, reality television often becomes increasingly controversial, with stars who stand out, often due to their outrageous behavior.

So television shows about teenage parents meet all the criteria that research shows the public wants in reality television. Now that we know the market exists, the next question to ask is, what is the impact that such shows have on teenage sexual decision making and behavior?

Some child development experts say that the adolescent brain is not properly wired for putting reality television into context. Others say that it is like any other form of media: Most children put it in the proper context, while just some do not.

Of course, if they are copying mannerisms, such as being rude to a friend, that is unkind, but not as life-changing as pregnancy and parenthood.

If you watch reality television, what shows have they been? What impact have these shows had on you? Have they influenced your behavior for the better? For the worse? Have the changed your awareness about certain issues? Have any reality shows encouraged you to make bad decisions? Have they encouraged you to make good decisions?

The articles in this issue make competing arguments about the influence of shows about teenage parenting and pregnancy. One article is a compelling opinion piece, while the other contains thoughtfully conducted research.

YES

Jessica Isner,
Annie Koval, and Lisa Paul

True-Life Teen Moms, Expert Say MTV's "Reality" Off the Mark

Once upon a time, Kelsey Kruse was an average high school sophomore in Yorkville.

She was a good Catholic, a good student, and she was dating a star athlete in the senior class. Technically, she wasn't allowed to date until she was 16, but that wasn't a problem—until she got pregnant.

Now a 19-year-old student and mother of two-year-old Halle, Kruse vividly recalls what it was like to be a pregnant teenager. And she can promise it was nothing like MTV portrays it on shows such as "Teen Mom" and "16 & Pregnant."

Kruse feels as though MTV stars like Amber Portwood and Jenelle Evans do not offer a realistic glimpse of young motherhood. Unfortunately, these shows have become so prominent on today's pop culture spectrum that Kruse worries they could be leading young high school students to believe that teen pregnancy is far more glamorous—and easy—than it actually is.

"These girls are living the life right now—they're being paid to get pregnant and have kids," she said. "To a teenage girl, that sounds pretty cool: I'm just going to get pregnant, go on one of these shows, and I'm going to be famous."

Kruse fears that the overexposure of teen pregnancy in the media could subtly encourage high school girls to get pregnant long before they are ready.

"It influences teens when [they] see their favorite celebrity out partying and drinking," she said. "When you see them shopping somewhere, you want to shop there. Celebrities being pregnant is no different from them doing those other things."

Teens today consume more media and are more tech savvy than ever, said Julie Dobrow, director of communications and media studies at Tufts University in Medford, MA.

"Media are an important source of information for teens about some topics," she said. "Particularly, things like sex—which are not taught well in school—are difficult for many to speak about with their parents and are embarrassing for them to talk about at all."

Whether teens are talking about it at home, pregnancy seems to be inescapable in the media. In recent years, young motherhood has become a pop culture trend, and this has not been lost on teens, said Emilie Zaslow, assistant professor of communication studies at Pace University in New York City.

"Generally, the research shows that there is not a direct link between media and behavior," she said, "but there is strong evidence that media does have an influence on attitudes and values, and how we see the world."

Some experts said that teens have the wherewithal to be critical of the media and make their own decisions, regardless of what they consume.

In other words, teens are not easily manipulated, suggested Eitan Schwarz, an adolescent and pediatric psychiatrist in Skokie.

"Media isn't a cause and effect—it's an indirect thing," he said. "Media doesn't cause anything. On the other hand, media tends to amplify things."

Schwarz suggested teenagers with low self-esteem could be more susceptible to the media's messages concerning pregnancy.

"Some of these girls want to have a baby because they want someone to love them—they are looking for love—and they are wanting it from the baby," he said. "Many times, these girls don't really have a lot to give because they want stuff for themselves—and that's not an equation that works for the baby or for mothers, either."

Still, there has been no conclusive evidence regarding the ways in which teens are influenced by specific television programming. National Campaign to Prevent Teen and Unplanned Pregnancy conducted a survey that found 82 percent of teens mentioned MTV's "Teen Mom" as a deterrent for teen pregnancy.

But 21-year-old student Matt Bridge, the father of Kruse's child, said society glorifies teen pregnancy, even if it doesn't necessarily encourage it.

"It portrays it like, 'Hey, if you get pregnant, your life is going to be a golden road because we're going to reward you for it,'" he said. "It seems like you get rewarded these days for being a teen and getting pregnant, when really it's not a good thing—if you don't get lucky and you're not one out of a million to get on that show."

Some organizations are seizing this opportunity to change the ways in which teenagers learn about safe sex, said Shireen Schrock, the community education director for Planned Parenthood of Illinois. TV shows and movies provide parents with the opportunity to have an open dialogue with their kids about sex.

"We are trying to use that to encourage parents, on an ongoing basis, to look for those teachable moments where they can have conversations about sexuality," she said. "Those TV shows and movies have actually really opened up those teachable moments and those conversations, which is a good thing."

But Zaslow suggested this type of discussion should begin in classrooms because media education is limited in our country, compared with the United Kingdom and Canada.

"The United States has some of the worst media education," she said. "And it is because we are the biggest producers of media—[producers] have a large strong hold."

Being able to determine fact versus fiction in terms of media messages is integral to adolescent decision-making.

"We want to work with young people about developing a filter for some of those media messages because we know that there are lots of different messages in the media about teen pregnancy," Schrock said. "We would like to use those TV shows as a way to help teens talk about real life and get them to really start thinking about how it would affect their own life in applying it."

To start, Kruse encouraged using education to defeat age-old stereotypes of teen mothers, many of which are perpetuated on TV.

"Just because you got pregnant at a young age, you can still go to college," Kruse said. "You can still have a good career, you can still have a good life for yourself.

Getting pregnant at a young age doesn't mean your life's over."

Jessica Isner, Annie Koval and **Lisa Paul** wrote this article for *NWI Parent,* which advertises that their publication provides Real Solutions for Real Families. The authors are concerned that MTV's episodes related to teenage parenthood fail to accurately capture the true challenges of teenage parenthood.

The National Campaign to Prevent
Teen and Unplanned Pregnancy

 **NO**

Evaluating the Impact of MTV's *16 and Pregnant* on Teen Viewers' Attitudes About Teen Pregnancy

Media Use

- American children ages 11–14 spend approximately 8 hours and 40 minutes with media every day—more than 5 hours are spent watching television.
- Teens age 15–18 spend nearly 8 hours with media every day—4 hours and 22 minutes are spent watching television.

Teens' Perspectives

New polling data, from a nationally representative survey commissioned by The National Campaign, asked teens their opinions on media and teen pregnancy and their views about *16 and Pregnant*. Findings from young people ages 12–19 include:

- Six in ten teens have watched at least some of *16 and Pregnant*.
- Among those teens who have watched the show, 82% think that the show helps teens better understand the challenges of teen pregnancy and parenthood, compared to 15% who believe that it glamorizes teen pregnancy.
- In addition, the clear majority of teen boys (67%) and girls (79%) agree with the statement, "When a TV show or character I like deals with teen pregnancy, it makes me think more about my own risk (of becoming pregnant/causing a pregnancy) and how to avoid it."

Introduction

Concerns exist about the sexual content in popular media and the influence these images and messages might have on young people's sexual behavior. Sexual content in the media has increased over the past several decades, and research has found that the sexual content in media can influence teens, attitudes about sex and contraception, and may also influence their sexual behavior. In fact, research has documented an association between exposure to sexual content on television and teen pregnancy.

Little research, however, has been conducted to better understand how media might also have positive effects

by, for example, decreasing risky sexual behavior and promoting healthier decisions among teens. Given that teens' use of media has increased over the past decade, and that the amount of sexual content in the media has also increased, it is reasonable to explore whether media might be used to help prevent teen pregnancy.

This *Science Says* presents results from an evaluation study designed to learn more about how watching and discussing episodes of the popular MTV documentary-style reality show *16 and Pregnant* influences teens, perceptions of getting pregnant, and becoming a parent at a young age. The document also includes new public opinion data that shed light on teens, perceptions of *16 and Pregnant*, in particular, and their views about how media might influence teens, decisions about sex more generally. Complete results from this new public opinion survey of both teens and adults will be available soon in a Campaign report entitled "With One Voice 2010."

About the Evaluation

The National Campaign worked with innovation, Research, and Training, Inc. (iRT) to learn more about teens, perceptions of the show *16 and Pregnant*, and whether or not watching and discussing the show affected their attitudes about teen pregnancy. In partnership with the Boys & Girls Clubs of America (see more information below), 18 clubs in one southern state participated in this research study. The clubs were randomly assigned to either see the episodes (treatment = nine clubs) or not (control = nine clubs). All participants obtained parental consent and completed questionnaires at baseline and again a week later. Teens in the treatment groups viewed three episodes of the first season of *16 and Pregnant* (the "Maci," "Amber," and "Ebony" episodes). Boys & Girls Club members watched one episode per day and the episodes were shown in different orders at different clubs. A group leader led a discussion of the shows with the teens each day. Control group teens did not view or discuss the episodes at the clubs, but did complete the pre- and post-test questionnaires.

A total of 162 teens participated and completed both the pre- and post-test questionnaires (78 from the control group and 84 from the treatment group). The average age of the participants was 13.5 years, ranging from 10 to 19 years. . . . Most participants were female (62%), and three-quarters (75%) were African American. Nearly three-quarters of all participants (73%) received reduced or free lunch at school. About one-third (34%) of the participants reported having had sex.

Television Shows vs. Prevention Programs

Television and other media alone do not cause—and cannot prevent—teen pregnancy. However, entertainment media can reach millions of teens with important messages about teen pregnancy. It is important to note that there is a critical distinction between this evaluation—which attempts to understand teens, views about teen pregnancy as a result of watching and discussing MTV's *16 and Pregnant*—versus an impact evaluation of a prevention program whose sole purpose is to reduce teen pregnancy. While evidence-based teen pregnancy prevention programs are guided by specific behavioral theories and have the explicit goal of changing behavior to reduce risk of teen pregnancy, television shows such as *16 and Pregnant* are created for entertainment with the goal of attracting viewers and keeping them engaged.

Key Findings

- *16 and Pregnant* got teens talking and thinking about teen pregnancy. The majority of teens who watched and discussed the show in a group also later talked to a friend about the show. More than one-third—40%—talked to a parent afterward and about one-third spoke to a sibling or girlfriend/boyfriend. Clearly, this show is an excellent conversation-starter for teens.
- The more teens talked about the show, the less likely they were to think that teen pregnancy and teen parenthood are commonplace, or to agree with the statement, "Most teens want to get pregnant." Parents and practitioners should be encouraged to talk about this show (and others like it) to the teens in their lives to help ensure that these young people know what the adults in their lives think about these shows and their messages.
- The teens in this study enjoyed watching and discussing the *16 and Pregnant* episodes and thought that the show was realistic. Neither the boys nor girls who watched the episodes wanted to imitate the teens in the episodes they watched. In fact, nearly all teens (93%) who watched the show agreed (53% strongly agreed) with the statement: "I learned that teen parenthood is harder than I imagined from these episodes." Although some have claimed that the show "glamorizes" teen pregnancy, the findings from this evaluation and the polling data noted above show that teens do not share that view.

Other Findings

A number of other findings emerged from this study. Analysis of the pre- and post-test questionnaires determined that regardless of whether or not they watched the episodes, girls had more realistic expectations than boys did about teen parenthood. In particular, many girls felt that becoming a teen parent would make it hard for them to finish high school, to attend college, and to achieve future career goals. Research shows that fewer than four in ten mothers who have a child before they turn 18 earn a high school diploma by age 22. Overall, girls disagreed more strongly than boys with the notion that becoming a teen parent would help to get their lives on track. Teen boys were less likely than the girls to believe that teen parenthood would have a negative impact on their educational or career goals.

In addition, teens who saw and discussed the episodes reported that they enjoyed watching and talking about the show and that they learned something new from doing so. The more they liked it, the more likely they were to have negative views about teen pregnancy.

Teens were eager to recommend the show to others; 89% of participants agreed (56% of those strongly agreed) with the statement: "I think all teenagers should watch a show like this." Many said they would recommend that friends participate in the discussion, too.

Cautionary Note

A few findings from the evaluation suggest that viewing *16 and Pregnant* could have an undesirable effect on some viewers. More specifically, teens who watched and discussed the episodes were more likely to believe that teens do want to get pregnant, compared to those in the group who did not watch or discuss the episodes. Note that discussing the episodes later with a friend seemed to moderate this finding somewhat. Also, among teens who had never had sex, those who viewed and discussed the episodes were more likely than those who had not to believe that most teens want to get pregnant, and that if they were to get pregnant or cause a pregnancy, that they "will be with the baby's mother/father forever."

In addition, regardless of whether they watched and discussed the episodes or not, sexually experienced teens were more likely than those teens who had not had sex to think that if they became a teen parent, their parents would help them raise the baby. Sexually experienced teens were also more likely to believe that people would view them as more mature if they had a child as a teen.

What It All Means

These types of shows reach a large number of teens and can be used in a positive way. The results of this project clearly support the idea that teens are interested in watching and discussing reality television shows about teen pregnancy, and that messages about the realities of teen pregnancy and parenting in these shows can influence teens, attitudes about the challenges of teen parenthood. Given the popularity of these shows, their messages clearly reach a large number of teens. For all these reasons, adults who work with teens should consider viewing and discussing episodes of such shows in their activities or programs that are designed to help reduce teen pregnancy and/or foster positive youth development more broadly.

Parents should use these shows to help them talk to their teens about sex, love, and relationships. According to the new polling data noted above, three-quarters of teens and adults agree that stories and events in TV shows and other media can be a good way to start conversations about sex, love, and relationships. This project provides further evidence to suggest that documentary-style shows, presented in ways that are appealing and interesting to teens, can be a useful way to start these conversations. Parents should be encouraged to watch these shows with their teens and use the story lines to openly discuss the challenges typically brought on by too-early pregnancy and parenthood.

If teens express positive views about teen pregnancy, talk to them about the benefits of waiting to start a family. Some teens might see pregnancy and parenthood as something that would make them seem more mature, would help them get their life on track, or would be a way to keep a boyfriend/girlfriend. It is crucial for parents and other adults to acknowledge that parenthood can be positive and rewarding, but that babies need and deserve adult parents, and that getting an education and having a stable, long-term partner can help them become good parents.

Groups such as Boys & Girls Clubs of America (BGCA) can play a valuable role in efforts to reduce teen pregnancy. The evaluation study summarized here shows that groups like the BGCA can be valuable leaders in preventing teen pregnancy because they work with many young people who are at high risk of teen pregnancy. Many of the BGCA facilitators enjoyed the sessions described here, although it is also true that some felt unprepared to lead the discussions. Training group discussion leaders could help to ensure that they feel comfortable in discussing the risks and problems associated with teen pregnancy and parenthood, and in dispelling the idea that teen pregnancy happens to most teen girls (it does not) or that early parenthood is a good way to get a teen's life on track. There is value in enlisting the help of health educators and experts in health communications who are well versed in adolescent development and youth culture particularly for community partners who may not be familiar with current media or with the topic of teen pregnancy.

THE NATIONAL CAMPAIGN TO PREVENT TEEN AND UNPLANNED PREGNANCY is dedicated to reducing teenage pregnancy. Their research reveals that teenagers who watch MTV's *16 and Pregnant* are more likely to express a negative view about the ways in which parenthood impacts a teen's life.

EXPLORING THE ISSUE

Do Reality Television Shows Have a Negative Influence on Teenage Pregnancy and Parenting?

Critical Thinking and Reflection

1. What are some arguments made by each side with which you agree or disagree?
2. What are the strengths and weaknesses of the two positions made in this issue? Compare and contrast the competing arguments made about reality television's impact on teens. What conclusions do you reach about the different narratives and research?
3. Think more broadly about the amount of reality television and teen parenthood. What is the impact in the end on how teenagers think about their long-term goals and behaviors?

Is There Common Ground?

While programming constantly changes, it is safe to assume that reality television, due to its low production costs, will remain a popular choice for television programmers. We may not all agree on the impact of such shows, but most would agree that we want children to be literate, aware, and thoughtful of the media that they are consuming. Chances are that much of the programming will become increasingly outrageous. What are adults doing to help children and adolescents navigate those messages? Should we teach critical media literacy in schools? In the home? How do we help children and adolescents put these shows into their proper perspective?

Additional Resources

"Why America Loves Reality TV" from *Psychology Today:* www.psychologytoday.com/articles/200109/why-america-loves-reality-tv

Reality TV World: www.realitytvworld.com/

The Case for Reality TV: www.theatlantic.com/magazine/archive/2007/05/the-case-for-reality-tv/5791/

The New Yorker: "Reality Television and American Culture": www.newyorker.com/arts/critics/atlarge/2011/05/09/110509crat_atlarge_sanneh

Create Central

www.mhhe.com/createcentral

Internet References . . .

National Campaign to Prevent Teen Pregnancy

www.thenationalcampaign.org/

Focus on the Family

www.focusonthefamily.org

CDC: Social Media and Teen Pregnancy

www.cdc.gov/TeenPregnancy/SocialMedia/

Selected, Edited, and with Issue Framing Material by:
David M. Hall, PhD, *Delaware Valley College*

ISSUE

Should There Be Harsh Penalties for Teens Sexting?

YES: Lisa E. Soronen, Nicole Vitale, and Karen A. Haase, from "Sexting at School: Lessons Learned the Hard Way," National School Boards Association, *Inquiry & Analysis* (February 2010)

NO: Julie Hilden, from "How Should Teens' 'Sexting'—The Sending of Revealing Photos—Be Regulated?" Findlaw.com (April 28, 2009)

Learning Outcomes
After reading this issue, you will be able to: • Identify arguments made for and against taking teen sexting seriously. • Compare and contrast the major arguments cited and analysis used in examining penalties for teen sexting. • Evaluate the ways in which teen sexting affects the lives of teens who participate.

ISSUE SUMMARY

YES: Lisa E. Soronen, Nicole Vitale, and Karen A. Haase are writing on legal issues for the National School Boards Association. This article encourages administrators to hand over cell phone sexting cases to the appropriate law enforcement agencies.

NO: Julie Hilden is a graduate of Harvard College and Yale Law School. A former clerk for Supreme Court Justice Stephen Breyer, she has more recently appeared on *Good Morning America*, Court TV, CNN, and NPR. Hilden argues that harsh penalties are extreme and unjust.

Sexting—the slang term for the use of a cell phone or other similar electronic device to distribute pictures or video of sexually explicit images. It can also refer to text messages of a sexually charged nature.

We know that teens participate in a significant amount of interaction electronically. In 2010, the average American teen, ages 13–17, sent 3,339 texts per month. This can be difficult for adults to understand, as they only send and receive approximately 10 text messages per day. As a result, a decidedly different level of communication occurs among teens while sending text messages.

Why do teens sext? Are the reasons similar? How often does it occur?

According to the National Campaign to Prevent Teen and Unplanned Pregnancy, this is how many teens ages 13–19 are engaging in sending or posting nude or seminude pictures or videos of themselves:

    20 percent of teens overall
    18 percent of teen boys

    22 percent of teen girls
    11 percent of young teen girls (ages 13–16)

How many teens are sending or posting sexually suggestive messages?

    39 percent of all teens.
    36 percent of teen girls.
    40 percent of teen boys.
    48 percent of teens say they have received such messages.

What accounts for the differences that we see in gender? Why are some teens not engaging in such behavior? Lack of technology? Personal morals? Lack of a trusted person to send such messages to? Once someone presses Send, these images can go anywhere, but who are the pictures, photos, and videos initially being sent to?

71 percent of girls and 67 percent of guys who have sent such images have directed them to their boyfriend or girlfriend.

21 percent of girls and 39 percent of boys have sent them to someone they wanted to hook up with or date.

15 percent have sent them to someone they only met online.

Do they understand the risks? They appear to. Over 70 percent of teens know that sending and posting such photos, videos, or messages "can have serious negative consequences."

Of course the biggest fear that most people have is that a person will share these images with others. How often does that occur?

44 percent of boys and girls say it is common for sexually explicit text messages to be shared with others.

36 percent of girls and 39 percent of boys say it is common for nude or seminude photos to be shared.

Does sexting affect their lives? Many say that it does. For example, 22 percent of teens say that they are more forward and aggressive via electronic communication than in real life; and 38 percent say it makes dating or hooking up more likely. In fact, 29 percent say that sending such messages means you are "expected" to date or hook up.

If that is the impact, what is the motivation? Over 60 percent say it is to be "fun or flirtatious." Over half of girls who send sexually explicit messages or photos were giving their significant other a "sexy present." Almost half sent them in response to something they had received. Even 40 percent of girls say that they sent such messages as a joke. One-third of girls do so to "feel sexy."

What about pressure from their peers? Fifty-one percent of girls say they send such messages due to pressure from a guy. Only 18 percent of teen boys report that pressure from a female. Close to one out of four teens post sexually explicit messages, photos, or videos as a result of being pressured by their friends.

If sexting is so common, what are some helpful guidelines to keep in mind when doing so? According to the National Campaign to Prevent Teen and Unplanned Pregnancy, these five steps should occur before pressing the Send button:

1. **Don't assume that anything you send or post will remain private.** Your messages and images will get passed around, even if you think they won't.

2. **There is no changing your mind in cyberspace—anything you send or post will never truly go away.** Something that seems fun and flirty on a whim will never really die. Potential employers, college recruiters, teachers, coaches, and parents, friends, enemies, strangers, and others may be able to find your past posts, even after you have deleted them.

3. **Don't give in to the pressure to do something that makes you uncomfortable, even in cyberspace.** Peer pressure is major motivation for sexting—a very bad motivation.

4. **Consider the recipient's reaction.** Not everyone will take the messages as you intend. For example, 40 percent of teen girls have sent a sexually explicit message as a joke, but 29 percent of boys take it as a sign that she wants to hook up or date.

5. **Nothing is truly anonymous.** Even if you think you are anonymous online, it may be easier to find you than you realize. Many people learn this the hard way when they think what they are doing will occur without their true identity ever being revealed.

It is not just teens. According to the American Association of Retired Persons (AARP), sexting is up among senior citizens. Relationship coach Susan Blake explains that seniors engage in sexting because they "want sexual activity. They want to flirt. It makes them feel healthy and young."

One senior citizen says that she likes to send sexually explicit messages because she feels that she has a "naughty secret. If you're sitting in a restaurant waiting for your food, you can just talk dirty to someone, and no one knows what you're doing. I would rather talk on the phone. But I'm also comfortable with hiding behind texting if I want to say something dirty."

However, senior citizens are not being charged with harsh penalties in response to their sexting. Teenagers, however, are sometimes finding that their lives will never be the same. Will harsh laws and a punishing adult reaction reduce the degree to which teens send sexually explicit messages? If not, what will?

In this issue, one side argues that schools need a harsh reaction to protect themselves. The opposing view is that we are being far too tough on teens with our treatment of them over sexting. See which argument you find most compelling.

YES

Lisa E. Soronen, Nicole Vitale,
and Karen A. Haase

Sexting at School: Lessons Learned the Hard Way

A 16-year-old boy asks his 15-year-old girlfriend to send him a naked photo of herself. She does so via text message, thinking that the photo will remain private and will show him how much she cares about him. Three weeks later, the couple breaks up, and her boyfriend forwards the text message to his friends, who quickly spread the image throughout the school. The girl is teased for months afterward, her grades plummet, and the formerly sunny teen refuses to go to school or to socialize with other students.

As many school attorneys and administrators know, this case is far from isolated. "Sexting," the practice by which teens forward sexually explicit images of themselves or their peers via text messaging, has become increasingly common nationwide. According to a frequently cited survey from the National Campaign to Prevent Teen and Unplanned Pregnancy, one in five teens have sent or posted nude or seminude photos of themselves online or via text message. Twenty-two percent of teens have received a nude or semi-nude photo of someone else. The study found that while most of the images are exchanged between boyfriends or girlfriends, 15 percent of teens have forwarded images to someone they only know online.

The potential detrimental effects that sexting can have on students are vast. Educators, child psychologists, and prosecutors agree that most teens do not understand the implications that sexting may have on their futures. While sexting often originates as a private exchange between a teen and his or her love interest, relationships can quickly deteriorate. Before long, the seemingly private images can be distributed throughout the school. These incidents can be highly embarrassing for students and, in some extreme cases, can have deadly consequences. At least two female students have committed suicide after the sexually explicit photos of themselves sent to a boy were disseminated to classmates. As discussed below, criminal prosecution—including being required to register as a sex offender—is another possible long-term negative consequence of sexting.

This article discusses a number of legal and practical issues related to sexting in schools. Specifically, this article discusses searching cell phones, what steps administrators can and should take upon discovering sexting, anti-sexting policies, and preventing sexting through education.

Searching Cell Phones

School administrators typically find out about sexting through the rumor mill. Of course, the only way administrators can determine if sexting actually has happened and who is involved is to ask students or to "see for themselves." In the ideal world, students will readily admit to being involved in sexting upon being questioned by administrators. In the real world, administrators may feel they need to search cell phones as part of a sexting investigation. Depending on the facts, searching a student's cell phone without a warrant may violate the Fourth Amendment. Likewise, it is at least arguable that searching open text messages on a cell phone without consent violates the Stored Communications Act. To avoid Fourth Amendment and Stored Communications Act issues, school administrators may always seek consent of a student and his or her parents before searching a cell phone as part of a sexting investigation.

Fourth Amendment Concerns

The U.S. Supreme Court held in *New Jersey v. T.L.O.* that school officials may search students as long as the search is reasonable; that is, the search must be justified at its inception and reasonable in scope. According to the Court:

> Under ordinary circumstances, a search of a student by a teacher or other school official will be "justified at its inception" when there are reasonable grounds for suspecting that the search will turn up evidence that the student has violated or is violating either the law or the rules of the school. Such a search will be permissible in its scope when the measures adopted are reasonably related to the objectives of the search and not excessively intrusive in light of the age and sex of the student and the nature of the infraction.

In no reported cases to date has a student challenged administrators searching his or her cell phone in a sexting investigation. However, in *Klump v. Nazareth Area School District*, a federal district court denied a school district's motion to dismiss on the basis of qualified immunity in a case involving a search of a student's cell phone. A teacher confiscated Christopher Klump's cell phone because he displayed the phone in violation of a school policy that prohibited the display or use of cell phones during school hours. The teacher and the assistant principal called other students in Christopher's phone directory to see if they were also violating district policy and accessed his text messages and voicemail.

Christopher asserted that these actions constituted an unreasonable search in violation of his Fourth Amendment rights. The court found that confiscation of the cell phone was justified because Christopher was caught violating the district's policy prohibiting the use or display of cell phones during school hours. However, the search of the cell phone violated Christopher's Fourth Amendment rights because: "They had no reason to suspect at the outset that such a search would reveal that Christopher Klump himself was violating another school policy; rather, they hoped to utilize his phone as a tool to catch other students, violations." The search of the cell phone, therefore, was not reasonable in scope.

It is not too difficult to imagine a fact pattern involving sexting where a school district could argue persuasively that an administrator's search of a student's text messages and pictures was justified at its inception and reasonable in scope. For example, let's say Christopher Klump showed an administrator an inappropriate picture a classmate texted him. As part of an investigation, the administrator should determine whether the named classmate actually sent Christopher the picture. It would seem a search of the classmate's text messages sent to Christopher Klump would be justified at its inception and reasonable in scope. Likewise, simply asking the classmate to present his cell phone to the administrator and calling the number in Christopher's phone associated with the text probably would be all the proof an administrator would need.

School administrators can take a few steps to make it more likely that searches of cell phones in sexting investigations pass Fourth Amendment muster. First, as described in the paragraph above, in some instances administrators can rely on information provided by technology—rather than just rumors—to determine whose phone to search and where to look. Second, while common sense indicates that sexting is a violation of school rules, explicitly prohibiting it in a school district policy or a student code of conduct will make it clear. Third, providing notice in the school district's cell phone policy that the administration may search cell phones if it has reasonable suspicion that a search will reveal that school rules have been violated, may also support a district's argument that a search was reasonable.

If school administrators ask school resource officers (SROs) to search a student's cell phone, the more demanding probable cause standard may apply. Likewise, if school administrators ask the police to search the student's phone, the probable cause standard likely will apply to the search.

In some instances, administrators may need to search to find a cell phone; for example, let's say Christopher's classmate in the example above denies having a cell phone at school. The time Christopher received the text message or a call to the student's parents about whether he generally brings a cell phone to school may cast doubt on the student's claim that his phone is not with him. If administrators search for the phone, they should consider T.L.O.'s requirement that the search be permissible in scope when determining where to look.

Stored Communications Act Concerns

In *Klump v. Nazareth Area School District*, Christopher Klump also argued that the school district violated Pennsylvania's version of the federal Stored Communications Act (SCA) by accessing his text messages, phone numbers, and call records. It is a violation of the federal SCA (which is very similar to Pennsylvania's statute) to: "(1) intentionally access without authorization a facility through which an electronic communication service is provided; or (2) intentionally exceed an authorization to access that facility; and thereby obtain, alter, or prevent authorized access to a wire or electronic communication while it is in electronic storage in such system."

The district court concluded that a call log and phone number directory are not "communications" under the statute, so searching them did not violate Pennsylvania's SCA. However, concluding that Christopher's "voice mail at least would have been stored by his cell phone provider and not in the cell phone itself," the court did not dismiss the unlawful access claims related to the voicemail or text messages.

While not argued in this case, under the federal SCA courts have held that open emails of which a recipient maintains a copy do not meet the definition of "electronic storage."

"Electronic storage" is defined as: "(A) any temporary, intermediate storage of a wire or electronic communication incidental to the electronic transmission thereof; and (B) any storage of such communication by an electronic communication service for purposes of backup protection of such communication." An open email is not in "temporary, intermediate storage"; instead, it is in "post-transmission storage." Open emails that users store on an Internet Service Provider's (ISP) system are not backup copies; backup copies are made by ISPs to protect the email from technical problems before it is transmitted.

Under this rationale, Christopher's opened text messages contained on his phone would not be in "electronic storage." Instead, they would be in post-transmission storage and are not "backups" maintained by his cell phone company to protect its system integrity. In other words, had the court analyzed this case by applying the definition of "electronic storage," it likely would have concluded Christopher's open text messages did not fall under the SCA.

The federal SCA allows users to authorize access to communications otherwise protected by the statute. To avoid possibly violating the SCA school districts may seek authorization from the student and his or her parents before searching a student's cell phone. If consent is denied, the federal SCA allows the government to compel the content of electronic communications from providers of "electronic communication service" and "remote computing service," which includes cell phone companies, after obtaining a search warrant, subpoena, etc.

Sexting Has Been Discovered . . . Now What?

When sexting arises in the school setting, it can have broad practical and legal implications. When school administrators discover sexting, they should consider at least the following: (1) telling the parents of all the students involved; (2) reporting the sexting to the police; (3) reporting the sexting as suspected abuse or neglect; (4) minimizing exposure to child pornography charges; (5) whether, who, and how to discipline the students involved; and (6) preventing the harassment and bullying of students involved in sexting. The rather dramatic story of a Virginia assistant principal charged with possession of child pornography and failure to report suspected child abuse after he asked a student to send him a seminude picture in the student's cell phone as part of a sexting investigation, illustrates what can happen when a school administrator fails to take the steps listed above.

Assistant principal Ting-Yi Oei explained that after he viewed an inappropriate picture contained in a student's cell phone, he showed the picture to the principal, who instructed him to transfer it to Oei's computer "in case we needed it later." Oei did not know how to do this, so the teen texted the picture to Oei's cell phone and told Oei how to forward it to his work email address. Oei could not identify the person in the photograph, concluded it was probably not a student at the school, told the principal what happened, and assumed the matter was closed.

Two weeks later, the boy caught with the photo was suspended for pulling down a girl's pants in class. Oei told the boy's mother about the sexting when he told her about the suspension. She was outraged that he had not informed her of the picture earlier and complained to the police. They conducted an investigation, and Oei showed them the photograph on his cell phone after he could not find it on his computer.

A month later, Oei was charged with failure to report suspected child abuse. The commonwealth (district) attorney dropped that charge but later charged him with possession of child pornography. The circuit court dismissed the child pornography charge finding that the picture—which at worst maybe showed a nipple—did not meet the definition of "sexually explicit visual material," pursuant to Virginia's child pornography statute.

Tell the Parents of All Students Involved

School administrators should notify parents promptly upon discovering that their child is the subject of, is in possession of, or has sent inappropriate pictures for many reasons. First, contacting parents immediately should demonstrate that the pictures were viewed for investigative purposes only, dissuading parents from pursuing child pornography charges. Second, as the Ting-Yi Oei incident illustrates, some parents want to know about sexting as soon as possible. Any concern regarding a parent's potential overreaction is outweighed by the district's duty to act in place of the parents while their children are at school. Parents should be told of this dangerous behavior, and administrators should follow abuse and neglect reporting statutes if they fear a parent's reaction might be violent.

Tell the Police

State law or school district policy may require school districts to report to the police certain crimes that have happened on school grounds. It may come as a surprise to school administrators that sexting in some states in some instances may be a crime. In fact, students in a number of states have been charged criminally and convicted of violating child pornography laws by sexting. For example, students likely could be prosecuted for sexting under Ohio's Illegal Use of Minor in Nudity-oriented Material or Performance statute, which prohibits "[p]hotograph[ing] any minor . . . in a state of nudity, or creat[ing], direct[ing], produc[ing], or transfer[ring] any material or performance that shows the minor in a state of nudity. . . ." Under the Ohio statute, it appears that both the girlfriend and the boyfriend from the example at the beginning of this article could be convicted. The girlfriend photographed herself nude and transferred the picture; the boyfriend further transferred the picture. The Ohio Legislature is considering adopting a statute specifically aimed at minors sexting.

Prosecutors across the country have taken various approaches to sexting. Parties who have been charged include the "victim," the recipient, and the disseminator. Prosecutors in some instances may not charge anyone at all or may recommend that those charged participate in a diversion program. Few reported cases discuss whether, and under what circumstances, students can be criminally prosecuted for sexting. . . . In this case, a school district discovered sexting and informed the district attorney. The parents of the girls depicted in the photographs successfully challenged the district attorney's threat to criminally prosecute them unless they participated in an education and counseling program. This case has been appealed to the Third Circuit.

District attorneys have been heavily criticized for prosecuting children engaged in sexting—particularly when the result is the child prosecuted being required to register as a sex offender. As one district attorney points out, child pornography laws were intended to prosecute child sexual predators, not minors who may not even know what child pornography is. Miller is a great example of backlash against district attorneys prosecuting sexting cases.

To respond to myriad concerns raised by sexting, in 2009, lawmakers in at least 11 states have introduced legislation addressing the issue, according to the National Conference of State Legislatures. At least two other states—Kentucky and Virginia—are expected to consider legislation in 2010. . . . To summarize, a number of states have adopted (Vermont, North Dakota) or proposed (Ohio, Pennsylvania) legislation that specifically addresses sexting as a crime separate from child pornography with lesser penalties. Other states have created (Nebraska) or proposed to create (New York) an affirmative defense to child pornography statutes for sexting in some circumstances. Two states have proposed to create (New Jersey, Pennsylvania) educational diversionary programs for students charged or convicted of sexting. Two other states (Colorado, Oregon) have amended their Internet sexual exploitation of a minor statutes to include texting. Finally, two states have proposed to educate students about sexting (New York, New Jersey).

Given that sexting is a new phenomenon and that most child pornography statutes were adopted before cell phones were widely used and sexting was a national problem, school attorneys in most instances will not be able to determine definitely whether a crime has been committed. For this reason, school districts are well-advised to inform the police of sexting so that they can conduct a criminal investigation. However, any school administrator who knows the facts of *Miller v. Skumanick* as described by the district court—where the district attorney threaten to charge the girls depicted in the photographs with felonies that could result in a long prison term, a permanent record, and registration as sex offenders—would think twice before telling the police about sexting. School administrators should not assume all district attorneys will prosecute all sexting cases or that school administrators will be unable to influence the district attorney. Sexting is a new crime. For this reason, many district attorneys likely would welcome input from school district officials on how to handle these cases. Particularly if the district is going to discipline the students involved, the district attorney may be amenable to not charging the students criminally depending on facts of the case.

It is always a good idea for school district officials to try to foster cooperation with local police and the prosecutors. The best time to approach the district attorney's office about this issue is before sexting occurs on campus and before a district attorney has had the chance to decide that prosecuting sexting cases will be the new "tough on crime" tactic. Likewise, part of building a good relationship with the district attorney's office may be asking for input on how the district should punish sexting and inviting the district attorney to participate in the district's sexting education and prevention efforts.

Report Sexting as Suspected Child Abuse and Neglect

A sexted image may constitute child abuse or neglect, depending on the state's definition of these terms and what is exactly depicted in the photograph. All states have child abuse and neglect reporting statutes which apply to school districts. Most, if not all, statutes include in the definition of child abuse and neglect sexual crimes against a child. For example, Virginia's definition of an abused or neglected child include one: "[w]hose parents or other person responsible for his care commits or allows to be committed any act of sexual exploitation or any sexual act upon a child in violation of the law." Virginia's Department of Social Services states that child abuse occurs when a parent: "[c]ommits or allows to be committed any illegal sexual act upon a child including incest, rape, fondling, indecent exposure, prostitution, or allows a child to be used in any sexually explicit visual material."

Ting-Yi Oei admitted that he did not think about the sexting incident in terms of whether it violated Virginia's child abuse and neglect reporting statute. It is unlikely Oei could have been successfully prosecuted under this statute for at least three reasons. First, he did not know the identity of the girl, though her identity was determined later. Second, he did not know she was only 16. Third, the circuit court ruled in Oei's possession of child pornography case that the picture was not "sexually explicit visual material." Had Oei known the girl's identity and age, and had the picture been more revealing, Oei likely would have had a reporting obligation under Virginia law.

In short, depending on the state's definition of abuse and neglect and depending on the visual depiction in the sexted photograph, school districts may have an obligation to report sexting under child abuse and neglect reporting statutes.

Minimize Exposure to Child Pornography Charges

School administrators should take steps to avoid being accused of possession of child pornography by prosecutors or disgruntled parents. This may simply involve turning over confiscated evidence of sexting to the police immediately. In fact, Oei may have avoided being charged altogether had he taken possession of the boy's phone and turned it over to the police promptly, like the school officials in Miller, instead of receiving and maintaining the photo on his own phone.

School administrators should also take steps to avoid charges of disseminating child pornography. As described later in this article, a lawsuit has been filed against a Washington state school district which rather cryptically accuses school officials of showing sexted photographs of a student to "other adults" in violation of Washington's dissemination of child pornography statute. The district denies doing so in its answer. Regardless of what actually happened in this case, it illustrates that a school administrator who discovers sexting should not share the images with other school employees much less non-employees.

The Utah legislature, likely in response to the Ting-Yi Oei incident, has passed a law to ensure that school employees and others cannot be liable "when reporting or preserving data" in a child pornography investigation. . . .

Discipline the Students Involved

As the case described below illustrates, school districts should consider disciplining all students involved in the sexting—the student featured in the image, students who received the image (unless they deleted it immediately), and students who disseminated the image—equally if possible.

The parents of a Washington state high school student are suing the school district for violating Washington's sexual equality statute for only punishing their daughter in a sexting incident. The parents admit in their complaint that their daughter took a naked picture of herself which was circulated among other students. The school district suspended her for one year from the cheer squad for violating the athletic code. Her parents alleged that the school district violated Washington's sexual equality statute by punishing only her and not the football players who possessed and viewed the picture of her. The school district responded that it did not discipline the football players because it did not know who sent, received, or forwarded the pictures. The daughter refused to tell the district because she did not "want to get anyone in trouble."

Whether the sexual equality claim is successful, plaintiffs do have a fair point that the boys who received and did not immediately delete the photograph of their daughter—or, worse yet, forwarded it—also should have received punishment. While a court likely will not be sympathetic to the daughter's refusal to inform the district of the football players who received and forwarded the picture of her, it likewise might not be sympathetic to the school district's failure to investigate further without her help.

Preventing Bullying and Harassment

Eighteen-year-old Jessica Logan committed suicide after being bullied and harassed after her ex-boyfriend forwarded to other students nude photos she took of herself and sent to him. Her parents are suing the school district, who was aware of the sexting, claiming that the district did not do enough to stop her from being harassed. Whether their claim against the district will be successful, it illustrates that districts should take measures to prevent harassment before and following a sexting incident.

Preventing bullying and harassment at school generally is a difficult task. At minimum, those involved in a sexting incident should be specifically instructed not to harass the "victims" of sexting. Likewise, before a sexting incident occurs, parents and school staff should be informed that sexting may occur, discipline will result, and harassment is prohibited. If an incident occurs, these messages might have to be reiterated. Finally, if harassment or bullying related to a sexting incident occurs, the district's anti-harassment/bullying policy should be followed and harassers should be disciplined.

Anti-sexting Policies

Adopting anti-sexting policies may be one approach school districts can take to prevent sexting. Obviously, no anti-sexting policy will stop sexting altogether, no matter how carefully written or widely circulated. However, an anti-sexting policy will put students and their parents on notice that sexting is unacceptable and has serious consequences.

School districts may take a variety of policy approaches to prevent sexting. Districts may revise existing policies addressing acceptable use, student codes of conduct, cell phones, harassment and bullying, or other similar subject areas, to prohibit sexting. School districts may ban cell phone use during school or cell phone possession at school altogether to prevent sexting. Some boards may decide that they need a separate policy addressing sexting.

Districts adopting a comprehensive anti-sexting policy should consider including the following elements. First, an anti-sexting policy should clearly state that the mere possession of sexually explicit digital pictures on any device is prohibited regardless of whether the state's child pornography law is violated. Second, the policy should state that all involved in sexting, unless they deleted images right away, will be punished. For example, student handbook language should prohibit "sending, sharing, viewing, or possessing pictures, text messages, emails, or other material of a sexual nature in electronic or any other form on a computer, cell phone, or other electronic device." Third, the policy should inform students that their parents and the police may be contacted and sexting may be reported as suspected child abuse or neglect. Fourth, the policy should put students on notice that administrators may search their cell phones if they have reasonable suspicion a student has been involved in sexting. Fifth, the consequences for sexting should be clearly stated but should include discretionary wording that allows administrators to adjust punishments up or down as appropriate. Finally, the policy should prohibit harassment and bullying related to sexting incidents and should punish nonconforming behavior.

Education as Prevention

Education professionals—including school lawyers—should make parents, staff, and students aware of the existence of and dangers of sexting. School districts should consider a variety of actions to raise awareness of and increase education about sexting. Districts may partner with other community organizations or public offices to provide staff trainings on bullying, cyber-bullying, and computer/Internet safety, including sexting and safety on social networking sites. This can include in-school assemblies for students, professional development for staff, training for school board members, distribution of school rules and policies through student handbooks, newsletters/correspondence to the community, meeting with parent groups, and resources on the school webpage and public forums.

Any education around sexting can and should be aimed at the whole community when possible. This means including students, board members, and staff as well as parents and community members. While the majority of recent press has involved middle and high school students, education regarding computer/Internet/technology safety should include younger children as appropriate. A variety of websites and documents provide information about sexting for students, parents, and educators.

Conclusion

The world of social interaction through new technologies is evolving at break-neck speed. Because young people are trendsetters—particularly when technology is involved—schools are affected by these changes. Disturbing, new technology trends like sexting have significant legal implications for school districts that may not be immediately obvious even to an experienced school administrator or school lawyer. However, sexting has been a growing problem long enough to give us the Ting-Yi Oei incident, Washington state case, and the Jessica Logan case, all of which are full of lessons learned about sexting. School attorneys must pass these lessons learned on to their clients.

LISA E. SORONEN, NICOLE VITALE AND KAREN A. HAASE are writing on legal issues for the National School Boards Association. This article encourages administrators to hand over cell phone sexting cases to the appropriate law enforcement agencies.

Julie Hilden    **NO**

How Should Teens' "Sexting"—The Sending of Revealing Photos—Be Regulated?

Recently, the *Wall Street Journal* and its law blog reported on a Pennsylvania controversy over "sexting"—the practice of sending nude or semi-nude photos of one-self or others via cell phone. After some "sexted" photos were confiscated from students at a high school, the local District Attorney threatened to file broad child-pornography charges if the teens were not willing to enroll in a five-week compulsory educational program covering topics such as "what it means to be a girl in today's society." (This topic is telling; sexting controversies often seem to be connected to adults' discomfort with girls' expression of their sexuality. It seems likely, too, that discomfort with gay teens' sexuality will eventually lead to a sexting controversy as well.)

The ACLU rightly responded with a lawsuit. Because First Amendment rights were at issue, the suit could properly be filed prior to charges being brought, in order to address the ongoing "chilling effect" on speech of the threat of prosecution hanging overhead. A federal judge has temporarily enjoined the D.A. from filing charges, with a hearing to occur in June.

These particular charges are ill-grounded in law, as the ACLU has pointed out. The photos at issue show teen girls in their bras or, in one case, topless. In contrast, child-pornography laws typically cover lascivious displays of the genitals and/or sexual activity. Thus, this is likely to be an easy case—as the judge's initial ruling, granting an injunction in the ACLU's favor in part because of its high likelihood of success on the merits, indicates.

This is not the first time that old laws have proven to be a bad fit with recent technology. But it's an especially worrying example of a general problem, because both criminal charges and First Amendment rights are at issue.

In this [article], I will consider how the law should respond when much harder cases regarding sexting come along, as they inevitably will. These cases would involve photos of underage teens having sex, displaying their genitals in a lascivious way, or both. Accordingly, these cases could validly form the basis for child-pornography charges. But should they always trigger charges? Or should the law be adjusted to take into account the factual nuances of the case?

Should There Be "Romeo and Juliet" and Age-Specific Exceptions for Sexting?

There is no question that if an adult traffics in photos that fit the child-pornography laws—that is, photos that include a lascivious display of an underage person's genitals, or show an underage person having sex—it is a very serious crime, as well as despicable behavior. Indeed, the Supreme Court recently issued an opinion allowing the prosecution of even those traffickers who offer virtual child pornography (involving no real children) but believe it is real—as I discussed in a prior column.

But what if teenagers take the photographs and do the trafficking, and the subjects and recipients of the photos are exclusively the teenagers themselves? Should the crime—and the penalties—be the same?

My answer is a strong "No." We should craft new laws specifically for sexting before old laws—designed for graver and much more morally bankrupt, dangerous, and exploitative contexts—are applied to sexting, and serious injustice results.

One good model for the regulation of teens' sexting might be the statutory rape laws—which sometimes offer a so-called "Romeo and Juliet" exception when the two parties to an act of sex are close in age (say, 18 and 16, or 17 and 15). If a 16-year-old "sexts" a photo of himself or herself at an 18-year-old high school class-mate's invitation, surely that is far less disturbing than if the 16-year-old does so at the invitation of a 40-year-old adult.

Such exceptions might accord well with our sense of when sexting is really disturbing, and appropriately deemed a crime, and when it is better addressed (if at all) with non-criminal remedies such as school suspension, paren-tal punishments, and the like. Notably, the ACLU, in the Pennsylvania case, has suggested that "sexting," in some cases, is not innocuous and may perhaps be penalized—but not through the criminal law.

The Tricky Issues of Consent That Sexting Raises, Especially with Respect to Forwarding

"Romeo and Juliet" exceptions in the sexting context probably will do more good than harm, in practice. But they will also have costs, if they are applied as bright-line rules.

That's because sexting is, in a way, more complicated than statutory rape. Statutory rape, by definition, comes out of a consensual act of sex; if it didn't, it would just be rape. The argument is that the young person's consent is not valid due to his or her immaturity, not that consent was not given. Thus, defining a crime as statutory rape moots out the consent issue. But often, the nature of sexting is intertwined with issues of consent and lack of consent that cannot be so easily put aside.

For instance, a 16-year-old sophomore girl might "sext" a nude photo she has taken of herself to her 18-year-old senior boyfriend, yet not intend that he share it with his 18-year-old friends. In my view, the girl's sexting the photo to the boyfriend would and should be immune from prosecution under a Romeo and Juliet exception—but one might argue that his forwarding of the photo to his same-age friends should not be immune (especially, but perhaps not only, if the girl did not consent to the forwarding). In other words, with respect to sexting, a pure age-based Romeo and Juliet exception, one that renders consent irrelevant, could be a refuge for scoundrels.

This example shows a strong tension between simple, bright-line age-based safe harbors for sexting, and a nuanced inquiry into whether the original "sexter" consented to forwarding. And there may be another nuance as well: Based on my admittedly limited knowledge as a member of Generation X and a viewer of the documentary *American Teen* (which covers a sexting story, among others), it seems to me that sexting in high school may be intimately bound up with issues of popularity, insecurity, and humiliation. And that explosive mix could lead to important and tricky issues regarding consent, particularly consent to forwarding.

For instance, a teen might authorize forwarding, but then later falsely claim that he or she did not consent,

if the forwarding was accompanied by the forwarder's humiliating commentary on his or her body or if such commentary by recipients led to humiliation at school. Parental disapproval—or ignorance—of teen relationships could lead to lying, too. In addition, a good-looking teen could deem it cooler to pretend that he or she was not, in fact, the driving force ensuring that a particularly flattering and explicit photo of him or her had ended up being "sexted" to the whole school but was "shocked, shocked to discover" that this had occurred.

In sum, I suspect that there is a whole complex anthropology here that it will be difficult for adults to fully understand. High-school communities might have unspoken "default rules," such as: "You can forward, but only with the photographer's—or subject's—okay." Or, "You can forward, but only to our clique, not to outsiders."

It's worth considering here that the worst sexting abuses, among teenagers, might lead to a civil claim for intentional infliction of emotional distress, or to expulsion from school. In light of these possible remedies, as well as the chance that parents will take action, it's possible that Romeo and Juliet exceptions, although not ideal, might be good enough.

Such exceptions would still allow authorities to crack down on the 18-year-old senior who takes and "sexts" a photo of a 13-year-old eighth-grader, and who truly is engaging in child pornography. Yet these exceptions would also avoid imposing stiff criminal penalties on more-or-less same-age kids for what is, in essence, ugly immaturity, not crime. Alternatively, a compromise solution would create low-level misdemeanor offenses relating to sexting—offenses that would ensure that teenagers, who are often impulsive, could not ruin their lives with a single, ill-considered forward.

Julie Hilden is a graduate of Harvard College and Yale Law School. A former clerk for Supreme Court Justice Stephen Breyer, she has more recently appeared on *Good Morning America*, Court TV, CNN, and NPR. Hilden argues that harsh penalties are extreme and unjust.

EXPLORING THE ISSUE

Should There Be Harsh Penalties for Teens Sexting?

Critical Thinking and Reflection

1. What are some arguments made by each side with which you agree or disagree?
2. What are the strengths and weaknesses of the two positions made in this issue?
3. Compare and contrast the competing arguments made about harsh responses to sexting. Think more broadly about teens' sexting. Is it healthy or unhealthy? Natural or dangerous? What are the larger implications of sexting behaviors? What conclusions do you reach about the different arguments cited?

Is There Common Ground?

No one wants to see teens feel humiliated as a result of sexting messages being shared, or even made public. Is the answer harsh penalties or education? Our laws are still evolving regarding how to respond to teen sexting. However, that shouldn't stop us from better educating children about digital citizenship. Are children receiving a proper education in this regard? Is this the job of schools? Parents? Places of worship? Can parents do a better job being aware of who their children are communicating with? Are there proper limits on electronic communication for children as they develop their digital citizenship skills? Should parents monitor what their children are posting? Do children know what their parents' expectations are of them online?

Create Central

www.mhhe.com/createcentral

Additional Resources

Psychology Today on teens' sexting:

www.psychologytoday.com/blog/teen-angst/201103/sexting-teens

ABC News and "Sexting Teens Going Too Far":

http://abcnews.go.com/Technology/WorldNews/sexting-teens/story?id=6456834

Pew Internet and American Life Project and teens' sexting research:

www.pewinternet.org/Reports/2009/Teens-and-Sexting.aspx

Safeteens.com provides sexting tips:

www.safeteens.com/teen-sexting-tips/

Internet References . . .

American Academy of Pediatrics: Talking to Kids and Teens about Social Media and Texting

www.aap.org/en-us/about-the-aap/aap-press-room/news-features-and-safety-tips/pages/Talking-to-Kids-and-Teens-About-Social-Media-and-Sexting.aspx

Momlogic: Teen Sexting

www.momlogic.com/resources/sexting.php

School Superintendent Association: Sexting

www.aasa.org/content.aspx?id=3390

Selected, Edited, and with Issue Framing Material by:
David M. Hall, PhD, *Delaware Valley College*

ISSUE

Are Open Relationships Healthy?

YES: Donald Dyson, from "Seeing Relationships Through a Wider Lens: Open Relationships as a Healthy Option," written for *Taking Sides: Family and Personal Relationships* (2009)

NO: Stanley Kurtz, from "Here Come the Brides: Plural Marriage Is Waiting in the Wings," *The Weekly Standard* (December 26, 2005)

Learning Outcomes

After reading this issue, you will be able to:

- Identify the major arguments made for and against open relationships.
- Compare and contrast the competing arguments made for and against open relationships in this issue.
- Evaluate the implications of open relationships on the stability of marriage and the larger fabric of American society.

ISSUE SUMMARY

YES: Donald Dyson is assistant professor of human sexuality education at Widener University and the national co-chair of the conference for the American Association of Sexuality Educators, Counselors, and Therapists. Dyson argues that there are essential qualities of a healthy relationship and that an open relationship can be successful.

NO: Stanley Kurtz, a writer and senior fellow at the Ethics and Public Policy Center, argues that allowing same-sex marriage will create a slippery slope, eventually leading to plural marriages. Kurtz contends that such marriages prove destructive to the institution of marriage itself.

During the nineteenth century, the U.S. Congress outlawed polygamy. Although all citizens of the United States were affected by this, the intent was to target members of the Church of Latter-Day Saints, otherwise known as Mormons. In fact, in order for Utah to join the union, the state first had to adopt anti-polygamy laws.

In the late 1870s, George Reynolds, a Mormon resident of Utah, was arrested for having multiple wives. He was convicted and sentenced to two years in prison and was fined $200. Reynolds challenged his conviction, and the case, *Reynolds v. United States,* reached the Supreme Court of the United States.

The Court ruled to uphold anti-polygamy and anti-bigamy laws, stating: "Polygamy has always been odious among the northern and western nations of Europe, and, until the establishment of the Mormon Church, was almost exclusively a feature of the life of Asiatic and of African people."

The bizarre, and frankly racist, choice of words in the Supreme Court opinion seemingly blames people of color, who were largely banned from the Mormon Church at that time, for white, Mormon polygamy. Aside from this language, this decision provides case law in addition to already existing statutory law stating that there is no right to plural marriages.

Although polygamy is illegal in the United States today, sex outside of a primary relationship—including sex outside marriage—occurs to a significant degree. Over the course of a heterosexual marriage, an estimated 24 percent of husbands and 18 percent of wives have sex outside marriage. The temptation to have sex outside marriage is clearly significant, and the practice is fairly common. These statistics reflect the frequency of sex outside marriage *without* the permission of one's spouse.

The difference between infidelity and an open relationship is that in an open relationship, sex occurs outside the marriage or relationship with the consent of one's partner or spouse. Open relationships have been referred to as wife swapping, swinging, and "the lifestyle." "Wife swapping" is perhaps the most misappropriated phrase. First, it implies that all open relationships are inherently heterosexual. Second, it indicates that men possess the power and that women are commodities being traded.

Heterosexual women in open relationships are often in high demand. Women in such relationships often find that they have a significant amount of power. In fact, in some relationships, the man might push to experiment with swinging, only to find that he does not care for it after seeing how sought-after his partner is by other men.

It is a challenge to find open relationships represented positively in television or film. A number of major American cities have swingers clubs that typically cater to heterosexual couples and single women. Due to the stigma associated with open relationships, most people within them work to conceal this from friends, family, and acquaintances.

Although open relationships exist, the majority of Americans believe that sex outside marriage is morally wrong and destructive. These individuals typically regard sexual intimacy and emotional intimacy as inseparable. They will often voice concerns that open relationships are bound to threaten the stability of a person's marriage or committed relationship.

When reading these articles, give some thought to historical factors that influence sexual morality today. Examine how your value system affects your reaction to these articles.

Sometimes the concept of open relationships is addressed in a cursory way by the popular media:

- On one episode of the sitcom *King of Queens*, Doug and Carrie, a married couple featured in the show, both agree that they can have sex outside their marriage with their dream person if the opportunity arises. They have to tell each other who that person is. Carrie shares first, disclosing a famous celebrity. Doug agrees to her choice, then shares his choice: a woman he works with. Amid laughter, Carrie refuses to accept his choice.
- On an episode of the cable series *Entourage*, Vincent Chase, a fictional Hollywood star, meets a woman in public and has sex with her in a nearby hotel room. He asks her whether they can see each other again. She explains she is engaged and can only do this once. She and her fiance both have a list of famous people they are allowed to have sex with.

Despite these examples from popular television shows, monogamy is treated as such a universal value that a significant number of readers may have never heard of polyamory or open relationships before reading this issue. What are some of the reasons that people are hesitant to discuss alternatives to monogamy? What is the impact, positive or negative, of this silence on individual relationships?

Aside from the diverse views of polyamory espoused by Dyson and Kurtz, this issue exposes fundamentally different philosophies. Dyson argues that open relationships can be positive. The argument portrays the impact of open relationships as self-contained to the individuals involved rather than assuming that such an arrangement will have a single, universal impact on all relationships. In contrast, Kurtz contends that any redefinition of marriage will be the start of a slippery slope that will ultimately affect everyone by causing the institution of marriage itself to disintegrate.

What do their views reveal about their position on the Political Ideology Continuum examined in the Introduction to this book? How do your views on this topic compare and contrast with other relationship issues raised in this book? The truth is that many people in open relationships are traditionally conservative, and many people committed to lifetime monogamy are quite liberal.

Regardless of the conclusion that you reach, this issue should help readers understand that one cannot make an assumption that relationship monogamy is a universal value. It is well advised for the reader to talk with a significant other at some point about his or her views on monogamy and relationships.

YES

Donald Dyson

Seeing Relationships Through a Wider Lens: Open Relationships as a Healthy Option

Introduction: The Current Cultural Context for Relationships

There are many ways in which human beings have learned to organize their daily relationships. People sometimes have family with whom they are very close; they have layers of social circles in which they operate, have friends, good friends, and intimate friends (some of whom may also be lovers). People have lovers and spouses; they have husbands and wives; they have partners and playmates. Each of these relationships involves a unique level of intimacy, the level of which is usually determined by the unique natures of the individuals involved.

Often, when people think of ideal relationship structures, they initially think of the types of relationships with which they are most familiar, or to which they have been most exposed. In Western cultures such as the United States, that relationship structure is most often a heterosexual, monogamous, married couple. In fact, so strong is the bias toward this one type of relationship structure, the questions of multiple partners or alternatives to monogamy are rarely discussed or considered.

Pile on top of this unquestioned assumption the cultural and clinical bias we see attached to sexual activity outside a monogamous pair bond. When one even considers sex with someone other than a primary partner, immediately the words "infidelity" and "cheating" spring to mind. Connected to those words are the culturally constructed ways in which people are supposed to respond to such things: anger, jealousy, hurt, rage. Indeed, such behaviors have many iconic images attached to them, including throwing a partner's belongings onto the front yard or cutting the partner's face out of pictures from a photo album.

Almost never does one instantly consider the possibility that the couple has agreed to a relationship style different from the monogamous monopoly. In the Clinton/Lewinsky scandal of the 1990s, in which Hillary Clinton was seen by some as a devoted wife who "stood by her man," and by others as a weak woman who should have divorced her husband for cheating on her—few considered the possibility that then-President Clinton and his wife might have had a different relationship style. Instead, people wondered why Mrs. Clinton remained with her spouse and conjectured that the president must have been a sex addict of some sort. This type of knee-jerk reaction clearly illustrates the monogamist (assuming that everyone is or should be monogamous) cultural bias in which we now live.

Add to this the prevailing cultural myth of "The One." This myth creates the expectation that somewhere, out there in the wide world, there is just one special person (think of the idea of a "soulmate") that is waiting for each of us. That person will meet all of our emotional, physical, intellectual, social, and sexual needs. That person will be the "yin" to our "yang." That one special person will become a person's "better half." That one individual, somewhere out there in the world, will "complete" another person. With every Disney movie supporting this romanticized ideal, how can we, as a culture, *not* believe that such a "One" exists?

Consider, then, where this leaves us. We are culturally programmed to consider only traditional, pair-bonded relationships that without question include sexual monogamy. We are taught that the proper definition of sex outside a committed relationship is cheating and it should be punished, or at least pathologized. We are brainwashed with the myth of "The One"; taught to believe that we must find that person within the billions of people in the wide world. In essence, people today are taught from early childhood to hold the highest of standards for potential partners, believing that this special person must be everything to them. Is it any wonder that the divorce statistics for traditional marriage relationships are so high?

One Possible Scenario: Consider This

The author's first experience with a couple who had an open relationship was in meeting a heterosexual married couple in their 60s. After a 30-year relationship, when they were in their 50s, the wife in the couple was diagnosed with a degenerative illness—one they were told would result in a loss of sensation in her sexual organs. In addition, the medicine that she took to slow the progression would result in a decrease in her interest in sex. Given this inevitability, the couple looked for viable alternatives.

Neither wanted to end their marriage; they were both still very much in love. They also continued to enjoy an active sex life, which was very important to both of them.

How could they resolve their dilemma? Was the wife to ask the husband to give up sex entirely for the rest of his life? Was the husband to foreswear sexual activity of any kind out of a grand gesture for his wife—a promise that would have been ripe for building resentment and bitterness?

This couple chose to open their relationship. The result was wonderful for both of them. They continued to be happy for 10 years after, and may still be enjoying the love they have nurtured for decades.

Alternatives: What Options Exist?

In reality, there are many "lifestyles" that people have adopted and adapted over time to suit their intimacy needs. In his 1985 work, Dr. William R. Stayton identified 17 different types of relationships. These included traditional monogamy, serial monogamy, singlehood, single parenthood, child-free marriage, polyamory, polyfidelity, open marriage, group marriage, swinging, synergamy, communal living, cohabitation/trial marriage, family clusters, secret affairs, celibate monogamy, and lifelong celibacy/chastity.

Of those 17, polyamory, polyfidelity, open marriage, group marriage, swinging, synergamy, family clusters, and secret affairs are relevant to this discussion. Briefly:

- "Polyamory" is a general term often used to describe all forms of multipartner relating.
- Polyfidelity is a form of group relationship where all the members agree to be faithful within their group and commit to exist as a family.
- Open marriage is when the primary couple agrees to engage in sexual activities with others outside the dyad. In these situations, couples usually make agreements that dictate the nature of relationships and sexual activities that would be deemed acceptable outside the primary relationship.
- Group marriage usually includes three or more people who agree to "marry" each other.
- Swinging is often a couple's experience and includes the practice of having sexual relationships with others, sometimes in groups, and is founded upon responsible, consensual sexual relating.
- Synergamy is when one or both people involved in a couple have an additional intimate relationship outside that pair. This arrangement often includes the establishment of more than one household and the full involvement of the individual in more than one family system.
- Family clusters include multiple family systems that are interdependent in social, relational, financial, and sometimes sexual functioning.

Secret affairs are relevant here because it is this type of "open relationship" that is most practiced in our current cultural milieu. Current statistics estimate that between 45

and 50 percent of married women and between 50 and 60 percent of married men engage in extramarital sex at some point during their relationships (Atwood and Schwartz, 2002). Although this type of relationship is the most common, it is also the most damaging. It is estimated that 60 to 65 percent of divorces result from secret affairs. In addition, the betrayal of trust, the lack of communication, and the resulting deceptions are often considered to be the most harmful outcomes of these experiences.

The Argument: Why Are Open Relationships Healthy?

With all of these options giving context to the argument, it must be acknowledged that no matter the specifics of the lifestyle or relationship choice, it is the practice of a relationship that makes any of them healthy or unhealthy. It is the behavior of the people involved that has the greatest effect on the relative healthiness of any given relationship style.

Whether checking dating and relationship Web sites, looking through marriage encounter brochures, perusing the outlines of pre-cana marriage classes, or flipping through the pages of *The Complete Idiot's Guide to a Healthy Relationship* (Kuriansky, 2001), each source includes three basic requirements for healthy and long-lasting relationships: trust, honesty, and communication. Although some sources include additional components, the universality of these three is striking.

Let us consider these three in reverse order, beginning with communication. The skills of good communication are the stuff of workshops, lesson plans, relationship and marriage seminars, and countless books and articles. These skills include using direct language, "I" statements, and active listening, among others. What is critically important here, though, is that these skills are not dependent on the type of relationship in which they are used. The same skills work effectively in conversations with one's parents, one's coworkers, and with one's sexual and relationship partners.

Good communication in open relationships is no different from good communication in monogamous ones. Instead, because of the many complexities inherent in dyadic communication, including significant others, those complexities increase exponentially. As a result of this explosion, open relationships might offer individuals increased opportunities for intimacy, as well as challenges to honing their communication skills.

Add to these multiple complexities the sensitive nature of the topics about which the individuals involved are communicating. Conversations are occurring about intimacy needs, sexual desires and fantasies, and personal preferences, as well as limitations, jealousy, attraction, and so much more. Many couples never brave these waters. For people involved in open relationships, they are necessary and sometimes daily conversations.

This level of communication leads directly into the next aspect of healthy relationships: honesty. As individuals broach subjects such as sexual desires, jealousies, and possibilities, the need for and reliance upon honesty increases. In the context of loving relationships, people can begin to express not only the ways that they feel fulfilled by a partner, but also the wants and needs that they are experiencing that are not being met by their primary partner. They can be honest about their sexual and emotional attractions to others. These are topics that are often avoided by other couples for fear of hurting one another or for fear of reprisals for having these types of feelings.

In this way, the honesty required within open relationships can be a very healthy benefit to the relationship overall. Secret keeping and lying take energy. So does honest communication . . .

Finally, the practice of open and honest communication requires a significant degree of vulnerability. As individuals express their wants and needs, their often secret desires and attractions, and their jealousy or fears of loss, the resulting vulnerability is incredibly acute. When this vulnerability is met with equal honesty and care, and when good communication is present and practiced, the result is a significant increase in trust and intimacy between the partners.

Trust, or the reliance upon the strength, integrity, ability, and surety of a person, is certainly a cornerstone of healthy relationships. It is usually built, bit by bit, within the shared experiences of vulnerability and care experienced by people within their relationships. In the context of open relationships, this trust is discussed, explored, and tested in ways that many in monogamous relationships never openly experience. As people practice honesty in their relationships, discuss sexual boundaries and limitations, acknowledge and explore their own desires, and allow their partners to do the same, that trust can increase, and the bonds between people can become stronger.

Summary

No type of relationship, in and of itself, is inherently or unequivocally healthy or unhealthy. It is the practice of relationships that give them their subjective qualification. Healthy relationships require effective, open communication; honesty; and trust. Open relationships can, indeed, be characterized by all of those things, thus characterizing them as healthy.

In addition, open relationships may offer some specific benefits. They can release individuals and relationships from the unspoken specter of monogamy. That is not to say that couples who discuss alternative relationship structures and choose monogamy are less healthy or self-aware. Instead, it demonstrates that the discussion

and intentional choices related to monogamy are opportunities for growth and increased intimacy.

Open relationships also have the power to allow individuals to be less "perfect" within their relationships and more human in their strengths and shortcomings. The pressure to be someone's "everything" and the resulting disappointment and resentment when that individual falls short of those expectations have surely been the demise of many potentially wonderful relationships. Exploring options for individuals to have their wants and needs met outside a dyadic relationship might well be the healthiest thing within a given relationship.

As people express their intimacy needs, their sexual fantasies, and their desires, they practice honesty in ways that many others never do. This exploration and reflection allow individuals to build increased levels of sexual awareness and self-awareness that have the potential to benefit not only themselves, but also all of their current and future partners.

And finally, open relationships by necessity include the constant practice of good communication skills. The opportunities to practice talking about all aspects of the relationship increase skills that are easily transferable to other situations. Healthy and honest communication is a benefit to every relationship. Open relationships are not a paradigm to be compared and contrasted with traditional monogamous ones. Instead, they are a paradigm all their own and should be measured against standards for good relationships, not monogamy.

For more information about open relationships, consider *Loving More: The Polyfidelity Primer*, by Ryam Nearing (PEP Publishing, 1992) or *The Ethical Slut*, by Dossie Easton and Catherine A. Liszt (Greenery Press, 1998).

References

J. D. Atwood and L. Schwartz, "Cyber-Sex: The New Affair Treatment Considerations," *Journal of Couple and Relationship Therapy* (vol. 1, no. 3, 2002).

J. Kuriansky, *The Complete Idiot's Guide to Healthy Relationships*, 2d ed. (Fort Smith, AZ: Alpha Books, 2001).

W. R. Stayton, "Alternative Lifestyles: Marital Options," in D. C. Goldberg and P. J. Fink, eds., *Contemporary Marriage: Special Issues in Couples Therapy* (Homewood, IL: Dorsey, 1985).

Donald Dyson is associate dean of School of Human Service Professions, director of Center for Human Sexuality Studies, and associate professor at Widener University and the national cochair of the conference for the American Association of Sexuality Educators, Counselors and Therapists. Dyson argues that there are essential qualities of a healthy relationship and that an open relationship can be successful.

Stanley Kurtz

 **NO**

Here Come the Brides: Plural Marriage Is Waiting in the Wings

On September 23, 2005, the 46-year-old Victor de Bruijn and his 31-year-old wife of eight years, Bianca, presented themselves to a notary public in the small Dutch border town of Roosendaal. And they brought a friend. Dressed in wedding clothes, Victor and Bianca de Bruijn were formally united with a bridally bedecked Mirjam Geven, a recently divorced 35-year-old whom they'd met several years previously through an Internet chatroom. As the notary validated a *samenlevingscontract*, or "cohabitation contract," the three exchanged rings, held a wedding feast, and departed for their honeymoon.

When Mirjam Geven first met Victor and Bianca de Bruijn, she was married. Yet after several meetings between Mirjam, her then-husband, and the De Bruijns, Mirjam left her spouse and moved in with Victor and Bianca. The threesome bought a bigger bed, while Mirjam and her husband divorced. Although neither Mirjam nor Bianca had had a prior relationship with a woman, each had believed for years that she was bisexual. Victor, who describes himself as "100 percent heterosexual," attributes the trio's success to his wives' bisexuality, which he says has the effect of preventing jealousy.

The De Bruijns' triple union caused a sensation in the Netherlands, drawing coverage from television, radio, and the press. With TV cameras and reporters crowding in, the wedding celebration turned into something of a media circus. Halfway through the festivities, the trio had to appoint one of their guests as a press liaison. The local paper ran several stories on the triple marriage, one devoted entirely to the media madhouse.

News of the Dutch three-way wedding filtered into the United States through a September 26 report by Paul Belien, on his Brussels Journal website. The story spread through the conservative side of the Internet like wildfire, raising a chorus of "I told you so's" from bloggers who'd long warned of a slippery slope from gay marriage to polygamy.

Meanwhile, gay marriage advocates scrambled to put out the fire. M.V. Lee Badgett, an economist at the University of Massachusetts, Amherst, and research director of the Institute for Gay and Lesbian Strategic Studies, told a sympathetic website, "This [Brussels Journal] article is ridiculous. Don't be fooled—Dutch law does not allow polygamy." Badgett suggested that Paul Belien had deliberately mistranslated the Dutch word for "cohabitation contract" as "civil

union," or even "marriage," so as to leave the false impression that the triple union had more legal weight than it did. Prominent gay-marriage advocate Evan Wolfson, executive director of Freedom to Marry, offered up a detailed legal account of Dutch cohabitation contracts, treating them as a matter of minor significance, in no way comparable to state-recognized registered partnerships.

In short, while the Dutch triple wedding set the conservative blogosphere ablaze with warnings, same-sex marriage advocates dismissed the story as a silly stunt with absolutely no implications for the gay marriage debate. And how did America's mainstream media adjudicate the radically different responses of same-sex marriage advocates and opponents to events in the Netherlands? By ignoring the entire affair.

Yet there is a story here. And it's bigger than even those chortling conservative websites claim. While Victor, Bianca, and Mirjam are joined by a private cohabitation contract rather than a state-registered partnership or a full-fledged marriage, their union has already made serious legal, political, and cultural waves in the Netherlands. To observers on both sides of the Dutch gay marriage debate, the De Bruijns' triple wedding is an unmistakable step down the road to legalized group marriage.

More important, the De Bruijn wedding reveals a heretofore hidden dimension of the gay marriage phenomenon. The De Bruijns' triple marriage is a bisexual marriage. And, increasingly, bisexuality is emerging as a reason why legalized gay marriage is likely to result in legalized group marriage. If every sexual orientation has a right to construct its own form of marriage, then more changes are surely due. For what gay marriage is to homosexuality, group marriage is to bisexuality. The De Bruijn trio is the tip-off to the fact that a connection between bisexuality and the drive for multipartner marriage has been developing for some time.

As American gay-marriage advocates were quick to point out, the cohabitation contract that joined Victor, Bianca, and Mirjam carries fewer legal implications and less status than either a registered partnership or a marriage—and Dutch trios are still barred from the latter two forms of union. Yet the use of a cohabitation contract for a triple wedding is a step in the direction of group marriage. The conservative and religious Dutch paper *Reformatorisch Dagblad* reports that this was the first known occurrence in the Netherlands of a cohabitation contract between a married couple and their common girlfriend. . . .

So the use of cohabitation contracts was an important step along the road to same-sex marriage in the Netherlands. And the link between gay marriage and the De Bruijns' triple contract was immediately recognized by the Dutch. The story in *Reformatorisch Dagblad* quoted J.W.A. van Dommelen, an attorney opposed to the De Bruijn union, who warned that the path from same-sex cohabitation contracts to same-sex marriage was about to be retraced in the matter of group marriage.

Van Dommelen also noted that legal complications would flow from the overlap between a two-party marriage and a three-party cohabitation contract. The rights and obligations that exist in Dutch marriages and Dutch cohabitation contracts are not identical, and it's unclear which arrangement would take precedence in case of a conflict. "The structure is completely gone," said Van Dommelen, as he called on the Dutch minister of justice to set up a working group to reconcile the conflicting claims of dual marriages and multipartner cohabitation contracts. Of course, simply by harmonizing the conflicting claims of dual marriages and triple cohabitation contracts, that working group would be taking yet another "small step" along the road to legal recognition for group marriage in the Netherlands.

The slippery-slope implications of the triple cohabitation contract were immediately evident to the SGP, a small religious party that played a leading role in the failed battle to preserve the traditional definition of marriage in the Netherlands. SGP member of parliament Kees van der Staaij noted the substantial overlap between marriage rights and the rights embodied in cohabitation contracts. Calling the triple cohabitation contract a back-door route to legalized polygamy, Van der Staaij sent a series of formal queries to Justice Minister Piet Hein Donner, asking him to dissolve the De Bruijn contract and to bar more than two persons from entering into cohabitation contracts in the future.

The justice minister's answers to these queries represent yet another small step—actually several small steps—toward legal and cultural recognition for group marriage in the Netherlands. To begin with, Donner reaffirmed the legality of multipartner cohabitation contracts and pointedly refused to consider any attempt to ban such contracts in the future. Donner also went so far as to assert that contracts regulating multipartner cohabitation can fulfill "a useful regulating function" (also translatable as "a useful structuring role"). In other words, Donner has articulated the rudiments of a "conservative case for group marriage."

The SGP responded angrily to Donner's declarations. In the eyes of this small religious party, Donner had effectively introduced a form of legal group marriage to the Netherlands. A party spokesman warned of an impending legal mess—especially if the De Bruijn trio, or others like them, have children. The SGP plans to raise its objections again when parliament considers the justice department's budget.

It's not surprising that the first English-language report was a bit unclear as to the precise legal status and significance of the triple Dutch union. The Dutch themselves are confused about it. One of the articles from which Paul Belien drew his original report is careful to distinguish between formal marriage and the cohabitation contract actually signed by Victor, Bianca, and Mirjam. Yet the very same article says that Victor now "officially" has "two wives."

Even Dutch liberals acknowledge the implications of the De Bruijn wedding. Jan Martens, a reporter and opinion columnist for *BN/DeStem*, the local paper in Roosendaal, wrote an opinion piece mocking opposition to group marriage by religious parties like the SGP. Noting the substantial overlap between cohabitation contracts and marriage, Martens said he agreed with the SGP that the De Bruijn triple union amounts to a "short-cut to polygamy." Yet Martens emphasized that he "couldn't care less if you have two, three, four, or sixty-nine wives or husbands."

Minority religious parties and their newspapers excepted, this mixture of approval and indifference seems to be the mainstream Dutch reaction so far. Not only has Justice Minister Donner articulated the beginnings of a conservative case for group marriage, but Green Party spokesman Femke Halsema, a key backer of gay marriage, has affirmed her party's support for the recognition of multipartner unions. The public has not been inclined to protest these developments, and the De Bruijn trio have been welcomed by their neighbors. . . .

When it comes to marriage, culture shapes law. (It's a two-way street, of course. Law also influences culture.) After all, Dutch same-sex marriage advocates still celebrate the foundational role of symbolic gay marriage registries in the early 1990s. Although these had absolutely no legal status, the publicity and sympathy they generated are now widely recognized as keys to the success of the Dutch campaign for legal same-sex unions and ultimately marriage. How odd, then, that American gay-marriage advocates should respond to the triple Dutch wedding with hairsplitting legal discourses, while ignoring the Dutch media frenzy and subsequent signs of cultural acceptance—for a union with far more legal substance than Holland's first symbolic gay marriages. Despite the denials of gay-marriage advocates, in both legal and cultural terms, Victor, Bianca, and Mirjam's triple union is a serious move toward legalized group marriage in the Netherlands.

Given the stir in Holland, it's remarkable that not a single American mainstream media outlet carried a story on the triple Dutch wedding. Of course the media were all over the Dutch gay marriage story when they thought the experiment had been a success. In late 2003 and early 2004, in the wake of the Supreme Court's *Lawrence v. Texas* decision, which ruled sodomy laws unconstitutional, and looming gay marriage in Massachusetts, several American papers carried reports from the Netherlands. The common theme was that Holland had experienced no ill effects from gay marriage, and that the issue was no longer contentious. . . .

Although the triple Dutch union has been loosely styled "polygamy," it's actually a sterling example of polyamory. Polyamorists practice "responsible nonmonogamy"—open, loving, and stable relationships among more than two people (see "Beyond Gay Marriage: The Road to Polyamory," *The Weekly Standard*, August 4/August 11, 2003). Polygamous marriages among fundamentalist Mormons or Muslims don't depend on a blending of heterosexuality and bisexuality. Yet that combination perfectly embodies the spirit of polyamory. And polyamorists don't limit themselves to unions of one man and several women. One woman and two men, full-fledged group marriage, a stable couple openly engaging in additional shifting or stable relationships—indeed, almost any combination of partner-number and sexual orientation is possible in a polyamorous sexual grouping.

Polyamorists would call the De Bruijn union a "triad." In a polyamorous triad, all three partners are sexually connected. This contrasts with a three-person "V," in which only one of the partners (called the "hinge" or "pivot") has a sexual relationship with the other two. So the bisexuality of Bianca and Mirjam classifies the De Bruijn union as a polyamorous bisexual triad. In another sense, the De Bruijn marriage is also a gay marriage. The Bianca-Mirjam component of the union is gay, and legalized gay marriage in Holland has clearly helped make the idea of a legally recognized bisexual triad thinkable. . . .

The germ of an organized effort to legalize polyamory in the United States can be found in the Unitarian Church. Although few realize it, the Unitarian Church, headquartered in Boston, played a critical role in the legalization of same-sex marriage in Massachusetts. Julie and Hillary Goodridge, lead plaintiffs in *Goodridge v. Department of Public Health,* were married at the headquarters of the Unitarian Universalists in a ceremony presided over by the Reverend William G. Sinkford, president of the Unitarian Universalist Association. Hillary Goodridge is program director of the Unitarian Universalist Funding Program. And Unitarian churches in Massachusetts played a key role in the struggle over gay marriage, with sermons, activism, and eventually with marriage ceremonies for same-sex couples. Choosing a strongly church-affiliated couple like the Goodridges as lead plaintiffs was an important part of the winning strategy in the *Goodridge* case.

It's a matter of interest, therefore, that an organization to promote public acceptance of polyamory has been formed in association with the Unitarian Church. Unitarian Universalists for Polyamory Awareness (UUPA) was established in the summer of 1999. At the time, the news media in Boston carried reports from neighboring Vermont, where the soon-to-be-famous civil unions case was about to be decided. And the echo effect of the gay marriage battle on the polyamory movement goes back even further. The first informal Unitarian polyamory discussion group gathered in Hawaii in 1994, in the wake of the first state supreme court decision favorable to same-sex marriage in the United States.

"Our vision," says UUPA's website, "is for Unitarian Universalism to become the first poly-welcoming mainstream religious denomination." Those familiar with Unitarianism's role in the legalization of gay marriage understand the legal-political strategy implicit in that statement. UUPA's political goals are spelled out by Harlan White, a physician and leading UUPA activist, on the society's website. Invoking the trial of April Divilbiss, the first American polyamorist to confront the courts, White says, "We are concerned that we may become the center of the next great social justice firestorm in America."

White maintains that American polyamorists are growing in number. An exact count is impossible, since polyamory is still surrounded by secrecy. Polyamorists depend on the Internet to connect. Even so, says White, "attendance at conferences is up, email lists and websites are proliferating, and poly support groups are growing in number and size." As for the Unitarian polyamorists, their email list has several hundred subscribers, and the group has put on well-attended workshops at Unitarian General Assemblies since 2002. And although the number of open polyamorists is limited, some Unitarian ministers already perform "joining ceremonies" for polyamorous families. . . .

Shortly after the second article appeared, UUA president Sinkford circulated a statement among Unitarians acknowledging that press interest in Unitarian polyamory had "generated a great deal of anxiety" among the church's leadership. "Many of us are concerned that such press coverage might impair our ability to witness effectively for our core justice commitments." Sinkford appeared to be expressing a concern that had been stated more baldly in the original *Chronicle* article. According to the *Chronicle,* many of the students and faculty at the Unitarians' key west-coast seminary, Starr King School for the Ministry, in Berkeley, see the polyamory movement as a threat to the struggle for same-sex marriage.

In other words, Unitarians understand that moving too swiftly or openly to legitimize polyamory could validate the slippery-slope argument against same-sex marriage. So with news coverage prematurely blowing the cover off the Unitarians' long-term plan to legalize polyamory, President Sinkford took steps to hold UUPA at arm's length. Sinkford issued a public "clarification" that distanced the church from any formal endorsement of polyamory, yet also left room for the UUPA to remain a "related organization." . . .

The other fascinating angle in the *San Francisco Chronicle*'s coverage of the Unitarian polyamorists was the prominence of bisexuality. Most members of UUPA are either bisexual or heterosexual. One polyamorist minister who had recently come out to his congregation as a bisexual treated polyamory and bisexuality synonymously. "Our denomination has been welcoming to gays and lesbians and transgendered people," he said. "Bisexuals have not received the recognition they deserve." In other words, anything less than formal church recognition of polyamory is discrimination against bisexuals.

Two developing lines of legal argument may someday bring about state recognition for polyamorous marriage: the argument from polyamory, and the argument from bisexuality. In a 2004 law review article, Elizabeth F. Emens, of the University of Chicago Law School, offers the argument from polyamory (see "Monogamy's Law: Compulsory Monogamy and Polyamorous Existence," *New York University Review of Law & Social Change*). Polyamory is more than the mere practice of multiple sexual partnership, says Emens. Polyamory is also a disposition, broadly analogous to the disposition toward homosexuality. Insofar as laws of marriage, partnership, or housing discriminate against polyamorous partnerships, maintains Emens, they place unfair burdens on people with "poly" dispositions. Emens takes her cue here from the polyamorists themselves, who talk about their "poly" inclinations the way gays talk about homosexuality. For example, polyamorists debate whether to keep their poly dispositions "in the closet" or to "come out."

Emens's case for a poly disposition was inspired by the radical lesbian thinker Adrienne Rich, who famously put forward a "continuum model" of lesbianism. Rich argued that all women, lesbian-identified or not, are in some sense lesbians. If women could just discover where they fall on the "lesbian continuum," then even those women who remain heterosexually identified would abandon any prejudice against homosexuality.

Following Rich, Emens argues that all of us have a bit of "poly" inside. By discovering and accepting our own desires for multiple sexual partners, then even those who remain monogamous would abandon their prejudice against polyamorists. Of course, some people fall at the extreme ends of these continuums. Some folks are intensely monogamous, for example. But by the same token, others are intensely polyamorous. Whether for biological or cultural reasons, says Emens, some folks simply cannot live happily without multiple simultaneous sexual partners. And for those people, Emens argues, our current system of marriage is every bit as unjust as it is for homosexuals. . . .

The second legal strategy available to the polyamorists is the argument from bisexuality. No need here to validate anything as novel-sounding as a "polyamorous disposition." A case for polyamory can easily be built on the more venerable orientation of bisexuality. While no legal scholar has offered such a case, the groundwork is being laid by Kenji Yoshino, a professor at Yale Law School and deputy dean for intellectual life.

Yoshino's 2000 *Stanford Law Review* article "The Epistemic Contract of Bisexual Erasure" has a bewildering title but a fascinating thesis. Yoshino argues that bisexuality is far more prevalent than is usually recognized. The relative invisibility of bisexuality, says Yoshino, can be attributed to the mutual interest of heterosexuals and homosexuals in minimizing its significance. But according to Yoshino, the bisexuality movement is on the rise and bound to become more visible, with potentially major consequences for the law and politics of sexual orientation.

Defining bisexuality as a "more than incidental desire" for partners of both sexes, Yoshino examines the best available academic studies on sexual orientation and finds that each of them estimates the number of bisexuals as equivalent to, or greater than, the number of homosexuals. Up to now, the number of people who actively think of themselves as bisexuals has been much smaller than the number who've shown a "more than incidental" desire for partners of both sexes. But that, argues Yoshino, is because both heterosexuals and homosexuals have an interest in convincing bisexuals that they've got to make an all-or-nothing choice between heterosexuality and homosexuality.

Heterosexuals, for example, have an interest in preserving norms of monogamy, and bisexuality "destabilizes" norms of monogamy. Homosexuals, notes Yoshino, have an interest in defending the notion of an immutable homosexual orientation, since that is often the key to persuading a court that they have suffered discrimination. And homosexuals, adds Yoshino, have an interest in maximizing the number of people in their movement. For all these reasons and more, Yoshino argues, the cultural space in which bisexuals might embrace and acknowledge their own sexual identity has been minimized. Yoshino goes on to highlight the considerable evidence for the recent emergence of bisexuality as a movement, and predicts that in our current cultural climate—and given the numerical potential—bisexuality activism will continue to grow.

In addition to establishing the numerical and political significance of bisexuality, Yoshino lays down an argument that could easily be deployed to legalize polyamory: "To the extent that bisexuals are not permitted to express their dual desires, they might fairly characterize themselves as harmed." Yet Yoshino does not lay out a bisexual defense of polyamory. Instead Yoshino attacks—rightly—the stereotype that treats all bisexuals as nonmonogamous. Yet the same research that establishes the monogamous preferences of many bisexuals also confirms that bisexuals tend toward nonmonogamy at substantially higher rates than homosexuals. (See Paula C. Rust, "Monogamy and Polyamory: Relationship Issues for Bisexuals," in Firestein, ed., *Bisexuality: The Psychology and Politics of an Invisible Minority*.) That fact could easily be turned by a bisexuality rights movement into an argument for legalized polyamory. . . .

In 2004, the *Journal of Bisexuality* published a special double issue on polyamory, also released as the book *Plural Loves: Designs for Bi and Poly Living*. It's clear from *Plural Loves* that the polyamory movement now serves as the de facto political arm of the bisexual liberation struggle. As one contributor notes, "the large number of bi people in the poly movement provides evidence that bisexuality is one of the major driving forces behind polyamory. In other words, polyamory was created and spread partly to satisfy the need for bisexual relationship structures. . . . [T]he majority of poly activists are also bisexual. . . . Poly activism is bi activism. . . . The bi/poly dynamic has the potential to move both communities towards a point of culture-wide visibility, which is a necessary step on the road to acceptance."

Clearly, visibility and acceptance are on the rise. This past summer, the *Baltimore Sun* featured a long, friendly article on the polyamorists' national conference, held in Maryland. In September, the *New York Times* ran a long personal account of (heterosexual) polyamory in the Sunday Styles section. But the real uptick in public bisexuality/polyamory began with the October 2005 release in New York of the documentary *Three of Hearts: A Postmodern Family.*

Three of Hearts is the story of the real-life 13-year relationship of two men and a woman. Together for several years in a gay relationship, two bisexual-leaning men meet a woman and create a threesome that produces two children, one by each man. Although the woman marries one of the men, the entire threesome has a commitment ceremony. The movie records the trio's eventual breakup, yet the film's website notes their ongoing commitment to the view that "family is anything we want to create." . . .

Of course, many argue that true bisexuality does not exist. In this view— held by a variety of people, from some psychiatrists to certain pro-gay-marriage activists— everyone is either heterosexual or homosexual. From this perspective, so-called bisexuals are either in confused transition from heterosexuality to homosexuality, or simply lying about their supposedly dual sexual inclinations. Alternatively, it's sometimes said that while female bisexuality does exist, male bisexuality does not. A recent and controversial study reported on by the *New York Times* in July 2005 claimed to show that truly bisexual attraction in men might not exist.

Whatever view we take of these medical/psychiatric/philosophical controversies, it is a fact that a bi/poly rights movement exists and is growing. Whether Koen Brand and Bianca and Mirjam de Bruijn are "authentic" bisexuals or "just fooling themselves," they are clearly capable of sustaining polyamorous bisexual V's and triads for long enough to make serious political demands. *Three of Hearts* raises questions about whether the two men in the triangle are bisexual or simply confused gays. But with two children, a 13-year relationship, and at one time at least a clear desire for legal-ceremonial confirmation, the *Three of Hearts* trio is a harbinger of demands for legal group marriage. Public interest in the De Bruijn triangle has already raised the visibility and acceptance of polyamorous bisexuality in the Netherlands. For legal-political purposes, acceptance is what matters. And given Yoshino's numerical analysis, the growth potential for self-identifying bisexuals is substantial.

Americans today respond to gay and bisexual friends and family members in a variety of ways. Despite stereotypical accusations of "homophobia," the traditionally religious generally offer a mixture of compassion and concern. Many other Americans, conservative and liberal alike, are happy to extend friendship, understanding, and acceptance to gay and bisexual relatives and acquaintances. This heightened social tolerance is a good thing. Yet somehow the idea has taken hold that tolerance for sexual minorities requires a radical remake of the institution of marriage. That is a mistake.

The fundamental purpose of marriage is to encourage mothers and fathers to stay bound as a family for the sake of their children. Our liberalized modern marriage system is far from perfect, and certainly doesn't always succeed in keeping parents together while their children are young. Yet often it does. Unfortunately, once we radically redefine marriage in an effort to solve the problems of adults, the institution is destined to be shattered by a cacophony of grown-up demands.

The De Bruijn trio, Koen Brand, the Unitarian Universalists for Polyamory Awareness, the legal arguments of Elizabeth Emens and Kenji Yoshino, and the bisexual/polyamory movement in general have been launched into action by the successes of the campaign for gay marriage. In a sense, though, these innovators have jumped too soon. They've shown us today—well before same-sex marriage has triumphed nationwide—what would emerge in its aftermath.

Liberals may now put behind-the-scenes pressure on the Dutch government to keep the lid on legalized polyamory for as long as the matter of gay marriage is still unsettled. The Unitarian polyamorists, already conflicted about how much recognition to demand while the gay marriage battle is unresolved, may be driven further underground. But let there be no mistake about what will happen should same-sex marriage be fully legalized in the United States. At that point, if bisexual activists haven't already launched a serious campaign for legalized polyamory, they will go public. It took four years after the full legalization of gay marriage in the Netherlands for the first polyamory test case to emerge. With a far larger and more organized polyamory movement in America, it might not take even that long after the nationalization of gay marriage in the United States.

It's easy to imagine that, in a world where gay marriage was common and fully accepted, a serious campaign to legalize polyamorous unions would succeed—especially a campaign spearheaded by an organized bisexual-rights movement. Yet win or lose, the culture of marriage will be battered for years by the debate. Just as we're now continually reminded that not all married couples have children, we'll someday be endlessly told that not all marriages are monogamous (nor all monogamists married). For a second time, the fuzziness and imperfection found in every real-world social institution will be contorted into a rationale for reforming marriage out of existence.

STANLEY KURTZ is a writer and senior fellow at the Ethics and Public Policy Center. Kurtz is a key contributor to American public debates and has written on issues for various journals, particularly National Review Online. Kurtz argues that allowing for same-sex marriage will create a slippery slope, eventually leading to plural marriages. Kurtz contends that such marriages prove destructive to the institution of marriage itself.

EXPLORING THE ISSUE

Are Open Relationships Healthy?

Critical Thinking and Reflection

1. What are some arguments made by each side with which you agree or disagree?
2. What are the strengths and weaknesses of the two positions made in this issue? Pick the side with which you most agree. What are some additional arguments you would make to strengthen the case for or against open relationships? Think more broadly of the issue of open relationships. What sort of attitudes exist about open relationships? How will this affect those who choose to participate? How might it affect other couples in which there is strong disagreement over whether open relationships are healthy?

Is There Common Ground?

What is your response to Dyson's argument that the impact depends on the individual relationship? What is your response to Kurtz's argument that same-sex marriage will lead to polyamory? Is the progression as inevitable as he contends? What are some other factors that influence your views related to monogamy and polyamory?

This issue specifically asks whether open relationships are healthy. Is there a universal definition for what is emotionally healthy regarding sexual partners? Specifically, is monogamy a universal value that should be practiced in all relationships? Is polyamory a universal value that should be practiced in all relationships? What, if anything, would you regard as a standard relationship model that all couples should aspire to? Is sex outside marriage cheating if your spouse approves of it? Most importantly in seeking common ground, what kind of communication is necessary to ensure that people are being honest about their feelings?

Create Central

www.mhhe.com/createcentral

Additional Resources

Polyamory Forum:

www.polyamory.com/forum/

Xeromag presents Polyamory 101:

www.xeromag.com/fvpoly.html

The Daily Beast reports on polyamory:

www.thedailybeast.com/newsweek/2009/07/28/only-you-and-you-and-you.html

Alternatives to Marriage Project presents polyamory:

www.unmarried.org/polyamory.html

Internet References . . .

Categories of Poly Resources

www.polyamory.org/SF/groups.html

Patheos: Strategies for Open Relationships

www.patheos.com/Resources/Additional-Resources/Bouquet-of-Lovers.html

WebMD: Open Marriages

www.webmd.com/sex-relationships/features/the-truth-about-open-marriage